I am particularly impressed by this book's attention to leveraging change at multiple levels of analysis – creating change for people, processes, and even the mentoring paradigm. The rich focus on a multiplicity of identities creates a sophisticated approach toward understanding mentoring dynamics. The deep dive into processes provides thoughtful approaches toward developing more diverse cohorts of organizational leaders. The willingness to question assumptions of hierarchy stimulates insightful discussion of the links between mentoring and social inequality. I strongly recommend this book to anyone seeking to understand the field of mentoring as well as the role of mentoring in leadership development.

Alison M. Konrad, *Corus Entertainment Chair in Women in Management, Ivey Business School, Western University, Canada*

This thought-provoking volume provides provocative insights and alternative paradigms that can spark important new dialogues between diversity and mentoring scholars and generate new research that explains the complex relationship between mentoring and diversity in the workplace.

Belle Rose Ragins, *Professor of Human Resource Management, University of Wisconsin-Milwaukee, USA*

MENTORING DIVERSE LEADERS

Mentoring Diverse Leaders provides up-to-date research on the impact of mentoring relationships in organizations, particularly as they relate to cultivating diverse leadership. Contributions from experts in the fields of psychology, business, law, non-profit management, and engineering draw connections between mentoring research, theory, and practice in both domestic and global organizations. Rather than standing apart from the broader goals and objectives of these organizations, they demonstrate the ways mentoring for diversity actually drives innovation and change, talent management, organizational commitment, and organizational success.

Audrey J. Murrell is Associate Dean, Kenneth R. Woodcock Faculty Fellow, and Director of the David Berg Center for Ethics and Leadership at the University of Pittsburgh, Katz Graduate School of Business and College of Business Administration.

Stacy Blake-Beard is the Deloitte Ellen Gabriel Chair of Women and Leadership and Faculty Affiliate at the Center for Gender in Organizations at the Simmons School of Management. She is also Visiting Faculty with the Vedica Scholars Programme for Women in New Delhi, India.

MENTORING DIVERSE LEADERS

Creating Change for People, Processes, and Paradigms

Edited by Audrey J. Murrell and Stacy Blake-Beard

Routledge
Taylor & Francis Group

NEW YORK AND LONDON

First published 2017
by Routledge
711 Third Avenue, New York, NY 10017

and by Routledge
2 Park Square, Milton Park, Abingdon, Oxon, OX14 4RN

Routledge is an imprint of the Taylor & Francis Group, an informa business

Library of Congress Cataloging in Publication Data
A catalog record for this book has been requested

ISBN: 978-1-138-81432-5 (hbk)
ISBN: 978-1-138-81433-2 (pbk)
ISBN: 978-1-315-74756-9 (ebk)

Typeset in Bembo
by Wearset Ltd, Boldon, Tyne and Wear

CONTENTS

CONTRIBUTORS

Estelle E. Archibold is a graduate of Simmons College School of Management and a PhD student in Organizational Behavior at Case Western Reserve University. Her current research focuses on transformational learning and leadership development of women within coaching and mentoring relationships. She has broad research interests in the sociology of organizations and organizational change theory.

Shereka Banton is a PhD candidate in the Wallace H. Coulter Department of Biomedical Engineering at Georgia Tech and Emory School of Medicine. Through her interest in the organizational culture of STEM fields in higher education settings, she has received a certificate in science policy and interned at the National Science Foundation.

Gilda Barabino is the Daniel and Frances Berg Professor and the Dean of The Gove School of Engineering at The City College of New York. Prior to City College, Barabino served as Professor and Vice Provost for Academic Diversity at Georgia Institute of Technology, and Professor and Vice Provost for Undergraduate Education at Northeastern University. She is the founder and Executive Director of the National Institute for Faculty Equity.

Ella L. J. Edmondson Bell-Smith is a Professor at the Tuck School of Business at Dartmouth College. She is also an author, managerial consultant, and advocate on women's workplace issues. She is the co-author of *Our Separate Ways: Black and White Women and the Struggle for Professional Identity* and the author of *Career GPS*. Edmondson Bell-Smith's scholarly work has been reported in the *Wall Street Journal*, *The Christian Science Monitor*, *Working Women*,

Black Enterprise and *Essence* magazines. She is considered by industry and the academy to be one of the leading experts in organizational change, and the management of race, gender, and class in organizational life.

Stacy Blake-Beard is the Deloitte Ellen Gabriel Chair of Women and Leadership and Faculty Affiliate at the Center for Gender in Organizations at the Simmons School of Management. Her research focuses on the challenges and opportunities offered by mentoring relationships, with a focus on how these relationships may be changing as a result of increasing workforce diversity.

Donna Maria Blancero is the Assistant Dean of Business Programs at Bentley University. She holds a PhD from Cornell University. Her research focuses on diversity with a special focus on Latinos and their experiences in the workplace. She is a national speaker on issues of Latino leadership.

Dorian Olivier Boncoeur is a doctoral student at the Naveen Jindal School of Management at the University of Texas at Dallas. His research focuses on how behaviors toward diversity impact team-based as well as organizational outcomes.

Meg A. Bond is Professor of Psychology and Director of the Center for Women & Work at the University of Massachusetts Lowell. As a community psychologist, her work adopts a social ecological framework for understanding interrelationships among issues of diversity, empowerment, and organizational dynamics. She serves on the editorial board of the *American Journal of Community Psychology* and is lead editor for a new APA *Handbook of Community Psychology* (2017). Bond is a former President of the Society for Community Research and Action (SCRA) and has received two SCRA career awards: for Special Contributions (2001) and Ethnic Minority Mentoring (2009).

Andrea R. Burton is an MBA graduate of Simmons College with research interests in the area of women leadership and mentoring. She currently works for the City of Brockton, Massachusetts in the Office of the Mayor as the Director of Community Relations.

Randie C. Chance, PhD, is an applied social psychological researcher based in the Sacramento, CA region. In addition to her organizational consulting work, Chance has been conducting research on social justice topics for more than ten years. Specifically, she has focused on scientifically examining social issues in the education field (elementary school and higher education) through services such as program evaluation, statistical consulting, and survey design/research.

Donna M. Chrobot-Mason, PhD, is an Associate Professor and Director of the Center for Organizational Leadership at the University of Cincinnati (UC). Her focus is on leadership across differences and strategies for creating organizational practices, policies, and a climate that supports diversity and fosters intergroup collaboration. Donna holds a PhD and Master's degree in Applied Psychology from the University of Georgia. She teaches undergraduate and graduate courses in Human Resources, Diversity, and Organizational Leadership and is co-director of the women's leadership development program, UC Women Lead.

Amanda Clinton is the Senior Director for the Office of International Affairs at the American Psychological Association. A licensed clinical psychologist and a credentialed school psychologist, Dr. Clinton has experience in academic, hospital, community, and policy settings. Dr. Clinton's scholarly work includes the edited volume titled *Integrated Assessment of the Bilingual Child* and numerous peer-reviewed papers and book chapters, as well as Associate Editorship of two journals. Her research interests include social-emotional learning, cultural adaptation, social justice, bilingualism, and learning disabilities.

Natalie C. Cotton-Nessler is an Assistant Professor of Management at Bentley University. She earned a PhD in Management and Sociology from the University of Michigan. She researches how people understand and use their relationships at work.

Stephanie J. Creary is an Assistant Professor of management and organizations at the Cornell University School of Hotel Administration. Her research examines questions related to identities and resources including how they emerge and affect workplace relationships, generativity, and the broader organizational environment. She earned her PhD in management with a concentration in organization studies from the Boston College Carroll School of Management.

Faye J. Crosby is a scholar, writer, consultant, and social activist. Most of her work concerns sex and race discrimination with a focus on remedies. She received her PhD in social psychology in 1976. Since 1997, Crosby has been Professor of Psychology at University of California, Santa Cruz. Previous faculty appointments included Rhode Island College, Yale University, The Kellogg School of Management, and Smith College. Crosby has authored or co-authored five books and has edited or co-edited another ten volumes. Her articles and chapters number about 200. She is the recipient of numerous professional awards. Crosby has held various administrative positions. She is the founder of Nag's Heart, an organization whose mission is the replenishment of the feminist spirit.

Diane Felicio is the Director of Resource and Business Development at Community Catalyst, a national healthcare consumer advocacy organization. She oversees fundraising and business development and did so during a time of significant growth for the organization, from an $11 million annual budget to $20 million. A social psychologist and mediator, Felicio has a knack for working effectively with non-profit professionals, academics, business executives, politicos, and policy wonks. She serves on the Advisory Board of the Equality Fund at The Boston Foundation and on the board of the Lesbian Political Action Committee (LPAC).

Katherine Giscombe is Consultant and Vice-President, Global Member Services, at Catalyst, a non-profit organization focused on advancement of women in the workplace. She led Catalyst's groundbreaking study, *Women of Color in Corporate Management: Opportunities and Barriers*, and several subsequent in-depth research projects on diverse women. She draws on her extensive corporate work experience, as well as academic theory, in directing consulting engagements. She also gives speeches and acts as media spokesperson for Catalyst, having been interviewed by National Public Radio, CNN-FN, CBS Radio, the Boston Globe, and ARISE News, among others.

Jessica Halem founded and leads the LGBT Office of Harvard Medical School within the Office for Diversity Inclusion and Community Partnership. Her research interests include LGBT leadership development and organizational change.

Kathy E. Kram is the Shipley Professor in Management Emerita at Boston University. Her primary interests are in the areas of adult development, relational learning, mentoring and developmental networks, leadership development, and change processes in organizations. In addition to her book, *Mentoring at Work: Developmental Relationships in Organizational Life*, she has published in a wide range of management and psychology journals. She is co-editor of *The Handbook of Mentoring at Work: Theory, Research, and Practice* with Dr. Belle Rose Ragins. Her most recent book, *Strategic Relationships at Work: Creating Your Circle of Mentors, Sponsors and Peers for Success in Business and Life*, was co-authored with Prof. Wendy Murphy.

Payal Kumar is an independent scholar based in Delhi, India. Her research interests include mentoring from a protégé perspective, Indian women leadership, and leadership from a follower-centric perspective.

Michelle Ann Kweder is a critical management scholar. Her primary focus is the critique of mainstream business school curricula and its exclusion of issues of poverty and inequality; this focus has led her to develop a method of intersectional, intertextual critical discourse analysis that she uses to analyze Harvard Business Publishing cases. She is an Affiliate at the Center for Gender in Organizations at Simmons College and the Administrative Director at the

Prison Legal Assistance Project at Harvard Law School. Kweder holds a BA in English and Women's Studies from Hamilton College, a MBA from Simmons College and a PhD in Business Administration, Organizations and Social Change from the University of Massachusetts – Boston.

Cheryl Leggon is an Associate Professor in the School of Public Policy at Georgia Institute of Technology; prior to that, she was a Staff Officer at the National Research Council/National Academy of Sciences. She was elected as a Fellow in the American Association for the Advancement of Science (AAAS) and Sigma Xi. As a sociologist, her research and evaluation work focus on under-represented race/ethnic/gender groups in the science and engineering workforces.

Audrey J. Murrell is Associate Dean, Kenneth R. Woodcock Faculty Fellow, and Director of the David Berg Center for Ethics and Leadership at the University of Pittsburgh, Katz Graduate School of Business and College of Business Administration. She conducts research on mentoring, career development, and social issues in management. This work has been published widely in journals, popular media and several books including: *Mentoring Dilemmas: Developmental Relationships within Multicultural Organizations* (with Crosby and Ely) and *Intelligent Mentoring: How IBM Creates Value through People, Knowledge and Relationships* (with Forte-Trummel and Bing).

Nisha Nair is a Clinical Assistant Professor of Business Administration at the Katz Graduate School of Business at the University of Pittsburgh. She has previously taught as a visiting faculty at the Cotsakos College of Business at William Paterson University and served as a tenured faculty member at the Indian Institute of Management (IIM) Indore. Her research interests are primarily in the dark side of employee behavior, namely work alienation and deviance. She is also interested in gender issues, managing conflict and emotions, and organizational development in the non-profit sector.

Stella M. Nkomo is a Professor in the Department of Human Resource Management at the University of Pretoria, South Africa. Her internationally recognized research on gender and diversity in organizations, human resource management, and leadership has been published in numerous journals and edited volumes. Current research interests focus on building knowledge and theory to understand race and gender issues in South Africa and Africa as well as continuing to interrogate taken-for-granted organizational concepts and relationships from critical management, postcolonial, and decolonial theoretical perspectives. She is currently President of The Africa Academy of Management.

Maureen O'Connor, PhD, JD, is the President of Palo Alto University, an institution dedicated to education and training in psychology. She spent nearly twenty years at the City University of New York (CUNY) as Professor and former Chair of Psychology at John Jay College and as Executive Director of the Doctoral Program in Psychology at the CUNY Graduate Center. Recent work has focused on evidence-based pedagogy development for doctoral students, and on innovative mentoring strategies. She is an APA Fellow and past-President of the Society for the Psychological Study of Social Issues.

Regina M. O'Neill is a Professor of Management at Suffolk University's Sawyer Business School. She studies mentoring, leadership, and career development in diverse settings, and her publications include race and gender in mentoring relationships, careers of women across ethnic identities, and leadership for social change. She consults for many corporate, educational, and non-profit organizations in the design and deliver of mentoring and leadership development programs focused on increasing organizational effectiveness through inclusiveness.

Karen L. Proudford is an Associate Professor of Management and Director of the Honors Program at the Graves School of Business and Management, Morgan State University. She is affiliated with the Center for Gender in Organizations, Simmons College and the Nonprofit Executive Leadership Institute, Bryn Mawr College. She received her BS from Florida A&M University and her PhD from the Wharton School, University of Pennsylvania. Before joining academia, she held positions at Honeywell and IBM.

Laura Morgan Roberts is a Professor in Antioch University's PhD Program in Leadership and Change. She is also a core faculty affiliate of the Center for Positive Organizations. Her research examines questions related to authenticity, identities, diversity, and best self engagement. She earned her MA and PhD (Organizational Psychology) from the University of Michigan.

Maureen Scully is a faculty member in the Organizations and Social Change area in the College of Management at the University of Massachusetts Boston. She is also a faculty affiliate of the Center for Gender in Organizations at the Simmons College School of Management and of the Aspen Institute for Business and Society. Her research explores how inequality is legitimated by meritocratic ideology and sometimes redressed by tempered radicals working for change from inside systems, with publications in *Academy of Management Journal*, *Human Relations*, *Organization*, *Organization Science*, and *Organization Studies*.

Jeannette E. South-Paul is the Andrew W. Mathieson UPMC Professor and Chair of the Department of Family Medicine at the University of Pittsburgh School of Medicine. She is a family physician responsible for the undergraduate medical education and faculty practices of three residencies and associated clinical sites. Her research focuses on cultural competence and reducing health disparities. She has served in leadership positions on national medical school and academic family medicine organizations. She is a graduate of the University of Pennsylvania and the University of Pittsburgh and was elected to the Institute of Medicine and the Gold Humanism Honor Society.

Margaret S. Stockdale (PhD Industrial-Organizational Psychology, Kansas State University) is Professor of Psychology and Chair, Department of Psychology at IUPUI. Dr. Stockdale is a Fellow of the American Psychological Association, the Society for Industrial/Organizational Psychology and the Society for the Psychological Study of Social Issues. Her research and consulting address gender issues in the workplace.

Neharika Vohra is a Professor of Organizational Behavior at IIM Ahmedabad, India. She completed her PhD in Social Psychology from the University of Manitoba, Canada. She has published over forty-five peer-reviewed research papers in top-level international and national journals and authored three books. She has research interests in the area of entrepreneurship, women leadership, change management, and education. She has been involved in competence building of executives in various sectors and across countries. She is currently the Chair of the Centre for Innovation and Incubation in Entrepreneurship Initiatives at IIMA, and is also on the advisory board of several companies, professional bodies, and academic institutes.

Montressa L. Washington is an Assistant Professor of Management–Arts, Entertainment and Media Management at the Harry F. Byrd, Jr. School of Business, Shenandoah University. She teaches courses in Organizational Behavior, Entrepreneurship, and Design and Innovation. Washington conducts mixed method research in the areas of strategic management, women's leadership, technology innovation, and social media.

PREFACE

Mentoring and Diversity—Challenges and Promises

Stacy Blake-Beard, Kathy E. Kram, and Audrey J. Murrell

> *It is not our differences that divide us. It is our inability to recognize, accept and celebrate those differences.*
>
> (Audre Lorde)

Overview

Mentoring continues to be of great interest to individuals who are navigating an increasingly complex world of work, and to organizations that need to identify, develop, and retain talent in order to maintain their competitive edge in this global economy. At the same time, scholars and practitioners recognize that our shared understanding of mentoring is limited by the relatively stable, hierarchical, and homogeneous context in which mentoring has been studied and practiced until quite recently. The purpose of this volume is to call attention to a number of challenges and promises that are posed by increased diversity at all levels of organization and society. We aim to illuminate the subtle yet powerful forces that can enhance or undermine the potential of mentoring to serve as a transformational tool for individuals of diverse backgrounds and organizations that must leverage diverse talent.

Foundations of Mentoring

We build on the shoulders of scholars and practitioners whose work over the last three plus decades has given us a solid understanding of the nature of mentoring as a developmental relationship, how it unfolds over time, and the possible outcomes of this developmental tool when its potential is realized. This work began with Kram's qualitative study of the relationships of eighteen pairs of mentors and protégés in one organizational context, summarized in *Mentoring at Work* (1985). Combined with subsequent empirical study (e.g., Chao, Walz, & Gardner, 1992; Noe, 1988a; Ragins & Cotton, 1999; Scandura, 1992), this foundational work illuminated the career and psychosocial functions that these developmental relationships offer those in need of mentoring, and how such relationships unfold over time. This early work illuminated how mentoring is a relational process, that under certain conditions would have a range of positive outcomes for both mentors and protégés.

Many scholars have built on this work during the ensuing decades to demonstrate first how the experiences of women differed from those of men (e.g., Burke & McKeen, 1990; Dreher & Ash, 1990; Noe, 1988b; Ragins, 1989, 1999; O'Neill & Blake-Beard, 2002), and then how the experiences of black and other racial minorities also differed from those of the white male majority, who were the primary subject of the earliest research on mentoring (Blake-Beard, 1999; Dreher & Cox, 1996; Murrell & Tangri, 1999; Thomas, 1990, 1993). Much progress has been made in our understanding of mentoring as evidenced in the publication of two major handbooks devoted to mentoring research and practice almost ten years ago (Allen & Eby, 2007; Ragins & Kram, 2007). These handbooks summarized extant literature on mentoring at work and in other settings and challenged scholars in the field to develop stronger theory, diverse methodologies, and expand the dialog of mentoring to include more diverse populations and organizational settings.

Concurrently, Mezias and Scandura (2005) pointed out the need for mentoring research to use data from contrasting cultures where mentoring dynamics are studied within the backdrop of a cultural context. Later, Ramaswami, Huang and Dreher (2014) examined the influence of power distance on mentoring and career attainment for men and women in Taiwanese and US cultures. They found interesting results in relation to power distance, gender, and nationality. For men, regardless of their power distance and their nationality, those who were involved in mentoring relationships did better in relation to their career attainment. This was not the case for women in the USA or in Taiwan. For the Taiwanese women, those with high power distance reported higher salaries than mentored women with low power distance. For the US women, the findings were the opposite—low power distance was critical for their career attainment. This study is one of many examples that speak to the importance of looking at diverse populations in diverse cultural contexts.

In addition to the context in which we are collecting data, we also have had opportunity to expand the outcomes that we are investigating. Kram and Ragins (2007) discussed the importance of expanding the outcomes explored beyond career-related outcomes. While it has been beneficial to understand the impact of mentoring on traditional outcomes such as performance, compensation, promotions, advancement, job attitudes, and career satisfaction, there are so many more outcomes that are germane to mentoring studies and research. New lines of inquiry that mentoring scholars can pursue include investigating the impact of mentoring on learning, relational competencies, personal development and growth, as well as physiological and other health-related outcomes. Kram and Ragins further expanded the discussion of potential outcomes by sharing how the work–family interface may be inter-related with mentoring, including attention to family interference with work and work enrichment of family. These outcomes reflect one way that the field and study of mentoring can be broadened and deepened; people are more than their careers and our studies of mentoring should reflect these broadened borders.

The promise of mentoring means that there has been increased interest in this process as a tool for organizations to support and develop their employees, in particular their pipeline of leadership. The positive effects of mentoring have been linked to the adoption of formal mentoring programs by many organizations, including 71 percent of the Fortune 500 (Holt, Markova, Dhaenens, Marler, & Heilmann, 2016). But the proliferation of mentoring programs has not been accompanied by the accompanying level of research on formal mentoring; the extant research has focused predominantly on informal mentoring relationships. The development and delivery of effective organizationally sponsored mentoring programs is another area of research in need of more attention. Chen, Liao, and Wen (2014) studied the experiences of 208 formal mentor–protégé dyads in the People's Republic of China, addressing the gaps in the literature on both formal mentoring and mentoring in other cultural contexts. They found a relationship between formal mentoring and the outcomes of affective commitment and turnover intention: those involved in formal mentoring reported higher levels of affective commitment and lower levels of turnover intention. They also noted that power distance mediated the relationship between formal mentoring and perceived psychological safety. However, the benefits of formal versus informal mentoring continue to be strongly debated (Henderson, 2003). Given the increase in the use of formal mentoring programs across the globe, more attention to their impact will be beneficial as organizations continue efforts to attract, retain, and advance diverse talent into leadership roles.

Over time, the complexities posed by gender, racial, and ethnic diversity have been examined further. It is now evident that it is not simply one's gender or race that alters the traditional mentoring processes discovered in the early 1980s, but also the relational dynamics and the surrounding organizational culture and practices that shape the experiences of mentoring, as well as the benefits and costs of engaging in such alliances. Most recently, new theoretical lenses including intersectionality (e.g., Crenshaw, 1991; Buzzanell, Long, Anderson, Kokini, & Batra, 2015; Holvino, 2001), Positive Organizational Scholarship (e.g., Cameron, Dutton, & Quinn, 2003; Dutton & Ragins, 2007; Roberts, 2006), Relational Cultural Theory (RCT) (e.g., Fletcher & Ragins, 2007; Jordan, Kaplan, Miller, Stiver, & Surrey, 1991; Kram, 1996; Miller,

1976), Critical Management Studies (CMS) (e.g., Alvesson & Willmott, 1992; Fournier & Grey, 2000; Zanoni, Janssens, Benschop, & Nkomo, 2010), and social network theory (Higgins & Kram, 2001; Murphy & Kram, 2014) have given us tools that enable us to highlight important nuances that powerfully affect the mentoring experience and its varied consequences.

A Roadmap for this Book

The contributors to this volume are women and people of color who recognize that our own dimensions of diversity have changed and challenged our views and experiences of mentoring. Thus, the chapters in this volume bring diverse voices and new theoretical perspectives to the discourse on mentoring. Our hope is that our own personal experiences, theoretical lenses, and understanding of extant scholarship and practice will lead to a new appreciation for the complexities that characterize the intersection of mentoring and diversity in a global context. Ultimately, we hope to offer a rich array of possibilities to effectively leverage mentoring as a tool for individual, leadership, and organizational transformation.

Our understanding of how mentoring is affected by and impacts on diversity has helped us to change how we approach the need to develop effective diverse leaders locally and globally. With this volume, we have created a global dialog across a number of scholars, colleagues, and collaborators in order to better understand the role of mentoring in creating change for people, processes, and paradigms. The chapters are organized into these three major themes.

Change for People

We start at the micro or individual level where there is a need to expand our knowledge of how mentoring impacts people at work and in their lives. We find a number of gaps in both the literature and organizational practice. Much of the mentoring literature is based on examining the experiences of majority individuals within a US-centric perspective. While previous work has examined mentoring through diversity dimensions, such as gender and race, there are aspects of diversity that remain untapped or even ignored. Thus, Donna Blancero and Natalie Cotton-Nessler share the experiences of Latino leaders, as they are navigating the changing nature of the psychological contract. Their work questions the use of traditional mentoring perspectives, which have been described as much more transactional; they apply RCT—Relational Cultural Theory—which by definition is a relational perspective, as more relevant to understanding the mentoring experiences of Latinos. Gilda Barbarino, Shereka Banton, and Cheryl Leggon examine the mentoring experiences of women striving to succeed within the non-traditional and male-dominated profession of academic engineering. Stacy Blake-Beard, Jessica Halem, Estelle Archibold,

Dorian Boncoeur, Andrea Burton, and Payal Kumar used their interviews of professional Indian women to better understand the interaction of gender, race, ethnicity, and culture on their subjects' mentoring relationships.

In addition, Stephanie Creary and Laura Morgan Roberts use a Positive Organizational Scholarship (POS) lens to discuss mentoring as a source of positive identity construction. Building on conceptual work applying the positive approach to mentoring (Ragins, 2012), Creary and Roberts position mentoring as a catalyst that may allow diverse leaders to enhance positive modes of thinking and behavior, and, as important, to temper/shift negative patterns of thought and action. Mentoring, from their perspective, is important because it supports increased personal leadership effectiveness through the development of positive identities. Their model of mentoring (G.I.V.E.) offers diverse leaders a space to cultivate positive identities to enhance their personal leadership effectiveness and a tool to contribute to their organizations from a position of strength.

Collectively, these authors' work highlights the importance of acknowledging that people across the spectrum of diversity may and do have different experiences of mentoring—that the relationship may evolve differently, may affect outcomes differently, and may be held differently in diverse contexts. Examining mentoring relationships across dimensions of difference provides a critical opportunity to enrich our knowledge about this developmental process, as well as its impact on producing positive versus negative outcomes for diverse groups.

Change for Processes

It is interesting to note that mentoring is a relational phenomenon that can be used to enhance a wide array of processes. Mentoring impacts organizational processes (e.g., recruitment, retention, leadership development), individual processes (e.g., involvement, commitment, satisfaction), and interpersonal processes (e.g., attachment, identification, and socialization). Most recently, mentoring has been linked to transformational processes such as globalization, inclusion, and innovation.

In the second section of this book, the use of mentoring as a "process to support processes" is explored. Each of these chapters raises important questions about how mentoring can change organizational systems, programs, structures, and approaches. Audrey Murrell and Jeannette South-Paul explore peer mentoring as a tool for social influence that may reposition diversity as a transformative tool within academic medicine. Katherine Giscombe offers guidance for how organizations can better leverage formal mentoring programs to support women of color as leaders throughout the organization. Nisha Nair and Neharika Vohra challenge us to rethink the intersection of mentoring, diversity, and inclusion, and remind us that we must look beyond the shores of North America with insights on mentoring as a tool for inclusion for women in India. Karen Proudford and Montressa Washington present a process view of sponsorship and offer a provocative notion of formal sponsorship as an organizational routine that can either inhibit or facilitate the progress of diverse leaders within an organization. Each one of these chapters speaks to the promise that examining mentoring as a process to support other processes offers much promise for future research and for future organizational practice.

Change for Paradigms

In the previous two sections, each chapter contributor attempts to advance our thinking on existing topics within the extant literature on mentoring. However, offering insights on how mentoring can create change for paradigms is quite different. We would be remiss if we did not take advantage of the opportunity to question the very fundamental assumptions and traditions underlying mentoring relationships, process, and valued outcomes. The foundations of mentoring theory and practice are created from the perspective, life experiences, and world-view of white, educated, upper economic level, employed, US-born men. To merely include diverse people within a research sample and compare the "differences" in research results ignores the fundamental truth that paradigms based on the reality of one group may not fit, support, or advance the experience of other diverse groups. This practice merely perpetuates the view of diverse groups as the "Other" and will not transform our thinking in meaningful ways about mentoring. Given the entrance of women and men of many different races and ethnicities into the global workforce and leadership ranks, it is time to question this traditional model and perhaps dismantle it.

We believe that mentoring provides an avenue to engage paradigm shifts of the kind that are called for when we look at global forces that are changing not only organizations but also our world. Maureen Scully, Stacy Blake-Beard, Regina O'Neill, and Diane Felicio talk about mentoring and class, using their chapter as a space to contextualize mentoring in the mythic meritocracy that is still representative of our current organizational context. They question the concept of mentoring itself, noting the ways that the process is "classed." They inquire about the need to contemplate mentoring as a metaphorical ladder in the contemporary organizational landscape. Michelle Kweder offers an adept application of Critical Management Studies (CMS) to critically assess mentoring. Her use of three precepts (questioning the performativity of intent, denaturalizing taken for granted organizational knowledge, and expecting a high level of reflexivity) from CMS to critique mentoring theory and practice is provocative. With Kweder, we are asked to consider whether mentoring is a powerful developmental tool for the uplifting and advancement of individuals or whether it is "a mechanism of the historically contextualized contemporary capitalist organization."

One of the most exciting aspects of this book is the identification of mentoring as a tool for transformation. For example, Faye Crosby, Margaret Stockdale,

Donna Chrobot-Mason, and Randie Chance share a model of peer mentoring via mentoring circles—Nag's Heart retreats. They discuss this alternative form of mentoring and the outcomes participants in Nag's Heart retreats reported. These outcomes include increased feelings of competence, greater empowerment, and enhanced inner strength. Most of all, Nag's Heart participants reported feeling not alone, validated, and strengthened by the community created by this process. Meg Bond, Maureen O'Connor, and Amanda Clinton explicitly encourage us to see mentoring as a catalyst for social justice, especially within the context of educational systems, which should be used as a vehicle for social mobility as well as equality. These papers, in particular, highlight the opportunity to broaden and deepen our knowledge of mentoring. Through them, we see glaring gaps in the literature, gaps that are painful to acknowledge because of the socio-historical discourse that often hinders collective understanding and collective action. However, it is necessary for us to look at these places where our very paradigms must be shifted—it is here that the future lays.

Final Thoughts

We offer this book as an invitation for dialog and as a resource for both research and practice. We invited our contributors to push the boundaries, challenge our assumptions, and apply a critical eye to existing research and organizational practice. We are interested in expanding the discourse on mentoring and diversity beyond a traditional focus on career outcomes and organizational effectiveness. We invite into this dialog challenging and complex issues such as social class, power, inclusion, as well as culture and organizational routines that perpetuate unequal access. Our work has gathered together a collection of innovative thinkers who embraced our challenge. We are thrilled to share their new theories, models, and ways of thinking about mentoring, particularly in terms of how these frameworks can shape and transform diverse leaders in global organizations into the future.

At the heart of this book is our belief and our hope that mentoring acts as a catalyst and tool of social change for authentic and ethical leaders. In his essay on authenticity, Warren Bennis (2013) shared his experience with mentoring as a container to both receive and develop this critical leadership competency. He talked about becoming the leader he is in large part because of the mentoring relationships that accompanied him through his graduate studies. Fries-Britt and Snider (2015) speak on the importance of authenticity specifically in the relationships of people of color; they suggest that standard mentoring relationships do not meet the needs of URMs—under-represented minorities. These articles each speak to the pivotal role that mentoring holds in the careers of all leaders. With access to this critical developmental relationship, leaders across the spectrum of age, race, gender, class, and nationality will have "personal learning, skill development, enhanced performance, and a rich array of other outcomes critical for the continued growth of individuals, groups and organizations" (Kram & Ragins, 2007: 687). Please join us in examining the complexities and promise of diversity and mentoring.

References

Allen, T. D., & Eby, L. T. (2007). *The Blackwell handbook of mentoring: A multiple perspectives approach*. Malden, MA: Blackwell Publishing.

Alvesson, M., & Willmott, H. (Eds.). (1992). *Critical management studies*. London: Sage.

Bennis, W. (2013). Authenticity. *Leadership Excellence Essentials, 30*(5), 3–4.

Blake-Beard, S. D. (1999). The costs of living as an outsider within: An analysis of the mentoring relationship and career success of Black and White women in the corporate sector. *Journal of Career Development, 26*, 21–36.

Burke, R. J., & McKeen, C. A. (1990). Mentoring in organizations: Implications for women. *Journal of Business Ethics, 9*, 317–332.

Buzzanell, P. M., Long, Z., Anderson, L. B., Kokini, K., & Batra, J. C. (2015). Mentoring in academe: A feminist, poststructural lens on stories of women engineering faculty of color. *Management Communication Quarterly, 29*(3), 440–457.

Cameron, K. S., Dutton, J. E., & Quinn, R. E. (Eds.). (2003). *Positive organizational scholarship: Foundations of a new discipline*. San Francisco, CA: Berrett-Koehler.

Chao, G. T., Walz, P. M., & Gardner, P. D. (1992). Formal and informal mentorships: A comparison on mentoring functions and contrast with nonmentored counterparts. *Personnel Psychology, 45*, 619–636.

Chen, C., Liao, J., & Wen, P. (2014). Why does formal mentoring matter? The mediating role of psychological safety and the moderating role of power distance orientation in the Chinese context. *International Journal of Human Resource Management, 25*(8), 1112–1130.

Crenshaw, K. (1991). Mapping the margins: Intersectionality, identity politics, and violence against women of color. *Stanford Law Review, 43*(6), 1241–1299.

Dreher, G. F., & Ash, R. A. (1990). A comparative study of mentoring among men and women in managerial, professional, and technical positions. *Journal of Applied Psychology, 75*(5), 539–546.

Dreher, G. F., & Cox, T. H. (1996). Race, gender, and opportunity: A study of compensation attainment and the establishment of mentoring relationships. *Journal of Applied Psychology, 81*(3), 297–308.

Dutton, J. E., & Ragins, B. R. (Eds.) (2007). *Exploring positive relationships at work: Building a theoretical and research foundation*. Mahwah, NJ: Lawrence Erlbaum.

Fletcher, J. K., & Ragins, B. R. (2007). Stone Center relational cultural theory: A window on relational mentoring. In B. R. Ragins, & K. E. Kram (Eds.), *The handbook of mentoring at work: Theory, research, and practice* (pp. 373–399). Thousand Oaks, CA: Sage.

Fournier, V., & Grey, C. (2000). At the critical moment: Conditions and prospects for critical management studies. *Human Relations, 53*(1): 7–32.

Fries-Britt, S., & Snider, J. (2015). Mentoring outside the line: The importance of authenticity, transparency, and vulnerability in effective mentoring relationships. *New Directions for Higher Education, 171*, 3–11.

Henderson, H. V. (2003, June). Why mentoring doesn't work. *Harvard Business Review*, C0306B-PDF-ENG.

Higgins, M. C., & Kram, K. E. (2001). Reconceptualizing mentoring at work: A developmental network perspective. *Academy of Management Review, 26*(2), 264–288.

Holt, D. T., Markova, G., Dhaenens, A. J., Marler, L. E., & Heilmann, S. G. (2016). Formal or informal mentoring. What drives employees to seek informal mentor? *Journal of Managerial Issues, 28*(1–2), 67–82.

Holvino, E. (2001). *Complicating gender: The simultaneity of race, gender and class in organizational change(ing)*. Center for Gender in Organizations Working Paper No. 14, Boston, MA.

Jordan, J. V., Kaplan, A. G., Miller, J. B., Stiver, L. P., & Surrey, J. L. (1991). *Women's growth in connection: Writings from the Stone Center*. New York: The Guilford Press.

Kram, K. E. (1985). *Mentoring at work: Developmental relationships in organizational life*. Glenview, IL: Scott, Foresman.

Kram, K. E. (1996). A relational approach to career development. In D. T. Hall (Ed.), *The career is dead—Long live the career: A relational approach to careers* (pp. 132–157). San Francisco, CA: Jossey-Bass.

Kram, K. E., & Ragins, B. R. (2007). The landscape of mentoring in the 21st century. *The handbook of mentoring at work: Theory, research, and practice* (pp. 685–692). Los Angeles, CA: Sage Publications.

Mezias, J., & Scandura, T. A. (2005). A needs-driven approach to expatriate adjustment and career development: A multiple mentoring perspective. *Journal of International Business Studies, 36*(5), 519–538.

Miller, J. B. (1976). *Toward a new psychology of women*. Boston, MA: Beacon Press.

Murrell, A. J., & Tangri, S. S. (1999). Mentoring at the margin. In A. J. Murrell, F. J. Crosby, & R. J. Ely (Eds.), *Mentoring dilemmas: Developmental relationships within multicultural organizations* (pp. 211–224). Mahwah, NJ: Lawrence Erlbaum.

Murphy, W., & Kram, K. E. (2014). *Strategic relationships at work: Creating your circle of mentors, sponsors, and peers for success in business and life*. New York: McGraw Hill Professional.

O'Neill, R. M., & Blake-Beard, S. D. (2002). Gender barriers to the female mentor–male protégé relationship. *Journal of Business Ethics, 37*(1), 51–63.

Noe, R. A. (1988a). An investigation of the determinants of successful assigned mentoring relationships. *Personnel Psychology, 41*(3), 457–479.

Noe, R. A. (1988b). Women in mentoring: A review and research agenda. *Academy of Management Review, 13*, 65–78.

Ragins, B. R. (1989). Barriers to mentoring: The female manager's dilemma. *Human Relations, 42*, 1–22.

Ragins, B. R. (1999). Gender and mentoring relationships: A review and research agenda for the next decade. In G. N. Powell (Ed.), *Handbook of gender and work* (pp. 347–370). Thousand Oaks, CA: Sage.

Ragins, B. R. (2012). Relational mentoring: A positive approach to mentoring at work. In K. S. Cameron, & G. M. Spreitzer (Eds.), *The Oxford handbook of positive organizational scholarship*. New York: Oxford University Press.

Ragins, B. R., & Cotton, J. L. (1999). Mentor functions and outcomes: A comparison of men and women in formal and informal mentoring relationships. *Journal of Applied Psychology, 84*(4), 529–550.

Ragins, B. R., & Kram, K. E. (Eds.) (2007). *The handbook of mentoring at work: Theory, research, and practice*. Thousand Oaks, CA: Sage.

Ramaswami, A., Huang, J. C., & Dreher, G. (2014). Interaction of gender, mentoring, and power distance on career attainment: A cross-cultural comparison. *Human Relations, 67*(2), 153–173.

Roberts, L. M. (2006). Shifting the lens on organizational life: The added value of positive scholarship. *Academy of Management Review, 31,* 241–260.

Scandura, T. A. (1992). Mentorship and career mobility: An empirical investigation. *Journal of Organizational Behavior, 13*(2), 169–174.

Thomas, D. A. (1990). The impact of race on managers' experiences of developmental relationships (mentoring and sponsorship): An intra-organizational study. *Journal of Organizational Behavior, 11*(6), 479–492.

Thomas, D. A. (1993). Racial dynamics in cross-racial developmental relationships. *Administrative Science Quarterly, 38,* 169–194.

Zanoni, P., Janssens, M., Benschop, Y., & Nkomo, S. M. (2010). Unpacking diversity, grasping inequality: Rethinking difference through critical perspectives. *Organization, 17*(1), 9–29.

PART I
Creating Change for People

1

G.I.V.E.-BASED MENTORING IN DIVERSE ORGANIZATIONS

Cultivating Positive Identities in Diverse Leaders

Stephanie J. Creary and Laura Morgan Roberts

Mentoring is a widely accepted practice for developing leaders around the world. Mentoring offers instrumental benefits, namely, promoting career advancement into (higher level) leadership positions (Blake-Beard, 1999, 2001; Murrell, Blake-Beard, Porter, & Perkins-Williamson, 2008; Murrell, Crosby, & Ely, 1999; Murrell & Tangri, 1999; Ragins & Kram, 2007). Mentoring also equips people to lead change more effectively within organizations, helping them to learn how to activate power and access resources that promote systemic change (Blake-Beard, 2001; Murrell et al., 2008; Ragins, 1997). In fact, in a survey of diversity management practices in fifty-nine large public and private companies, we found that nearly 60 percent of these companies were using formal mentoring programs to develop leaders from under-represented, non-prototypical groups (hereafter, "diverse leaders") in the United States and approximately 30 percent of these same companies were using formal mentoring programs to develop diverse leaders in other geographic locations around the world. Yet, in spite of these efforts, developing diverse leaders continues to be a challenge around the world.

One reason why developing diverse leaders is difficult—and why mentoring is so important—is that these leaders face unique challenges in cultivating positive identities at work. Diverse leaders experience challenges having their leadership claims validated and authenticated by others who view them and their leadership as different from the "norm" (Roberts, Cha, Hewlin, & Settles, 2009). Identity construction is central to leadership—in order to mobilize and influence others, a "leader" must be viewed as credible by his/her followers. The act of leadership involves putting forth a claim by asserting oneself as an influential or authoritative actor, which is then granted (or accepted) through the other person's followership. This claiming/granting process takes place more smoothly for people who fit into prototypical profiles of leaders; meaning, they embody the commonly held or stereotypical characteristics of those in organizational leadership roles. In fact, there has been a shocking convergence around the prototypical characteristics of leadership, which include dominance and assertiveness, as well as demographic traits and characteristics of race (i.e., White), gender (i.e., male), and age (Eagly & Karau, 2002; Ensari & Murphy, 2003; Rosette, Leonardelli, & Phillips, 2008). Leaders from under-represented, non-prototypical groups do not fit the mold of "typical" characteristics and features associated with leaders (Lord & Maher, 1991). For instance, Rosette and colleagues (2008) found that people are more likely to designate White individuals as leaders and to evaluate them as being effective leaders relative to African American, Hispanic American, and Asian American individuals. Even when non-prototypical leaders succeed, they receive less personal credit for leadership effectiveness; their success is likely attributed to external factors (e.g., the rest of the team, external conditions, etc.).

Diverse leaders who struggle to feel validated, authenticated, and credible at work may also find it difficult to understand and manage these negative experiences in constructive ways. For instance, they may internalize and personalize negative encounters, which not only jeopardizes their ability to maintain positive relationships at work, but also their ability to lead well (Roberts, 2007b). Mentorship may be critical for buffering the impact of negative workplace experiences on diverse leaders' assessment of the organizational climate (for evidence of the positive buffering function of mentoring, see Zagenczyk, Gibney, Kiewitz, & Restubog, 2009). We propose that mentorship serves an additional related function: helping diverse leaders to change negative patterns of thought and action around internal experiences, interactions, and behaviors to those that are more positive and constructive. In other words, mentors help diverse leaders develop greater *personal leadership effectiveness* even in the face of identity challenges. When mentors engage in leadership development practices (e.g., coaching, strategic career planning, networking) that encourage diverse leaders to G.I.V.E. (i.e., *Grow, Integrate diverse identities at work, engage in Virtuous action at work, and affirm their sense of worth and Esteem*), diverse leaders will be better positioned to contribute creatively at work from positions of strength.

In this chapter, we focus on positive identity cultivation as a key mechanism for increasing personal leadership effectiveness, and describe several ways that mentors can help diverse leaders understand and manage their internal experiences, interactions, and behaviors while navigating challenging experiences at work through G.I.V.E.-based mentoring. We begin with a discussion of positive identity cultivation and how it generates the social and emotional resources that are key to personal leadership effectiveness. Then, we reveal how mentoring can facilitate this process of positive identity cultivation for diverse leaders who face challenging experiences at work. We propose that positive identity cultivation enables mentors and protégés to generate valuable resources for their organizations; therefore, both protégés and mentors benefit from G.I.V.E.-based mentoring. We conclude with our characterization of G.I.V.E.-based mentoring as a form of relational leadership. Hereafter, we explore these ideas in more detail.

Understanding Positive Identity Construction

Scholars in the fields of psychology, sociology, organizational studies, race/ ethnic studies, and gender studies have explored identities extensively (for an interdisciplinary discussion of identity features, see Roberts & Creary, 2011). Though these varied traditions examine different facets of identity construction and identity-related outcomes, common threads weave together a general understanding of identity. In brief, identities are the answers to the questions, "Who am I? Who are you? Who are we? Who are they?" Identities matter because they evoke thoughts, activate emotions, and guide behavior. These cognitions, emotions, and behaviors mutually influence one another to shape our reality. Our identities also help us to understand how we fit into our social world, based on our defining characteristics as well as our relationships with others. Some defining characteristics are personally distinctive qualities, such as being driven and compassionate, but most identities become meaningful through relative comparisons and relationships with other people. For example, role identities help us to understand who we are, within the context of our relationships to other people (e.g., mother *of Isaiah*, manager *of the sales department*, mentor *of junior-level women scholars of color*). Our social identities also help us to understand and appreciate our connections to groups, communities, and organizations (e.g., Native *of Gary, Indiana*, IBM*'er*, graduate of *The University of Michigan*, fan of the *Boston Celtics*). Our personally distinctive qualities, role identities, and social identities constitute a unique constellation of characteristics and affiliations that shape our perspectives, feelings, and actions. Importantly, our various identities also shape our interactions with others.

In general, identities are co-created and co-constructed through both transformative experiences and through micro-encounters with other people (DeRue & Ashford, 2010; Ibarra, 1999; Pratt, Rockmann, & Kaufmann, 2006). Throughout the course of our lives, we learn about ourselves from interpersonal feedback, and we grow and change through our experiences. For leaders, the process of identity co-creation is especially important, as leaders cannot assert power, authority, and influence in a vacuum. Research by DeRue and Ashford (2010) indicates that the process of leadership emergence and leadership identity development is a process of claiming and granting, as described earlier. Likewise, all identities are also negotiated on an ongoing basis, from day to day, moment to moment, and encounter to encounter. For example, a professor negotiates her identity as "teacher" when she stands in front of the classroom, responding to a question from a student. A newcomer negotiates his identity as "high potential" when he introduces himself on the first day of orientation. An investment banker negotiates her identity as a "financial expert" when she presents her firm's bid to cover an industry leader's IPO. A scientist negotiates his identity when he presents his research discoveries at an academic conference. In each scenario, the other parties are evaluating the diverse leader's identity claims: Can this person lead the initiative? Do I trust their ability? Are they capable of wise decision-making? In this respect, diverse leaders' identities—and subsequent effectiveness—depend not only on their own self-views, but also on the perceptions that others have of them.

The vast majority of healthy, functioning people want to develop and establish a positive sense of self (for a collection of recent articles that develop these claims, see Roberts & Dutton, 2009). Notwithstanding the small percentage of individuals who have very negative self-views, and seek confirmatory feedback about these negative self-views, most people seek to hold positive self-views (Gecas, 1982), desire to be viewed positively by others (Swann, Pelham, & Krull, 1989), and, as a result, seek to construct *positive* identities—those that consist of a self-definition that is favorable or valuable in some way (Roberts & Dutton, 2009). Positive identity construction is the process of (re)defining a personal or collective identity using images, stories, and descriptions that are considered to be positive or valuable in some way.

Positive Identity Construction and the Generation of Social and Emotional Resources at Work

Positive identities provide people with essential social and emotional resources for effecting desirable changes within their own patterns of thought and action (for a review of the benefits of positive work identities, see Dutton, Roberts, & Bednar, 2010). By "resources," we mean "entities valued in their own right" or "entities that act as a means to obtain centrally valued ends" (Hobfoll, 2002: 307). To this end, *social resources* are "the valuable assets that inhere in the structure, content, and quality of the connections individuals have with others at work" (Hobfoll, 2002: 307). All humans require social resources for vitality; as a species, individuals have a fundamental desire and need for belonging, as they cannot exist in isolation independently. Research on mentoring supports the importance of building social resources (Higgins & Kram, 2001; Kram, 1985), and that cross-race relationships often provide less of this valuable social support than same-race relationships (Hayes-James, 2000; Thomas, 1990). Positive identities help individuals to build relationships across difference in ways that facilitate healthy outcomes and thriving in the workplace and beyond. Positive identities equip people to endure hardship and build relationships with others, who can support them in times of challenge.

Positive identity cultivation also activates and diffuses positive emotions (Dutton et al., 2010). Namely, positive identity cultivation activates positive emotion pathways, which help to broaden and build *emotional resources*. Like social resources, emotional resources help individuals to access other resources. According to the broaden-and-build theory of positive emotions (Fredrickson, 1998, 2001), positive emotions widen the range of thoughts and actions that come to mind, which enables the building of other personal resources including physical and intellectual resources. Positive emotions also enable individuals to cope with negative emotions, foster psychological resiliency, and trigger upward spirals of positive emotions toward enhanced emotional well-being (Fredrickson, 1998, 2001). Through seeing oneself, and being seen by others, in more favorable and/or valuable ways, people experience more positive emotions. As a consequence, they start to notice and embrace more resources that enable them to innovate, create, and even nurture more relationships in the environment that they otherwise would have overlooked (Fredrickson, 2009).

Mentoring Diverse Leaders for Personal Leadership Effectiveness

Mentors are important for helping diverse leaders cultivate positive identities that will enable them to develop greater personal leadership effectiveness at work. Herein, we use the G.I.V.E. model of positive identity construction (Roberts, 2014; Dutton et al., 2010) to reveal four key pathways through which mentors can help protégés develop personal leadership effectiveness. G.I.V.E. stands for **G**rowing, **I**ntegrated, **V**irtuous, and **E**steemed selves. Each pathway indicates how diverse leaders might establish a more positive sense of self at work, and lends insight into how mentors can facilitate the process of positive identity construction. Below, we briefly define the four pathways, and then detail each pathway as it applies to mentoring diverse leaders.

> *Growing*: I am becoming more like my desired self (for example, progressing in positive ways at work).

> *Integrated*: The different parts of my identity (such as work roles, demographic characteristics, family status and relationships, and organizational memberships) are connected in compatible and enriching ways.

> *Virtuous*: I possess virtuous qualities (such as courage, wisdom, integrity, humility, and compassion) and I display these virtues at work.

> *Esteemed*: I am worthy of positive regard (for example, I feel positively about my defining characteristics and/or group affiliations, and I believe others understand and appreciate my authentic self at work).

Cultivating Growth

The first pathway reflects the most common emphasis of mentoring—promoting growth and development. Many diverse leaders engage in self-protective behavior, afraid to display their vulnerability, and they therefore miss opportunities to learn and grow from their mistakes or more negative experiences in general (Giscombe, 2015; Roberts, 2007a). Mentors can help diverse leaders establish and/or affirm a more positive sense of self as evolving, adapting, and contributing in positive ways at work. Mentors can help diverse leaders to grow by creating a safe space in which learning and adaptation can take place.

Constructive Developmental Theory (CDT) (Kegan, 1980, 1982) proposes that individuals have the capacity to change, adapt, and attain optimal well-being throughout the lifespan by evolving in their meaning-making systems. Kegan reveals six stages in a developmental process that reflect a person's ability to balance his or her own perceptions and impulses relative to the needs of others. The incorporative (Stage 0) and impulsive stages (Stage 1) are marked by complete or substantial dependency on others to meet one's own needs and manage one's own behavior. The imperial stage (Stage 2) and the interpersonal stage (Stage 3) are marked by greater self-sufficiency, but people in these stages need clear direction and a lot of structure provided by others in order to grow in their abilities. In contrast, the institutional stage (Stage 4) is marked by an increased sense of self as distinct from others. A person in Stage 4 has a greater ability to self-author and own one's behavior without being bound to the current surroundings. Thus, the role of the Other for those in the institutional stage is to encourage and validate, while helping individuals to see their encounters as opportunities for growth. Finally, the interindividual stage (Stage 5) is marked by an orientation toward the process of transformation itself and a view that negative experiences are just as important as positive ones to transformation.

Mentorship is more effective when the mentor is aware of protégé's developmental needs. Mentors of diverse leaders can be especially helpful in facilitating challenging transitions from the socialized mind (CDT Stage 3), in which a diverse leader is driven by social pressures and desires at work, to a self-authoring mind (CDT Stage 4), in which a diverse leader is an active creator of his or her work experiences. For example, when transitioning into a new leadership role, leaders must overcome ego defensive routines that are often triggered by identity threats (Roberts, 2007a) by emphasizing forward movement along a growth trajectory.

While learning from one's negative experiences can be advantageous for diverse leaders, developmental readiness influences how receptive a protégé may be toward developing the Growing Self. Avolio and Hannah (2008) define developmental readiness as "both the ability and the motivation to attend to, make meaning of, and appropriate new knowledge into one's long term member structures." Developmental readiness is comprised of goal orientation, developmental efficacy, self-awareness and clarity, leader complexity, and meta-cognitive ability, which are all important to leadership growth and development. The first three components of developmental readiness are most amenable to the positive influence of mentors. Research shows that a learning goal orientation (Dweck, 2006, 2000) (vs. performance goal orientation) promotes psychological safety (Edmondson, 1999, 2012), because mistakes are viewed as part of the learning process. In this respect, diverse leaders with a learning goal orientation as opposed to a performance goal orientation may be more likely to interpret negative feedback as being developmental and useful rather than as a sign of failure.

Mentors can play a critical role in helping diverse leaders to frame negative feedback using a learning goal orientation. For example, as is the case with leader–follower relationships, when mentors demonstrate humility (Owens & Hekman, 2012; Owens, Johnson, & Mitchell, 2013), they can help diverse leaders to learn how to grow. By being more transparent about their own challenges, mentors can help to legitimate diverse leaders' developmental journeys and facilitate learning from them.

Mentors can play an important role by helping protégés to make sense of their negative experiences in ways that increase clarity and build efficacy. Developmental efficacy represents a leader's level of confidence that he or she can develop a specific leadership ability or skill. Efficacy helps diverse leaders to envision successful outcomes from developmental experiences, reflect on their learning, seek more performance feedback, and engage more generally (Avolio & Hannah, 2008; Hannah, Avolio, Luthans, & Harms, 2008; VandeWalle, Cron, & Slocum, 2001). Self-awareness and clarity can enable diverse leaders to understand the root causes of their negative career experiences, and use these insights to increase their leadership effectiveness. Self-reflection is critical to this process. Avolio, Wernsing, Chan, and Griffeth (2007) proposed that leaders can engage in either adaptive or maladaptive self-reflection. Mentors can help to facilitate adaptive self-reflection, which is a constructive process of reflection characterized by openness, positivity, and a learning goal orientation that promotes leadership development. In contrast, maladaptive self-reflection is more of a destructive process of reflection characterized by negative emotions such as anxiety, self-doubt and fear, focus on what did not work as opposed to what can be changed, and an excessive focus on self versus task. Through interpersonal sharing with mentors, diverse leaders can reflect upon the emotions that arise from their negative experiences and how those emotions are influencing their thoughts, behaviors, existing identities, and possible selves. These examples show how mentorship and positive identity construction work in conjunction to promote greater willingness to grow and develop among diverse leaders.

Cultivating Integration

Mentors can also help diverse leaders establish and/or affirm a more positive sense of self by helping them to view the different parts of their identity (including those aspects that are non-prototypical) as being connected in compatible and enriching ways. Diverse leaders can bring distinctive contributions to organizations by virtue of their diverse identities. Under-represented and non-prototypical identities generate several forms of "non-dominant cultural capital," including: symbolic capital (e.g., racial and cultural physically distinctive features that symbolize virtues), social capital (e.g., racial and cultural identity group experiences that help to build relationships), psychological and intellectual capital (e.g., racial and cultural identity perspectives that inform work processes or outcomes) (Roberts & Cha, 2016). These forms of non-dominant cultural capital equip leaders to draw upon marginalization to promote self-reliance, creativity, diligence, perseverance, biculturalism, attunement to others' perceptions, and relationships with constituencies (Roberts & Cha, 2016). Yet these aspects of diverse leaders' selves—and the forms of capital or resources that they generate—can be overlooked or even suppressed due to assimilation pressures. Identity integration (vs. segmentation or suppression) is important because it promotes effective coping (Caza & Wilson, 2009) and boundary spanning (Uhl-Bien, Marion, & McKelvey, 2007). Integration also stimulates creativity (Cheng, Sanchez-Burks, & Lee, 2008; Ely & Thomas, 2001), by tapping into novel insights and perspectives based on varied identity experiences. Further, integration is important because it enhances authenticity (Roberts et al., 2009). As people are more authentic, they experience fewer physical and depressive symptoms, lower anxiety, lower stress, and greater subjective vitality. They also experience more personal engagement, which builds stronger (more intimate) relationships (Kahn, 1990).

In this respect, integration can help diverse leaders to increase personal effectiveness even when they are struggling to feel validated, authenticated, and credible at work. Embracing non-prototypical identities in particular can generate a broader, more diverse social network that provides greater access to social resources, fosters resilience, and equips people to practice cross-cultural leadership more effectively. Rather than ignoring or suppressing identity differences, mentors can provide or introduce diverse leaders to the support that will enable them to view their non-prototypicality as an asset or resource to their work and their organizations, as opposed to being something that is more of a hindrance or a personal cost. Establishing positive connections between non-prototypical identities and work selves in this way enables diverse leaders to respond differently and more positively to the challenges they face at work, which increases their personal leadership effectiveness at work (Roberts, Wooten, & Davidson, 2015a). For example, Carla Harris, an African American Managing Director of Morgan Stanley, acknowledges the role that her colleagues have played in encouraging her to bring her multifaceted self to work, especially in client-centered jobs. In her book, *Expect to Win*, she wrote about how she became more comfortable with bringing her artistic and spiritual identities into her interactions with co-workers and clients. Harris shared the following example:

> The year I got promoted to managing director, another division asked me to sing at their holiday party. Up to that point, I had tried to keep invest-ment banker Carla and gospel singing Carla somewhat separate. When they approached me, my first thought was, "No way!" [...] But then as I considered it a little longer, I began to have second thoughts [...] So I told them yes; I agreed to sing at the party. As I was exiting the stage after my song, there was a guy waiting for me at the bottom of the stage steps. "Carla," he said, smiling at me and extending his hand, "I've heard so much about your voice. That was really terrific!" He introduced himself as a very senior person in that division [... and] we ended up having a long *business*-oriented discussion that gave him the opportunity to know me as a professional, as a banker [...] Days later, when I was being dis-cussed in the promotion committee, this person who recently had had a positive personal experience with me had a point of reference when he heard what was said about me. I feel strongly that my authentic self *really* paid off that day!
>
> (Harris, 2009: 23–24)

Mentorship (and sponsorship) is critical for creating opportunities for diverse leaders to bring their authentic selves to work projects and work relationships. Diverse leaders often assume that their "non-work" identities are irrelevant for work tasks, and therefore may be reluctant to mention or showcase them. Mentors (with their protégés permission) can elevate diverse leaders' profiles by highlighting their multifaceted selves as valued attributes that will increase their positive distinctiveness and create new opportunities for forging connections.

Cultivating Virtue

Mentors can help diverse leaders establish and/or affirm a more positive sense of self by helping them to display virtuous qualities or character strengths at work (e.g., wisdom, courage, compassion, integrity, hope, zest, gratitude, love, and curiosity). Research suggests that character strengths not only increase life satis-faction (Park, Peterson, & Seligman, 2004a, 2004b), but they also engender prosocial behavior. For example, individuals who define themselves as caring or compassionate are said to have a "prosocial identity" (Grant, Dutton, & Rosso, 2008). Scholars suggest that individuals with a prosocial identity are more likely to help and act benevolently toward others at work (Grant et al., 2008). Similarly, individuals with a moral identity are more likely to increase sympathy toward outgroup members (Reed & Aquino, 2003), interact with outgroup members (Dutton et al., 2010), and care about the well-being and suffering of others including outgroup members (Detert, Treviño, & Sweitzer, 2008). As such, cultivating virtue can help diverse leaders minimize in-group and outgroup divides and engage in more prosocial behavior at work.

Mentors can help diverse leaders to cultivate virtue and engage in more prosocial behavior at work by encouraging them to practice servant leadership (Joseph & Winston, 2005). According to Laub, servant leadership,

> promotes the valuing and development of people, the building of community, the practice of authenticity, the providing of leadership for the good of those led and the sharing of power and status for the common good of each individual, the total organization and those served by the organization.
>
> (Laub 1999: 81)

Volunteering is one way to practice servant leadership. Volunteering has been described as a type of prosocial behavior that has been linked both to employees' turnover decisions at work (Grant, 2012) and an organization's ability to create and maintain a reputation as a good corporate citizen (Marquis, Glynn, & Davis, 2007). Some diverse leaders who have a passion for social justice and/or identify as community activists outside of work may participate in corporate volunteering programs, believing that these programs will enable them to express a virtuous self and display leadership competencies at work. Yet, other diverse leaders may refrain from engaging in these programs when they believe that doing so will undermine their credibility as leaders. Notably, servant leadership runs the risk of "getting disappeared" at work in favor of those behaviors that prioritize individualism, independence, and authoritarianism (Fletcher, 2007). In general, relational practice is often associated with the feminine, softer side of organizational practice, which is often not recognized as leadership (Fletcher, 1999). As such, individuals who engage in relational practices that aim to help others to achieve their goals (such as volunteering) may be perceived as less credible and powerful than those who prioritize their own achievement, for instance.

Hence, one way in which mentors can help diverse leaders to cultivate a virtuous self at work is by helping them to be wise and strategic in how they engage in prosocial work. Namely, mentors can help diverse leaders create a narrative around how their engagement in organizationally sponsored and community-based volunteering programs benefits the organization. At the same time, mentors can also advocate for diverse leaders' prosocial behavior at work by narrating it as *leadership* behavior in their encounters with powerful and influential organizational members (Hewlett, Luce, & West, 2005). By increasing recognition and appreciation of virtuous acts, mentors help reinforce the linkages between developing others and leadership effectiveness. Mentors can also help to counter the negative effects of stereotyping and devaluation on diverse leaders' self and professional images, by making virtuous qualities more salient. Such mentoring support can enable diverse leaders to feel empowered to change overly *self*-focused patterns of thought and action around negative internal experiences, interactions, and behaviors at work to those that are positively focused on the development of *others*, thereby helping diverse leaders to generate more possibilities for becoming extraordinary at work.

Cultivating Esteem

Finally, mentors can help diverse leaders establish and/or affirm a more positive sense of self by helping them to feel more positively about their strengths and contributions, especially those related to their non-prototypicality. In general, individuals like to feel positively about themselves and are motivated to favorably distinguish themselves from others (Gecas, 1982; Baumeister, 1999). Positive self-regard is important not only because it is associated with higher life satisfaction, and lower depression and hopelessness (Crocker, Luhtanen, Blaine, & Broadnax, 1994), but because it also helps to generate social and emotional resources. For example, people who have high self-regard are viewed as more attractive, more popular, and receive more help (Scott & Judge, 2009). When people practice self-affirmation, they are less defensive in responding to threat (Steele, 1988), and more receptive to feedback and differing opinions (Correll, Spencer, & Zanna, 2004). People with higher self-regard engage in more prosocial behavior (Grant et al., 2008), and even more important in diverse work settings, they are less likely to stereotype others (Fredrickson, 2009; Johnson & Fredrickson, 2005; Waugh & Fredrickson, 2006). In these ways, the Esteemed Self works in tandem with the other pathways for positive identity construction via positive self-regard. Positive self-regard facilitates the Growing Self by providing a secure base for learning (Steele, 1988), stimulates the Integrated Self through more willingness to embrace of non-prototypical identities into work tasks (Ely & Thomas, 2001; Roberts, 2005), and catalyzes the Virtuous Self by prompting prosocial behavior, even across identity groups. Conversely, experiencing a sense of personal growth, integration, and engaging in virtuous action also fosters more positive self-regard (Roberts, 2013).

Given the reciprocal relationship between the esteemed self and other positive identity bases, mentors should be especially attuned to their ability to practice "authentic affirmation" with diverse leader protégés. Authentic affirmation refers to "sincere expressions of praise, appreciation, or gratitude for a person's, dyad's, group's, or organization's qualities and/or behaviors" (Roberts, Wooten,

Davidson, & Lemley, 2015b). Research supports that authentic affirmation is rare: across the globe, workers focus more on weaknesses and shortcomings than strengths and contributions (Hodges & Clifton, 2004). This finding is consistent with psychology research which supports that "bad is stronger than good" in our recall and interpretation of events (Baumeister, Bratslavsky, Finkenauer, & Vohs, 2001). To override this tendency toward focusing on deficiencies, relational partners (such as mentors) should offer 3–5 times more positive than negative verbal and non-verbal feedback (Fredrickson, 2009).

Mentors can help apply this among non-prototypical leaders; they may cultivate more esteemed selves through incorporating authentic affirmation into their coaching conversations. Evidence-based discussions of strengths and contributions are more compelling than sweeping generalizations or glowing praise (Roberts, Dutton, Spreitzer, Heaphy, & Quinn, 2005). In coaching conversations, mentors can help leaders to engage in a three-step process of authentic affirmation: (1) identify their peak moments, or times when they activated their best selves at work; (2) examine the personal and social factors that enabled them in peak moments; and (3) develop an action plan for benchmarking best practices, which involves identifying the resources needed to strategically activate their best selves in future situations. These discussions can also focus on how diverse leaders successfully engage their non-prototypical identities as sources of strength, assets, and personal and organizational resources. Such conversations will help mentors and diverse leaders to foster a culture of intelligence (Wiseman, Bradwejn, & Westbroek, 2014; Wiseman & McKeown, 2010) by asking: In what ways is this person smart? This view of intelligence is not based on elitism, scarcity and stasis, but assumes generativity and growth potential.

Another way in which mentors can help diverse leaders to experience deeper affirmation is by encouraging diverse leaders to become part of an employee resource group (also called "affinity networks"). For women and racial/ethnic minorities in particular, these groups often provide social support and leadership opportunities to members as well as opportunities to meet with other women and/or racial/ethnic minorities, who can help them to navigate and adapt to their organizations (Friedman & Holtom, 2002). In this respect, employee resource/network groups can provide diverse leaders with access to social resources that can help them establish and/or maintain positive alignment between their non-prototypical selves and work selves. At the same time, employee resource/network groups can be useful for helping diverse leaders to practice cross-cultural leadership more effectively. This mutually reinforces the integrated and esteemed selves.

For example, at General Electric (GE), the African American Forum (AAF) is an employee affinity network that was originally developed "to acculturate African American employees while allowing them to maintain their personal identities" but, over time, also became focused on helping GE to rethink its model of business in Africa (Thomas & Creary, 2011: 5). Upon learning, in 2010, that GE's African employees possessed unique knowledge on how to build commerce on the continent, AAF leaders, who were African American and several of whom were also senior leaders at GE, engaged in efforts to begin acculturating and developing African leaders for GE's businesses in Africa (Thomas & Creary, 2011). This example demonstrates how employee resource groups can not only provide diverse leaders with the validation, authentication, and credibility that they are lacking in other aspects of their work lives, but can also provide them with opportunities to exercise leadership in visible ways.

Hence, mentors can help diverse leaders deepen their experiences of affirmation and integration by helping them to access and gain social resources like employee resource groups; these mentoring practices can support diverse leaders in responding constructively at work to their non-prototypicality and any negative experiences that arise from it.

We have proposed that in order to attain greater personal leadership effectiveness at work, diverse leaders need to establish and/or affirm a more positive sense of self. Mentors can help diverse leaders develop a more positive sense of self by helping them to feel more positively about/embrace their non-prototypical identities and distinctive contributions at work (i.e., cultivate esteem), encouraging them to integrate the insights and experiences they have gained from their identity experiences into work-based tasks and processes (i.e., cultivate integration), and helping them to engage in more prosocial behavior at work (i.e., cultivate virtue). In so doing, mentors can help diverse leaders develop in positive ways at work (i.e., cultivating growth). Beyond yielding positive benefits to protégés, using the G.I.V.E. model can also positively affect the quality of mentor–protégé relationships, which is important for organizational growth and positive organizational change.

We propose that mentoring via the G.I.V.E. model can unlock and generate valuable social and knowledge resources that are important for developing high-quality mentor–protégé relationships. Our insights extend from relational theories that explain resource dynamics within workplace relationships including

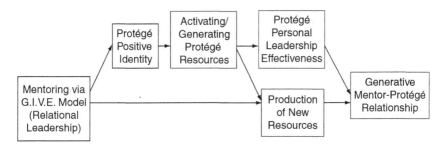

FIGURE 1.1 G.I.V.E.-Based   Mentoring   and   High-Quality   Mentor-Protégé Relationships

leader–member exchange (LMX) theory (Graen & Schiemann, 1978; Liden & Graen, 1980; Liden, Sparrowe, & Wayne, 1997), a POS perspective on positive relationships at work (Dutton & Heaphy, 2003; Dutton & Ragins, 2007; Rousseau & Ling, 2007; Stephens & Carmeli, forthcoming), and relational-cultural theory (RCT) (Fletcher, 2007; Miller, 1986; Miller & Stiver, 1997) as well as identity theories that link identities to resource dynamics at work (Caza & Wilson, 2009; Creary, Caza, & Roberts, 2015; Dutton et al., 2010; Roberts et al., 2015a). We build specifically on the work of Creary, Caza, and Roberts (2015) by examining the relationship between identity management, resources, and relational quality but within the context of "generative" mentoring relationships.

G.I.V.E.-Based Mentoring and Resource Production

Creary, Caza, & Roberts (2015) characterized manager and subordinate behavior in terms of the strategies each person may use for managing the subordinate's identities. Herein we adopt this perspective on identity management by positioning G.I.V.E.-based mentoring as an "inclusionary" identity management strategy that can "increase the relevance of one or more of the subordinate's identities in work-based tasks and activities" (Creary et al., 2015: 544). G.I.V.E.-based mentoring represents a form of strategy alignment, such that a mentor and a protégé both welcome the integration or inclusion of the protégé's non-prototypical identities at work. By encouraging the protégé to integrate his or her experiences as a diverse leader into work-based tasks and processes, the mentor invites a protégé to define and establish the ways in which his or her non-prototypical identity enables him or her to grow and lead effectively at work. In facilitating a transition from the socialized mind, in which a diverse leader views his or her diverse identity as a liability or as a source of discomfort, to self-authoring mind in which a diverse leader views his or her diverse identity as an asset at work, a mentor encourages a protégé to embrace and include his or her non-prototypical identity at work.

Consistent with Creary et al., we propose that this aligned and inclusionary form of identity management generates "resource production," which is characterized by "the mutual investment of resources, including those previously used or underutilized, to generate new resources" (2015: 550). The resource production occurs through a process of heedful interrelating (see also Weick & Roberts, 1993) in which both mentors and protégés are attentive to how their actions affect the functioning of the system (Caza & Wilson, 2009; Creary, 2015; Creary et al., 2015; Dutton et al., 2010; Ely & Thomas, 2001). In our theorizing, a mentor invests socio-emotional resources through G.I.V.E.-based support; in exchange, the mentor and protégé combine knowledge and/or social capital resources associated with the protégé's non-prototypical identity to develop new ideas and produce new resources. In this respect, G.I.V.E.-based mentoring is also a form of *relational leadership* in which patterns of interactions between leaders with formal role-based authority (i.e., mentors) and followers with less formal authority (i.e., protégés) are characterized by mutual and multi-directional influence (Fletcher, 2007; Stephens & Carmeli, forthcoming), respectful engagement, and caring (Stephens & Carmeli, forthcoming). The next section describes this identity management process of resource production in more detail.

In the first stage of the process of heedful interrelating, the mentor indicates that the protégé's non-prototypical identity is relevant and valuable at work and the protégé, who feels the same, decides to integrate his or her experiences as a diverse leader into work-based tasks and processes. For example, a protégé with a prosocial identity and passion for social justice develops and shares an idea with his or her mentor to create a program in the protégé's company designed to engage high-potential Millennial employees in community development initiatives that will also provide these employees with visible leadership opportunities. The mentor likes the idea because it also has the potential to support the company's leadership development platform and reputational goals. The mentor also believes that he or she can introduce the protégé to prominent leaders in the community whom he or she respects and might be interested in working with the protégé and his or her company. Thus, the mentor encourages the protégé to develop the idea further by drafting a brief project proposal.

In the second stage, the protégé's knowledge is combined with the mentor's resources. For example, the mentor uses his or her social capital to introduce the protégé to community leaders who are interested in meeting informally to discuss the protégé's proposal. The community leaders like the idea and agree to support it if the company approves it. Hence, both the mentor and protégé invest resources from their respective resource pools (e.g., Hobfoll, 1989, 2011) to develop support from community leaders for the proposed project.

In the third stage, new ideas are generated. For example, the protégé presents the proposal to his or her manager who schedules a meeting with senior leadership to discuss the proposal. At the meeting, senior leadership proposes that the program be designed to engage a broader base of employees in community development work while also targeting specifically high-potential Millennial employees who are interested in leadership development opportunities. Thus, the combination and recombination of resources (i.e., protégé's, mentor's, community leaders', and managers') enable learning, new work resources, and collaborative practices to endure.

Resource Production and a Generative Mentor–Protégé Relationship

Existing research proposes that the behavior of both persons in a relationship influences relational quality (e.g., Creary et al., 2015; Ragins & Dutton, 2007;

Miller & Stiver, 1997). In this respect, we propose that G.I.V.E.-based mentoring not only enables resource production but also creates a generative mentor–protégé relationship. Traditional relationships emphasize the role of the mentor as resource provider for the protégé (e.g., social capital, socio-emotional support, career guidance). Generative mentor–protégé relationships are characterized by the perception of equal resource contribution and mutual growth-in-connection (Creary et al., 2015). In addition, both individuals feel psychologically safe in the generative relationship, in that they can be or open, authentic, and direct with one another in their elaborated roles as mentor and protégé. In other words, the mentor and protégé both express vulnerability and humility in service of collaborative learning and innovation. Finally, both the mentor and protégé experience a feeling of increased vitality, aliveness, and energy from connecting to one another; they are motivated to act in the moment and experience an increased sense of worth from their mutual engagement in the relationship; and they desire to connect and engage more with each other and establish similar connections with others (Baker & Dutton, 2007; Dutton & Heaphy, 2003; Miller & Stiver, 1997). Based on our previous example, both the mentor and the protégé perceive that each person is making an equal contribution to the relationship because both parties are contributing resources that relate specifically to and extend beyond their functional roles, such as mutual engagement in the development of a project proposal for the protégé's company. Essentially, by introducing the protégé to community leaders, the mentor is acting as more than just someone who gives advice or other forms of socio-emotional support typically expected of mentors (Edmondson, 1999; Nembhard & Edmondson, 2011). Likewise, by engaging the mentor in the development of the project, the protégé is inviting the mentor to serve concretely in a generative (possibly collaborative) capacity rather than simply as a source of less tangible support. Both the mentor and the protégé accepted these elaborated roles because they feel psychologically safe in their relationship and desire to connect and engage with one another in different ways. Thus, actually experiencing the benefits of their relationship in terms of an enhanced project proposal enables them to feel an increased sense of worth from being in the relationship and an overall experience of generativity.

Further, the mutuality of generative mentor–protégé relationships extends beyond resource sharing and work outcomes. Experiencing this generative relationship can also positively affect how mentors see themselves as leaders. Through intentionally affirming and enhancing diverse leaders' identities, mentors can begin to cultivate their own sense of growth—becoming a more effective developer of people. They may expand the breadth of their own identities at work, including characteristics and experiences that stem from their own distinctiveness or non-prototypicality (cultural or otherwise). Mentors who practice G.I.V.E.-based mentoring with diverse leaders may also engage in more socially conscious behavior, promoting organizational equity and inclusion, which can bolster their virtuous selves. Through establishing a higher quality relationship, they will also carry over the feeling of esteem—being known and understood and valued by the protégé. This mutual dynamic stands in contrast with top-down leadership approaches as a relational approach that recognizes the centrality of relationship quality in influencing interpersonal and group interactions.

Conclusion

Mentors play a unique role in helping diverse leaders to generate more viable, robust, and sustainable pathways for increasing personal leadership effectiveness. Diverse leaders often struggle to feel validated, authenticated, and credible at work, and find it difficult to understand and manage these negative experiences in constructive ways. Mentors can help diverse leaders to develop greater personal leadership effectiveness by helping to buffer negative experiences and by helping to change negative patterns of thought and action around internal experiences, interactions, and behaviors to those that are more positive and constructive. In this chapter, we have explained how mentors can help to cultivate more positive identities with diverse leaders, thereby generating valuable social and emotional resources that facilitate personal leadership effectiveness. Further, we proposed that positive identity cultivation is a key mechanism through which mentors and their diverse protégés can develop higher quality, resource-generating relationships that benefit both parties and their organizations. When mentors engage in G.I.V.E.-based leadership development practices (e.g., coaching, strategic career planning, networking) that encourage diverse leaders to: *Grow, Integrate diverse identities at work, engage in Virtuous action at work, and affirm their sense of worth and Esteem*, they will be better positioned to contribute creatively at work from positions of strength. The mutuality of positive identity construction and resource exchange shows how G.I.V.E.-based mentoring is an act of relational leadership that is essential for developing diverse talent in twenty-first-century organizations.

References

Avolio, B. J., & Hannah, S. T. (2008). Developmental readiness: Accelerating leader development. *Consulting Psychology Journal: Practice and Research, 60*(4), 331.

Avolio, B., Wernsing, T., Chan, A., & Griffeth, J. (2007). A theory of developing leader self-awareness. *Unpublished manuscript, University of Nebraska—Lincoln.*

Baker, W., & Dutton, J. E. (2007). Enabling positive social capital in organizations. In J. Dutton, & B. R. Ragins (Eds.) *Exploring positive relationships at work: Building a theoretical and research foundation* (pp: 325–346). Mahwah, NJ: Lawrence Erlbaum and Associates.

Baumeister, R. F. (1999). The self. In D. T. Gilbert, S. T. Fiske, & G. Lindzey (Eds.) *The handbook of social psychology* (4th ed.). Boston: McGraw-Hill.

Baumeister, R. F., Bratslavsky, E., Finkenauer, C., & Vohs, K. D. (2001). Bad is stronger than good. *Review of General Psychology*, *5*(4), 323.

Blake-Beard, S. D. (1999). The costs of living as an outsider within: An analysis of the mentoring relationships and career success of black and white women in the corporate sector. *Journal of Career Development*, *26*(1), 21–36.

Blake-Beard, S. D. (2001). Taking a hard look at formal mentoring programs: A consideration of potential challenges facing women. *Journal of Management Development*, *20*(4), 331–345.

Blake-Beard, S. D., & McGowan, E. (2000, April). Insights from multiple perspectives: Mentor and protégé reflections on a formal high school mentoring program. Paper presented at the American Educational Research Association National Conference, New Orleans, LA.

Caza, B. B., & Wilson, M. G. (2009). Me, myself, and I: The benefits of work-identity complexity. In L. M. Roberts, & J. E. Dutton (Eds.), *Exploring Positive Identities and Organizations: Building a Theoretical and Research Foundation* (pp. 99–123). New York: Routledge Taylor and Francis Group.

Cheng, C.-Y., Sanchez-Burks, J., & Lee, F. (2008). Connecting the dots within creative performance and identity integration. *Psychological Science*, *19*(11), 1178–1184.

Correll, J., Spencer, S. J., & Zanna, M. P. (2004). An affirmed self and an open mind: Self-affirmation and sensitivity to argument strength. *Journal of Experimental Social Psychology*, *40*(3), 350–356.

Creary, S. J. (2015). *Making the most of multiple worlds: Multiple organizational identities as resources in the formation of an integrated health care delivery system*. Doctoral dissertation, Boston College.

Creary, S. J., Caza, B. B., & Roberts, L. M. (2015). Out of the box? How managing a subordinate's multiple identities affects the quality of a manager-subordinate relationship. *Academy of Management Review*, *40*(4), 538–562.

Crocker, J., Luhtanen, R., Blaine, B., & Broadnax, S. (1994). Collective self-esteem and psychological well-being among White, Black, and Asian college students. *Personality and Social Psychology Bulletin*, *20*(5), 503–513.

DeRue, D. S., & Ashford, S. J. (2010). Who will lead and who will follow? A social process of leadership identity construction in organizations. *Academy of Management Review*, *35*, 627–647.

Detert, J. R., Treviño, L. K., & Sweitzer, V. L. (2008). Moral disengagement in ethical decision making: A study of antecedents and outcomes. *Journal of Applied Psychology*, *93*(2), 374.

Dutton, J. E., & Heaphy, E. D. (2003). The power of high-quality connections. In K. S. Cameron, J. E. Dutton, & R. E. Quinn (Eds.), *Positive organizational scholarship: Foundations of a new discipline* (pp. 263–278). San Francisco, CA: Berrett-Koehler Publishers.

Dutton, J. E., & Ragins, B. R. (2007). Positive relationships at work: An introduction and invitation. In J. E. Dutton, & B. R. Ragins (Eds.), *Exploring positive relationships at work: Building a theoretical and research foundation* (pp. 3–25). New York: Lawrence Erlbaum Associates.

Dutton, J. E., Roberts, L. M., & Bednar, J. (2010). Pathways for positive identity construction at work: Four types of positive identity and the building of social resources. *Academy of Management Review*, *35*, 265–293.

Dweck, C. (2006). *Mindset: The New Psychology of Success*. New York: Random House.

Dweck, C. S. (2000). *Self-theories: Their role in motivation, personality, and development*. Philadelphia, PA: Psychology Press.

Eagly, A. H., & Karau, S. J. (2002). Role congruity theory of prejudice toward female leaders. *Psychological Review, 109*(3), 573.

Edmondson, A. (1999). Psychological safety and learning behavior in work teams. *Administrative Science Quarterly, 44*, 350–383.

Edmondson, A. C. (2012). *Teaming: How organizations learn, innovate, and compete in the knowledge economy*. New York: John Wiley & Sons.

Ely, R. J., & Thomas, D. A. (2001). Cultural diversity at work: The effects of diversity perspectives on work group processes and outcomes. *Administrative Science Quarterly, 46*(2), 229–273.

Ensari, N., & Murphy, S. E. (2003). Cross-cultural variations in leadership perceptions and attribution of charisma to the leader. *Organizational Behavior and Human Decision Processes, 92*(1), 52–66.

Fletcher, J. K. (1999). *Disappearing acts: Gender, power and relational practice at work*. Cambridge, MA: MIT Press.

Fletcher, J. K. (2007). Leadership, power, and positive relationships. In J. E. Dutton, & B. R. Ragins (Eds.), *Exploring positive relationships at work: Building a theoretical and research foundation* (pp. 347–371). New York: Lawrence Erlbaum Associates.

Fredrickson, B. L. (1998). What good are positive emotions? *Review of general psychology, 2*(3), 300.

Fredrickson, B. L. (2001). The role of positive emotions in positive psychology: The broaden-and-build theory of positive emotions. *American Psychologist, 56*(3), 218.

Fredrickson, B. L. (2009). *Positivity*. New York: Three Rivers Press.

Friedman, R. A., & Holtom, B. 2002. The effects of network groups on minority employee turnover intentions. *Human Resource Management, 41*(4), 405–421.

Gecas, V. (1982). The self-concept. *Annual Review of Sociology, 8*, 1–33.

Giscombe, K. (2015). Resilience and failure. In L. M. Roberts, L. P. Wooten, & M. N. Davidson (Eds.), *Positive organizing in a global society: Understanding and engaging differences for capacity building & inclusion* (pp. 85–89). New York: Routledge.

Graen, G., & Schiemann, W. (1978). Leader–member agreement: A vertical dyad linkage approach. *Journal of Applied Psychology, 63*, 206–212.

Grant, A. M. (2012). Giving time, time after time: Work design and sustained employee participation in corporate volunteering. *Academy of Management Review, 37*(4), 589–615.

Grant, A. M., Dutton, J. E., & Rosso, B. D. (2008). Giving commitment: Employee support programs and the prosocial sensemaking process. *Academy of Management Journal, 51*(5), 898–918.

Hannah, S. T., Avolio, B. J., Luthans, F., & Harms, P. D. (2008). Leadership efficacy: Review and future directions. *The Leadership Quarterly, 19*(6), 669–692.

Harris, C. A. (2009). *Expect to win: Proven strategies for success from a Wall Street vet*. New York: Plume.

Hayes-James, E. (2000). Race-related differences in promotions and support: Underlying effects of human and social capital. *Organizational Science, 11*(5), 493–508.

Hewlett, S. A., Luce, C. B., & West, C. (2005). Leadership in your midst. *Harvard Business Review, 83*(11), 74–82.

Higgins, M. C., & Kram, K. E. (2001). Reconceptualizing mentoring at work: A developmental network perspective. *Academy of Management Review, 26*(2), 264–288.

Hobfoll, S. E. (1989). Conservation of resources: A new attempt at conceptualizing stress. *American Psychologist, 44*, 513–524. DOI: 10.1037/0003-066X.44.3.513.

Hobfoll, S. E. (2002). Social and psychological resources and adaptation. *Review of General Psychology, 6*, 307–324.

Hobfoll, S. E. (2011). Conservation of resource caravans and engaged settings. *Journal of Occupational & Organizational Psychology*, *84*(1), 116–122. DOI: 10.1111/j.2044-8325. 2010.02016.x.

Hodges, T. D., & Clifton, D. O. (2004). Strengths-based development in practice. In P. A. Linley, & S. Joseph (Eds.), *International handbook of positive psychology in practice: From research to application* (pp. 256–268). Hoboken, NJ: Wiley and Sons.

Ibarra, H. (1999). Provisional selves: Experimenting with image and identity in professional adaptation. *Administrative Science Quarterly*, *44*, 764–791.

Johnson, K. J., & Fredrickson, B. L. (2005). "We All Look the Same to Me" Positive Emotions Eliminate the Own-Race Bias in Face Recognition. *Psychological Science*, *16*(11), 875–881.

Joseph, E. E., & Winston, B. E. (2005). A correlation of servant leadership, leader trust, and organizational trust. *Leadership & Organization Development Journal*, *26*(1), 6–22.

Kahn, W. (1990). Psychological conditions of personal engagement and disengagement at work. *Academy of Management Journal*, *33*(4), 692–724.

Kegan, R. (1980). Making meaning: The constructive-developmental approach to persons and practice. *The Personnel and Guidance Journal*, *58*(5), 373–380.

Kegan, R. (1982). *The evolving self: Problem and process in human development*. Cambridge, MA: Harvard University Press.

Kram, K. E. (1985). *Mentoring at work: Developmental relationships in organizational life*. Glenview, IL: Scott, Foresman & Co.

Laub, J. A. (1999). *Assessing the servant organization: Development of the servant organizational leadership assessment (SOLA) instrument*: Florida Atlantic University; 0119.

Liden, R. C., & Graen, G. (1980). Generalizability of the vertical dyad linkage model of leadership. *Academy of Management Journal*, *23*, 451–465.

Liden, R. C., Sparrowe, R. T., & Wayne, S. J. (1997). Leader-member exchange theory: The past and potential for the future. In G. R. Ferris (Ed.), *Research in personnel and human resources management*, Vol. 15 (pp. 47–119). Oxford: Elsevier Science/JAI Press.

Lord, R. G., & Maher, K. J. (1991). Cognitive theory in industrial and organizational psychology. *Handbook of industrial and organizational psychology*, *2*, 1–62.

Marquis, C., Glynn, M. A., & Davis, G. F. (2007). Community Isomorphism and Corporate Social Action. *Academy of Management Review*, *32*(3), 925–945.

Miller, J. B. (1986). *Toward a new psychology of women* (2nd ed.). Boston, MA: Beacon Press.

Miller, J. B., & Stiver, I. P. (1997). *The healing connection*. Boston, MA: Beacon Press.

Murrell, A. J., Blake-Beard, S., Porter, D. M., & Perkins-Williamson, A. (2008). Interorganizational formal mentoring: Breaking the concrete ceiling sometimes requires support from the outside. *Human Resource Management*, *47*(2), 275–294.

Murrell, A. J., Crosby, F. J., & Ely, R. J. (1999). *Mentoring dilemmas: Developmental relationships within multicultural organizations*. Mahwah, NJ: Lawrence Erlbaum Associates.

Murrell, A. J., & Tangri, S. S. (1999). Mentoring at the margin. In A. J. Murrell, F. J. Crosby, & R. J. Ely, (Eds.), *Mentoring dilemmas: Developmental relationships within multicultural organizations* (pp. 211–224). Mahwah, NJ: Lawrence Erlbaum Associates.

Nembhard, I., & Edmondson, A. (2011). Psychological safety: A foundation for speaking up, collaboration and experimentation. In K. S. Cameron, & G. M. Spreitzer (Eds.), *The Oxford handbook of positive organizational scholarship* (pp. 490–503). New York: Oxford University Press.

Owens, B. P., & Hekman, D. R. (2012). Modeling how to grow: An inductive examination of humble leader behaviors, contingencies, and outcomes. *Academy of Management Journal*, *55*(4), 787–818.

Owens, B. P., Johnson, M. D., & Mitchell, T. R. (2013). Expressed humility in organizations: Implications for performance, teams, and leadership. *Organization Science*, *24*(5), 1517–1538.

Park, N., Peterson, C., & Seligman, M. E. (2004a). Strengths of character and well-being. *Journal of Social and Clinical Psychology*, *23*(5), 603–619.

Park, N., Peterson, C., & Seligman, M. E. (2004b). Strengths of character and well-being: A closer look at hope and modesty. *Journal of Social and Clinical Psychology*, *23*(5), 628–634.

Pratt, M. G., Rockmann, K. W., & Kaufmann, J. B. (2006). Constructing professional identity: The role of work and identity learning cycles in the customization of identity among medical residents. *Academy of Management Journal*, *49*(2), 235–262.

Ragins, B. R. (1997). Diversified mentoring relationships in organizations: A power perspective. *Academy of Management Review*, *22*(2), 482–521.

Ragins, B. R., & Kram, K. E. (2007). *The handbook of mentoring at work: Theory, research, and practice*. Los Angeles, CA: Sage Publications.

Reed, A., & Aquino, K. F. (2003). Moral identity and the expanding circle of moral regard toward out-groups. *Journal of Personality and Social Psychology*, *84*(6), 1270.

Roberts, L. M. (2005). Changing faces: Professional image construction in diverse organizational settings. *Academy of Management Review*, *30*(4), 685–711.

Roberts, L. M. (2007a). Bringing your whole self to work: Lessons in authentic engagement from women leaders. In B. Kellerman, & D. L. Rhode (Eds.), *Women and leadership: The state of play and strategies for change* (pp. 329–360). San Francisco, CA: Jossey-Bass.

Roberts, L. M. (2007b). From proving to becoming: How positive relationships create a context for self-discovery and self-actualization. In L. M. Roberts, & J. E. Dutton (Eds.), *Exploring positive relationships at work: Building a theoretical and research foundation* (pp. 29–45). New York: Lawrence Erlbaum Associates.

Roberts, L. M. (2013). Reflected best self engagement at work: Positive identity, alignment, and the pursuit of vitality and value creation. In I. Boniwell, S. A. David, and A. Conley Ayers (Eds.), *The Oxford handbook of happiness* (pp. 767–782). New York: Oxford University Press.

Roberts, L. M. (2014). Cultivate Positive Identities. In J. E. Dutton, & G. M. Spreitzer (Eds.), *How to Be a Positive Leader* (pp. 55–64). San Francisco, CA: Berrett-Koehler Publishers.

Roberts, L. M., & Cha, S. (2016). Sources of strength: Mobilizing minority racial, ethnic and cultural identities as resources. In L. M. Roberts, L. Wooten, & M. Davidson (Eds.), *Positive Organizing in a Global Society*. New York: Taylor & Francis.

Roberts, L. M., Cha, S. E., Hewlin, P. F., & Settles, I. H. (2009). Bringing the inside out: Enhancing authenticity and positive identity in organizations. In L. M. Roberts, & J. E. Dutton, *Exploring positive identities and organizations: Building a theoretical and research foundation* (pp. 149–170). New York: Routledge.

Roberts, L. M., & Creary, S. J. (2011). Positive identity construction: Insights from classical and contemporary theoretical perspectives. In K. S. Cameron, & G. M. Spreitzer (Eds.), *The Oxford handbook of positive organizational scholarship* (pp. 70–83). New York: Oxford University Press.

Roberts, L. M., & Dutton, J. E. (2009). *Exploring positive identities and organizations: Building a theoretical and research foundation*. New York: Routledge.

Roberts, L. M., Dutton, J. E., Spreitzer, G. M., Heaphy, E. D., & Quinn, R. E. (2005). Composing the reflected best-self portrait: Building pathways for becoming extraordinary in work organizations. *Academy of Management Review*, *30*(4), 712–736.

Roberts, L. M., Wooten, L., & Davidson, M. (2015a). *Positive organizing in a global society: Understanding and engaging differences for capacity-building and inclusion.* New York: Routledge.

Roberts, L. M., Wooten, L. P., Davidson, M., & Lemley, A. (2015b). Authentic affirmation? Considering the cultural relevance of strength-based practices in global organizations. In L. M. Roberts, L. P. Wooten, & M. Davidson (Eds.), *Positive organizing in a global society: Understanding and engaging differences for capacity-building and inclusion.* New York: Routledge.

Rosette, A. S., Leonardelli, G. J., & Phillips, K. W. (2008). The White standard: Racial bias in leader categorization. *Journal of Applied Psychology, 93*(4), 758.

Rousseau, D., & Ling, K. (2007). Commentary: Following the resources in positive organizational relationships. In J. E. Dutton, & B. R. Ragins (Eds.), *Exploring positive relationships at work: Building a theoretical and research foundation* (pp. 373–384). New York: Lawrence Erlbaum Associates.

Scott, B. A., & Judge, T. A. (2009). The popularity contest at work: Who wins, why, and what do they receive? *Journal of Applied Psychology, 94*(1), 20.

Steele, C. M. (1988). The psychology of self-affirmation: Sustaining the integrity of the self. In L. Berkowitz (Ed.), *Advances in Experimental Social Psychology*, Vol. 21 (pp. 261–302). San Diego, CA: Academic Press.

Stephens, J. P., & Carmeli, A. (forthcoming). Relational leadership and creativity: The effects of respectful engagement and caring on meaningfulness and creative work involvement. In S. Hemlin, & M. D. Mumford (Eds.), *Handbook of Research on Creativity and Leadership.* Northampton, MA: Edward Elgar Publishing.

Swann, W. B., Pelham, B. W., & Krull, D. S. (1989). Agreeable fancy or disagreeable truth? Reconciling self-enhancement and self-verification. *Journal of Personality and Social Psychology; Journal of Personality and Social Psychology, 57*(5), 782.

Thomas, D. A. (1990). The impact of race on managers' experiences of developmental relationships. *Journal of Organizational Behavior, 11*(6), 479–492.

Thomas, D. A., & Creary, S. J. (2011). *Renewing GE: The Africa Project* (A). Boston, MA: Harvard Business School Publishing.

Uhl-Bien, M., Marion, R., & McKelvey, B. (2007). Complexity leadership theory: Shifting leadership from the industrial age to the knowledge era. *The Leadership Quarterly, 18*(4), 298–318.

VandeWalle, D., Cron, W. L., & Slocum, J. W. (2001). The role of goal orientation following performance feedback. *Journal of Applied Psychology, 86*(4), 629.

Waugh, C. E., & Fredrickson, B. L. (2006). Nice to know you: Positive emotions, self–other overlap, and complex understanding in the formation of a new relationship. *The Journal of Positive Psychology, 1*(2), 93–106.

Weick, K., & Roberts, K. (1993). Collective Mind in Organizations: Heedful Interrelating on Flight Decks. *Administrative Science Quarterly, 38*, 357–381.

Wiseman, L., Bradwejn, J., & Westbroek, E. M. (2014). A new leadership curriculum: The multiplication of intelligence. *Academic Medicine, 89*(3), 376–379.

Wiseman, L., & McKeown, G. (2010). Bringing out the best in your people. *Harvard Business Review* (May), 117–121.

Zagenczyk, T., Gibney, R., Kiewitz, C., & Restubog, S. (2009). Mentors, supervisors and role models: Do they reduce the effects of psychological contract breach? *Human Resource Management Journal, 19*(3), 237–259.

2

MENTORING RELATIONSHIPS OF PROFESSIONAL INDIAN WOMEN

Extending the Borders of our Understanding at the Intersection of Gender and Culture

Stacy Blake-Beard, Jessica Halem, Estelle E. Archibold, Dorian Olivier Boncoeur, Andrea R. Burton, and Payal Kumar

A rapidly changing economy and an increasingly competitive and diverse business landscape represent two of many forces that have created both an opportunity and a need for the inclusion of professional Indian women in India's workforce (Haynes & Ghosh, 2012; Ravindran & Baral, 2014; Srinivasan, Murty, & Nakra, 2013). The issue of gender diversity in Indian firms has recently gained attention given that over 400 million women are employed in different sectors in India (Buddhapriya, 2013). More than one-third (35%) of Indian women have successfully completed bachelor's degrees, 15 percent have completed master's degrees in academic fields, and 7.8 percent have completed professional degrees (Li, Mardhekar, & Wadkar, 2012). Fairly recently (within the past three decades), Indian women have been entering a number of professions, including engineering, information technology, financial services, management, civil services, and police/armed forces (Nath, 2000). Nath suggests that this rapid movement of women to paid labor outside of the home is "revolutionary" (2000).

In spite of these advances, Indian women face a number of challenging dynamics in relation to their workforce participation. Indian women must navigate a puzzling paradox. On the one hand, there is an acknowledgment of the importance of increasing the participation of women in the Indian labor market. Yet, these women still face very traditional conceptions of what roles are appropriate and accepted for them in Indian society (Haynes & Ghosh, 2012; Ravindran & Baral, 2014). For Indian women, the roles of mother, wife, and daughter are still believed to be predominant; there is an expectation that childcare, housework, and care of elderly relatives are squarely in their domain (Valk & Srinivasan, 2011; Wesley, Muthuswarmy, & Darling, 2009). A commonly cited reason for career interruption for Indian women is the predominance of familial responsibilities (childcare, elder care, and spousal relocation) (Bharathi & Baral, 2012). Managing the boundaries between family and work is a significant factor in the career progression of Indian women and merits attention.

In this chapter, we offer an exploration of the role that mentoring plays in helping women navigate their professional and domestic realms. For many of the Indian women in this study, successfully managing the paradox inherent in the challenging dynamics of workforce participation and Indian cultural experience lies in their ability to develop strategies and tools that allow the successful synthesis of multiple identities across their familial/social and work lives. Broadly, we explore the opportunities that mentoring offers to professional Indian women. We are specifically interested in how mentoring relationships may be affected by dynamics occurring at the intersection of gender and culture. How do these women develop effective mentoring practices that incorporate cultural and familial values, perspectives, and identities? Using accounts of their mentoring experiences across both familial and workplace contexts, we hope to show how these women identify and build mentoring relationships, while navigating the expectations and pressures resulting from cultural norms and practices.

In the following sections, we discuss the mentoring literature to acquaint readers with this developmental process that we believe can be used as a tool to support professional Indian women in their career journeys. We also review the literature on mentoring in India, to provide greater depth on the study of this developmental process in context. Findings regarding how these women use mentoring will be shared. We conclude the chapter with insights gained from the findings as well as suggestions for future research.

A Mentoring Theoretical Framework

Mentoring is most commonly known as the process through which an employee (protégé) develops a relationship with a professional colleague (mentor), which typically contributes to the development and career growth of both (Kram, 1983). Mentors are generally defined as individuals with advanced experience and knowledge who are committed to providing upward mobility and career support to their protégés, leading to behaviors reflecting positive career advancement (e.g., sponsorship, coaching, exposure/visibility, protection, and the provision of challenging assignments) and job attitudes (e.g., role modeling, counseling, friendship, and acceptance) (Kram, 1985).

Mentoring relationships yield many benefits. Protégés receive more promotions (Bachman & Gregory, 1993; Dreher & Ash, 1990; Scandura, 1992), have higher incomes (Chao, Walz, & Gardner, 1992; Whitely, Dougherty, & Dreher, 1991), and report more career satisfaction (Fagenson, 1989) and mobility (Scandura, 1992) than non-protégés. Mentoring has also been found to be related to positive outcomes such as organizational socialization (Chao et al., 1992; Ostroff & Kozlowski, 1993), career commitment (Bachman & Gregory, 1993), positional power (Fagenson, 1988), and to moderate negative outcomes such as turnover intentions (Scandura & Viator, 1994), job stress (Ford & Wells, 1985), work alienation (Koberg, Boss, Chappell, & Ringer, 1994), and role stress and burnout (Ford & Wells, 1985).

The importance of mentoring relationships has been widely documented and connected to career advancement at all levels of professional life. Such relationships have been classified into two types. Formal mentoring is when the mentor–mentee connection is set up by the organization and is central in reaching the short-term goals relevant to the mentee's position at that time (Geiger-DuMond & Boyle, 1995), and informal mentoring is a situation where the mentor handpicks a protégé to whom she can relate and forms a role model for the latter in an unstructured fashion. It also should be noted that mentors may or may not be employed in the same organization as their protéges, or be in their protégés' chain of command (Ragins, 1997). There is, however, little that we know of mentors that stem from direct familial bonds, representing another gap in the literature.

Strong gender disparities exist in relation to access to proper career guidance and to psychological support for employees. Mentoring has been established as a contributing factor related to the advancement of men (Barnier, 1982; Orth & Jacobs, 1971). Mentorship that takes place in the earlier years of adulthood for men corresponds to an earlier launch of their careers, which does not hold true for women (Missirian, 1982). Women structurally experience difficulty in establishing mentoring relationships due to various individual or organizational factors (Noe, 1988). The reasons why women are hindered from enjoying the perks of mentoring include: lack of access to informal networks, tokenism, stereotypes and attributions, socialization practices, norms regarding cross-gender relationships, and reliance on ineffective power bases (Noe, 1988).

Kumar and Blake-Beard assert that within a "feminine model of mentoring, human growth occurs through relational connections with others" (2012: 88). Further, mentoring outcomes can be differentiated among positive and negative mentoring experiences. They cite several positive outcomes associated with mentoring, including higher job satisfaction, an accelerated learning curve, and greater promotion and job prospects. Kumar and Blake-Beard also identify negative mentoring experiences, ranging from cloning behavior to physical withdrawal from the workplace (as reflected in absenteeism and turnover). While there can be positive and negative outcomes for the mentor as well, the focus of this chapter is on the benefits and outcomes for the protégé, and how the mentoring process may act as a cushion for women navigating the paradox inherent in tensions between Indian familial culture and professional/corporate cultures.

Mentoring in India: The Importance of Culture

Interest in mentoring in the workplace continues to gain ever-growing attention in India (Arora & Rangnekar, 2014; Haynes & Ghosh, 2012; Ramaswami & Dreher, 2010; Seema & Sujatha, 2015; Woszczynski, Dembla, & Zafar, 2016), as more practitioners embrace its potential for supporting career success. Recently, Arora and Rangnekar's (2014) empirical study found that psychosocial mentoring acts as a predictor of career resilience. Woszczynski and her colleagues suggest that mentors may give women access to informal networking opportunities and act as a sounding board for changing societal expectations. Understanding the nature of relationship-building that women undertake, as well as the opportunities and hurdles they experience in international contexts, can identify and define emerging patterns of mentorship that go beyond what has been assessed in the extant literature.

Over the last two decades, India in particular has emerged as a developing country of interest because of the increasing number of women entering the job market. Economic growth during this time has been unprecedented. The size of the middle class has quadrupled, and each year 1 percent of the poor has moved out of poverty (Chakrabarti & Cullenberg, 2003; Woszczynski et al., 2016). As a result of increasing globalization, shifting social norms, and economic reform, women are entering the job market at an accelerated pace. But these women are not entering a vacuum as their workplace relationships are affected by cultural dimensions.

There are several cultural factors that, in their interaction with gender, may affect mentoring relationships in India. Hofstede, who defined culture as "the collective programming of the mind which distinguishes the members of one category of people from those of another" (Hofstede, 1984: 1), identified four dimensions of national culture. These dimensions, from his original 1980 study, included individualism/collectivism, power distance, uncertainty avoidance, and masculinity/femininity.

Collectivism is one dimension that may impact mentoring. Considered to be a historically collectivist culture, Indian community ties and networks are essential within this context (Batra & Bhaumik, 2004). Ramaswami and Dreher describe collectivism as: "a general tendency toward interdependent self-construal. In other words, people view themselves as bound within the same collective and value relationships, connectedness, and social context over individuals' separateness and uniqueness" (2010: 521). This emphasis on interdependence rather than the individualism that we typically see in Western cultures may have an impact on the building of mentoring relationships across cultural contexts. Cultivating mentoring relationships, which have typically been seen as tools for individual development and advancement, may be more challenging in a cultural context that is set around attention to the needs of the many rather than focus on the needs of one. Another Indian cultural value related to collectivism is captured by the term "*apane log*" which translates to "one of us" or "in-group" (Ramaswami & Dreher, 2010). They hypothesize that this preference for interacting with in-group members and promoting *apane log* may affect mentoring relationships such that the initiation and development of mentoring may happen more easily with in-group members. Given that women are still relatively new to organizations and relatively scarce in the upper echelons, their access to mentoring may be hindered by this cultural dimension.

The masculinity/femininity dimension is another cultural factor that may affect mentoring relationships. Cultures that are high on the dimension of masculinity are characterized by strong societal gender roles—with men acting as the breadwinners and women managing the household (Hofstede & Hofstede, 2005). Within this dimension, some attention to the issue of marriage structure is warranted (Desai, Chugh, & Brief, 2014). In traditional Indian culture, most marriages are arranged, that is, they are negotiated by parents and extended family who screen potential spouses. In these cases, marriage is seen as a union between two families, not just two individuals. Within marriage, there are a number of expectations of Indian women. They are expected to place their families first and their careers should be secondary. Women are primarily responsible for care of the children and aging parents. So Indian women face the same work–family balancing act that women around the world face yet, compounded by culture. All of these demands in the familial sphere may have an impact on their ability and capacity to build mentoring relationships to support their careers. High levels of masculinity, which characterize Indian culture, may be a barrier to career pursuit for Indian women (Woszczynski et al., 2016).

A final cultural dimension that may interact with gender and mentoring is that of power distance. Power distance represents the degree of equality, or inequality, between people in the country's society. A high power distance suggests that inequalities of power and wealth are very present within the society. In contrast, a low power distance indicates that there is a de-emphasis in differences between citizens in relation to power and wealth, with a focus on equality and opportunity for all. Apospori, Nikandrou, and Panayotopoulou's (2006) study of the mentoring experiences of 297 Greek women provides a compelling example for understanding dimensions of culture and their potential impact on mentoring relationships. While they found that mentoring did have a positive effect on career advancement, they argued for the importance of paying attention to the impact of culture on mentoring. Apospori and her colleagues note that Greece, like India, has been identified as a culture that is strongly characterized by high power distance. As a result, there is a concentration of power and control in the hands of those in the highest levels of management. They suggest that because relationships in Greek culture are reflective of high power distance, it is more challenging to engender mentoring. Mentoring requires a degree of reciprocity and candid discussion that is not encouraged by high power distance dynamics. Particularly, high power distance has been found to impede upward and downward communication, to discourage personalization of the relationships between superiors and subordinates, and to reduce the amount of participative goal-setting done by management (Apospori et al., 2006).

Each one of these conditions (high collectivism, high masculinity, and high power distance) may negatively impact on the potential presence and quality of mentoring relationships. Through our research, we explored how women navigate this paradox of increasing opportunity juxtaposed against cultural norms and expectations for roles that they hold in relation to their family responsibilities and their work duties. We found that women in our study appreciated access to mentoring relationships to support them in their career; they also noted instances where mentoring raised dilemmas and challenges as a result of their clash with cultural norms, like power distance and masculinity. In the following section, we share information on how the data for this research was collected.

Research Overview

Women in our study represent two groups. The first group was MBA students, recruited from the pool of students at the Indian School of Business (ISB). The second group was recruited through snowballing technique of the first author as part of her research for a Fulbright grant focused on the careers and mentoring experiences of professional Indian women. The women in the second group were specifically selected because they had more work experience than the ISB MBA students. These women were interviewed in four cities: Hyderabad, Delhi, Mumbai, and Bangalore. These respondents were recruited through partnerships with several large organizations (both MNCs and IEs—multinational corporations and Indian enterprises). The total number of women interviewed was ninety-one. Of those, thirty-eight were MBA students and fifty-three were women who were more advanced in their careers, with experience ranging from five to thirty years.

Participants were interviewed using an IRB approved protocol that included questions on respondents' career journey, their conceptualization of mentoring, and their mentoring experiences. The first author conducted all the interviews, which were taped and transcribed. A team of coders was assembled and worked together to review and synthesize themes across the interviews. Codes were developed from reviewing a portion of the interviews as well as from themes in the emerging literature on women's careers in developing nations. The Dedoose qualitative software package was used to code the interviews and to develop memos to synthesize broader themes emerging across the interviews.

The Many Paths of Mentorship

Across the interviews, a number of interesting strategies that the women took up to manage their careers, and their family and work domains emerged. These strategies included actions and perspectives that the women adopted in support of their efforts. They also included support from critical familial connections, including their spouses, parents, and their spouses' parents. Using the lens of mentoring, we can see how vital relationships with others for learning, support, and feedback are crucial to navigating critical areas of their lives.

The Vital Role of Mentoring at Work

The vital role mentoring played in the women's careers was discussed at length throughout all of the interviews. Both informally and formally, mentors were crucial in their ability to teach the women the actual functions of the job at hand, navigate their role and career progression, and even offer a relationship to talk through the anxieties and personal issues that came up at work. The Indian women interviewed showed a thoughtfulness, even an assertiveness, toward seeking out mentors, whether in an informal or formal way, and took the relationship seriously:

> Keep saying that you want mentoring, even though you may not be getting it. Keep that issue alive. If you are not receiving mentoring from your direct supervisor, or whoever it may be, you should keep mentioning it somewhere or the other—maybe in your appraisal or at the appropriate moment—so that the person realizes that this is an important issue. Don't let it die down. I think that does have some effect—it may not be today; it may be a year or two down the line, but keep the issue alive so that people realize that you think this is something that is important. It is important.

Utilizing the mentors as the key to understanding new job functions or roles was very common among the women interviewed. While some of the women interviewed felt comfortable going to their actual supervisors with questions, others sought out someone else in the organization to show them the ropes. But they all described mentors or role models who were pivotal to their success:

> What I gained [from mentors] was the basic business acumen you know, how to do business, nobody in my family has ever done business, so I think I learned how to make money, and how to run this particular company. How to deal with people who we trying to get a contract from, what are the good companies, basic business strategy, and yes I had people

on my speed dial, who I could call up any hour of the day or night, that was big, big comfort. So that was a big comfort and cushion you know that I knew that I had people that I could call up.

Discussing mentors who were women and mentors who were men brought out some of the more personal aspects of these work relationships. While women mentors were less frequent due to a lack of senior women in the workplace, the desire and need for women role models was no less prevalent. Those interviewees who did have women as mentors described the crucial ability to discuss personal matters with them:

My first boss—and to this day, even if I haven't talked to her for 5–6 years, when we talk, it's like (snaps fingers)—she is the first one, who taught me that you dress in what you are comfortable in. And for her, it didn't matter in which part of the world she was, she was in a sari, and to me, that's made a lot of difference, and a lot of what I do today is primarily because of her. I think she's been a person who, from the start, has been very professional, very incisive, well groomed.

It is not surprising that most of the mentors discussed were male and for many of the women interviewed, gender differences were not a cause of concern. The women were clear in their need for guidance from someone higher up in the organization and were able to seek out whomever would aid them in their careers regardless of their gender. One participant describes the guidance from a male mentor:

One thing I want to share that today I came for the Interview because of the mentor. He gave me all this confidence that "you can do it." Otherwise I was very shy, that "no no no." See when I entered also I entered … I was not very comfortable. But still I came, with the confidence that I can manage it. So this is all because of my mentor, I feel. And lot of things I really feel that he … I knew he used to think such a way, he taught me to think different way. So this is one part I feel it was really good for me and today I am here.

Many of the women interviewed were clear about how mentors—both formal and informal—aided their career. Examples of knowledge sharing, network expansion, and confidence building abound in these women's stories of life inside and outside work. For those who had not considered the role of mentors in their life, when asked to reflect on their careers and individuals who may have played a role, they were able to see the impact of relationships from colleagues as pivotal to their success.

The Family as First Mentor

Woszczynski and her colleagues (2016) note that the first role models and mentors for girls are their families. Young women who succeed credit their families with valuing education and supporting them in their endeavors (Gupta, 2008). The role of the study participants' extended family was often discussed as an integral part of their work lives. Their ability to be successful was directly proportional to the support they received at home to pursue their careers; it was as important to acknowledge the potential conflict which might arise when family members saw themselves as the women's guides (or ultimate gatekeeper).

The crucial role of family in this "collectivist" culture differs from the more "individualistic" culture here in the USA. It isn't that family is not also important in individualistic cultures; family is influential for young people, across culture. What differentiates this collectivist stance is the continued influence and predominance of the family. Some researchers have noted that there continues to be a preference for the involvement of parents and extended family in making significant life decisions such as marriage and career aspirations (Jejeebhoy, Santhya, Acharya, & Prakash, 2013). The women interviewed for this study describe their family members as influential in this manner:

> I think family has been my biggest first and foremost help, whether it was my parents, my sisters, you know—I mean my—and then my husband and husband's family, my in-laws. So all along there has been a lot of support there. Of course, there were a few things that I had to—I would not say fight but make [them understand things] better. I had to say that this is what I did and given a situation like this, if I want to continue my career how were you gonna support me. So some of these challenging items were not something that were just swiped under the carpet but I actually brought it out for discussion out on the table and saying, okay I'm interested in having a career so how was everybody going to help me out here. And I feel that I could only come to work if I was sure that I had a support back home.

The role of men was a constant and interesting piece of the family theme throughout the interviews and in the women's lives. Whether they were fathers, brothers, or uncles—men were key to mentoring women as they navigated their first jobs, learned how to do their jobs, or thought through their next steps in life.

> When I started my business, two of my family friends, I mean uncles were there, so they would guide me every step of the way for initial 15 months, and even now, when you know when I find myself stuck then they have

been around in this business for 25–30 years, because each size of 300–400, so they have seen it all, so they do let me know when I am not making the right choice.

The role of family becomes even more interesting as women add or potentially replace their family of birth with their husbands and their families resulting from marriage. The Indian women interviewed had varied and fascinating relationships with their husbands when it came to mentoring and career support. All of the women interviewed had the support of their husbands for pursuing careers; most of them also received crucial daily support and mentoring for their jobs:

> The husband-spouse relationship could be a mentoring relationship, especially for a woman in our culture, I think. Until you are married, you get your directions from your parents; after that, you get your directions from your husband. I mean your allegiance is first to the family, then to the husband, so then that becomes a mentoring relationship and a source of advice. A lot of us, I think, are where we are because our husbands are supportive—they've said: "Go ahead and do it."

One of the most complicated and potentially interesting relationships in any Indian woman's life is that with her mother-in-law. Many of the women interviewed connected the question of mentoring to their first experience of being mentored by their mother-in-law. Often through arranged marriages (about half of the women in this study were in arranged marriages) and at a young age, women learn how to maintain a home and care for the men they have married from their mothers-in-law. Women in India most often go from their parent's home to their in-law's home. Getting their mothers-in-law on board with their career ambitions was paramount to their success:

> I did some conscious steps, the first year of marriage and they live in Mumbai ... we are in Bangalore, so when they came down to Bangalore I took them to my office, introduce to my boss, introduce them to my colleague, showed them my work area, for them to, you know, change their whatever level of thinking, what typical office environment is because their ideas around office environment were really, you know, from Hindi movie oriented and movies you see. So that I consciously took to, kind of, you know, involve them in whatever I was doing, so I would tell them what I do in office, what is my responsibility, who are my close colleagues, I mean, just like, you know, children coming from school telling everything to their parents, what they did, I used to do that with my mother-in-law.

Sharp Delineation between Work and Family, a Precarious Juggling Act

There are some impossibilities when it comes to keeping the work and family spheres separate. Mostly, it is a stressful, juggling act to continue to hold the role of wife/mother and professional career woman all running smoothly and successfully. For women in the burgeoning professional class of India, often employed by multinational corporations or starting their own small businesses, the demands on their time seem to never end. While many of the women in this study were of a class that employed staff, running a household with staff did not necessarily make their lives easier. Managing staff is a job unto itself.

The specific cultural and gendered world women in India live and work in creates challenges for which the women in the study sought to have mentoring. A recurring thread through the interviews was this yearning for a mentor or role model who is a woman—someone who is able to "do it all." While these relationships were generally appreciated and fruitful, they predominantly focused on careers and job functions:

> Ideally, I would love to have a mentor who would herself be a name to reckon with or a person whose life I would eventually be leading one day, you know. I don't want to give up my career, but at the same time I would be wanting to have a home, a husband, kids, right. And if she's been able to do this miraculously, then I would say she would fit the role of mentor.

Most of the women in the study consistently maintained their family lives intact, no matter the work in front of them:

> Indian culture? I would say we, I mean as a family, we tend to kind of finish work, go back home then get wear the homemaker hat or mom hat or whatever you are. And you kind of—there are two different switches. You switch on here and switch off there so those kinds of things. Probably that cut-off time probably is an inhibition at certain points because you can't network as much. I mean the meeting after the meeting and, those kinds of things don't happen as much as with men. So whatever happens, happens between nine to five.

A clear delineation exists for most of the women in our study. Throughout the interviews, we heard strategies to gain support from their extended family, thus ensuring women's ability to enter the workforce. But in the end, they questioned their ability to go back and forth easily and maintain both spheres equally well; they spoke of the predominance of family over all other concerns:

And that, part of the reason is because we're so rooted in our, in our culture that family and family relationships are paramount to us. So today, I'm, I'm saying that I think I'm doing fairly well in my career, come some place, need to go somewhere else and all of that, but in a heartbeat I'd drop all of these if I think my family would suffer.

Extending the Boundaries

Each one of our findings is an invitation to stretch and grow our understanding of mentoring as we extend this concept across national boundaries and cultural norms. The findings challenge the assumptions and norms that we have inherited from mentoring research set in Western contexts; these findings also ask that we re-examine and question the relevance and currency of cultural norms created more than three decades ago.

Invitation to Extend the Definition of Mentoring

From the first finding, we learn of the importance of mentoring to the professional Indian women whom we interviewed. Just as we see with studies conducted in Western contexts, we heard these participants speaking of the benefits of their participation in mentoring relationships.

This observation was similar to Ramaswami and Dreher's (2010) study where they reported findings similar to those in the Western literature. In this study, women participants reported seeking and valuing their mentoring relationships; their connections with their mentors were important because, in a sense, they gave these women permission and even encouragement to be in the work domain.

But does the prevalence of this Western framework overshadow the space for other, Indian, definitions of the concept of mentoring? When the participants were asked specifically about mentoring from an Indian context, several of them referred to the *guru-shishya* relationship (Pio, 2005; Ramaswami & Dreher, 2010; Vaidyanathan, 1989). Ramaswami and Dreher describe the roles in this relationship: "The *guru* is someone who guides the *shishya* in his or her own journey of self-discovery and mastery by building skills, enhancing knowledge, and understanding oneself" (2010: 504). The traditional and somewhat instrumental perspective of mentoring that dominates the US literature is very different from this Indian model of mentoring.

This finding of the importance of mentoring to these women also pushes against the concept of collectivism, the notion of the collective over the individual. This finding leads to a question about the relevance and currency of Hofstede's work. His work was conducted in the 1980s—given the rapid changes and transformation of Indian culture, is it time to revisit the classification of India along Hofstede's dimensions? Orr and Hauser suggests that

Hofstede's research should be re-examined; we appreciate that their critique: "is not meant to criticize Hofstede, but instead to pinpoint fallacies to enable researchers to build from his work in more appropriate directions" (2008: 1). Some scholars are noting a change—Bhattacharyya and Ghosh (2012) suggest that globalization has led to an "individualizing capacity" in the workplace that is contributing to the redefining of traditional gender norms. Haq indicates that Western influences have been connected to women: "challenging the traditional, religious, patriarchal interpretations of women's domestic roles, education levels, and economic participation" (2013: 172). These are important questions because as the workforce continues to change, and as more women return to the labor market and advance in their careers, it will be critical to understand how cultural norms support and challenge their career aspirations and their interest in and capacity to build mentoring relationships.

Invitation to Broaden the Network of Mentoring Providers

A recent trend in the mentoring literature has been a focus on moving from one mentor to multiple mentors (Murphy & Kram, 2014; Kram & Higgins, 2009). Interestingly, in talking about using a network perspective of developmental relationships, the focus has been predominantly on professional relationships. We appreciate that with the Indian women in this study, they were availing themselves of a network of mentors by drawing on family. This finding mirrors results from Ramaswami and Dreher's (2010) study where they found that 40 percent of their respondents indicated that their mentors were family members. Their acknowledgment of their families as sources of mentoring may be a powerful reminder or indicator to those of us in other contexts to broaden the pool of people who are considered as sources of developmental support. Higgins and her colleagues (Higgins & Kram, 2001; Higgins & Thomas, 2001) shared learning from mentoring as a constellation or network. There are a number of benefits that accrue from enlarging the pool of potential mentoring support. A larger pool of mentors offers greater opportunity for support. Broadening the pool of mentors may also encourage a synthesis or blending of professional and personal spheres, if support is drawn from both personal and professional domains. Given women's interest in and valuing of mentoring relationships, alternatives to creating more access to mentoring support may be a critical resource for supporting their careers.

The literature is also clear that there are some challenges that arise with the dependence on familial mentoring. The issue of high power distance has been found to have some negative consequences for mentoring relationships. Ramaswami and Dreher (2010) note that mentoring relationships characterized by mentors assuming a paternalistic/parental role may be over-involved in their protégés' professional and personal lives. Protégés may also develop an overdependence on these familial mentors. Because of the traditional hierarchical and paternalistic nature of Indian culture, it may also be difficult for protégés to question or challenge mentors in these types of relationships. And these relationships tend to be focused on the protégé (Ramaswami & Dreher, 2010), so there is not the level of explicitly expressed and acknowledged reciprocity that accompanies high-quality relational mentoring.

Invitation to Question Work–Family Balance

As these women were interviewed about their mentoring experiences and their professional careers, the predominance of their attention to and their focus on family over career was striking. This finding is in line with a key lesson that Haynes and Ghosh's identified in their work on mentoring and Indian women: "women's careers are affected by bifurcated demands in their work and family" (2012: 190). It is interesting to note that even in this lesson, the domain of work is listed first. Our observation, based on our data, is that not only were women required to pay attention to work and family, but that they also felt compelled to put family first. The message was clear from our respondents that concentration had to be dedicated to their familial domain before they could focus on their professional lives. This focus on the family, possibly at the cost of career focus, has implications for mentoring relationships and for the women themselves.

In terms of mentoring, the pervasive expectation that women are primarily responsible for the domestic domain means that women may not be as available to do the critical work necessary to build effective mentoring relationships. Woszczynski et al. note that: "Women may be unable to work long and late hours, failing to develop an informal network of peers and mentors, and thus keeping them from receiving information regarding opportunities in the organization" (2016: 510).

This high level of masculinity and the accompanying expectations also have implications for the women. The changing labor market dynamics, and the emerging individualization, may be acting as a liberating force from traditional patriarchal constraints (Bhattacharyya & Ghosh, 2012), like the expectations that accompany high masculine norms. Srinivasan et al. (2013), Haynes and Ghosh (2012), Haq (2013), and Bhattacharyya and Ghosh (2012) all speak of a "new Indian woman" who is evolving. Haynes and Ghosh (2012) trace the evolution of the Indian organizational women across five decades. This historical perspective starts in the 1950s, when women entered the workforce primarily in secretarial and administrative positions, and moves to the current decade, where millennial women are described as progressing to being a successful professional who is adept at managing both familial and professional roles. But this shifting dynamic of moving from a focus on being "wife/mother" to "professional" brings its own challenges; Srinivasan and her colleagues (2013) suggest that younger women pursuing careers and moving away from feminine roles in the home may face an "identity crisis." They call for a deeper understanding of the "new Indian woman" which could mean further expansion of our models and approaches to mentoring (Blake-Beard, 2015).

As we reviewed the literature on the challenges facing Indian women due to being embedded in a high masculine culture, we saw one suggestion offered over and over again—get more female mentors. While there is an acknowledgment that the senior ranks in Indian organizations are still predominantly occupied by men, researchers identified the benefits of having female mentors for women who are traversing their careers. Woszczynski et al. (2016) suggest that without women as mentors, young women are less likely to pursue their careers and they may feel excluded from important developmental networks. Paquin and Fassinger (2011) indicate that women provide both task-oriented and personal/emotional support in their mentoring, in contrast to men, who tend to focus on the task-oriented aspects of mentoring. They also found that there was a difference in the mentoring functions provided by male and female mentors; in their work, they report that women receive more advice on negotiating the intersection of home and work domains from female than male mentors. Haynes and Ghosh (2012) note that, given Indian culture, it is essential that women have the opportunity to both mentor and be mentored by other women. From our findings, it is evident that women, the organizations in which they are rising, and the very culture of India are all undergoing transformation that will impact mentoring relationships.

Conclusion

This study delving into the mentoring relationships of professional Indian women offers several insights. We found that mentoring relationships were critical to our study respondents; much like findings that we see in the research set in Western contexts, they acknowledged the importance of these relationships in supporting their careers and offering much needed advice and guidance. We also found differences in the mentoring relationships shared by these women. Consistent with traditionally held Indian cultural values, familial mentors were identified as a key source of support; these women drew extensively from the perspective and experience of their fathers, mothers, husbands, uncles, and mothers-in-law. The benefits of familial mentoring are tempered by the challenges that getting support and advice from those who are very close can engender: overprotection, overdependence, bad advice, challenges with challenging, and reduced reciprocity. And finally, we found that the masculine nature of India's culture constrains these women; in the fight for the "work–family" balance, family comes first. The expectation that they will subordinate their careers for their families can make building mentoring relationships more challenging, as they may not be as available to do the work that is needed to create high-quality, rich mentoring relationships.

Our findings also raised some questions about how or whether we should be using the traditional dimensions of culture that are attributed to India as we study mentoring and gender. In some instances, we saw these traditional dimensions being represented. Our data supports a representation of India as high power distance and masculine. But the dimension of collectivism seems to be shifting; the women in our study spoke of the conflict of strong career aspirations clashing with equally strong societal expectations of women's roles as the holders of the domestic domain. Our belief is that these findings suggest that we continue to look at the impact of culture, with some attention to the changes that are certain to accompany a world that is becoming a global village. Ramaswami and Dreher offer a powerful rationale, "While modernization and the diversity in India may limit the extent to which these characteristics are actually manifested, they remain influential and are pertinent to organizational relationships" (2010: 504). Even with the subtle shifts and rapid changes that are happening in India, we still need to pay attention to culture as we are studying mentoring and gender.

This topic also merits attention because the stakes are high. India is not fully utilizing the intellectual capital and breadth of its women; there is a cost accompanying this missed opportunity. Inderfurth and Khambatta (2012) provide compelling numbers regarding India's gender gap. The percentage of women in India's workforce is 24 percent. Women make 62 percent of their male counterparts' salary. Senior level representation of women is 5 percent, in contrast with a global average of approximately 20 percent. And of those women who are working, 48 percent drop out before they reach the middle of their career. This leakage of women from the talent pipeline, which happens at junior and middle levels, is attributed to familial pressure and cultural norms. Woszczynski and her colleagues share the practical costs of this gender gap for India: "giving women more opportunities in India could boost economic growth by 4% [...] With estimated GDP of over $1800 billion in 2013, having fewer opportunities available for women may translate to a loss of about $72 billion per year" (Woszczynski et al., 2016: 510). The call to include women in the workforce is strengthened by the importance of this movement, not only for women but also for India. Mentoring relationships, with all of the accompanying benefits and challenges, represent a critical tool to support the development and advancement of women in the Indian workforce and the continued emergence of India as a developing nation/world power.

References

Apospori, E., Nikandrou, I., & Panayotopoulou, L. (2006). Mentoring and women's career advancement in Greece. *Human Resource Development International, 9*(4), 509–527.
Arora, R., & Rangnekar, S. (2014). Workplace mentoring and career resilience: An empirical test. *The Psychologist-Manager Journal, 17*(3), 205–220.

Bachman, S. I., & Gregory, K. (1993). Mentor and protégé gender: Effects on mentoring roles and outcomes. Paper presented at the Society for Industrial and Organizational Psychology Conference, San Francisco, CA.

Barnier, L. A. (1982). *A study of the mentoring relationship: An analysis of its relation to career and adult development in higher education and business.* Dissertation Abstracts International, *42*(7-A), 3012–3013.

Batra, S., & Bhaumik, K. (2004). Intergenerational relationships: A study of three generations. *Indian Journal of Gerontology, 18*(3/4), 432–448.

Bharathi, R., & Baral, R. (2012). Women's career exit and reentry: A qualitative study. In *13th International Academy of Management and Business (IAMB) Conference,* Bali, Indonesia, September 12–14.

Bhattacharyya, A., & Ghosh, B. N. (2012). Women in Indian information technology (IT) sector: A sociological analysis. *IOSR Journal of Humanities and Social Science, 3*(6), 45–52.

Blake-Beard, S. (2015). Confronting paradox: Exploring mentoring relationships as a catalyst for understanding the strength and resilience of professional Indian women. In P. Kumar (Ed.), *Unveiling women's leadership: Identity and meaning of leadership in India* (pp. 25–43). London: Palgrave Macmillan.

Buddhapriya, S. (2013). Diversity management practices in select firms in India: A critical analysis. *Indian Journal of Industrial Relations, 48*(4), 597–611.

Chakrabarti, A., & Cullenberg, S. (2003). *Transition and development in India.* New York: Routledge.

Chao, G. T., Walz, P. M., & Gardner, P. D. (1992). Formal and informal mentorships: A comparison on mentoring functions and contrast with non-mentored counterparts. *Personnel Psychology, 45,* 619–636.

Desai, S. D., Chugh, D., & Brief, A. P. (2014). The implications of marriage structure for men's workplace attitudes, beliefs, and behaviors toward women. *Administrative Science Quarterly, 59*(2), 330–365.

Dreher, G. F., & Ash, R. A. (1990). A comparative study of mentoring among men and women in managerial, professional, and technical positions. *Journal of Applied Psychology, 75*(5), 539–546.

Fagenson, E. A. (1988). The power of a mentor: Proteges' and non-proteges' perceptions of their own power in organizations. *Group and Organization Studies, 13,* 182–194.

Fagenson, E. A. (1989). The mentor advantage: Perceived career/job experiences of protégés versus non-protégés. *Journal of Organizational Behavior, 10,* 309–320.

Ford, D. L., & Wells, L. (1985). Upward mobility factors among black public administrators: The role of mentors. *Centerboard, 3*(1), 38–48.

Geiger-DuMond, A. H., & Boyle, S. K. (1995). Mentoring: A practitioner's guide. *Training and Development, 49*(3), 51–54.

Gupta, V. (2008). An inquiry into the characteristics of entrepreneurship in India. *Journal of International Business Research, 7,* 53–69.

Haq, R. (2013). Intersectionality of gender and other forms of identity: Dilemmas and challenges facing women in India. *Gender in Management: An International Journal, 28*(3), 171–184.

Haynes, R. K. & Ghosh, R. (2012). Towards mentoring the Indian organizational women: Propositions, considerations, and first steps. *Journal of World Business, 47,* 186–193.

Higgins, M. C., & Kram, K. E. (2001). Reconceptualizing mentoring at work: A developmental network perspective. *Academy of Management Review, 26*(2), 264–288.

Higgins, M. C., & Thomas, D. A. (2001). Constellations and careers: Towards understanding the effects of multiple developmental relationships. *Journal of Organizational Behavior, 22*(3), 223–247.

Hofstede, G. (1984). *Culture's consequences: International differences in work-related values.* Beverly Hills, CA: Sage.

Hofstede, G., & Hofstede, G. J. (2005). *Cultures and organizations: Software of the mind.* New York: McGraw-Hill.

Inderfurth, K. F., & Khambatta, P. (2012). India's economy: The other half. *US-India Insight, 2*(2), 1–3. Washington, DC: Center for Strategic & International Studies. Retrieved from www.csis.org/analysis/indias-economy-other-half.

Jejeebhoy, S. J., Santhya, K. G., Acharya, R., & Prakash, R. (2013). Marriage-related decision-making and young women's marital relations and agency: Evidence from India. *Asian Population Studies, 9*(1), 28–49.

Koberg, C. R., Boss, R. W., Chappell, D., & Ringer, R. C. (1994). Correlates and consequences of protégé mentoring in a large hospital. *Group and Organization Management, 19,* 219–234.

Kram, K. E. (1983). Phases of the mentor relationship. *Academy of Management Journal, 26,* 608–625.

Kram, K. E. (1985). *Mentoring at work: Developmental relationships in organizational life.* Glenview, IL: Scott, Foresman & Co.

Kram, K. E., & Higgins, M. C. (2009). A new mindset on mentoring: creating developmental networks at work. *MIT Sloan Management Review*, (15 April), 1–7.

Kumar, P., & Blake-Beard, S. (2012). What good is bad mentorship? Protege's perception of negative mentoring experiences. *Indian Journal of Industrial Relations,* 79–93.

Li, M., Mardhekar, V., & Wadkar, A. (2012). Coping strategies and learned helplessness of employed and non-employed educated married women from India. *Health Care for Women International, 33,* 495–508.

Missirian, A. K. (1982). *The corporate connection: Why women need mentors to reach the top.* Englewood Cliffs, NJ: Prentice-Hall.

Murphy, W., & Kram, K. E. (2014). *Strategic relationships at work: Creating your circle of mentors, sponsors, and peers for success in business and life.* New York: McGraw Hill Professional.

Nath, G. (2000). Gently shattering the glass ceiling: Experiences of Indian women managers. *Women in Management Review, 15,* 44–52.

Noe, R. A. (1988). An investigation of the determinants of successful assigned mentoring relationships. *Personnel Psychology, 41*(3), 457–479.

Orr, L. M., & Hauser, W. J. (2008). A re-inquiry of Hofstede's cultural dimensions: A call for 21st century cross-cultural research. *Marketing Management Journal, 18*(2), 1–19.

Orth, C. D., & Jacobs, F. (1971). Women in management: A pattern for change. *Harvard Business Review, 49*(4), 139–147.

Ostroff, C., & Kozlowski, S. (1993). The role of mentoring in the information gathering processes of newcomers during early organizational socialization. *Journal of Vocational Behavior, 42,* 170–183.

Paquin, J. D., & Fassinger, R. E. (2011). Male managers' perceptions of the role of mentoring in women's career advancement in the chemical industry. *Journal of Women and Minorities in Science and Engineering, 17*(1), 51–68.

Pio, E. (2005). The Guru–Shishya process for radiating knowledge in organizations. *Knowledge and Process Management, 12*(4), 278–287.

Ragins, B. R. (1997). Diversified mentoring relationships in organizations: A power perspective. *Academy of Management Review, 22*(2), 482–521.

Ramaswami, A., & Dreher, G. F. (2010). Dynamics of mentoring relationships in India: A qualitative, exploratory study. *Human Resource Management, 49*(3), 501–530.

Ravindran, B., & Baral, R. (2014). Factors affecting the work attitudes of Indian re-entry women in the IT sector. *Vikalpa, 39*(2), 31–42.

Scandura, T. A. (1992). Mentorship and career mobility: An empirical investigation. *Journal of Organizational Behavior, 13*(2), 169–174.

Scandura, T. A., & Viator, R. E. (1994). Mentoring in public accounting firms: An analysis of mentor–protégé relationships, mentorship functions, and protégé turnover intentions. *Accounting, Organizations and Society, 19*(8), 717–734.

Seema, A., & Sujatha, S. (2015). Impact of mentoring on career success: An empirical study in an Indian context. *International Journal of Engineering Technology Science and Research, 2*, 29–48.

Srinivasan, V., Murty, L. S., & Nakra, M. (2013). Career persistence of women software professionals in India. *Gender in Management: An International Journal, 28*(4), 210–227.

Vaidyanathan, T. G. (1989). Authority and identity in India. *Daedalus, 118*(4), 147–169.

Valk, R., & Srinivasan, V. (2011). Work-family balance of Indian women software professionals: A qualitative study. *IIMB Management Review, 23*, 39–50.

Wesley, J. R., Muthuswamy, P. R., & Darling, S. (2009). Gender difference in family participation and family demand in dual career families in India: An empirical study. *Vilakshan, XIMB Journal of Management,* (September), 49–62.

Whitely, W., Dougherty, T. W., & Dreher, G. F. (1991). Relationship of career mentoring and socioeconomic origin to managers' and professionals' early career progress. *Academy of Management Journal, 34*(2), 331–350.

Woszczynski, A. B., Dembla, P., & Zafar, H. (2016). Gender-based differences in culture in the Indian IT workplace. *International Journal of Information Management, 36*(4), 507–519.

3

MENTORING LATINOS

An Examination of Cultural Values through the Lens of Relational Cultural Theory

Donna Maria Blancero and Natalie C. Cotton-Nessler

I would warn any minority student today against the temptations of self-segregation: take support and comfort from your own group as you can, but don't hide within it.

Sometimes, idealistic people are put off by the whole business of networking as something tainted by flattery and the pursuit of selfish advantage. But virtue in obscurity is rewarded only in heaven. To succeed in this world, you have to be known to people.

— Sonia Sotomayor

The words of Justice Sonia Sotomayor speak directly to the mentoring of Latino Leaders. The Latino community in the USA is 55 million strong and represents over 17 percent of the United States population. Importantly, 23.4 percent of the US population under the age of twenty-five identifies as Latino, indicating that the future pipeline of American leaders will be increasingly Latino. By 2050, Latinos will make up over 26 percent of the total US population (US Census, 2015). While the US workforce is increasingly Latino, there is a lack of representation in management and executive positions of business organizations. A mere 3 percent of Fortune 500's corporate board seats are filled by Latinos (HACR, 2013) and only 20.6 percent of Latinos work in management or professional occupations, as compared to 38 percent in the general population (US Bureau of Labor Statistics, 2014). Indeed, some have suggested that Latinos have lower levels of career success as compared to other major racial and ethnic groups (Blancero, DelCampo, & Marron, 2007; Cruz, 2012; Kochhar, 2005; Mundra, Moellmer, & Lopez-Aqueres, 2003). This differential outcome is reflected in the fact that Latinos comprise just over 8 percent of all those working in management and professional occupations, and less than 5 percent of all chief executives (US Bureau of Labor Statistics, 2014).

At the same time, more and more is known regarding mentoring and the benefits of developmental relationships and networks, especially for diversity and inclusion. Mentoring matters, that is certain. Those who are mentored have higher levels of career achievement, higher salaries, higher job satisfaction, and are more likely to stay in their organizations (for a more detailed discussion of this, see Tong & Kram, 2013). Thus, in order to improve the outcomes of Latinos, exploring what makes formal programs that focus on mentoring Latino employees effective is critical. How we can better understand the differences among cultural groups and whether mentoring relationships that are successful for Latinos have a different structure than those for non-Latinos will be the primary focus of this chapter.

Formal Mentoring and Diversity

Although there is a range of different types of mentoring relationships, both formal and informal mentoring are commonly understood as developmental relationships that involve both career and psychosocial functions (Ragins & Cotton, 1999). The extant literature on mentoring has substantially evolved over the past several decades (see Allen, Eby, Poteet, Lentz, & Lima, 2004). More recent research has examined the use of different approaches to mentoring within organizations such as facilitated peer mentoring (McManus & Russell, 2007), reverse mentoring (Murphy, 2012), and virtual mentoring (Ensher, Heun, & Blanchard, 2003). Others have examined hybrid approaches such as inter-organizational formal mentoring (Murrell, Blake-Beard, Porter, & Perkins-Williamson, 2008), or facilitated peer group mentoring (Stockdale, Chrobot-Mason, Chance, & Crosby, 2017: Chapter 12).

The distinction and benefits of formal versus informal mentoring have also been a focus within existing research and practice (Chao, 2009). Informal relationships with mentors and sponsors can be quite powerful and have been found in some research to be more effective than formalized relationships (see Noe, Greenberger, & Wang, 2002). Others argue that formal mentoring efforts are particularly important when mentoring seeks to impact the development of women as leaders (Giscombe, 2017: Chapter 8) or diversity and inclusion goals within the organization (Murrell & South-Paul, 2017: Chapter 5). Prior research is clear that one key barrier for women and people of color is lack of access to informal networks that include the opportunity for informal mentoring (Ortiz-Walters & Gilson, 2013). Thus, it may be the case that formalized programs offer a critical tool for equalizing access to key relationships within the organization that provide an opportunity for diverse mentoring relationships to be facilitated. For example, empirical research has shown that mentors of minority executives often became powerful sponsors later in the minority executives' careers, even recruiting them repeatedly to new positions (Thomas, 2001).

While we suggest that formal mentoring can have a transformative impact on diverse mentoring relationships, few scholars have critically and theoretically examined the possible role of formal mentoring in the development of diversity and inclusion that is specific to the needs and culture of Latinos. This critical examination is important if we are to see the full potential of mentoring to transform individuals, groups, organizations, and communities in meaningful ways (Ragins & Kram, 2007). Unfortunately, mentoring theory and practice have not evolved in a way that moves us from a traditional US-centric developmental model toward a relational approach that takes into account the needs of different cultures for mentors, mentees, and their interactions.

Clearly, cultural values impact on how individuals behave and these behaviors have implications for relationships at work, including mentoring relationships. In this chapter, we explore different cultural values and provide insight into best practices for mentoring Latino leaders who support diversity and inclusion throughout the organization. Certainly, Latinos are not a monolithic group, yet they share common features related to their cultural identity (Marin & Marin, 1991; Marin & Triandis, 1985; Quintana & Scull, 2009; Stone, Stone-Romero, & Johnson, 2007). We consider cultural values of Latinos as a singular group, recognizing that there are many differences among different Latino ethnicities; however, the cultural values we discuss are those that are considered central for Latinos.

Latinos have different cultural values from other racio-ethnic groups in the USA, which means that in order to be effective, mentoring programs need to take these values into account. We begin by discussing several key cultural values that we believe will impact mentoring relationships. We then move on to discuss what specific elements of mentoring programs need to be reconsidered given these cultural values. While much of the research on mentoring suggests that informal mentoring is most effective, we will explore formal mentoring as we believe that it is more effective for cross-cultural relationships. We end with recommendations for organizations.

Cultural Values of Latinos and Relational Cultural Theory

The cultural identity of Latinos consists of connections to the Spanish language and group-specific cultural values. Central are those of collectivism and allocentrism (Hofstede, 1980), which stress the significance of cohesion within the culture and the priority of group goals (i.e., family members) over individual goals (Arbona, 1995; Fouad & Bingham, 1995; Flores, Navarro, & Ojeda, 2006). While these group-specific cultural values are important, they need to be examined within a framework that is sensitive to relational aspects of culture. One way of conceptualizing Latino cultural values is to consider Relational Cultural Theory (RCT), sometimes referred to as the Stone Center relational model. This theory was created as an alternative view of the psychological development of women (Miller, 1976) but it can be used to examine other marginalized groups. RCT is a framework that considers processes and outcomes within a larger context of social and cultural factors and suggests that, due to experiences, members of marginalized groups develop stronger relational skills (O'Brien, Biga, Kessler, & Allen, 2008). This relational perspective not only provides context for group-specific values within the Latino culture, but also points to how mentoring experiences may be different for Latinos as mentors or protégés.

In particular, when examining mentoring relationships of Latinos, this theory can be useful. Fletcher and Ragins (2007) used this same lens when discussing relational mentoring, and considered gender as a cultural difference. Ruiz (2005) utilized RCT as a way of understanding Latino cultural values and personality development, suggesting that traditional theories are not culturally relevant. We agree with both views, and although Ruiz examined personality development, it is equally relevant to utilize RCT to provide a comprehensive overview of Latino cultural values within the context of mentoring diverse leaders.

A key aspect of RCT is the notion of mutually empathic relationships, or mutuality, in contrast to traditional theories that focus more on individuality and competition when analyzing relationships (Comstock, Hammer, Strentzsch, Cannon, Parsons, & Salazar, 2008). This framework takes into account the experiences of Latinos with regard to collectivism as well as other cultural values. It speaks to the notion of a two-way relationship where both parties work to understand each other and share their feelings. The positive outcome here is growth for both parties, not merely the protégé; thus, it is a reciprocal relationship. The mentoring research has grown from the "mentor guru" model to that of developmental networks (Kram & Higgins, 2009; Murphy & Kram, 2014) and, in our view, having such mutually empathic relationships aids in the development of strong mentoring relationships. Without such relationships, there are more likely to be disconnections (Ruiz, 2005) that can lead to isolation. As Jordan states:

> When we cannot represent ourselves authentically in relationships, when our real experience is not heard or responded to by the other person, then we must falsify, detach from, or suppress our response. Under such circumstances we learn that we cannot have an impact on other people in the relationships that matter to us. A sense of isolation, immobilization, self-blame, and relationship incompetence develops.
>
> (Jordon, 2004: 11)

Isolation is a strong concern of Latinos in the workplace, often due to being the only Latino in their department or entire unit/organization (Blancero et al., 2007). Clearly, it is in no one's interest to have talented leaders feeling isolated or detached. Having authentic and mutually empathic mentoring relationships is one way of ensuring more engaged Latino leaders. Considering a new paradigm to think about mentoring relationships for Latinos includes reflecting on the cultural values that many Latinos hold. We will discuss here the ones that we believe are the most salient with regard to mentoring relationships. These include: collectivism, family orientation or *familismo*, higher power distance (including *respeto*), *machismo*, and *simpatia*.

Collectivism

Latinos are often viewed as collectivistic due to the strong importance put on the needs and objectives of the whole community (or organization) rather than on themselves. They have higher levels of interdependence and are willing to sacrifice personal goals for the goals of the larger group. Also, Latinos prefer interpersonal relationships that are caring and nurturing (Triandis, Marin, Lisansky, & Betancourt, 1984). Collectivism is compared to individualism, which is the dominant perspective in Western culture, and primarily focuses on the goals of the individual. The implication for mentoring individuals from a collectivistic culture is that the non-Latino (often in the dominant role) needs to understand that, for the Latino, considering the department's or the organization's goals before one's own goals is not a result of being weak or not having a view, but is merely a reflection of Latino values. Perhaps similar to the mentor who clearly sees how the individual's goals "should" be considered first, a Latino mentor may clearly see just the opposite. This is a perfect example of why RCT is a powerful theoretical lens through which we can examine diverse mentoring relationships. The mentor and protégé should develop trust in order to share personal experiences and viewpoints, so that they can understand each other and develop respect for their cultural differences. According to Stone et al. (2007), collectivistic viewpoints will likely result in the protégé highly valuing mentoring opportunities that help the organization and will place greater importance on the relational aspects (e.g., psychosocial functions) of mentoring than their non-Latino counterparts.

Family Orientation/Familismo

The Latino culture places a very high premium on family relationships and the importance of taking care of family. According to Marin and Marin (1991), this value can translate into considering family members as role models, as well as a sense of obligation to care for family, and the reciprocal understanding that they have their family to rely on for support. Similar research has discussed this dynamic for Indian women. These women face very traditional conceptions of what roles (e.g., wife, mother) are appropriate and accepted for them which often conflict with career aspirations or work outside of the home (Blake-Beard,

Halem, Archibold, Boncoeur, Burton, & Kumar, 2017: Chapter 2; Haynes & Ghosh, 2012; Ravindran & Baral, 2014). For these cultures, there is an expectation that childcare and housework take precedence and are a commonly cited reason for career interruptions. Thus, managing the sometimes conflicting boundaries between family and work is a significant factor in the career progression of women from cultures that have a family orientation, especially for women in that culture.

Higher Power Distance (including respeto)

Power distance speaks to the difference in the degree to which individuals view the power differentials among individuals, with a high power distance promoting deference and respect to those in authority (Hofstede, 1980). More so than Western culture, Latinos place a high value on conformity vs. non-Latinos who value power over equality. Coupled with this is the notion of *respeto* (respect) which speaks to the strong value of the expectation of showing respect to those in authority and wanting to earn respect back from such individuals (Ruiz, 2005). While mentoring relationships have been examined based on power dynamics (Ragins, 1997), the issue of power within the Latino culture can be quite different. Once again, Relational Cultural Theory's notion of mutuality supports this value and can provide a useful lens to examine these dynamics within mentoring relationships.

Machismo

Machismo speaks to a cultural value that incorporates both gender and power, as well as a hierarchical structure (Jacobson & Jacobson, 2012). The Latino culture is highly gendered and traditional roles suggest that women are expected to defer to men. Such a value may result in both Latinas and Latinos assuming that men should take the dominant role and this can impact mentoring relationships. Due to the acceptance of traditional gender roles, special care should be taken when facilitating mentors and protégés in cross-gender and cross-cultural relationships. This value speaks to the notion of women being humble and nurturing their family through self-sacrifice (Flores et al., 2006; Ruiz, 2005). These behaviors may be misinterpreted within mentoring relationships that cross cultural and gender boundaries, creating perceptions that Latina women in particular lack initiative or are passive. As with any value, there are varying degrees of belief, so we do not want to overgeneralize; however, often Latinos are socialized with both the *marianismo* (the cultural value that women must be strong and caring for their family, but subordinate to men) and *machismo* values that may differentially impact diverse mentoring relationships.

Simpatia

The importance of relationships that are free of conflict are inherent in the cultural value of *simpatia* (Delgado, 1981). Relational Cultural Theory (RCT) supports this value due to the reciprocal nature of *simpatia*. Positive behaviors, including an emphasis on treating others with respect and empathizing with others' feelings are highly valued over such behaviors that would be considered negative, such as acting in a condescending or demeaning manner (Ruiz, 2005). An important factor to consider, according to Flores et al. (2006) is that many of these values make Latinos good colleagues and employees; but for individuals unfamiliar with these values, Latinos can appear weak and indirect in their communication style, especially in public settings. In the case of mentoring relationships, if we also couple the cultural value of *simpatia* with power distance, individuals may be more likely to develop close relationships with colleagues and peers, but tend to be more formal with mentors who have higher positions or rank within the organization. This is an example of the importance of both parties in the relationship understanding the need for learning about each other's cultural values and how they impact diverse mentoring relationships.

If the values and dynamics of mentoring relationships vary by culture, then it is reasonable to posit that perceptions of career success may be different for Latinos compared to the traditional career success. Traditionally, the career success literature consists of two dimensions: objective and subjective career success. Objective career success consists of the specific and measurable accomplishments that include income, rate of promotion, and level within the organization (Ng, Eby, Sorensen, & Feldman, 2005). Contrasting this is subjective career success, which, while broadly defined, is most often associated with one's own perception of career success, organizational commitment, and career satisfaction (Abele & Spurk, 2009; Hall, 1976). As stated earlier in this chapter, we recognize the distinctive role that cultural values have for Latinos at work and we believe that these same cultural influences will enhance subjective perceptions of career success. As Blancero and Cruz (2014) suggest, we agree that Latinos will view career success subjectively rather than via objective dimensions of career success that are traditionally valued by the individualistic work culture of the United States. This is similar to other cultural groups as Thomas (2001) also reports for minority executives who are more likely to define success based on their personal growth (subjective career success), rather than external rewards (objective career success). As such, this perspective will have an influence on the goals that Latino protégés have for their mentoring relationships that may differ from the goals of their non-Latino counterparts. As discussed in the next sections, mentors, protégés, and organizations need to be aware of this.

Formal Mentoring Programs and Cultural Values

Given that cultural values can significantly impact mentoring relationships, it is necessary to examine how formal mentoring programs may need to be adjusted in order to meet the needs of diverse groups. Thus, we outline several major aspects of mentoring programs that should be considered in light of Latino cultural values. First, the goals of the mentoring program to guide how the program is understood by both participants and observers. Within organizations, we must acknowledge that these goals are affected by cultural values. Second, how the program defines and creates mentoring relationships should be considered in light of these cultural values. Third, the structure and target outcomes of the program should be chosen thoughtfully, both to take into account Latino cultural values and to accommodate differences in cultural values between mentors and protégés. Finally, how organizational decision makers evaluate the mentoring program on an ongoing basis should be affected by a thoughtful consideration of cultural values as the impact of perceived success among diverse groups.

Goals of Formal Mentoring Programs

The fundamental goals of a formal mentoring program focus on improving the career outcomes and retention of protégés. However, how we define or envision career success is affected by cultural values. In traditional American business culture, career success is understood in terms of promotions and material success or what some label as objective career success. A mentoring program relying on non-Latino cultural values places priority on promotion of protégés as its purpose, and recruits protégés with the promise of enhancing opportunities for advancement. An examination of mentoring through an RCT lens shifts the focus from instrumental or transactional interactions to a relational exchange that may have different experiences based on cultural values.

As mentioned earlier, by contrast, Latino American cultural values emphasize relational dimensions along with subjective career success rather than transactional exchange or objective success and material rewards. The idea of "moving up the corporate ladder" may be appealing but not at the expense of relational outcomes. Thus, the goals of gaining expertise and personal growth should receive substantial importance based on culture. As a result, a mentoring program described as a way to help employees get promoted and attain higher ranks in the organization or as only focused on sponsorship, may be at variance with Latino employees' own career aspirations and cultural values. This is not to say that Latino career aspirations do not involve promotion, but rather, that promotion is not the main purpose and way one evaluates success; and so to pursue mentoring for the purpose of promotion would be a less worthy goal.

This issue becomes more complicated as a result of both gender dynamics and cultural values. Promotions and greater responsibility in mainstream business culture usually require a greater commitment of time to work and less work/life balance. Latinas' cultural orientation toward family (*familismo*) is important here. Among Latinas, having more time for personal relationships and being able to raise children are important goals (O'Neill, Shapiro, Ingols, & Blake-Beard, 2013). These responsibilities are particularly important for Latina women. This value is certainly in tension with the traditional business assumption that those who are in leadership positions should devote more time and energy to the interests of the organization and thus may conflict with the cultural values of diverse groups.

Thus, formal mentoring programs should become more receptive to Latino career aspirations by broadening notions of career success and valued outcomes. Mentoring programs that balance skill development, intellectual challenge, work/life balance, and generating greater impact for protégés would fit more with Latinos' own career aspirations. This more inclusive approach to career success will encourage Latino employees to want to participate in the program and increase its overall effectiveness. Put differently, a formal mentoring program that is designed to enhance leadership at all levels of the organization can be embraced by a wider set of culturally diverse employees.

However, this approach may at first seem counter-intuitive. After all, much of the impetus for this chapter is the observation that Latinos are not adequately represented in the higher ranks of organizations. This dearth of representation means that we should have addressing the inequality in the promotion of Latinos as a goal. Providing an inclusive set of goals does not exclude promotion and career advancement as being necessary and valued for Latinos. Having a more inclusive approach to career development will gain greater commitment from and increase the comfort level of Latino protégés and mentors. Over time, as protégés pursue greater career impact and skill development, they will also achieve higher rates of promotion, strong relationships, and positive work-related attitudes. All of these are important in serving organizational goals as well as individual career goals.

Another cultural difference to consider is the collective orientation of Latinos. While those with an individualistic orientation are motivated to pursue rewards that benefit and develop the self, those with collective orientation are also motivated to improve the group in addition to seeking individual benefit. Traditionally, mentoring programs are described as benefiting the protégé, and a prospective protégé would choose to participate in a mentoring program in order to enhance his or her individual success. In fact, many organizations rely on individual one-to-one mentoring as their standard approach to mentoring, especially for the development of future leaders. A mentoring program that works to improve the diverse definitions of career success for protégés, while also benefiting mentors and the organization as a whole, should engender strong support from individuals with a collective orientation culture.

Yet how people define or make sense of the benefit of participating in mentoring programs will be influenced by cultural frames and values. In traditional individualistic cultures, people are encouraged to be ambitious, seeking individual success, and defining performance based on individual level achievement and competition. With this cultural frame, prospective mentors are encouraged to look at mentoring at the individual mentee level almost without regard to more group-orientated goals, needs, and values. By contrast, employing a collectivistic cultural frame would mean that mentors and protégés are recruited by characterizing involvement as good organizational citizenship that equally benefits both the organization and the self. Outcomes that are valued may include contribution to the team or level of collaboration rather than an exclusive focus on individual achievement or success.

At the organization level, another benefit of mentoring programs designed specifically for Latinos (or other people of color), might be to increase cross-cultural understanding and inclusiveness. Given that mentors are likely to be non-Latino and from higher ranks, the mentoring relationships created may increase management's knowledge of Latinos' career advancement and distinct cultural values. This knowledge may be important in helping transform an organization into one that is more inclusive and has improved retention rates of Latinos and other diverse groups (Douglas & McCauley, 1999). Through mentoring relationships, mentors may learn to recognize culturally based attitudes and behaviors and have a greater opportunity to take the perspective of someone from a different cultural background. This access to different experiences may help mentors think critically about whether the organizational environment supports or obstructs the career and professional development of its diverse employees.

Given the above discussion of Latino cultural values, gender, and the effect of cultural values and gender on definitions of career success, we emphasize that formal mentoring programs should be altered in three specific ways: First, we examine the aspects of the formal mentoring programs in terms of the matching of mentor–protégé pairs taking into account cultural values that facilitate effective relational outcomes. Second, we discuss structural aspects of formal mentoring programs, especially in terms of communication, trust, and exchange within cross-cultural relationships. Third, we discuss the outcomes of formal mentoring programs and how definitions of success and effectiveness should take into consideration the cultural values of diverse protégés and mentors within these programs as well as the organization as a whole.

Connecting Mentors and Protégés across Culture

An important aspect of formal mentoring programs is the selection/matching of mentors and protégés (Blake-Beard, O'Neill, & McGowan, 2007). Given the importance of the relational aspects of mentoring, the matching process can have a tremendous effect on the outcomes for diverse protégés, particularly from cultures that are different from their mentor. If mentors and protégés are not appropriately matched, the result can create awkward relationships that do not involve commitment or mutual understanding, thus interfering with positive outcomes. How this matching process is conducted may vary considerably from formal program to program. We focus on whether race, ethnicity, and gender are considered in matching individuals. This should be considered thoughtfully by organizational decision makers when creating a formal mentoring program for Latinos.

When choosing appropriate mentors for protégés, a question to consider is whether mentoring pairs will be chosen to match or be compatible with a protégé's social identity. Having similarity of social identity (e.g., along race, ethnicity, and/or gender lines) can make relationships more comfortable due to shared cultural backgrounds, and similar interests and perceptions. Based on RCT, when social and cultural similarity exists within a mentoring pair, one would expect the relationship to be more close and have a higher commitment than when identities conflict or are ignored, which in turn would translate into positive outcomes for protégés. However, there is considerable conflicting evidence on whether matching mentors to protégés based on race and/or gender produces positive outcomes. Some studies find matching similar identities to be beneficial, whereas others do not (for comprehensive reviews of the literature on matching, see Blake-Beard, Bayne, Crosby, & Muller, 2011). Considering the conflicting results across studies, it is difficult to conclude that matching or not matching social identity is best. However, based on RCT, taking social identities and culture into account or helping mentors develop a sense of cultural competence can facilitate positive mentoring relationships and outcomes.

On the other hand, one could argue that when it comes to matching by race, previous studies have primarily focused on understanding the effects of racial matching (i.e., White–Black versus Black–Black mentoring dyads within American culture) but have not typically included Latinos as part of the examinations. Thus, participants in those studies had largely similar American cultural values. It is possible that because Latino culture is significantly different from non-Latino American culture, providing Latino mentors to Latino protégés may result in different and perhaps more positive outcomes for protégés as compared to providing non-Latino mentors. Based on RCT, we argue that mutual understanding and synergy may be more difficult in cross-cultural mentoring relationships. However, without further empirical evidence, we cannot know this for sure.

Based on these ideas, organizational decision makers may consider matching Latino protégés to Latino mentors or developing cultural awareness among non-Latino mentors whenever possible. Particularly if one of the mentoring program's goals is to enhance awareness and understanding of diversity by providing greater cross-cultural exposure, this may require having cross-cultural mentoring pairs. However, if same-culture mentoring dyads prove to have more positive outcomes than cross-cultural mentoring dyads, Latino protégés may be disadvantaged by having a formal mentoring program which does not give them exposure to non-Latino mentors, who may be at higher levels within the organization and thus a source of critical sponsorship. When a Latino protégé has a non-Latino mentor as part of a formal mentoring program, the protégé may also seek Latino mentors throughout the company to augment his or her overall developmental network of mentors. In fact, for Latinos and other minorities, forging relationships with peer minorities can especially provide psychosocial support, and having a balanced network of majority and minority members has been argued to be ideal (Ibarra, 1995). While more empirical work is needed, it may be that the best way of supporting Latino employees is through formal mentoring programs that focus on facilitating both same and cross-cultural mentoring relationships in order to provide a balance between instrumental support and psychosocial forms of support.

In sum, there are a variety of perspectives to take into account on this issue, and it is reasonable to pursue a relational strategy that favors matching based on social identities within some aspects of formal mentoring efforts within the organization. We are agnostic on this issue: we do believe that cross-cultural mentoring can be a positive aspect of a portfolio of formal mentoring programs. Deciding how to proceed on this issue should involve considering the ultimate goals of the mentoring program. One limitation to strictly matching based on cultural similarity is that in most cases, there aren't enough Latinos in the higher ranks of the organization to provide an adequate supply of mentors. Thus, matching alone will not drive the overall effectiveness of formal mentoring programs for Latinos. We must examine other factors such as the overall program structure.

Structure of Formal Mentoring Programs

The structure of formal mentoring programs varies considerably. Aspects that differ include: guidelines for how mentoring pairs are to communicate and interact; how frequently meetings are to happen; and what type of role mentors are to play in protégés' development. Much of how mentors and protégés conduct their relationship will be decided by the individuals involved. However, effective formal mentoring programs may provide guidance and/or training to help facilitate awareness and positive interactions.

Cultural values of both protégés and mentors will influence and shape the expectations of how mentoring relationships operate in terms of how to effectively communicate within the relationship. In particular, power distance and *machismo* are important to consider here. Given high power distance, Latino protégés will defer more to the demands of mentors compared to non-Latino protégés. This tendency may be further complicated by cross–gender mentoring, such that male dominant cultural expectations (*machismo*) can conflict when the mentor is a non–Latina female and the protégé is a Latino male. As a result, this dynamic can introduce a barrier to mentoring success, as Latino protégés are less likely to vocalize a desire to alter the parameters of the mentoring relationship if they are not in line with protégés' needs. Since formal authority is honored, particularly if they cross gender lines, protégés are less likely to press their need even when both the mentor and protégé agree that the protégé should be proactive. Especially when non–Latino mentors occupy high status positions within the organization, it can be difficult to obtain access and so the high power distance values of protégés can be perceived as passive or reactive instead of showing proper respect for someone in status or authority. This behavior is exacerbated by the cultural values of non–Latino mentors, for whom lower power distance is typical, as they may assume that when protégés are silent that they are not invested in the mentoring relationship.

As a result, mentoring programs should have a mechanism for explicit discussions about how to interact, what the roles of mentor and protégé are, and how the goals of the mentoring relationship should be negotiated across different cultural values (e.g., power distance, *machismo*). Consistent with RCT, ongoing training in cross–cultural relationship awareness would be an important element to include in the overall structure of any formal program.

Thus, when mentoring pairs include a non–Latino as a mentor, it is important to discuss cultural differences openly at the beginning of the relationship. Discussions of cultural differences and the sharing of perspectives about what it is like to be culturally different in that organization are vital when taking a relational approach such as outlined by RCT. Non-Latino mentors, and especially those at leadership levels, may shy away from such difficult discussions, as they may be anxious to not offend their partners or cause conflict within the organization. This behavior is called "protective hesitation" and is an important consideration in cross–cultural interactions (Thomas, 2001). Protective hesitation is when individuals are not as open with sensitive issues for fear of being regarded as biased or appearing racist. Of course, this can happen from the mentor's or the protégé's perspective. This hesitation can prevent important discussions between mentors and protégés that are vital for effective relationship cultivation. Yet, these open discussions are key opportunities for meaningful cross–cultural understanding. To prevent protective hesitation from stunting mentoring relationships, mentoring programs should provide ongoing and meaningful cross–cultural training to all program participants as part of the overall structure. This training would provide a mechanism for having safe, mutually respectful, and tolerant conversations that are considered the cornerstone of effective relationships according to RCT.

Mentors and protégés should especially discuss issues of power distance and gender dynamics (*machismo*) and come to an agreement about how they will communicate on issues of time, mutual respect, and resolving disagreements when they occur. For example, high power distance impedes good mentoring by reducing the flow of information (Blake-Beard, 2009), and if both partners understand this, they can take steps to improve communication channels. These expectation-setting discussions should happen both at the beginning of the mentoring relationship and also at various "checkpoints" throughout the relationship. This proactive planning can help reduce protective hesitation, which can inhibit positive interactions within diverse mentoring relationships.

Another challenge for mentoring pairs is that expectations of the meaning of the relationship may vary. This differential understanding points to the cultural value of *simpatia* and how formal versus informal the partners take the relationship to be as illustrated by levels of empathy and trust. This differing perception leads to several key questions that should be addressed between the mentor and protégé. What are the acceptable boundaries between personal and professional issues? What is the level of closeness and how much emotion is shared in the relationship? What is the correct balance between work and friendship within the mentoring relationship? Given that the Latino culture emphasizes *simpatia*, valuing relationships, trust, empathy, and emotional connection may be seen as appropriate and necessary within the workplace. Yet when mentoring pairs involve mentors who are higher ranked in the organization (thus, power distance is emphasized), Latino protégés will expect a more formal (less close) relationship than with peers or culturally similar mentors. By contrast, traditional American cultural values emphasize informality between individuals, regardless of power or status. Ironically, despite this informality, traditional American cultural values do not prioritize relationships in the workplace, and personal issues and emotion are avoided. These differences in both power distance and *simpatia* can surface in how the mentoring pair addresses each other, how/which activities are engaged in, how much personal information is shared, and how conflicts are resolved. When the mentoring pair has different expectations of the meaning or the level of formality of the relationship and how to build and maintain trust, these differences can cause discomfort for either or both parties, resulting in protective hesitation that reduces the potential for mutually beneficial relationships.

Protective hesitation can be exacerbated by gender effects. Not only are mentoring pairs likely to be cross-cultural, but for Latina protégés, the relationship is also likely to be cross-gender. Given the gendered nature of Latino culture, Latinas are less likely to share openly with male mentors than with female mentors. Thus, cross-gender relationships may tend to be kept more formal than same-gender mentoring. As a result, Latina protégés may have a difficult time initiating, cultivating, and maintaining effective mentoring relationships because of gender constrained behaviors (Blake-Beard, 2009). Mentoring programs can alleviate these challenges by providing workshops or training which sensitize both mentors and protégés to how mentoring relationships can alter expectations about the level of formality and closeness that can differentially influence male versus female participants' comfort level within cross-gender relationships.

Navigating across cultural boundaries should be part of the overall structure within formal mentoring programs. Moreover, mentoring programs should provide recommendations for effective relationship management rather than leaving this important aspect as unspecified. For example, it is suggested that there be regular check-ins and follow-up meetings between the mentor and the protégé as a way to legitimatize the contact between diverse mentoring partners and to ensure that cultivation actually takes place (Murrell et al., 2008). Having more frequent check-ins and meetings is especially beneficial for cross-cultural mentoring pairs. When frequent interactions do not take place, the protégé can remain "Othered" (Ortiz-Walters & Gilson 2013). In order to create cross-cultural understanding, frequent meetings should be encouraged, particularly in the beginning of the relationship. In fact, research shows that having more frequent meetings enhances the protégé's satisfaction with the mentoring relationship (Lyons & Oppler 2004).

Finally, we note that apart from issues such as formality, communication, and interaction levels, mentoring pairs may differ in exactly how support is perceived and received within the relationship. Therefore, another issue for mentors and protégés that should be addressed within the structure of formal programs is the set of expectations each has for how to proceed at the beginning of the mentoring relationship. This support might include discussing issues such as the appropriate focus on career versus personal development. For example, will the mentor sponsor the protégé, introducing her or him to others in the organization, and providing access to high visibility tasks in addition to providing emotional support and validation? Will the mentor provide skill development for the protégé along with serving as a sounding board for issues such as work–life–family balance? Will the mentor expect the protégé to be ambitious, take advantage of the mentor's network, and aim for promotion, or focus on relationship cultivation and satisfaction? To a certain extent, the expectations of mentors and protégés with regard to how support will be provided will depend on critical aspects of culture that have been discussed such as collectivism, *simpatia*, and gender role behavior. A non-Latino mentor may find it surprising when a protégé chooses to focus on personal development more than career advancement, thus providing a response of protective hesitation by the mentor. It is important that mentors and protégés identify not only what their desires are for the relationship, but also why and how this fits into culture-based expectations of the mentor and the protégé.

In sum, considering Latino cultural values and the challenges of cross-cultural relationships, it is important that mentoring programs consider providing more structure, guidelines, and training to both mentors and protégés. This support should include cross-cultural training, training on best practices for how to engage in mentoring relationships, and a mechanism for having open discussions that set the tone for effective mentoring cultivation that allows Latino protégés to voice their needs and expectations within the relationship.

Evaluating Program Outcomes

Finally, evaluation of a formal mentoring program that supports both the career and personal development of Latinos should be based on how well the program is meeting its key goals within the context of key cultural dimensions. In particular, differences in career aspirations specific to Latinas may lead programs to adopt broader effectiveness measures. These outcomes may include not just promotions and material success, but also measures of impact, personal development, and subjective career success.

As a result, when assessing the outcomes of a formal mentoring program for Latinos, organizational decision makers should seek to include a variety of indicators of career, personal, and relational development. These measures may include aspects that have to do with skill development and knowledge, including how well protégés perceive support that they receive as appropriate and valuable along with important career sponsorship. Measures of protégés' informal influence within the organization, such as having wider and more positive reputations within the organization and greater size and scope of their social networks, may be useful for determining mentoring impact. In addition, organizational decision makers should also consider how satisfied protégés are with their careers and development equally across work, life, and family dimensions. In all, there are many ways to assess career development, and evaluators should look to include as many as possible to obtain a comprehensive understanding of the effect of the mentoring program and how they might include different dimensions of culture.

Over time, an effective formal mentoring program can create change throughout the organization, not just on the outcomes of individual mentor–protégé pairs. For example, improved retention rates for Latino employees along with an increase in the percentage of Latinos achieving higher ranks in the organization are ways in which the composition and dynamics can be changed through an effective formal mentoring program. Moreover, a successful formal mentoring program should impact mentors as well as protégés. Through their exposure to diverse protégés, non-Latino mentors may develop greater cultural awareness and sensitivity. These mentors could become advocates for cross-cultural understanding, diversity, and inclusion throughout the company. Therefore, organizational decision makers should also consider assessing the outcomes for mentors when evaluating the impact of a formal mentoring program.

Based on principles of RCT, as mentors are influenced by protégés and vice versa, one may expect some cumulative impact in terms of organizational culture change over time. This change may take the form of enhanced cultural sensitivity, a stronger relational culture, or increased value placed on an inclusive culture. Thus, employees of all backgrounds are beneficiaries of these broader outcomes of effective mentoring. In this way, a successful mentoring program for Latinos can also have a positive influence on others throughout the organization. As Latino cultural values come to have greater influence within the organization, this inclusion may help organizations devote more resources and attention toward the positive outcomes and an inclusive workplace. In evaluating any formal mentoring program, organizational decision makers should consider to what degree the existence and support of the program has contributed to broader organizational cultural change.

Conclusion

In reality, when good mentoring happens—regardless of the cultural values of the program—all participants benefit through the relationships created. Recent research shows that high-quality mentoring relationships provide important benefits to mentors, not just to protégés. For many mentors, the notion of leaving a legacy can be strong (Ragins & Scandura, 1999). Additionally, mentors can learn specific, work-related information, such as technology knowledge, from their protégés (Mullen, 1994). Additional benefits include a rejuvenation of their careers, keeping abreast of what is going on in the organization, and loyalty from their protégés (Kram, 1985). For example, a recent meta-analysis suggested that mentors received five types of subjective career outcomes from mentoring: job satisfaction, organizational commitment, turnover intent, job performance, and career success. The findings also suggested that mentors were more satisfied with their jobs and had greater organizational commitment (Ghosh & Reio, 2013).

While research shows that mentoring can be a powerful tool, little work has focused on the unique experience of Latinos from a relational perspective. Given aspects of culture (e.g., collectivism, *machismo*, family orientation, *simpatico*), the dynamics between mentor and protégé are sensitive to cultural differences. Aspects of formal mentoring programs such as mentor–mentee matching, expectations, structure and evaluation of outcomes may have to be redefined for an increasing diverse workforce within the USA and globally. Consistent with principles of RCT, the effective support and structure of diverse mentoring relationships across culture can benefit both the mentor and the protégé, and the overall organization as well.

Our goal for this chapter was to provide an examination of Latino cultural values and how they can be used to develop effective mentoring programs for Latinos. A focus on effective formal mentoring is essential as we seek to develop the pipeline of diverse leaders within the organization that include Latinos. Clearly, the implementation of such programs will require thoughtful planning and an organizational culture that fosters cross-cultural skills. Our view is that such mentoring programs can serve as a pillar for organizational change efforts that includes embracing diversity and the development of the next generations of diverse leaders.

References

Abele, A. E., & Spurk, D. (2009). How do objective and subjective career success interrelate over time? *Journal of Occupational & Organizational Psychology, 82*(4), 803–824.

Allen, T. D., Eby, L. T., Poteet, M. L., Lentz, E., & Lima, L. (2004). Career benefits associated with mentoring for protégé: A meta-analysis. *Journal of Applied Psychology, 89*, 127–136.

Arbona, C. (1995). Theory and research on racial and ethnic minorities: Hispanic Americans. In F. T. L. Leong (Ed.), *Career development and vocational behavior of racial and ethnic minorities* (pp. 37–66). Mahwah, NJ: Lawrence Erlbaum Associates.

Blake-Beard, S. (2009). Mentoring as a bridge to understanding cultural difference. *Adult Learning, 20*(1), 15.

Blake-Beard, S., Bayne, M. L., Crosby, F. J., & Muller, C. B. (2011). Matching by race and gender in mentoring relationships: Keeping our eyes on the prize. *Journal of Social Issues, 67*(3), 622–643.

Blake-Beard, S., Halem, J., Archibold, E. E., Boncoeur, D. O., Burton, A. R., & Kumar, P. (2017). Mentoring relationships of professional Indian women: Extending the borders of our understanding at the intersection of gender and culture. In A. J. Murrell, & S. D. Blake-Beard (Eds.), *Mentoring diverse leaders: Creating change for people, processes and paradigms.* New York: Routledge Press.

Blake-Beard, S. D., O'Neill, R. M., & McGowan, E. M. (2007). Blind dates?: The importance of matching in formal mentoring programs. In B. R. Ragins & K. E. Kram (Eds.), *The handbook of mentoring at work: Theory, research, and practice* (pp. 617–632). Thousand Oaks, CA: Sage.

Blancero, D. M., & Cruz, J. L. (2014). Latina and Latino career success: The role of acculturation. In Urbina, M. G. (Eds.) *Twenty-First century dynamics of multiculturalism: Beyond post-racial America* (pp. 115–152). Springfield, IL: Charles C. Thomas Publisher.

Blancero, D. M., DelCampo, R. G., & Marron, G. F. (2007). Perception of fairness in psychological contracts by Hispanic business professionals: An empirical study in the United States. *International Journal of Management, 24*(2), 364–375.

Chao, G. T. (2009). Formal mentoring: Lessons learned from past practice. *Professional Psychology: Research and Practice, 40*(3), 314.

Comstock, D. L., Hammer, T. R., Strentzsch, J., Cannon, K., Parsons, J., & Salazar, G. (2008). Relational-cultural theory: A framework for bridging relational, multicultural, and social justice competencies. *Journal of counseling and development, 86*(3), 279.

Cruz, J. L. (2012). Latinas in the legal profession: Challenges and catalysts to their career success. In D. M. Blancero, & R. G. DelCampo (Eds.), *Latina/os at work: A collection of research, theory, and application* (pp. 189–225). Hauppauge, NY: Nova Science Publishers.

Delgado, M. (1981). Hispanic Cultural Values: Implications for Groups. *Small Group Behavior, 12*(1), 69–79.

Douglas, C. A., & McCauley, C. D. (1999). Formal developmental relationships: A survey of organizational practices. *Human Resource Development Quarterly, 10*, 203–220.

Ensher, E. A., Heun, C., & Blanchard, A. (2003). Online mentoring and computer-mediated communication: New directions in research. *Journal of Vocational Behavior, 63*, 264–288.

Fletcher, J. K., & Ragins, B. R. (2007). Stone Center relational cultural theory: A window on relational mentoring. In B. R. Ragins, & K. E. Kram (Eds), *The handbook of mentoring at work: Theory, research, and practice* (pp. 373–399). Thousand Oaks, CA: Sage.

Flores, L. Y., Navarro, R. L., & Ojeda, L. (2006). Career counseling with Latinas. In W. B. Walsh, & M. J. Heppner (Eds.), *Handbook of career counseling for women* (pp. 271–313). Mahwah, NJ: Lawrence Erlbaum Associates.

Fouad, N. A., & Bingham, R. P. (1995). Career counseling with racial and ethnic minorities. *Handbook of vocational psychology, 2*, 331–366.

Ghosh, R., & Reio, T. G. (2013). Career benefits associated with mentoring for mentors: A meta-analysis. *Journal of Vocational Behavior, 83*(1), 106–116.

Giscombe, K. (2017). Creating more effective mentoring programs for women of color. In A. J. Murrell, & S. D. Blake-Beard (Eds.), *Mentoring diverse leaders: Creating change for people, processes and paradigms*. New York: Routledge Press.

Hall, D. T. (1976). *Careers in organizations*. Pacific Palisades, CA: Goodyear Publishing Company.

Haynes, R. K., & Ghosh, R. (2012). Towards mentoring the Indian organizational women: Propositions, considerations, and first steps. *Journal of World Business, 47*, 186–193.

Hispanic Association on Corporate Responsibility (HACR). (2013). HACR Corporate Governance Study. Retrieved from http://issuu.com/hacr/docs/2013_hacr_corporate_governance_stud.

Hofstede, G. (1980). *Culture's consequences: International differences in work-related values*. Newbury Park, CA: Sage.

Ibarra, H. (1995). Race, opportunity, and diversity of social circles in managerial networks. *Academy of Management Journal, 38*(3), 673–703.

Jacobson, K. J. L., & Jacobson, R. P. (2012). The effects of machismo values on organizational outcomes among Hispanic professionals: A research agenda. In D. M. Blancero & R. G. DelCampo (Eds.), *Hispanics@Work: A Collection of Research, Theory, and Application* (pp. 3–20). Hauppauge, NY: Nova Science.

Jordan, J. V. (2004). Toward competence and connection. The complexity of connection. In J. V. Jordan, L. M. Hartling, & M. Walker (Eds.), *The complexity of connection: Writings from the Stone Center's Jean Baker Miller Training Institute* (pp. 11–27). New York: The Guilford Press.

Jordan, J. V., Kaplan, A. G., Miller, J. B., Stiver, I. P., & Surrey, J. L. (1991). *Women's growth in connection: Writings from the Stone Center*. New York: The Guilford Press.

Kochhar, R. (2005). The occupational status and mobility of Latina/os. Washington, DC: Pew Latina/o Center. Retrieved from http://pewLatina/o.org/files/reports/59.pdf.

Kram, K. E. (1985). *Mentoring at work: Developmental Relationships in Organizational Life*. Greenville, IL: Scott, Foresman & Co.

Kram, K. E., & Higgins, M. C. (2009). A new mindset on mentoring: creating developmental networks at work. *MIT Sloan Management Review*, (April 15), 1–7.

Lyons, B. D., & Oppler, E. S. (2004). The effects of structural attributes and demographic characteristics on protégé satisfaction in mentoring programs. *Journal of Career Development, 30*(3), 215–229.

Marin, J., & Marin, B. (1991). *Research with Hispanic Populations.* Newbury Park, CA: Sage.

Marin, G. & Triandis, H. C. (1985). Allocentrism as an important characteristic of the behavior of Latin Americans and Hispanics. In R. Diaz-Guerro (Ed.), *Cross-cultural and national studies in social psychology.* Amsterdam: North Holland.

McManus, S. E., & Russell, J. E. A. (2007). Peer mentoring relationships. In B. A. Ragins and K. E. Kram (Eds), *The handbook of mentoring at work: Theory, research, and practice* (pp. 273–295). Thousand Oaks, CA: Sage Publications.

Miller, J. B. (1976). *Toward a new psychology of women.* Boston, MA: Beacon Press.

Mullen, E. J. (1994). Framing the mentoring relationship as an information exchange. *Human Resource Management Review, 4*(3), 257–281.

Mundra, K., Moellmer, A., & Lopez-Aqueres, W. (2003). Investigating Latina/o under-representation in managerial and professional occupations. *Latina/o Journal of Behavioral Sciences, 25*(4), 513–529.

Murphy, W. M. (2012). Reverse mentoring at work: Fostering cross-generational learning and developing millennial leaders. *Human Resource Management, 51*(4), 549–574.

Murphy, W. & Kram, K. E. (2014). *Strategic relationships at work: Creating your circle of mentors, sponsors, and peers for success in business and life.* New York: McGraw Hill Professional.

Murrell, A. J., Blake-Beard, S., Porter, D. M., & Perkins-Williamson, A. (2008). Inter-organizational formal mentoring: Breaking the concrete ceiling sometimes requires support from the outside. *Human Resource Management, 47*(2), 275–294.

Murrell, A. J., & South-Paul, J. E. (2017). The emerging power of peer mentoring within academic medicine. In A. J. Murrell, & S. D. Blake-Beard (Eds.), *Mentoring diverse leaders: Creating change for people, processes and paradigms.* New York: Routledge Press.

Noe, R. A., Greenberger, D. B. & Wang, S. (2002). Mentoring: What we know and where we might go from here. In G. R. Ferris, & J. J. Martocchio (Eds.), *Research in personnel and human resources management,* Vol. 21 (pp. 129–173). Oxford: Elsevier.

Ng, T. W. H., Eby, L. T., Sorensen, K. L., & Feldman, D. C. (2005). Predictors of objective and subjective career success: A meta-analysis. *Personnel Psychology, 58*(2), 367–408.

O'Brien, K. E., Biga, A., Kessler, S. R., & Allen, T. D. (2008). A meta-analytic investigation of gender differences in mentoring. *Journal of Management, 36*(2), 537–554.

O'Neill, R. M., Shapiro, M., Ingols, C., & Blake-Beard, S. (2013). Understanding Women's Career Goals across Ethnic Identities. *Advancing Women in Leadership, 33,* 214.

Ortiz-Walters, R., & Gilson, L. L. (2013). Mentoring Programs for Under-Represented Groups. In J. Passmore, D. B. Peterson, & T. Freire (Eds.), *The Wiley-Blackwell handbook of the psychology of coaching and mentoring* (pp. 266–282). Oxford: Wiley-Blackwell.

Quintana, S. M., & Scull, N. C. (2009). Latino ethnic identity. *Handbook of US Latino Psychology: Developmental and Community-Based Perspectives,* 81–98.

Ragins, B. R. (1997). Diversified mentoring relationships: A power perspective. *Academy of Management Review, 229,* 482–521.

Ragins, B. R. & Cotton, J. L. (1999). Mentor functions and outcomes: A comparison of men and women in formal and informal mentoring relationships. *Journal of Applied Psychology, 84,* 529–550.

Ragins, B. R., & Kram, K. E. (2007). The roots and meaning of mentoring. In B. R. Ragins, & K. E. Kram (Eds.), *The handbook of mentoring at work: Theory, research, and practice* (pp. 3–15). Los Angeles, CA: Sage Publications.

Ragins, B. R., & Scandura, T. A. (1999). Burden or blessing? Expected costs and benefits of being a mentor. *Journal of Organizational Behavior, 20*(4), 493–509.

Ravindran, B., & Baral, R. (2014). Factors affecting the work attitudes of Indian re-entry women in the IT sector. *Vikalpa, 39*(2), 31–42.

Ruiz, E. (2005). Hispanic Culture and Relational Cultural Theory. *Journal of Creativity in Mental Health, 1*(1), 33–55.

Stockdale, M. S., Chrobot-Mason, D. M., Chance, R. C., & Crosby, F. J. (2017). Peer mentoring retreats for addressing dilemmas of senior women in STEM careers: The Nag's Heart Model. In A. J. Murrell, & S. D. Blake-Beard (Eds.), *Mentoring diverse leaders: Creating change for people, processes and paradigms.* New York: Routledge.

Stone, D. L., Stone-Romero, E. F., & Johnson, R. D. (2007). The moderating effect of ethnicity on relations between cultural values and the importance of job attributes. *The Business Journal of Hispanic Research, 1*(2), 42–53.

Thomas, D. A. (2001). Race Matters. *Harvard Business Review, 79*(4), 99–107.

Tong, C., & Kram, K. E. (2013). The efficacy of mentoring—The benefits for mentees, mentors, and organizations. In J. Passmore, D. B. Peterson, & T. Freire (Eds.), *The Wiley-Blackwell handbook of the psychology of coaching and mentoring* (pp. 217–242). Oxford: Wiley-Blackwell.

Triandis, H. C., Marin, G., Lisansky, J., & Betancourt, H. (1984). Simpatia as a cultural script of Hispanics. *Journal of Personality and Social Psychology, 47*(6), 1363.

US Department of Labor, Bureau of Labor Statistics. (August, 2014). Labor force characteristics by race and ethnicity, 2013. Retrieved from www.bls.gov.

US Census Bureau, Population Division (2015). Annual Estimates of the Resident Population by Sex, Age, Race, and Hispanic Origin for the United States and States: April 1, 2010 to July 1, 2014. Retrieved from http://factfinder.census.gov/faces/table services/jsf/pages/productview.xhtml?pid=PEP_2014_PEPALL6N&prodType=table.

4

MOVING BEYOND THE HEROIC JOURNEY MYTH

A Look at the Unique Experiences of Black Women in Academic Engineering

Gilda Barabino, Shereka Banton, and Cheryl Leggon

Access to mentoring for women and unrepresented minority groups remains elusive within the technical professions such as engineering. Breaking down the barriers that cause access to mentoring to remain elusive for diverse groups has important implications for key outcomes such as career progression and advancement of diverse leaders. However, few studies address the lived mentoring experiences of these under-represented groups. In this chapter we combine evidence from the literature and personal experience to probe and illuminate the lived experience of African American (Black) women in academic engineering and the role that mentoring plays in career development. We posit that examining mentoring in engineering through the lens of race and gender provides nuanced insights that can be applied across all demographic groups. We ask the questions: (1) How are Black women represented in engineering and how does that affect their experience? (2) How have traditional approaches to mentoring helped or hindered the ability of Black women to overcome barriers? and (3) What are meaningful mentoring strategies for the advancement of women (and minorities) within academic engineering? The authors are uniquely positioned to address these questions as African American females engaged in the practice of engineering and the study of women and under-represented minorities in science, technology, engineering, and mathematics (STEM). Dr. Barabino is the first African American female to serve as engineering dean at a non–HBCU (Historically Black College and University) institution and the doctoral advisor and mentor for co-author, Shereka Banton. Dr. Leggon, a sociologist and international expert on STEM shares a long-time collaboration with Dr. Barabino on cross-disciplinary research and initiatives for minority women in engineering. We reflect both on our collective experiences and existing research to examine this critical issue for mentoring diverse leaders.

Engineering as a Social and Organizational Enterprise

When one thinks of an engineer, one typically imagines a person who applies basic concepts to build and create technologies. Most often, this person has been imagined as a White male. This social conditioning appears to begin at even the elementary or middle school level as the majority of children who were asked to draw engineers in separate studies drew men (Karatas, Micklos, & Bodner, 2011; 2008; Capobianco, Diefes-Dux, Mena, & Weller, 2011).

In examining its historical origin, we note that the word engineer (along with the words ingenuity and engine) is derived from the Latin word *ingenium*, meaning natural talent or capacity. While the definition of engineering has evolved over time, as with the meaning of science, it has always carried a connotation of being a quantitative and exacting discipline and the social nature of the field is overlooked. However, social dynamics can influence who becomes an engineer or scientist, and how one is able to navigate a career path and contribute to the field. Fox (1991) notes that science is both social and organizational. The influence of social-organizational (also referred to as institutional, environmental, and structural) factors in combination with individual characteristics on women's mentorship, participation, and status in the field, ability to translate creative ideas into products are all seen as critical for career advancement (Fox, 2010; Fox & Fonseca, 2006; Fox & Mohapatra, 2007). A recent study examining why female students leave engineering reveals that gender dynamics in team-based work projects and settings whereby women are subjected to stereotypes relegating them to menial tasks, dampens female students' enthusiasm for the field (Seron, Silbey, Cech, & Rubineau, 2015). Women in engineering, and women of color in particular, are confronted with stereotypes and structural impediments that must be recognized and addressed to ensure that engineering is a field that embraces women and benefits from the full spectrum of the nation's talent.

Status of Black Women in Engineering

In 2010, Black women comprised just 0.6 percent of individuals with at least a bachelor's degree working as engineers in the United States (National Science Foundation SESTAT, 2010). Conversely, their male counterparts comprised 2.9 percent of engineers and White men and women were 64 percent and 8 percent of the employed engineers, respectively. More than 7,500 institutions that participate in the United States government's federal student financial aid program are required to report the number of bachelor's, master's, and doctoral degrees awarded each year to the Department of Education's National Center for Education Statistics Integrated Postsecondary Education Data System Completion Survey. The number of engineering degrees conferred to Black women has been flat, never greater than 1,500 per year and less than the number conferred to Black men from 1989–2013 (Ginder & Kelly-Reid, 2013). Conversely, since 2009, the number of engineering degrees conferred to White women has increased, suggesting that recruiting and retention efforts are likely more successful at targeting this group. Moreover, evidence shows that Black women, and women in general, persist in engineering programs at essentially the same rate as men by the eighth semester of undergraduate enrollment (Lord, Camacho, Layton, Long, Ohland, & Washburn, 2009). This suggests that one issue may be the recruitment and enrollment of Black women in academic engineering. A variety of factors (e.g., availability of mentors, self-selection, departmental climate, etc.) can contribute to attrition. Issues of under-representation, recruitment, and retention of Black females ultimately impact on the diversity of students within engineering and limit the number of these women who advance to faculty or leadership ranks. Lastly, the lack of Black female faculty as role models or visible signs of diversity can further challenge the long-term persistence of Black women in engineering professions (Leggon & Barabino, 2015; Berry, Cox, & Main, 2014).

For the few numbers of Black women who do persist in the engineering profession, career progression does not occur at the same rate as it does for other groups. Using median salaries for women working in engineering occupations as a proxy for career progression, Black women experience peak salary in their thirties with their salaries decreasing thereafter and well below the median salary for all women (National Science Foundation Report, 2010). Conversely, all other ethnic groups of women experience an increase in median salary as they progress along their careers. Black women aged forty and above make below the median salary for all women. This difference suggests the presence of significant barriers unique to the experience of African American women in engineering. Identifying whether the gap in median salary present for African American female engineers older than forty may be due to a lack of social network formation and mentoring is necessary. We need to uncover the specific social and professional experiences, particularly mentoring, of Black female engineers across all sectors (i.e., academia, industry, non-profit, and government) that may reduce this gap and facilitate career progression within engineering. Understanding this differential experience requires moving beyond grouping women and minorities into one category rather than disaggregating by race/ethnicity and gender, so that African American and other minority women do not fall through the cracks and remain invisible (Leggon, 2010). For example, Ohland and colleagues (2011) demonstrated that for students in engineering, trajectories of persistence are non-linear, gendered, and racialized, and that these differences would be masked and the findings skewed toward the experience of White males if the data were aggregated (Ohland, Brawner, Camacho, Layton, Long, Lord, & Washburn, 2011). Thus, we focus on the unique experiences of African American women in academic engineering and the role that inclusive mentoring can play in helping them overcome the challenges they face.

Academic Culture as Context

Since introduction into the engineering profession traditionally starts within an academic setting with the attainment of an undergraduate education, the focus on higher education as a critical point of entry is appropriate. Therefore, we were particularly interested in what factors in the academy/academic culture propagate the under-representation of Black female engineers. Social constructivists would contend that training and working in engineering (and the sciences) is a social, political, and intellectual process because individuals are not value-free and impartial. As scholars and educators, our beliefs, preferences, and experiences drive how we identify and define problems, how we choose groups to include in research studies, how we approach problem solving, and how our research results are reported and used to shape society (Leggon, 2010). The under-representation or marginalization of Black women within academic engineering can exclude their voices, unique talents, perspectives, and skills from the creation of knowledge and practice within the profession that this group can offer.

For Black women, the intersectionality of race and gender uniquely defines a set of differential experiences, especially given their small numbers within the field (Ong, Wright, Espinosa, & Orfield, 2011). These few women currently in engineering can experience isolation, marginality, and lack of access to important or influential networks. As a group, African American women are also the least likely to receive mentoring which is instrumental in the ability of individuals to get promotions in their fields (Dreher & Ash, 1990; Scandura, 1992). Ironically, they are also the most likely to be overburdened by administration and service including advising and mentoring others (Griffin & Reddick, 2011; Turner, 2002). Thus, we focus on the power of mentoring experiences for African American women that provide a unique and critical lens through which to view and gain insights that would be useful to all women.

Mentoring Experiences of Black Women in Academic Engineering

Mentoring is cited as a key factor for successful careers in engineering and other fields (Scandura, 1992; Boyle & Boice, 1998; Ragins & Cotton, 1999; Moody 2004). However, a clear understanding of what constitutes effective mentoring and how individual and structural characteristics influence mentoring is critical. Gendered mentoring experiences of women are well recognized within prior research and these experiences can be more pronounced in engineering given the under-representation of African American women, particularly among the senior ranks within higher education institutions. Lack of mentoring, or gendered mentoring, impacts on the careers of African American women that span entire career paths from training as a student to joining the engineering workforce as an academic or practitioner to becoming a leader within the academy or university (Blake-Beard, Bayne, Crosby, & Muller, 2011; Chesler & Chesler, 2002).

Traditionally, mentoring is defined as a relationship between a more senior and knowledgeable individual (mentor) and a junior less experienced individual (protégé); the mentor is seen as one who provides guidance and support within the domains of career development, psychosocial development, and role modeling (Kram, 1985; Tillman, 2001; Blake-Beard et al., 2011). We agree with those that view mentoring as a relational process that evolves over time in phases within a contextual setting (see Higgins & Kram, 2001). We recognize that mentoring can be informal or formal, and can occur through one-to-one relationships, peer groups, a network of multiple mentors, or through electronic means. Mentoring can also be dynamic or vertically integrated as in the case where a professor, for example, mentors a graduate student who in turn mentors an undergraduate student. For both mentors and protégés, mentoring can be a mutually rewarding experience. However the form, mentoring relationships are embedded in an organizational context reflecting the culture of the organization and reflect the norms, attitudes, and values of its members (Wanburg, Welsh, & Hezlett, 2003). Thus, we must draw attention to the importance of understanding same-race and cross-race mentoring along with same-gender and cross-gender mentoring (Thomas, 2001; Tillman, 2001; Syed, Azmitia, & Cooper, 2011). The context of under-representation and marginalization, together with the complex and relational perspective of mentoring, provides the backdrop for our exploration of African American women within academic engineering.

In preparing for this chapter, we were struck by the absence of experiences and voices of African American females within the history of and the bodies of work in engineering, especially within the literature on mentoring. The extant literature on women in engineering overwhelmingly represents White women's experiences and perspectives, and fails to account for differential experiences based on race. This gap is also true for other factors that shape the experiences of mentors and protégés such as cultural backgrounds, religious preferences, social class, and other aspects of diversity or social identity. There are a few exceptions. For example, Leslie, McClure, and Oaxaca (1998), through a life sequence analysis, found that earlier life experiences and early socialization impact on behaviors in science and engineering and that for women and minorities, a particular individual (typically a mentor) was instrumental in their persistence and success. Johnson (2007) found that science professors were often discouraging to women of color by the lack of encouragement, the lack of quality personal interactions, and the failure to acknowledge that science is not race-, ethnicity-, and gender-neutral. The importance of more research and scholarship on African American women is clear. Effective mentoring can be beneficial to the same degree that ineffective mentoring is detrimental. Therefore, those in a position to mentor must be aware of their actions and behaviors, and the consequences of those actions and behaviors; they must be sensitive to differences based on race and ethnicity, gender and other characteristics. While the need for and benefits of mentoring are known, the specific approach to mentoring for African American women and other under-represented groups matters.

The Heroic Journey Mentoring Model in Academic Engineering

The traditional male-dominated mentorship style in engineering embraces a gender-specific conception of the mentor who is the dominant (alpha) male behavior within the relationship. This conception is defined by valuing competition over collaboration, being separated from rather than integrated into one's group, and the measuring of success at the individual rather than group level (Chesler & Chesler, 2002). This style of mentoring does not necessarily value or provide psychosocial support and is more focused on advice-giving around technical and career-related issues. A common feature of this mentorship style is the "heroic journey" narrative (also known as sink or swim) in which protégés are challenged to navigate their work independently and competitively in order to "test their manhood" and their strength, therefore validating themselves and their abilities (Chesler & Chesler, 2002). We should mention that the presence of the sink or swim narrative of mentoring in engineering and the hierarchal nature of training in the field necessitates rethinking how we structure formal mentoring programs as part of engineering education programs. For example, a formal graduate advisor–graduate student relationship is not necessarily an effective mentoring relationship if the student (the protégé) does not have access to both career as well as psychosocial support on matters of academic, career, and personal development. As Bozeman and Feeney state, "If the instruction is part of the formal requirements of the job (or the supervisory relationship), it does not qualify as mentoring" (2007: 731). We cannot presume that complete or inclusive mentoring occurs in this traditional context, particularly for women and under-represented groups whose experiences are shaped not only by their academic and professional bodies of work, but also by the influence of their experience of gender and/or racial identity as they navigate through the field. Ensuring that multiple opportunities for diverse mentoring experiences exist, especially for under-represented groups, is critical given the dominant narrative within academic engineering. Thus, the heroic journey perspective of mentoring does not provide adequate support and may signal to African American women that they do not fit within the engineering profession.

Inclusive Mentoring Approaches in Academic Engineering

Race, gender, and other identities matter, as do organizational politics and culture, when mentoring women and minorities in engineering. There are a few examples of mentoring approaches tailored to diverse women that suggest inclusive mentoring can be an effective strategy in retention and career development within engineering. These examples point to several common threads, such as a balance between formal and informal mentoring opportunities, use of different types of mentoring relationships, and a balanced focus between career and psychosocial functions within the mentoring relationships (Leggon & Barabino, 2015; Mondisa, 2014, 2015; Gibson, 2006; Girves, Zepeda, & Gwathmey, 2005). Here, we highlight examples of programs that tailor the mentoring approach to the unique needs of diverse groups such as African American women and then discuss three underlying theoretical frameworks (unconscious bias, identity conflict, and leadership challenges) that can help us better understand the potential success of these inclusive approaches to mentoring.

One example is the Meyerhoff Scholars Program at the University of Maryland Baltimore County, which has been highly successful in recruiting and retaining under-represented minority undergraduate and graduate students in STEM fields (Summers & Hrabowski, 2006). Mentorship between students and faculty in the form of students working in laboratories and partaking in face-to-face meetings or group activities with other participants is a central part of the program. A second example is the National Science Foundation's Louis Stokes Alliances for Minority Participation (LSAMP) and Alliances for Graduate Education and the Professoriate (AGEP) programs, which are focused on diversifying the student population in undergraduate and graduate STEM programs at specific institutions, as well as nationally through the adoption of exemplars' successful practices. Funded, hands-on research experiences for students are also a key component of programs for both LSAMP and AGEP institutions. A third example instituted at the faculty level is the NSF ADVANCE Cross-Disciplinary Initiative for Minority Women Faculty. Authors Barabino and Leggon developed a national model for mentoring minority women in academic engineering that includes crossing disciplines and institutions as part of this unique program (Leggon & Barabino, 2015). The goal across all of these formal programs is to socialize participants into their fields, provide personal contact via relational support, and offer advice and resources that support career and professional development. Expanding access to diverse mentoring experiences (formal, informal, peer-to-peer, group, one-on-one) is another advantage of these programs in meeting the unique needs of African American women.

While these example programs have been recognized as models for other institutions, we must be cautious to note that mentoring in engineering for women and under-represented minorities is fraught with challenges, given the dearth of women and minorities and the limited opportunities for authentic, informal relationships to develop between those who share the same gender and cultural background. This dearth of opportunity produces a demand on African American women within these programs to continually navigate cross-racial and cross-gender relationships to receive mentoring support that their counterparts do get to experience. This dynamic was described by Girves, Zepeda, and Gwathmey (2005), who point to limited access to mentors, the tendency for spontaneous relationships to form between those with social characteristics in common, resistance to assimilation (losing one's identity), and mixed outcomes as barriers for women engaged in cross-gender and cross-race mentoring. On the contrary, Blake-Beard and her colleagues (2011) acknowledge the benefits of same-gender and same-race mentoring and note that there can be mixed outcomes when other areas of similarity between mentors and protégés, beyond race and gender, are taken into consideration.

Theoretical Frameworks

We argue that the success or failure of mentoring programs and mentoring relationships for African American women rests on the awareness of an explicit effort to address key barriers within these cross-race, cross-gender relationships. Understanding how key factors can intervene within diverse mentoring relationships can help us break down the barriers reflected in the heroic mentoring journey narrative that is so pervasive within academic engineering. Thus, we discuss three key theoretical frameworks that can elucidate our perspectives on the unique experiences of African American women and other under-represented groups: unconscious bias, identity conflict, and presumed meritocracy.

Unconscious Bias

Unconscious (implicit) bias has devastating consequences for African American women and can affect the quality of their mentoring relationships. Defined as attitudes or stereotypes that affect one's behavior in an unconscious manner, unconscious bias leads to exclusion, devaluation, and stigmatization of African American women that impacts academic outcomes, impedes career progression, and often results in premature departures from the field (Easterly & Ricard, 2011). Stereotypes about the innate talent (or lack of talent) of women and African Americans may create unwillingness by mentors to offer critical support such as sponsorship. This unwillingness can help explain their under-representation in STEM (science, technology, engineering, and math) fields where practitioners believe that innate talent is the primary requirement for success (Leslie, Cimpian, Meyer, & Freeland, 2015). For example, Jacoby-Senghor and colleagues (2016) demonstrated a link between instructors' unconscious/implicit bias and academic outcomes such that instructor bias predicted diminished performance for African American students, but not for

White students (Jacoby-Senghor, Sinclair, & Shelton, 2016). Thus, it is not surprising that African American women may hesitate to enter the field; when they do enter, these biases continue to create a sense of stereotype threat and a sense of not belonging that limits the effectiveness of mentoring relationships.

In the academy, African American women's marginalized position facilitates isolation, exclusion, and the undervaluation or devaluation of their scholarly work (Henderson, Hunter, & Hildreth, 2010), which serves to reinforce biases. Further, without perceived competence and value, African American women are excluded from important social and community building activities that foster collegiality, collaboration, and career development. The absence of recognition of African American women as intellectuals allows stereotyped viewpoints to operate (e.g., nurturing "mammy," angry woman, affirmative action candidate), limiting support and engagement within mentoring relationships. In addition, the sink or swim narrative within academic engineering accentuates the unconscious biases and judgment that African American women "just can't cut it." The lack of numerical representation of African American women reinforces the bias that they are not "native" to the academy, and are therefore seen as an exception and not entitled to the access and resources that other groups receive (Harley, 2008; Henderson et al., 2010).

For African American women who are able to succeed and achieve the ranks of professor, they continue to face the impact of not being perceived as talented and contributing members of the academic community. Evidence shows that they carry heavy teaching and service (e.g., diversity) loads, bear the mentoring responsibilities for marginalized groups, are considered the go-to for diversity issues, and ultimately are not being recognized during tenure and promotion decisions (Harley, 2008; Henderson et al., 2010). These teaching, service, and mentoring responsibilities are additive to Black female professors' scholarly duties, particularly in research-intensive institutions. Because of this burden, any failure to produce "adequate" scholarship further reinforces the idea of lesser value to the academy, when the time and energy spent on these extra activities is often ignored or discounted. However, failure to do these activities would also call into question their contributions as organizational citizens which can negatively impact career progression, especially in being selected for academic leadership positions. This extra conflicting set of demands can also lead to African American women being burdened by the Superwoman complex with unreasonable expectations for strength and resilience. What arose as a means of survival and of counteracting negative stereotypes continues to take a toll on African American women in the academy in terms of unrealistic demands, persistent barriers, and expectations and detrimental effects on well-being because of these unconscious biases (Mullings, 2005).

Identity Conflict

Kimberlee Crenshaw (1989) is credited with coining the term intersectionality when she used it to convey the interconnectedness of race, gender, and class, and how different types of oppression and discrimination interact. We use the concept of intersectionality here to highlight the critical intersections of social statuses, disciplines, individual characteristics, social-organizational factors, history, and lived experiences when seeking to examine issues like the mentoring of under-represented groups within academic engineering. For African American women in particular, these intersections lead to multiple identities being experienced simultaneously and sometimes one identity may conflict with another.

Identity is lived experience and is produced by social norms as well as social interactions. It is influenced by race and gender (Carlone & Johnson, 2007), and as described by Gee (2000), identity is defined by social perceptions about the nature and social group membership of individuals. How one sees herself as an engineer is not fully under her control as described by Malone and Barabino (2009). For African American women and other women of color, minority status impacts on identity formation through invisibility, social isolation, and the inability to integrate their personal, social, and professional identities. In describing how identity shapes the experiences of women of color engineering students, Tate and Linn (2005) report that students report feelings of being different, of not belonging, and behaving as "outsiders within." The absence of those who share similar identities adds to feelings of isolation and marginalization, and can limit the pool of mentors who can serve as role models and who can help shape or refine personal as well as professional identity. Same-gender and same-race mentors can play an important role in helping protégés develop self-confidence, gain political insight, socialize into the profession, and develop as leaders (Tillman, 2001; Syed et al., 2011) in a manner that serves to reinforce identity formation and integrate personal and professional identities.

Presumed Meritocracy

Presumed meritocracy that exists in academic engineering and the myth of the highly individualized heroic journey imply that one's body of work, innate talent, and drive should be the dominant criteria for acceptance as leaders and professional advancement. However, Castilla and Benard (2010) have found that an organizational setting that prides itself on its meritocracy often enables those in managerial positions to make decisions that are actually influenced by their prejudices and biases rather than objective criteria such as merit or performance. Also called the "paradox of meritocracy," this framework involves the espousing of the meritocratic ideal and employees' internalization of the ideal and can create a culture of perceived objectivity in decision-making that may not actually exist. We contend that African American women have to meet not only the criteria set on paper within their organizations or groups, but are also impacted by subjective and unspoken criteria that are used to evaluate performance and interfere with cross-race and cross-gender mentoring. Arguably, the *maximum* criteria for advancement that other groups must meet may actually be the *minimum* criteria that Black women must reach to advance professionally, assume leadership roles, or be supported when they assume leaderships roles. Cech and Blair-Loy (2010) provide an *alternate* explanation for the gender inequality evident in male-dominated fields and point to career success as an indicator of one's perception of structural factors rather than meritocratic ideologies accounting for a perceived glass ceiling for women. Their findings suggest that women's beliefs about gender inequality vary, based on their career and family circumstances, and influence whether or not they would be inclined to help remove structural barriers imposed on themselves and protégés or embrace meritocratic ideologies and thus, reinforce the glass ceiling. In this situation, whether one has already reached the upper echelons in their profession can influence her perception of those who are in lower-level positions, adding an additional layer to her biases, preferences, and views. When the experiences of Black women in engineering are considered, it becomes clear that the reward structure in the academy, and likely other sectors, is not as meritocratic as it is perceived to be. This can affect the dynamics of their professional and mentoring experiences, whether they are a mentor or protégé, because their acceptance as legitimate contributors to engineering is conditional to factors other than the merit of their work.

Toward an Inclusive Approach to Mentoring: Personal Reflections

As with new friends and old friends where one is silver and the other is gold, this dynamic may also characterize mentoring relationships; this is the case with mentor, Gilda Barabino and protégé, Shereka Banton. It was a freshman Biomedical Engineering problem-based learning class where Professor Barabino served as the faculty facilitator for a student team that Shereka was a member of that brought Barabino and Banton together. Shereka was a quiet force behind her team's success and immediately stood out to Professor Barabino, not only because of her academic skills, but also because she was one of a very few Blacks in biomedical engineering. Having been in solo status throughout her career as one of a small population of African American female engineers, Barabino was eager to reach out to Banton as a mentor and invited Shereka to join her lab as an undergraduate researcher. Following her award-winning success at undergraduate research, Shereka joined Dr. Barabino's lab as a graduate student and is working toward her doctorate in biomedical engineering while pursuing her interests in public policy. Shereka has received prestigious fellowships for her engineering research as well as her policy work and she is poised for success in a number of career paths. Were it not for Dr. Barabino's encouragement, Shereka would have likely passed on the opportunity to attend graduate school and not had access to the various enrichment activities during her graduate experience. She would be remiss not to emphasize just how much having Dr. Barabino, as an experienced and caring mentor in her corner, has changed her life. She knows that she can always depend on Dr. Barabino to provide support and advisement for scientific, professional, and personal development and that the support will be lifelong.

When asked about the power of their mentoring relationship, both Barabino and Banton state that there are clear benefits to same-gender and same-race mentoring, to shared cultural and professional experiences, to mutual interests and to a shared world-view. For example, Barabino herself is interested and involved in public policy as an engineer, so is more likely to be supportive of Banton's efforts in this arena. When Barabino accepted a position as Dean of Engineering that necessitated a move to another institution, there was no question in Banton's mind that she wouldn't move with her advisor/mentor. The Barabino–Banton mentoring relationship continues to flourish and serves as a model for effective mentoring and for understanding the multiple dimensions of mentoring associated with race and ethnicity, gender and organizational contexts.

When she received her PhD in chemical engineering in 1986 from Rice University after being the first African American male or female admitted to the doctoral program in chemical engineering, Dr. Barabino learned that she was only the fifth in the nation. This is notable given that Marron William Fort was the first African American to receive a PhD in any engineering discipline when he was awarded a PhD in chemical engineering from MIT in 1933. It wasn't until 1979 that an African American female, Jenny Patrick, received a PhD in chemical engineering from MIT and just prior to that time, another African American female, Lilia Abron received her PhD in chemical engineering from the University of Iowa in 1978. Early in her career, Dr. Barabino and Dr. Patrick were co-workers in a chemical company and later Dr. Barabino had occasions to interact professionally with Dr. Abron at conferences and other settings. When Dr. Barabino began her academic career as a tenure-track assistant professor of chemical engineering in 1989, she was thought to be the first and only at that time.

Whether by choice or not, the sheer scarcity of African American females in chemical engineering and in other engineering fields positioned Barabino as a role model and leader, in her case roles that were taken extremely seriously. Motivated by her own solo experience and desire to make a difference for others who were similarly situated, drawing on the legacy of African American women turning to sister networks for support (Green & King, 2001), and recognizing the need for interdisciplinary approaches joining the social sciences with engineering to address issues of under-representation and career advancement, Barabino reached out to her colleague, Leggon, for the implementation of the Cross-Disciplinary Initiative for Minority Women Faculty (XD). Examining the socialization and career advancement of minority women in academic engineering through a research-driven professional development initiative, Barabino and Leggon found that mentors are necessary, but not sufficient for career advancement (Leggon & Barabino, 2015). In addition to mentors, there is a clear need for sponsors and champions with enough influence and contacts to advance the career of the protégé. Mentoring requires individualized approaches that accommodate changing needs over time and there is no one-size-fits-all approach. It is wise to have simultaneous or multiple mentors (Murphy & Kram, 2014) as well as sequential or serial mentors as no one person can mentor on all aspects of the protégé's personal and professional life and different mentors are needed at different career stages.

For Barabino, the XD reinforced her experiences in the academy to date and followed on career-long efforts to mentor members of under-represented groups in engineering. The lack of mentors and the acuteness of the gaps in meeting the needs of women of color in engineering became vividly clear for Barabino during her sabbatical at Georgia Tech in 2003. In response to daily lines outside her office door of African American and other women of color seeking guidance from one who shared their background, to increase her reach, Barabino established regular support group meetings. Over time, these meetings evolved and formed the basis of subsequent focus groups and individual interviews as part of a collaborative research project with psychologist Kareen Malone to examine the science identity formation for women of color (Malone & Barabino, 2009).

Conclusion

We ended by describing a very effective mentoring relationship for African American women in academic engineering that reinforces the notion that inclusive mentoring can be an effective strategy for developing women of color as engineers. Mentoring for career progression and leadership works best when using a holistic approach. This means moving beyond the myth of the individual heroic journey by attending to both the protégé's and mentor's personal and professional developmental needs. In addition, this holistic approach involves recognizing that the life experiences, individual characteristics, and social and structural influences impact Black women differently than their peers. Thus, multiple mentors playing different roles at different times to meet protégé needs is effective. However, it is best to have at least one mentor who shares many characteristics with the protégé and who can provide long-term support. Thus, it would make sense that diversity in the types of mentoring relationships that are available for African American women is critical to provide both career and psychosocial support for developing them for life and work within academic engineering. The unparalleled success achieved in the mentor–protégé relationship between Barabino and Banton provides an illustration of the benefits that are produced from effective mentorship, including same-gender and same-race mentoring. These benefits include access to opportunities, attention to personal and professional needs, shared lived experiences, goals and interests, and mutual respect. Barabino reached out to Banton as an undergraduate student and has become a lifelong advisor, mentor, and advocate. Barabino's understanding of engineering and career attainment in the field as a social process and of how culture is perpetuated along with her lived experiences as a Black woman solidly positioned her to provide the type of mentoring for Banton that allowed her to fully develop her talent and thrive. Banton's talent, along with her recognition of the type of mentor and mentorship needed to ensure her success, enabled her to propel from an undergraduate researcher to graduate studies in biomedical engineering and public policy. Both Banton and Barabino recognize that there are social-organizational factors beyond their relationship that determine career attainment and they are prepared to build upon their relationship to draw in others and push the confines of structures designed to limit their advancement. Together this example of effective mentoring serves as a model of how to navigate through unconscious bias, identity conflict, and presumed meritocracy toward a more inclusive organization that supports and values the contribution of their diverse members and leaders.

References

Berry, C. A., & Cox, M. F., & Main, J. B. (2014). Women of Color Engineering Faculty: An Examination of the Experiences and the Numbers. Paper presented at 2014 ASEE Annual Conference, Indianapolis, Indiana. Retrieved from https://peer.asee.org/23314.

Blake-Beard, S., Bayne, M. L., Crosby, F. J., & Muller, C. B. (2011). Matching by race and gender in mentoring relationships: Keeping our eyes on the prize. *Journal of Social Issues, 67*(3), 622–643.

Boyle, P., & Boice, B. (1998). Systematic mentoring for new faculty teachers and graduate teaching assistants. *Innovative Higher Education, 22*(3), 157–179.

Bozeman, B., & Feeney, M. K. (2007). Toward a useful theory of mentoring a conceptual analysis and critique. *Administration & Society, 39*(6), 719–739.

Capobianco, B. M., Diefes-Dux, H. A., Mena, I., & Weller, J. (2011). What is an engineer? Implications of elementary school student conceptions for engineering education. *Journal of Engineering Education, 100*(2), 304.

Carlone, H. B., & Johnson, A. (2007). Understanding the science experiences of successful women of color: Science identity as an analytic lens. *Journal of Research in Science Teaching, 44*(8), 1187–1218.

Castilla, E. J., & Benard, S. (2010). The paradox of meritocracy in organizations. *Administrative Science Quarterly, 55*(4), 543–676.

Cech, E. A., & Blair-Loy, M. (2010). Perceiving glass ceilings? Meritocratic versus structural explanations of gender inequality among women in science and technology. *Social Problems, 57*(3), 371–397.

Chesler, N. C., & Chesler, M. A. (2002). Gender-informed mentoring strategies for women engineering scholars: On establishing a caring community. *Journal of Engineering Education, 91*(1), 49–55.

Crenshaw, K. (1989). Demarginalizing the intersection of race and sex: A black feminist critique of antidiscrimination doctrine, feminist theory and antiracist politics. *University of Chicago Legal Forum, 140*, 139–167.

Dreher, G. F., & Ash, R. A. (1990). A comparative study of mentoring among men and women in managerial, professional, and technical positions. *Journal of Applied Psychology, 75*(5), 539–546.

Easterly, D. M., & Ricard, C. S. (2011). Conscious Efforts to End Unconscious Bias: Why Women Leave Academic Research. *Journal of Research Administration, 42*(1), 61–73.

Fox, M. F. (1991). Gender, environmental milieu, and productivity in science. In J. C. Ziuckerman, & J. Bruer (Eds.), *The Outer Circle: Women in the Scientific Community* (pp. 188–204). New York: W. W. Norton.

Fox, M. F. (2010). Women and men faculty in academic science and engineering: Social-organizational indicators and implications. *American Behavioral Scientist, 53*(7), 997–1012.

Fox, M. F., & Fonseca, C. (2006). Gender and mentoring of faculty in science and engineering: Individual and organisational factors. *International Journal of Learning and Change, 1*(4), 460–483.

Fox, M. F., & Mohapatra, S. (2007). Social-organizational characteristics of work and publication productivity among academic scientists in doctoral-granting departments. *The Journal of Higher Education, 78*(5), 542–571.

Gee, J. P. (2000). Identity as an analytic lens for research in education. *Review of Research in Education, 25*(1), 99–125.

Gibson, S. K. (2006). Mentoring of women faculty: The role of organizational politics and culture. *Innovative Higher Education, 31*(1), 63–79.

Ginder, S. A., & Kelly-Reid, J. E. (2013). *2012–2013 Integrated Post-Secondary Education Data System (IPEDS) Methodology Report*. National Center for Educational Evaluation and Regional Assistance, (NCES 2013–293). Washington, DC: US Department of Education.

Girves, J. E., Zepeda, Y., & Gwathmey, J. K. (2005). Mentoring in a post-affirmative action world. *Journal of Social Issues, 61*(3), 449–479.

Green, C. E., & King, V. G. (2001). Sisters mentoring sisters: Africentric leadership development for Black women in the academy. *Journal of Negro Education, 70*(3), 156–165.

Griffin, K. A., & Reddick, R. J. (2011). Surveillance and sacrifice gender differences in the mentoring patterns of Black professors at predominantly White research universities. *American Educational Research Journal, 48*(5), 1032–1057.

Harley, D. A. (2008). Maids of academe: African American women faculty at predominately white institutions. *Journal of African American Studies, 12*(1), 19–36.

Henderson, T. L., Hunter, A. G., & Hildreth, G. J. (2010). Outsiders within the academy: Strategies for resistance and mentoring African American women. *Michigan Family Review, 14*(1).

Higgins, M. C., & Kram, K. E. (2001). Reconceptualizing mentoring at work: A developmental network perspective. *Academy of Management Review, 26*(2), 264–288.

Jacoby-Senghor, D. S., Sinclair, S., & Shelton, J. N. (2016). A lesson in bias: The relationship between implicit racial bias and performance in pedagogical contexts. *Journal of Experimental Social Psychology, 63*, 50–55.

Johnson, A. C. (2007). Unintended consequences: How science professors discourage women of color. *Science Education, 91*(5), 805–821.

Karatas, F. O., Micklos, A., & Bodner, G. M. (2011). Sixth-grade students' views of the nature of engineering and images of engineers. *Journal of Science Education and Technology, 20*(2), 123–135.

Kram, K. E. (1985). *Mentoring at work: Developmental Relationships in Organizational Life.* Greenville, IL: Scott, Foresman & Co.

Leggon, C. B. (2010). Diversifying science and engineering faculties: Intersections of race, ethnicity, and gender. *American Behavioral Scientist, 53*(7), 1013–1028.

Leggon, C. B., & Barabino, G. A. (2015). Socializing African American female engineers into academic careers. In J. B. Slaughter, Y. Tao, and W. Pearson Jr. (Eds.), *Changing the Face of Engineering: The African American Experience* (pp. 241–255). Baltimore, MD: Johns Hopkins University Press.

Leslie, L. L., McClure, G. T., & Oaxaca, R. L. (1998). Women and minorities in science and engineering: A life sequence analysis. *Journal of Higher Education, 69*(3), 239–276.

Leslie, S., Cimpian, A., Meyer, M. & Freeland, E. (2015). Expectations of brilliance underlie gender distributions across academic disciplines. *Science, 347*(6219), 262–265.

Lord, S. M., Camacho, M. M., Layton, R. A., Long, R. A., Ohland, M. W., & Washburn, M. H. (2009). Who's persisting in engineering? A comparative analysis of female and male Asian, Black, Hispanic, Native American, and White students. *Journal of Women and Minorities in Science and Engineering, 15*(2), 167–190.

Malone, K. R., & Barabino, G. (2009). Narrations of race in STEM research settings: Identity formation and its discontents. *Science Education, 93*(3), 485–510.

Mondisa, J. (2014, June). *Mentoring Minorities: Examining Mentoring from a Race and Gender Lens.* Paper presented at 2014 ASEE Annual Conference, Indianapolis, Indiana. Retrieved from https://peer.asee.org/22832.

Mondisa, J. L. (2015). *Increasing Diversity in Higher Education by Examining African-American STEM Mentors' Mentoring Approaches.* Proceedings of 2015 International Conference on Interactive Collaborative Learning, 321–326.

Moody, J. (2004). *Faculty Diversity: Problems and Solutions.* New York: Routledge Falmer.

Mullings, L. (2005). Resistance and resilience: The sojourner syndrome and the social context of reproduction in Central Harlem. *Transforming Anthropology, 13*(2), 79–91.

Murphy, W., & Kram, K. E. (2014). *Strategic relationships at work: Creating your circle of mentors, sponsors, and peers for success in business and life.* New York: McGraw Hill Professional.

National Science Foundation. (2010). National Center for Science and Engineering Statistics, Scientists and Engineers Statistical Data System (SESTAT), 2010. Retrieved from www.nsf.gov/statistics/sestat/.

Ohland, M. W., Brawner, C. E., Camacho, M. M., Layton, R. A., Long, R. A., Lord, S. M., & Washburn, M. H. (2011). Race, gender, and measures of success in engineering education. *Journal of Engineering Education, 100*(2), 225.

Ong, M., Wright, C., Espinosa, L., & Orfield, G. (2011). Inside the double bind: A synthesis of empirical research on undergraduate and graduate women of color in science, technology, engineering, and mathematics. *Harvard Educational Review, 81*(2), 172–209.

Ragins, B. R., & Cotton, J. L. (1999). Mentor functions and outcomes: A comparison of men and women in formal and informal mentoring relationships. *Journal of Applied Psychology, 84*(4), 529.

Scandura, T. A. (1992). Mentorship and career mobility: An empirical investigation. *Journal of Organizational Behavior, 13*(2), 169–174.

Seron, C., Silbey, S. S., Cech, E., & Rubineau, B. (2015). Persistence is cultural: Professional socialization and the reproduction of sex segregation. *Work and Occupations, 43*(2), 178–214.

Summers, M. F., & Hrabowski III, F. A. (2006). Preparing minority scientists and engineers. *Science, 311*(5769), 1870–1871.

Syed, M., Azmitia, M., & Cooper, C. R. (2011). Identity and academic success among underrepresented ethnic minorities: An interdisciplinary review and integration. *Journal of Social Issues, 67*(3), 442–468.

Tate, E. D., & Linn, M. C. (2005). How does identity shape the experiences of women of color engineering students? *Journal of Science Education and Technology, 14*(5–6), 483–493.

Thomas, D. A. (2001). The truth about mentoring minorities: Race matters. *Harvard Business Review, 79*(4), 98–107.

Tillman, L. C. (2001). Mentoring African American faculty in predominantly White institutions. *Research in Higher Education, 42*(3), 295–325.

Turner, C. S. V. (2002). Women of color in academe: Living with multiple marginality. *Journal of Higher Education, 73*(1), 74–93.

Wanburg, C. R., Welsh, E. T., & Hezlett, S. (2003). Mentoring research: A review and dynamic process model. In G. R. Ferris (Ed.), *Research in Personnel and Human Resource Management*, Vol. 22 (pp. 39–124). Oxford: Emerald Group Publishing.

PART II

Creating Change for Processes

5

THE EMERGING POWER OF PEER MENTORING WITHIN ACADEMIC MEDICINE

Audrey J. Murrell and Jeannette E. South-Paul

In the address at the 126th annual meeting of the AAMC (Association of American Medical Colleges), Board Chair Peter L. Slavin, MD, and AAMC President and CEO Darrell G. Kirch, MD, told the leaders of the nation's medical schools and teaching hospitals that:

> crossing the inequality chasm is imperative if America is to achieve better health for all. Equity has too often been overlooked or politicized, instead of being treated as a defining test of whether we're meeting our responsibility to deliver quality care to everyone who needs it. The simple truth is that we cannot achieve quality without addressing inequality.[...] Targeting inequality actually raises the quality of care for everyone.
>
> (AAMC, 2015)

These comments are in the backdrop of recent reports finding that while almost half of all students who graduate from US and Canadian medical schools are women, few women are advancing into leadership roles such as full professors, department chairs, deans, and presidents (Valentine, Grewal, Candy, Moseley, Shih, Stevenson, & Pizzo, 2014). In addition, few minority medical students report interest in pursuing careers within the academic medicine profession (Sanchez, Peters, Lee-Rey, Strelnick, Garrison, Zhang, Spencer, Ortega, Yehia, Berlin, & Castillo-Page, 2013).

Challenges Facing Academic Medicine

Many scholars note that the future of academic medicine is at risk because of its failure to attract and retain diverse women and people of color into the profession (Borges, Navarro, Grover, & Hoban, 2010; MacPhee, Chang, Lee, & Spiri, 2013; Strong & Cornelius, 2012). Evidence to support this perspective is provided by high rates of dissatisfaction, burn-out and aging faculty exacerbated by higher intent to leave and higher dissatisfaction among women and minority faculty members (Pololi, Krupat, Civian, Ash, & Brennan, 2012). These conditions are correlated with factors such as heavy workloads, lack of opportunities for professional advancement, low salary, work–life/work–family imbalance, lack of recognition, and overall discontent with leadership (Cropsey, Masho, Shiang, Sikka, Kornstein, & Hampton, 2008). The persistent domination of men at upper levels of leadership within academic medicine points to a critical pipeline problem that continues to inhibit diverse talent from getting into positions of influence or visibility within health care institutions (Valentine et al., 2014). The critical question that will be the central focus in this chapter is how emerging forms of mentoring, specifically peer mentoring, can be a tool for addressing negative trends within the academic medicine profession.

The lack of diversity within the pipeline and leadership ranks within academic medicine also negatively impacts the overall effectiveness of healthcare organizations. Faculty and leaders within academic medicine not only provide clinical care but also help to shape the educational and training experience for the next generation of researchers, faculty, and healthcare professionals. Issues such as quality of patient care, reduced number of tenure-track faculty positions, and the ability to provide culturally competent care have been linked to the lack of diversity within academic medicine centers and healthcare organizations (Borges et al., 2010). In addition, the impact of faculty turnover has been shown to account for 5 percent of the annual budget for an academic health center (Schloss, Flanagan, & Culler, 2009), and costs for faculty replacement are significant.

Academic medicine as a profession and academic health centers as organizations are viewed as the nucleus of health care within the USA and globally. This suggests that solutions to the recruitment, retention, and advancement of diverse professionals within the healthcare industry are critical to identify, develop, and effectively implement. Whether in terms of recruitment of medical students into the pipeline for careers in academic medicine, the retention of new talent as clinicians and faculty researchers, or development of diverse leaders within healthcare organizations and academic health centers, formal and informal mentoring has been consistently identified as one effective solution (Kashiwagi, Varkey, & Cook, 2013; Straus, Johnson, Marquez, & Feldman, 2013; Sambunjak, Straus, & Marusic, 2006; Straus, Chatur, & Taylor, 2009; Tillman, Jang, Abedin, Richards, Spaeth-Rublee, & Pincus, 2013).

Mentoring in Academic Medicine

Informal mentoring relationships as well as formal mentoring programs have a rich history within academic medicine and are a frequent tool for recruitment, retention, and leadership development. Mentoring within medical and health-care professions has been shown to impact career choice, personal development, research productivity, and career advancement (Sambunjak et al., 2006; Straus et al., 2013; Pololi & Knight, 2005). There is little debate over the importance of mentoring programs within academic medicine; however, questions remain over the most effective aspects of program design, program delivery and evaluation metrics (Sambunjak et al., 2006; Straus, Straus, & Tzanetos, 2006). Most systematic reviews of existing literature find that mentoring produces faculty who are more productive, promoted more quickly, and are more likely to stay in their academic institutions than those who do not have access or choose not to participate in formal mentoring efforts (Sambunjak et al., 2006; Straus et al., 2013).

To date, a majority of formal programs within academic medicine tend to take the form of traditional one-to-one mentoring (Sambunjak, Straus, & Marusic, 2009). However, Pololi and Knight (2005) argue that the decline in the number and diversity of clinical and research faculty causes a significant reduction in the available pool of senior mentors that are needed using this traditional approach. Few junior faculty will have access to a senior mentor for one-to-one matching within a formal program and lack of willingness may further limit access to informal mentoring relationships. Diverse senior mentors are an extremely scarce resource and expectations for these individuals to be involved in multiple formal and informal mentoring relationships can produce an unfair burden or "mentoring tax" for these faculty members and clinicians (Blake-Beard, Murrell, & Thomas, 2007).

In addition to the lack of diverse senior mentors who are available and willing to be part of formal and/or informal mentoring relationships, Pololi and Knight (2005) argue that traditional one-to-one mentoring can produce a range of issues, including unequal power dynamics, diversity clashes, over-dependency, and "cloning" behavior rather than meaningful developmental relationships. These behaviors are similar to the ones identified within the typology of negative mentoring relationships outlined by Eby and her colleagues (Eby, Butts, Lockwood, & Simon, 2004). Factors such as exploitation, unconscious bias, or more overt forms of discrimination can contaminate hierarchical dyadic mentoring relationships. The failure of traditional mentoring dyads to move beyond the embedded hierarchical structure and relationships that are found in most academic medicine institutions needs to be addressed by employing different forms or approaches to traditional mentoring within these organizations. The exclusive reliance on hierarchical dyadic relationships may also perpetuate homogeneity and produce little change if mentors are allowed to select or are matched to mentees who are similar to themselves, which merely perpetuates "sameness" within academic medicine (DeCastro, Sambuco, Ubel, Stewart, & Jagsi, 2013).

Some research finds that facilitated peer-to-peer mentoring offers significant benefits to participants versus traditional hierarchical mentoring dyads (e.g., Bussey-Jones, Bernstein, Higgins, Malebrance, Paranjape, Genao, Lee, & Branch, 2006). In fact, peer mentoring was identified as the most valued experience by senior faculty members within a study of academic medical centers (Pololi & Knight, 2005). Peer mentoring has been used within academic medicine and as some argue can lead to valuable personal feedback, long-lasting friendships, and feelings of support that can fill some of the gap left by a lack of access to senior mentors (Bussy-Jones et al., 2006). These findings suggest that paying attention to the impact of peers is an important area for innovation, especially for developing diverse leaders within the pipeline of academic medicine. While mentoring in general has received attention within academic medicine, a closer examination of the potential impact of peer mentoring on the development of diverse leaders within academic medicine warrants further exploration.

Peer Mentoring

Recent mentoring work has expanded the types of relationships beyond the traditional senior–junior mentoring to include a peer mentoring (Kram & Isabella, 1985; McManus & Russell, 2007), virtual mentoring (Ensher, Heun, & Blanchard, 2003), group mentoring (Friedman, 1996; Friedman, Kane, & Cornfield, 1998), and reverse mentoring (Murphy, 2012). Some argue that given the changing nature of organizations in terms of being more networked and flat, peer or lateral mentoring is more readily available within the environment and provides critical career and social support (Eby, 1997; Ensher, Thomas, & Murphy, 2001; Higgins & Kram, 2001; Higgins & Thomas, 2001). Peer mentoring relationships provide both important job-related and technical knowledge (Eby, 1997), and have been shown to be a valuable resource for knowledge transfer and learning (Bryant & Terborg, 2008; Young & Perrewe, 2000, 2004). Thus, peer mentoring can be a powerful conduit for the transfer of tacit knowledge into explicit knowledge (Nonaka, 1994) given that much of the knowledge shared between peers is learned from personal experience and thus not typically part of the formal knowledge management processes within the organization (Swap, Leonard, Shields, & Abrams, 2001). In fact, some argue that peers can actually compensate for an absence of traditional mentors because peer mentoring is less dependent on status, power, and access to organizational resources (Ensher et al., 2001).

Clearly there is an important contribution to be made by examining peer mentoring as a source of support and also a tool for advancing research development within academic medicine. First, it responds to a number of scholars who call for greater attention to the diverse types of mentoring and their impact on key career and organizational outcomes (Murrell, Crosby, & Ely, 1999; Noe, Greenberger, & Wang, 2002; Wanberg, Welsh, & Hezlett, 2003). Second, it draws attention to the importance of reciprocity as a defining feature of peer mentoring that distinguishes it from traditional hierarchical types of mentoring (McManus & Russell, 2007). Third, peer or lateral mentoring relationships could meet the needs of the millennial and later generations for whom structure, position, and hierarchy are not strongly emphasized (Bussey-Jones et al., 2006). Fourth, studying peer mentoring can leverage different methodologies such as social network analysis as a tool to assess and evaluate dynamic mentoring networks within academic medicine instead of an exclusive focus on traditional survey or interview approaches. This would move research and practice within academic medicine from the individual unit of analysis to the relationship unit of analysis. Using reciprocal relationships as well as multiple ties is also consistent with scholars who argue that mentoring relationships should be defined and studied as complex relationships that involve mutuality, multiple functions, as well as relationship networks or constellations (see Baugh & Scandura, 1999, or Higgins & Kram, 2001). Thus, we explore three different types of relational ties among peers and outline the implications for future directions in research and practice for academic medicine.

Kram and Isabella (1985) provided an early examination into different types of peer relationships as one vehicle for effective mentoring. They argued that peer relationships can serve the same functions as traditional senior–junior mentoring relationships, yet can be more readily available to individuals because of both sheer numbers and overall accessibility. In addition, Kram and Isabella (1985) suggest that peer relationships may achieve a greater degree of communication, support, and collaboration than traditional mentoring relationships. They examined peers across a variety of career stages and conducted in-depth interviews of a "focal person" along with significant others who were identified during the interviews. Their results supported the notion that peer mentoring provides much of the same range of career and psychosocial support functions as traditional one-to-one mentoring relationships. Peer relationships were shown to provide information sharing, career advice, exposure, coaching, and sponsorship as well as emotional support, feedback, and friendship.

Interestingly, Kram and Isabella (1985) identify a number of peer relationships that help to capture the range of mentoring functions provided during peer exchanges that are relevant for academic medicine. *Information peers* focus on the exchange of information or knowledge about work and the organization. These types of peer relationships involve very little personal exchange and may have moderate to infrequent amounts of contact between individuals. Kram and Isabella argue that individuals can maintain a large number of these types of relationships, which appear to be important for socialization, knowledge development, and information sharing. In contrast, *special peers* involve strong interpersonal ties along with a sense of bonding between individuals. Unlike information peers, special peers are involved in more self-disclosure, intimacy, and emotional connection. Thus, as Kram and Isabella argue, there may be fewer special peers at work compared to information peers. Lastly, they identify *collegial peers* that involve both moderate amounts of self-disclosure and information sharing. While not to the extent of special peers, the personal exchange among collegial peers allows for the development of trust and opportunity for honest feedback. Their results find that collegial peers tend to be people with whom a person has worked, shared information, and formed some type of identification through the relationship as both knowledge and personal information were being shared. The findings from the interviews conducted by Kram and Isabella (1985) also showed that during early career stages, collegial peers helped individuals define themselves in terms of professional role and job performance.

Since this early descriptive and conceptual work, a focus on peer mentoring or what has been labeled "lateral mentoring" has received only modest attention (Eby, 1997; McDougall & Beattie, 1997; McManus & Russell, 2007). Thus, peer mentoring relationships have been an important but somewhat overlooked source of both career and psychosocial support until fairly recently (see Murphy & Kram, 2014). However, the conceptual argument provided by Kram and Isabella (1985) is compelling. Peer mentors can provide the same core functions (career and psychosocial) that have been identified in previous mentoring research (Kram, 1985). A good deal of work has been devoted to the measurement and validation of these two categories of mentoring functions (Chao, 1998; Ragins & Cotton, 1999; Scandura, 1992), as well as understanding the outcomes associated with career versus psychosocial functions of mentoring (for reviews, see Noe et al., 2002; and Wanberg et al., 2003; and for a review and meta-analysis, see Allen, Eby, Poteet, Lentz, & Lima, 2004). Thus, peer relationships may be an untapped source of both career and psychosocial functions of mentoring involving individuals who may differ in position or function within the organization, but are similar or equivalent within the organizational hierarchy (Pullins & Fine, 2002).

Individuals may have a number or a network of peers as well as other types of mentoring relationships throughout their professional lives. However, McManus and Russell (2007) draw a clear distinction between the benefits of traditional mentoring versus peer mentoring, the latter involving some degree of mutuality or reciprocity. While traditional mentoring relationships are frequently conceptualized and measured as unidirectional (typically from the perspective of the mentee), peer mentorships are described as uniquely multidirectional (McDougall & Beattie, 1997), or reciprocal (McManus & Russell, 2007). In fact, McManus and Russell go as far as to predict that mutuality will be more commonly found in peer compared to traditional one-to-one mentoring relationships.

While this notion of reciprocity has been noted as important for effective mentoring relationships in general (Young & Perrewe, 2000, 2004), we agree that reciprocity defined in a manner similar to McManus and Russell (2007) that includes reciprocity is essential in the case of peer mentoring. While Ensher et al., (2001) argue that what may be important is what is being reciprocated rather than the presence or absence of reciprocity in direct comparisons of traditional versus peer mentoring, the three distinct types of peer mentoring (information, collegial, and special peers) identified by Kram and Isabella (1985) and later by McDougall and Beattie (1997) have, embedded within their definitions, the notion of reciprocity among peers engaged in these lateral mentoring relationships.

Assuming reciprocity among peers means that within the study and application of peer mentoring to professions such as academic medicine, one must acknowledge the importance of relational or social ties between peers that are acknowledged by both parties. This acknowledgment provides evidence of some degree of social exchange (Gouldner, 1960) or social influence (Meyer, 1994). For example, utilizing social network analysis could provide a valuable tool for identifying peer relationships that are reciprocal in nature, thus distinguishing them from relationships that are distant, one-sided, and non-reciprocal. While the strength of these peer mentoring relationships may vary across time and among different individuals, the presence of a reciprocal social tie could be a key indicator of effective peer mentoring as well as social influence. Assumptions of reciprocity have not been the case for traditional dyadic mentoring. The focus on reciprocity and social exchange that may distinguish peer from traditional mentoring relationships also points to the potential benefit that peers can serve. Peers may also influence the behavior of others in ways that can support individuals' personal and professional development.

Peers as a Source of Social Influence

Looking at peers from a relational view can provide a unique perspective that regards these relationships as not simply a resource for support or information but also has an impact on shaping attitudes and behaviors. The idea that peer mentors can act as agents of social influence is supported by several well-known theoretical perspectives that include social learning theory (Bandura, 1986), social information processing theory (Salancik & Pfeffer, 1978), and social comparison theory (Festinger, 1954).

Bandura's (1986) social learning theory emphasizes the importance of observing and modeling the behaviors, attitudes, and emotional reactions of others in learning and personal development. For instance, a study by Bommer, Miles, and Grover (2003) showed that employees' performance of organizational citizenship behaviors was related to the frequency and consistency of organizational citizenship behavior performance by other peer employees in their workgroup. Ibarra (1999) demonstrated that investment bank and management consulting firm employees who made the transition from entry-level to management positions observed and interacted with peer employees whom they admired in order to learn what behaviors, attitudes, and perceptions helped the admired employees to be successful. These studies show that social learning can influence the behavior, attitudes, and perceptions of peers who share relational ties. Thus, we would expect that peer relationships, particularly those characterized by strong ties and some level of reciprocity, to involve social learning about issues concerning the organization and its values and culture. Seeing peer relationships as a valuable source of knowledge and learning challenges traditional one-to-one approaches within academic medicine that often assume the only meaningful learning comes from more senior experts within the organization. For example, Files and her colleagues conducted a pilot program for the advancement of women in academic medicine and found that peer mentoring facilitated academic productivity, promotion in academic rank, and enthusiasm for the profession as critical outcomes (Files, Blair, Mayer, & Ko, 2008).

Social information processing also plays a key role in shaping perceptions, attitudes, and behaviors in organizations. The core argument of social information processing theory is that because organizations are complex and ambiguous environments, perceptions are influenced by the social context in which they are formed. This belief is especially relevant for academic medicine where the types of knowledge that are needed are complex, dynamic, and contextual in nature (Jarvis-Selinger, Pratt & Regehr, 2012; MacPhee et al., 2013). This type of influence may occur as a result of direct statements from peers or through intentional or unintentional behavioral cues (Salancik & Pfeffer, 1978). According to this theory, social information affects how individuals: (1) learn to react to social cues; (2) form perceptions by focusing attention on some aspects of the work environment but away from others; (3) construct their interpretations of organizational events; and (4) understand the requirements of their jobs. This understanding is most clearly illustrated in the preceptor model that is currently used within training programs for medical and healthcare professionals (Sachdeva, 1996).

Earlier, Coleman, Katz, and Menzel (1966) found that doctors' decisions to prescribe a new drug were similar to the decisions of professional associates with whom they had talked about the drug. Mark and her colleagues reviewed several innovative mentoring programs that each showed evidence of peer influence on recruitment, retention, and development for female junior faculty within academic medicine (Mark, Link, Morahan, Pololi, Reznik, & Tropez-Sims, 2001). Other studies have shown that employees' attitudes toward new technology were similar to the attitudes of individuals with whom they communicate frequently (Burkhardt, 1994). Meyer (1994) found that employees had similar perceptions of organizational coordination to employees with whom they communicated frequently. Finally, Dabos and Rousseau (2004) showed that faculty members' beliefs regarding promises made to them by their university were similar to the beliefs of individuals with whom they maintained direct peer relationships. Overall, this research supports the idea that social information processing results in social similarity among individuals' attitudes, perceptions, and behaviors. Therefore, utilizing peer mentoring within academic medicine should enhance necessary skills such as critical thinking, ethical decision-making, and effective problem-solving (Jarvis-Selinger et al., 2012).

We argue that social information processing will occur through peer mentoring relationships because peers share information and knowledge related to the completion of their work through such ties (Ibarra & Andrews, 1993). For example, peer advice networks are characterized by cognitive trust or the belief that another has the ability and competence to provide help (McAllister, 1995). Therefore, asking a peer for advice and looking to them as an example of excellent performance are both an indication of respect for the opinion of that individual and an expectation that help from that individual is available and useful (Hansen, 1999). These expectations suggest that peer mentoring, through the exchange of information can help individuals understand and interpret the complexity of the profession and their specific organization. The practice of sharing information highlights an important process that may explain how peer mentoring relationships can serve as a mechanism for social influence that is relevant for enhancing diversity within academic medicine.

Social influence among peers can occur when individuals draw comparisons between themselves and other individuals in order to better understand ambiguous situations (Sparrowe, Liden, Wayne, & Kraimer, 2001). Social comparison theory (Festinger, 1954) suggests that: (1) individuals learn about themselves through comparison with others; (2) individuals who have similar demographic characteristics are often chosen for comparison; and (3) social comparisons will have strong effects when objective nonsocial comparisons are unavailable and when others' evaluations are important to the individual. These tendencies are clearly relevant to the notion of lateral mentoring that has already been shown to help with early socialization, learning, moral support, and the need to have safe conversations about the complex dynamics that impact their careers (DeCastro et al., 2013).

Social comparison is prevalent in organizations because, in many cases, evaluations regarding individual job performance within the organization are subjective. Social comparison can result in similar perceptions between individuals when one identifies with his or her peers. However, such social comparison may also lead to negative identity when there are status differences as is the case for traditional one-to-one mentoring, particularly when power and aspects of diversity intersect (Ragins, 1997). In these cases, identity discordance or conflict can provide negative signals that the individual does not fit within the organization or the profession. Social comparison processes could be one explanation for research showing a relationship between lack of diversity and disinterest in academic medicine among medical students (Sanchez et al., 2013). However, when peers provide feedback on another's performance, this input can seem less threatening and serve as signal to the individual regarding how she or he should interpret the other more formal evaluations within both academic health professions and healthcare organizations (DeCastro et al., 2013).

Thus, peer relationships are often used for social comparison because they develop between individuals with similar attributes or aspirations (Marsden, 1988; Gibson, 2003, 2004). For instance, Wheeler and Miyake (1992) showed that social comparison was most frequent among close friends, followed by peers with whom individuals were somewhat close, and least likely among individuals who were not friends. Peer relationships defined by friendship ties involve expressions of personal affect, social support, and a sense of identity and personal belongingness (Coleman, 1988, 1990). Individuals depend on peers for counseling and companionship, especially for sensitive issues (Sias & Cahill, 1998). For example, Morrison (2002) found that peer network size was positively related to organizational commitment, while advice network size was not. Krackhardt and Stern (1988) demonstrated that individuals were more likely to share resources with peers from other departments than with non-peers during a simulated organizational crisis. Finally, individuals tend to make career decisions that are similar to those of their peers (Kilduff, 1990). This tendency to engage in social comparisons has led some to structure peer mentoring groups as a tool for facilitating collaboration among junior faculty as providing peer support which is found to be critical during early career stages (Bussey-Jones et al., 2006).

Overall, these theoretical perspectives (social learning, social information processing, and social comparison theories) provide the basis for our argument that peer relationships serve as an important source of social influence. Prior evidence suggests that individuals make social comparisons with their peers, identify with individuals they consider models or exemplars of what they would like to become themselves, and exchange knowledge and information with peers they see as knowledgeable (Zagenczyk, Gibney, Murrell, & Boss, 2008). Individuals are therefore likely to compare their professional and job-related perceptions to those with whom they have advice, peer and/or friendship ties, particularly when these relationships are strong (versus weak), and reciprocal (versus unidirectional) in nature (Ostroff & Kozlowski, 1992). Given that access to diverse peers may be much more readily available within healthcare organizations, opportunities for peer support, feedback, and knowledge transformation among diverse individuals maybe greater than for traditional hierarchical mentoring alone (Varkey, Jatoi, Williams, Mayer, Ko, Files, Blair, & Hayes, 2012).

Future Directions within Academic Medicine

The need to examine different types of mentoring relationships is an emerging topic for research and practice within academic medicine. We argue that the categories of peer relationships identified in the original research by Kram and Isabella (1985) actually represent a continuum of relational ties among peers that provide a range of diverse mentoring functions. For example, information peers help the individual learn the ropes by helping to provide information on how to get the job done or other key work-related knowledge. These peer mentoring relationships support the exchange of information about work and can be a valuable source of knowledge that benefits career outcomes such as research productivity and professional expertise. Special peers appear to focus more on emotional support or provide psychosocial functions of mentoring than information peers. These special peers help the individual to understand expectations because they provide social support and can be critical for outcomes such as retention, satisfaction, and overall level of engagement. Collegial peers are unique because they are characterized by both strong personal exchange and knowledge sharing. These peer mentors can help individuals develop a sense of competence within the workplace and often are a source of identification, role definition, and clarity. This variety of what is provided by different types of peers suggests that a diverse network of peer mentoring relationships is not only important for an individual's personal and professional development, but can also help to address the critical need for more effective recruitment, retention, and advancement of diversity within academic medicine.

We argue that peer mentors are sources of social influence who shape individuals' experiences and perceptions of the organization and the profession. The information, knowledge, and opinions shared through peers, coupled with the self-disclosure and affect associated with strong and reciprocal ties, are an important combination available within this type of mentoring. Clearly, the exchange of knowledge and information together with self-disclosure and emotional support provides a unique impact that peer mentoring relationships may have, which may not always be provided by traditional hierarchical mentoring. It may also be the case that knowledge exchange, social support, and identification are critical features that can be provided through formal peer mentoring relationships provided by the organization through a well-designed portfolio of mentoring programs (Murrell, Forte-Trammel, & Bing, 2008). This information is consistent with other research on peer mentoring relationships (Eby, 1997) as well as work on similarity in pro-social organizational behavior among peers (Bommer et al., 2003) and knowledge sharing among peer group members (Liang, Moreland, & Argote, 1995).

Interestingly, McDougall and Beattie offer a category of peer mentoring they label as a "holistic peer mentor" (1997: 430), that involves high levels of both work and personal aspects of learning. These holistic peers have complementary knowledge, skills, and ability, yet also share core values as each is able to address the other's unique developmental needs. There is a significant focus on the exchange and co-creation of knowledge among this type of peer relationship. While Kram (1985) focuses on notions of empathy within peer relationships,

McDougall and Beattie (1997) add a focus on collaborative knowledge sharing (Hansen, 1999). Perhaps the notion of a holistic peer mentor reflects some combination of all three types of peer mentoring relationships previously identified in Kram's work. Thus, holistic peers are characterized by the exchange of emotional support (collegial peers), professional identification (special peers), together with the reciprocal exchange of knowledge and advice (information peers). Although not explicitly labeled within their work, research on junior faculty doing sponsored medical research suggests that numerous roles were available either in peer mentoring relationships or throughout diverse peer mentoring networks (DeCastro et al., 2013).

This research indicates that strong and reciprocal ties within peer relationships are critical dimensions that provide a source of social support, knowledge exchange, and social influence. Past mentoring research within academic medicine has mainly considered the effects of single and unidirectional relationships, but has not considered the importance of reciprocity and multiplicity in peer relationships. While a great deal of empirical research has examined the nature of traditional senior-to-junior mentoring relationships, we suggest that understanding the power of strong, reciprocal, and multiple peer relationships is a critical step toward advancing our understand of mentoring within academic medicine. Given the changing nature of organizations (Arthur & Rousseau, 1996), the role of peer mentors within one's development network is critical, especially for diverse segments of employees (Murrell, Blake-Beard, Porter, & Perkins-Williamson, 2008).

The inclusion of social influence as a factor within peer mentoring relationships is also valuable for future research and practice. Prior social influence research reveals that one's social ties are related to perceptions of and attitudes toward the profession or organization (Granovetter, 1973), including perceptions of organizational justice (Umphress, Labianca, Brass, Kass, & Scholten, 2003); attitudes toward technology (Burkhardt, 1994); decisions regarding job interviews (Kilduff, 1990); social identity among under-represented groups (Mehra, Kilduff, & Brass, 1998); and beliefs about organizational coordination (Meyer, 1994). However, prior research had not explored the possibility that perceptions of support are also subject to social influence through peers. This connection is critical as academic medicine attempts to address the declining interests by women and people of color in careers within the profession. Given the minimal growth in diversity within the health professions during the past decade, changing negative perceptions, removing barriers, and providing ongoing support are critical endeavors if we want to reverse this negative trend (Sanchez et al., 2013). Perhaps peer relationships can be a valuable tool for social influence and change.

One area for additional focus in future work is in the measurement of effective mentoring relationships. Berk and his colleagues argue that there has been a lack of clarity about the measurement of critical characteristics and outcomes of mentoring relationships (Berk, Berg, Mortimer, Walton-Moss, & Yeo, 2005). Research and practice lack acceptable and rigorous tools for measuring the complexity of mentoring relationships, which they argue has led to a superficial examination of mentoring. Moving beyond traditional definitions of one-to-one hierarchical mentoring to newer mentoring models complicates the issue. Measuring peer mentoring as a diverse array of reciprocal relationships outlines the usefulness of a social networks methodology as valuable tool for assessing effectiveness and outcomes (Marsden, 1990; Marsden & Campbell, 1984). Defining peer mentoring as a social network allows researchers to answer a number of questions about these relationships, such as: what outcomes are associated with having diverse types of peers?; what characteristics or attributes are related to peers as a source of social influence?; how do social influence processes shape outcomes among diverse peers?; how many peers and of what types should individuals have based on career stage?; and, how are different types of peer relationships influential with respect to specific work outcomes? These are all exciting questions that should generate interest for future research within the area of peer mentoring relationships using social network analysis.

Conclusion

This chapter began with the limitations of traditional hierarchical mentoring relationships and the need to support diversity and diverse leadership development within academic medicine. Within traditional research on mentoring, peers are categorized as part of the broad array of developmental assistance that includes career support, psychosocial support, and role modeling functions. Higgins and Kram (2001) argue that a social network approach is needed to advance our understanding of how these various types of developmental relationships can impact an individual's career as well as organizational outcomes. We agree with Higgins and Kram's (2001) assertion that one's developmental relationships are a subset of an entire social network that is important to career development as well as to work-related outcomes. This perspective also connects the ideas of mentoring to social influence processes that are known to occur across one's social network. Some social networks research examining social influence indicates that individuals who maintain peer relationships with one another are more likely to have similar perceptions and attitudes than employees who do not maintain these relationships (e.g., Umphress et al., 2003; Dabos & Rousseau, 2004). This relational perspective leads to several important questions outlined in this chapter that should help shape meaningful future research on and practice of mentoring within academic medicine.

National trends show that under-represented minorities and non-traditional faculty are less likely to be represented within the basic sciences or be nurtured in those academic disciplines with traditions highly organized around hierarchical mentoring and apprenticeship programs. Indeed, under-represented minorities are less likely to be represented among medical school faculty, and if they are there, are more likely to be in the clinical disciplines. Clinical faculty are less likely to experience formal faculty development and are more at risk of leaving academia mid-career than non-clinical colleagues—likely because they are more comfortable in the clinical setting than in the classroom or the lab and perceive more immediate rewards in daily patient care rather than in the assorted responsibilities of being a faculty member (Cropsey et al., 2008).

Medical educators have adapted and transformed school curricula over time in order to keep pace with changes in science as well as to meet the needs of an increasingly diverse patient population. More scientific disciplines and fewer social science and public health disciplines have been added to the curricula providing a clear message regarding what is valued in medical academia. Furthermore, most mentoring efforts have retained a traditional focus on one-to-one hierarchical relationships with status, power, and demographic differences seen as the necessary price to pay for developmental relationships. We have argued in this chapter that change within the profession requires change in our perspective and approaches to mentoring. Unlocking the power of diverse peer mentoring relationships offers a great deal of promise for helping change the composition of academic medicine and reversing current negative trends.

There is general consensus that lasting improvements in the health of a population requires an increase in the diversity of individuals within academic, research, and clinical activities. This issue is not merely one of diversity within the profession but is linked to overall quality of health care as part of the national and global public healthcare agenda. While organizations like the Association of American Medical Colleges (AAMC) have articulated a commitment to the development of minority faculty for more than two decades, more needs to be done. We see great potential for peer mentoring as a source of knowledge sharing, career advice, and social support within academic medicine.

References

AAMC (2015, November 8). AAMC Chair and President Call on the Nation's Medical Schools and Teaching Hospitals to Address Health Care Inequalities. Association of American Medical Colleges. Retrieved from www.aamc.org/newsroom/news releases/448308/11082015.html

Allen, T. D., Eby, L. T., Poteet, M. L., Lentz, E., & Lima, L. (2004). Career benefits associated with mentoring for protégé: A meta-analysis. *Journal of Applied Psychology*, *89*, 127–136.

Arthur, M. B., & Rousseau, D. M. (1996). Introduction: The boundaryless career as a new employment principle. In M. B. Arthur, & D. M. Rousseau (Eds.), *The boundaryless career: A new employment principle for a new organizational era* (pp. 3–20). New York: Oxford University Press.

Bandura, A. (1986). *Social foundations of thought and action*. Englewood Cliffs, NJ: Prentice Hall.

Baugh, S. G., & Scandura, T. A. (1999). The effect of multiple mentors on protégé attitudes toward the work setting. *Journal of Social Behavior and Personality*, *14*, 503–521.

Berk, R. A., Berg, J., Mortimer, R., Walton-Moss, B., & Yeo, T. P. (2005). Measuring the effectiveness of faculty mentoring relationships. *Academic Medicine*, *80*(1), 66–70.

Blake-Beard, S. D., Murrell, A. J., & Thomas, D. A. (2007). Unfinished business: The impact of race on understanding mentoring relationships. In B. R. Ragins, and K. E. Kram (Eds.), *The handbook on mentoring at work: Theory, research, and practice*. Thousand Oaks, CA: Sage Publications.

Bommer, W. H., Miles, E. W., & Grover, S. L. (2003). Does one good turn deserve another? Coworker influences on employee citizenship. *Journal of Organizational Behavior*, *24*, 181–196.

Borges, N. J., Navarro, A. M., Grover, A., & Hoban, J. D. (2010). How, when and why do physicians choose careers in academic medicine? A literature review. *Academic Medicine*, *85*(4), 680–686.

Bryant, S. E., & Terborg, J. R. (2008). Impact of peer mentor training on creating and sharing organizational knowledge. *Journal of Managerial Issues*, *20*(1), 11–29.

Burkhardt, M. E. (1994). Social interaction effects following a technological change: A longitudinal investigation. *Academy of Management Journal*, *37*, 869–898.

Bussey-Jones, J., Bernstein, L., Higgins, S., Malebrance, D., Paranjape, A., Genao, I., Lee, B., & Branch, W. (2006). Repaving the road to academic success: The IMeRGE approach to peer mentoring. *Academic Medicine*, *81*(7), 674–679.

Chao, G. T. (1998). Invited reaction: Challenging research in mentoring. *Human Resource Development Quarterly*, *9*, 333–338.

Coleman, J. S. (1988). Social capital in the creation of human capital. *American Journal of Sociology*, *94*, 95–120.

Coleman, J. S. (1990). *Foundations of Social Theory*. Cambridge, MA: Harvard University Press.

Coleman, J. S., Katz, E., & Menzel, H. (1966). *Medical innovation: A diffusion study*. New York: Bobbs-Merrill.

Cropsey, K. L., Masho, S. W., Shiang, R., Sikka, V., Kornstein, S. G., & Hampton, C. L. (2008). The committee on the status of women and minorities. Why do faculty leave? Reasons for attribution of women and minority faculty from a medical school: Four-year results. *Journal of Women's Health*, *17*, 1111–1118.

Dabos, G. E., & Rousseau, D. M. (2004). Social interaction patterns shaping employee psychological contracts. *Academy of Management Best Papers Proceedings*, OB, N1–N6.

DeCastro, R., Sambuco, D., Ubel, P. A., Stewart, A., & Jagsi, R. (2013). Mentor networks in academic medicine: Moving beyond a dyadic conception of mentoring for junior faculty researchers. *Academic Medicine*, *88*(4), 488–496.

Eby, L. T. (1997). Alternate forms of mentoring in changing organizational environments: A conceptual extension of the mentoring literature. *Journal of Applied Psychology*, *75*, 539–546.

Eby, L. T., Butts, M., Lockwood, A., & Simon, S. A. (2004). Proteges' negative mentoring experiences: Construct development and nomological validation. *Personnel Psychology*, *57*, 411–447.

Ensher, E. A., Heun, C., & Blanchard, A. (2003). Online mentoring and computer-mediated communication: New directions in research. *Journal of Vocational Behavior*, *63*, 264–288.

Ensher, E. A., Thomas, C., & Murphy, S. E. (2001). Comparison of traditional, step-ahead, and peer mentoring on protégés support, satisfaction and perceptions of career success: A social exchange perspective. *Journal of Business & Psychology, 15,* 419–438.

Festinger, L. (1954). A theory of social comparison processes. *Human Relations, 7,* 117–140.

Files, J. A., Blair, J. E., Mayer, A. P., & Ko, M. G. (2008). Facilitated peer mentorship: A pilot program for academic advancement of female medical faculty. *Journal of Women's Health, 17,* 1009–1015.

Friedman, R. (1996). Defining the scope and logic of minority and female network groups: Does separation enhance integration? In G. Ferris (Ed.), *Research in personnel and human resource management* (pp. 307–349). Greenwich, CT: JAI Press.

Friedman, R., Kane, M., & Cornfield, D. B. (1998). Social support and career optimism: Examining the effectiveness of network groups among Black managers. *Human Relations, 51*(9), 1155–1177.

Gibson, D. E. (2003). Developing the professional self-concept: Role model construals in early, middle, and late career stages. *Organization Science, 14,* 591–610.

Gibson, D. E. (2004). Role models in career development: New directions for theory and research. *Journal of Vocational Behavior, 65,* 134–156.

Gouldner, A. W. (1960). The norm of reciprocity: A preliminary statement. *American Sociological Review, 25,* 161–178.

Granovetter, M. (1973). The strength of weak ties. *American Journal of Sociology, 78,* 1360–1380.

Hansen, M. T. (1999). The search-transfer problem: The role of weak ties in sharing knowledge across organization subunits. *Administrative Science Quarterly, 44,* 82–111.

Higgins, M. C., & Kram, K. E. (2001). Reconceptualizing mentoring at work: A developmental network perspective. *Academy of Management Review, 26*(2), 264–288.

Higgins, M. C. & Thomas, D. A. (2001). Constellations and careers: Toward understanding the effects of multiple developmental relationships. *Journal of Organizational Behavior, 22,* 223–247.

Ibarra, H. (1999). Provisional selves: Experimenting with image and identity in professional adaptation. *Administrative Science Quarterly, 44,* 764–791.

Ibarra, H., & Andrews, S. B. (1993). Power, social influence, and sensemaking: Effects of network centrality and proximity on employee perceptions. *Administrative Science Quarterly, 38,* 277–303.

Jarvis-Selinger, S., Pratt, D. D., & Regehr, G. (2012). Competency is not enough: Integrating identity formation into the medical education discourse. *Academic Medicine, 87*(9), 1185–1190.

Kashiwagi, D. T., Varkey, P., & Cook, D. A. (2013). Mentoring programs for physicians in academic medicine: A systematic review. *Academic Medicine, 88*(7), 1–9.

Kilduff, M. (1990). The interpersonal structure of decision-making: A social comparison approach to organizational choice. *Organizational Behavior and Human Decision Processes, 47,* 270–288.

Krackhardt, D., & Stern, R. N. (1988). Informal networks and organizational crises: An experimental simulation. *Social Psychology Quarterly, 51,* 123–140.

Kram, K. E. (1985). *Mentoring at work: Developmental relationships in organizational life.* Glenview, IL: Scott, Foresman & Co.

Kram, K. E., & Isabella, L. A. (1985). Mentoring alternatives: The role of peer relationships in career development. *Academy of Management Journal, 28*(1), 110–132.

Liang, D. W., Moreland, R. L., & Argote, L. (1995). Group versus individual training and group performance: The mediating role of transactive memory. *Personality & Social Psychology Bulletin, 21*, 383–393.

McAllister, D. J. (1995). Affect- and cognition-based trust as foundations for interpersonal cooperation in organizations. *Academy of Management Journal, 38*, 24–59.

McDougall, M., & Beattie, R. S. (1997). Peer mentoring at work: The nature and outcomes of non-hierarchial developmental relationships. *Management Learning, 28*, 423–437.

McManus, S. E., & Russell, J. E. A. (2007). Peer mentoring relationships. In B. A. Ragins, & K. E. Kram (Eds), *The handbook of mentoring at work: Theory, research, and practice* (pp. 273–295). Thousand Oaks, CA: Sage Publications.

MacPhee, M., Chang, L., Lee, D., & Spiri, W. (2013). Global health care leadership development: Trends to consider. *Journal of Healthcare Leadership, 5*, 21–29.

Mark, S., Link, H., Morahan, P. S., Pololi, L., Reznik, V., & Tropez-Sims, S. (2001). Innovative mentoring programs to promote gender equity in academic medicine. *Academic Medicine, 76*(1), 39–42.

Marsden, P. V. (1988). Homogeneity in confiding relations. *Journal of Social Networks, 10*, 57–76.

Marsden, P. V. (1990). Network data and measurement. *Annual Review of Sociology, 16*, 435–463.

Marsden, P. V., & Campbell, K. E. (1984). Measuring tie strength. *Social Forces, 63*, 482–501.

Mehra, A., Kilduff, M., & Brass, D. J. (1998). At the margins: A distinctiveness approach to the social identity and social networks of underrepresented groups. *Academy of Management Journal, 41*, 441–452.

Meyer, G. W. (1994). Social information processing and social networks: A test of social influence mechanisms. *Human Relations, 47*, 1013–1047.

Morrison, E. W. (2002). Newcomer's relationships: The role of social networks ties during socialization. *Academy of Management Journal, 45*, 1149–1160.

Murphy, W. M. (2012). Reverse mentoring at work: Fostering cross-generational learning and developing millennial leaders. *Human Resource Management, 51*(4), 549–574.

Murphy, W., & Kram, K. E. (2014). *Strategic relationships at work: Creating your circle of mentors, sponsors and peers for success in business and life.* New York: McGraw-Hill Professional.

Murrell, A. J., Blake-Beard, S. A., Porter, D. M., & Perkins-Williamson, A. (2008). Interorganizational formal mentoring: Breaking the concrete ceiling sometimes requires help from the outside. *Human Resource Management, 47*(2), 275–294.

Murrell, A. J., Crosby, F. J., & Ely, R. J. (1999). *Mentoring dilemmas: Developmental relationships within the multicultural organization.* Mahwah, NJ: Lawrence Erlbaum Associates.

Murrell, A. J., Forte-Trammel, S., & Bing, D. (2008). *Intelligent Mentoring: How IBM adds value through people, knowledge and relationships.* Boston, BA: Pearson Publishers.

Noe, R. A., Greenberger, D. B., & Wang, S. (2002). Mentoring: What we know and where we might go from here. In G. R. Ferris, & J. J. Martocchio (Eds.), *Research in personnel and human resources management*, Vol. 21 (pp. 129–173). Oxford: Elsevier.

Nonaka, I. (1994). A dynamic theory of organizational knowledge creation. *Organization Science, 5*, 12–37.

Ostroff, C., & Kozlowski, S. W. J. (1992). Organizational socialization as a learning process: The role of information acquisition. *Personnel Psychology, 45*, 849–874.

Pololi, L. H., & Knight, S. (2005). Mentoring faculty in academic medicine: A new paradigm? *Journal of General Internal Medicine, 20,* 866–870.

Pololi, L. H., Krupat, E., Civian, J. T., Ash, A. S., & Brennan, R. T. (2012). Why are a quarter of faculty considering leaving academic medicine? A study of their perceptions of institutional culture and intentions to leave at 26 representative U.S. medical schools. *Academic Medicine, 87*(7), 859–869.

Pullins, E. B., & Fine, L. M. (2002). How the performance of mentoring activities affects the mentor's job outcomes. *Journal of Personal Selling & Sales Management, 22,* 259–272.

Ragins, B. R. (1997). Diversified mentoring relationships: A power perspective. *Academy of Management Review, 229,* 482–521.

Ragins, B. R., & Cotton, J. L. (1999). Mentor functions and outcomes: A comparison of men and women in formal and informal mentoring relationships. *Journal of Applied Psychology, 84,* 529–550.

Sachdeva, A. K. (1996). Preceptorship, mentorship and the adult learning in medical and health sciences education. *Journal of Cancer Education, 11.* 131–136.

Salancik, G. R., & Pfeffer, J. (1978). A social information processing approach to job attitudes and task design. *Administrative Science Quarterly, 23,* 224–253.

Sambunjak, D., Straus, S. E., & Marusic A. (2006). Mentoring in academic medicine: A systematic review. *Journal of the American Medical Association, 296*(9), 1103–1115.

Sambunjak, D., Straus, S. E., & Marusic, A. (2009). A systematic review of qualitative research on the meaning and characteristics of mentoring in academic medicine. *Journal of General Internal Medicine, 25*(1), 72–78.

Sanchez, J. P., Peters, L., Lee-Rey, E., Strelnick, H., Garrison, G., Zhang, K., Spencer, D., Ortega, G., Yehia, B., Berlin, A., & Castillo-Page, L. (2013). Racial and ethnic minority medical students' perceptions of an interest in careers in academic medicine. *Academic Medicine, 88*(9), 1299–1307.

Scandura, T. A. (1992). Mentorship and career mobility: An empirical investigation. *Journal of Organizational Behavior, 13*(2), 169–174.

Schloss, E. P., Flanagan, D. M., & Culler, C. L. (2009). Some hidden costs of faculty turnover in clinical departments in one academic medical center. *Academic Medicine, 84,* 32–36.

Sias, P. M., & Cahill, D. J. (1998). From coworkers to friends: The development of peer friendships in the workplace. *Western Journal of Communication, 62,* 273–299.

Sparrowe, R. T., Liden, R. C., Wayne, S. J., & Kraimer, M. L. (2001). Social networks and the performance of individuals and groups. *Academy of Management Journal, 44,* 316–325.

Straus, S. E., Chatur, F., & Taylor, M. (2009). Issues in the mentor–mentee relationship in academic medicine: A qualitative study. *Academic Medicine, 84,* 135–139.

Straus, S. E., Johnson, M. O., Marquez, C., & Feldman, M. D. (2013). Characteristics of successful and failed mentoring relationships: A qualitative study across two academic health centers. *Academic Medicine, 88*(1), 82–89.

Straus, S. E., Straus, C., & Tzanetos, K. (2006). Career choice in academic medicine. *Journal of General Internal Medicine, 21,* 1222–1229.

Strong, C. G., & Cornelius, L. A. (2012). Preparing the next generation in academic medicine: Recruiting and retaining the best. *Journal of Investigative Dermatology, 132,* 1018–1025.

Swap, W. D., Leonard, D., Shields, M., & Abrams, L. (2001). Using mentoring and storytelling to transfer knowledge in the workplace. *Journal of Management Information Systems, 18,* 95–114.

Tillman, R. E., Jang, S., Abedin, Z., Richards, B. F., Spaeth-Rublee, B., & Pincus, H. A. (2013). Policies, activities, and structures supporting research mentoring: A national survey of academic health centers with clinical and translational science awards. *Academic Medicine, 88*(1), 90–96.

Umphress, E. E., Labianca, G., Brass, D. J., Kass, E., & Scholten, L. (2003). The role of instrumental and expressive social ties in employees' perceptions of organizational justice. *Organization Science, 14*, 738–753.

Valentine, H. A., Grewal, D., Candy, M., Moseley, J., Shih, M. C., Stevenson, D., & Pizzo, P. A. (2014). The gender gap in academic medicine: Comparing results from a multifaceted intervention for Stanford faculty to peer and national cohorts. *Academic Medicine, 89*(6), 904–911.

Varkey, P., Jatoi, A., Williams, A., Mayer, A., Ko, M., Files, J., Blair, J., & Hayes, S. (2012). The positive impact of a facilitated peer mentoring program on academic skills of women faculty. *BMC Medical Education, 12*(14), 1–8.

Wanberg, C. R., Welsh, E. T., & Hezlett, S. A. (2003). Mentoring research: A review and dynamic process model. In G. R. Ferris, & J. J. Martocchio (Eds.), *Research in personnel and human recourses management*, Vol. 22 (pp. 39–124). Oxford: Elsevier.

Wanous, J. P., Reichers, A. E., & Hudy, M. J. (1997). Overall job satisfaction: How good are single-item measures? *Journal of Applied Psychology, 82*, 247–252.

Wheeler, L., & Miyake, K. (1992). Social comparison in everyday life. *Journal of Personality and Social Psychology, 62*, 760–773.

Young, A. M., & Perrewe, P. L. (2000). The exchange relationships between mentors and protégés: The development of a framework. *Human Resource Management Review, 10*, 117–209.

Young, A. M., & Perrewe, P. L. (2004). The role of expectations in the mentoring exchange: An analysis of mentor and protégé expectations in relation to perceived support. *Journal of Managerial Issues, 16*, 103–126.

Zagenczyk, T. J., Gibney, R., Murrell, A. J., & Boss, S. (2008). Friends don't make friends good citizens, but advisors do. *Group & Organization Management, 33*, 760–780.

6

RE-CONCEPTUALIZING SPONSORSHIP OF WOMEN LEADERS AS AN ORGANIZATIONAL ROUTINE[1]

Karen L. Proudford and Montressa L. Washington

Sponsorship of women who aspire to be corporate officers and CEOs is imperative for those organizations that are committed to assembling diverse leadership teams. A unique set of impediments blocks women's advancement to the most senior levels in organizations. Eagly and Carli conclude that: "when you put all the pieces together, a new picture emerges for why women don't make it into the C-suite. It's not the glass ceiling, but the sum of many obstacles along the way" (2007: 63). Hewlett, Peraino, Sherbin, and Sumberg (2010) state the case succinctly:

> Women just aren't making it to the very top. Despite making gains in middle and senior management, they hold just 3% of Fortune 500 CEO positions. In the C-suite, they are outnumbered 4-to-1. They account for less than 16% of all corporate officers, and comprise only 7.6% of Fortune 500 top earner positions.
>
> (Hewlett et al., 2010: i)

Even women who enter organizations with identical academic credentials may lack "the powerful backing necessary to inspire, propel, and protect them through the perilous straits of upper management. Women lack, in a word, sponsorship" (Hewlett et al., 2010: i). Navigating the corporate landscape can be complicated, confusing, and disorienting for those women who do not have the benefit of the tools and support necessary to help make sense of the complex journey to the top.

Though female participation in the workforce has increased, the gender diversity that exists throughout many organizations in the lower and also the middle levels (Cotter, Hermsen, Ovadia, & Vanneman, 2001: 656–657) has not reached the highest echelons. Structured interventions, such as mentoring programs, have done little to change this intractable pattern (Silva & Carter, 2011). Instead, the "unseen and unbreachable barrier [...] keeps minorities and women from rising to the upper rungs of the corporate ladder, regardless of their qualifications or achievements" (Federal Glass Ceiling Commission, 1995: 4). The glass ceiling has been recast as the concrete ceiling for African Americans (Hayes, 2006), the adobe ceiling for Hispanics (DelCampo & Blancero, 2008), and the bamboo ceiling for Asians (Mundy, 2014), in order to reflect the unique barriers encountered by people, and especially women, of color (Murrell, Blake-Beard, Porter, & Perkins-Williamson, 2008). Furthermore, evidence suggests that this enduring pattern is a global phenomenon, rather than country-specific (Festing, Knappert, & Kornau, 2015).

Both the academic and business communities have maintained a lengthy focus on ways to advance women in the workplace since the 1986 *Wall Street Journal* "Corporate Woman" column first introduced the term "glass ceiling" into the lexicon (Federal Glass Ceiling Commission, 1995). Subsequent initiatives at the federal level and in the business community were aimed at establishing a foundation for increased opportunities and advancement, including mentoring as a critical lever.

The narrative would, it was thought, unfold in this manner: Men advance in organizations largely because they have trusted individuals who provide the advice and coaching necessary to help them understand "the ropes." By contrast, women had few such advisors to assist them in understanding the written and unwritten codes of conduct that govern advancement. Companies largely accepted this argument and designed programs that matched mentors with women protégés. It was expected that these efforts would yield substantial gains in women's careers by the early 2000s. There is evidence that mentoring does have a significant impact on improving the advancement of women in organizations. One notable study is the longitudinal work by Kalev, Dobbin, and Kelly (2006), which shows that mentoring is more effective than diversity training programs in facilitating career development, especially for black women.

However, the results of the Carter and Silva (2010) study of male and female graduates of elite MBA programs run counter to the proposed story. The authors indicate, "Reports of progress in advancement, compensation, and career satisfaction are at best overstated, at worst just plain wrong" (Carter & Silva, 2010: 19). Similarly, other research finds that though women are as likely as men to get mentored, women tend to have mentors who are at lower levels in the hierarchy, and that their mentoring relationships are less likely to yield the desired career advancement (Ibarra, Carter, & Silva, 2010). Silva and Carter (2011) argue:

> Good mentoring is undeniably valuable to junior managers trying to learn the ropes of an organization—but our research shows it is certainly not a

golden ticket. High-potential women actually have more mentors than men, yet the promotion and pay gap persists. A closer look reveals that men's mentors tend to be more senior, putting men in a better position to receive sponsorship.

(Silva & Carter, 2011)

Research indicates that women are less likely to be assigned "game-changing experiences" or "mission critical" assignments that give men the opportunity to showcase their talent (Silva & Ibarra, 2012: 19). This distinction is important because "a 2011 McKinsey report noted that men are promoted based on potential, while women are promoted based on past accomplishments" (Barsch & Yee, 2011, cf. Sandberg & Scovell, 2013: 8). The very nature of how women are viewed for advancement begins to illuminate why a comprehensive strategy is needed.

Such a strategy is needed in order to address the enduring obstacles blocking women's rise on career ladders. Ibarra et al. (2010) shifted the dialogue about gendered career patterns by making a distinction between mentorship and sponsorship: The authors assert that a sponsor "goes beyond giving feedback and advice and uses his or her influence with senior executives to advocate" for the junior member (Ibarra et al., 2010: 82). Companies have taken hold of sponsorship as a critical mechanism for pushing through the proverbial glass ceiling, and programs aimed at "matching" high-potential women with senior members willing to use their influence have been initiated (see, for example, Foust-Cummings, Dinolfo, & Kohler, 2011). Despite the increasing interest, the notion of sponsorship has received limited theoretical attention in the literature, although Friday, Friday, and Green (2004) did broach the topic somewhat in their study. Turner's (1960) sponsored-mobility model of career advancement posited that status is granted rather than earned, on the basis of criteria determined by those in top positions. The sponsored approach was believed to be more efficient than the contest mobility approach (Wayne, Liden, Kraimer, & Graf, 1999) under which individuals have equal opportunity to rise in the organization. Wayne et al. found support for the sponsored mobility model, noting its close relationship with leader–member exchange theory. They found that leader–member exchange was positively related to salary progression, the supervisor's perception of the subordinate's promotability, and the subordinate's career satisfaction.

Higgins and Kram note that: "in much of the mentoring research of the past three decades, researchers have conceptualized mentoring as the developmental assistance provided by a more senior individual within a protégé's organization, that is, a single dyadic relationship" (2001: 264). However, as Hewlett et al. (2010) suggest, the role of a mentor differs from that of a sponsor. While it is possible for a senior leader to act as both a mentor and a sponsor, the expectations and desired outcomes associated with each role are distinct. The central concern of this chapter, then, is to examine sponsorship theoretically in order to suggest ways in which it generates mechanisms for women's career advancement. The first section of this chapter posits sponsorship as a routine nested within organizational and talent management routines. Next, we discuss the impact of gender, as intertwined with legitimacy, on sponsorship routines. We then consider the ways in which sponsorship routines can be disrupted in order to bring about change, before addressing the implications for contemporary organizations seeking to identify and support the advancement of talented women and men.

Sponsorship as a Talent Management Routine

Because our understanding of sponsorship has been driven largely by practical rather than theoretical interest, it follows that current conceptualizations are built upon notions of mentoring, which focus on the identification of a mentor, a protégé, and the establishment of an ongoing developmental relationship between the two. Similarly, current thinking about sponsorship centers around a role-based, non-routine view that includes the identification of a sponsor and a high-potential candidate (HPC), and the subsequent matching and relationship-building efforts between the two actors. This role-based view (depicted in Figure 6.1) emphasizes the characteristics of each actor, the degree of similarity and/or affinity between the two, and their capacity to co-create developmental opportunities for the candidate. The role of organizational leadership is to identify potential sponsors and potential candidates, institute a process for matching sponsors with candidates, and then provide guidance regarding the coaching, potential for stretch assignments, and other activities that would lead to enhanced performance and advancement.

Though sponsor-candidate dyads may receive encouragement, guidance, and support from the organization, each relationship has unique elements shaped primarily by the sponsor and candidate. Their interactions are not necessarily

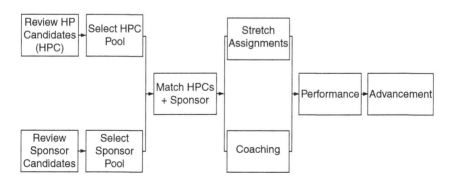

FIGURE 6.1 A Role-Based, Non-Routine View of Sponsorship

tied to organizational habits and routines. Instead, the dyads may prefer less formal or loosely structured interactions as a method of building their relationship. This ad hoc approach offers flexibility for the sponsor and candidate, higher levels of accountability regarding the desired outcomes of the relationship, and lower levels of accountability regarding the sponsorship process.

We suggest a process-based, routine perspective on sponsorship that focuses on the sequence of interactions carried out by multiple individuals engaged in the identification and development of high-potential talent. Process-based approaches institutionalize the ways in which high-potential talent is sourced within the organization.

In contrast, role-based approaches depend upon the organization sourcing specific types of employees in order to affect this process. Thus, the role-based, non-routine view posits sponsorship as a set of expectations fulfilled by an individual committed to the advancement of his/her assigned protégé. These sequences of interactions that characterize a process-based perspective are embedded in the talent management processes within the organization (see Figure 6.2), which comprise a set of routines (Nelson & Winter, 1982) that are "repetitive, recognizable patterns of interdependent actions, carried out by multiple actors" (Feldman & Pentland, 2003: 95). Such routines are "recognizable if the steps within each performance follow from one to the next, like the notes of a song. For a routine to be repetitive, these recognizable patterns must be retained from one performance to the next" (Pentland, Feldman, Becker, & Liu, 2012: 1485). Increasingly, researchers are studying routine dynamics in order to understand actions, patterns, actors, change, and stability in the organizational context (Feldman, Pentland, D'Adderio, & Lazaric, 2016).

Routines clear a path toward accomplishing work, are a critical element of organizational behavior (Feldman, 2000), and are impacted by demographic differences that exist at the societal, organizational, group, and individual levels. This nested view of the sponsorship routine process acknowledges the impact and influence of context. It is worth noting that talent management and diversity and inclusion (D&I) efforts may exist in separate (i.e., not nested) domains in organizations. In those cases, the impact of D&I may not be readily apparent to those who believe that the existing talent management processes are effective in identifying the company's top talent.

In our view, however, talent management, in as much as it is nested within organizational and societal routines, is necessarily intertwined with diversity. In turn, attracting, developing, and retaining top, diverse talent is a core objective of the talent management processes (Rothwell, 2011), and a primary strategic imperative of companies seeking to compete in a dynamic, global arena. As Kesler notes, having a strong pipeline of leadership talent "is a steady, ongoing labor that requires discipline, decisiveness, and responsible risk-taking" (2002: 32). In distinguishing between succession planning and replacement planning, Kesler asserts that effective programs should not develop as a disparate activity.

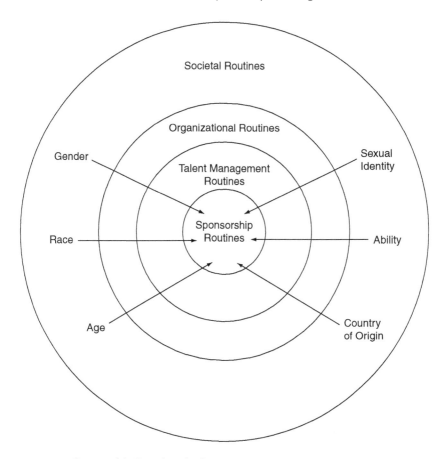

FIGURE 6.2 Sponsorship Routines in Context

Instead, talent development should be viewed as "the result of placing talented people in the right stretch assignments, supported by effective bosses and coaches" (Kesler, 2002: 33).

As illustrated in Figure 6.3, the process-based, routine view of sponsorship relies on shared ownership of the sponsorship activities. The group (i.e., the decision makers or leadership team) share the responsibility for reviewing and identifying HPCs and determining the mentoring, coaching, and stretch assignments and other opportunities that might guide the candidate toward enhanced performance and career advancement.

Dialogue among the leadership team, rather than between a designated sponsor and candidate, is central to this view, as is the presence of feedback loops. During the first part of the process, when HPCs are identified and selected, the decision makers can examine their individual unconscious biases and, as a group, review their assumptions (e.g., about the criteria used to

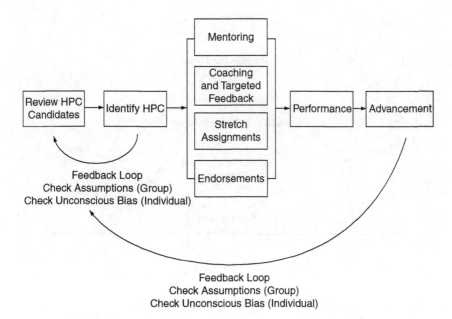

FIGURE 6.3 A Process-Based, Routine View of Sponsorship

evaluate and select candidates). A second feedback loop occurs as the candidate's performance and advancement is being monitored, such that decision makers can revisit any potential biases and assumptions as they assess the candidate's progress. In our view, sponsorship is an activity embedded in the culture of the organization. A low degree of embeddedness is characteristic of largely informal sponsorship actions, driven by unchallenged assumptions and occurring among an indeterminate number of participants. By contrast, a high degree of embeddedness is characteristic of largely formal sponsorship actions, prescribed by practice and policies, governed by stated assumptions, and occurring among an identifiable number of participants. Routinized sponsorship processes are highly embedded in the organizational context.

In suggesting that sponsorship is a routine, we seek to decouple the role of sponsor from the activity of sponsorship. Further, we posit that multiple actors can engage in sponsorship of an individual. This differs considerably from the view that a single sponsor determines the career trajectory of his/her protégé. In our view, sponsorship takes place in the midst of the conversation, with multiple actors evaluating and re-evaluating an individual's potential, rather than one individual advocating on behalf of an individual—though the latter may occur as well. The reputational risk associated with advocating on behalf of a specific individual makes it less likely that most influencers would do so, absent considerable resources to mitigate against potential losses in status, reputation, or resources:

The hallmark of sponsorship is its inherently public nature. Sponsors stick their neck out. They'll "put their name next to your performance," making their support highly visible. In contrast, "you can mentor and coach someone who is awful without risking your reputation."

(Hewlett et al., 2010: 5)

The willingness to attach one's name and reputation to an employee is the critical difference, and this leads to the realization that an effective sponsor must have a certain amount of social and political capital within an organization.

Therefore, when weighing the impact of a potential sponsor, it is important that a sponsor be "in a position to attend [meetings] that can make or break the career of an employee; their authority allows them to speak to your strengths, make a case for your advancement, and be heard in your absence" (Hewlett et al., 2010: 5). Their assertion is based on a role-based, non–routine view of sponsorship; however, the suggestion that sponsorship is public in nature is consonant with the process-based, routine view being proposed here. The level of risk is lower when a process-based approach is used for two key reasons: first, responsibility and accountability are shared among decision makers; and second, decision makers are actively revisiting the criteria for candidate selection and opportunity matching, yielding the greater insight that group reflection often provides. Both aspects of the group interaction are especially important practices to adopt if strategic gains are to be made in increasing the number of women ascending to higher levels in the organization.

Gender, Legitimacy, and Sponsorship Routines

Catalyst reports that "the core components of talent management are linked in ways that disadvantage women, creating a vicious cycle in which men continually dominate executive positions" (2009: 9). Senior leadership has a significant effect on talent management programs and practices, which ultimately affects who gets promoted. In addition, organizations may describe their talent management systems as formalized, customized, and centralized, but still fall short when it is necessary to implement checks and balances that minimize gender bias. In short, the gaps between the design and execution of talent management programs compound the disadvantages faced by women, especially those seeking professional development and advancement (Catalyst, 2009). For example, decisions to implement talent management systems and the processes that support talent management are often made by people who do not test their biases, and as a result they tend to recreate themselves in their own image. Kaczmarek, Kimino, and Pye found that the characteristics of board nomination committees "are significant antecedents of board diversity, hence the composition of the [nomination committee] is an important step and prerequisite for assembling a diverse board" (2012: 474). Given this finding, one could expect that appointing women to a nomination committee could lead to a greater representation of women on the full board. Because new leaders are likely to demonstrate the traits and biases of the senior leaders who chose them, new routines must be established in the form of checks and balances that ensure that biases and assumptions do not continue to drive sponsorship actions in a way that reinforces male privilege (Catalyst, 2009).

There is a large body of research that indicates that men are seen as more capable, stronger leaders, more strategic, and more effective than women in roles of influence and authority (Hurst, Leberman, & Edwards, 2016; Cuadrado, Garcia-Ael, & Molero, 2015; Gupta & Turban, 2012; Johnson, Murphy, Zewdie, & Reichard, 2008; Scott & Brown, 2006). In many instances, the current routines help to establish legitimacy, for example, the organizational processes and routines reinforce the belief that masculine talent attributes are legitimate while feminine talent attributes lack legitimacy. Gender diversity among decision makers is not sufficient to eliminate existing notions of legitimacy attached to established sponsorship routines. Existing routines can absorb diversity in ways that do not challenge assumptions or beliefs about the status, competence, capabilities, and potential of men and women. The need to reconsider established sponsorship routines rests largely upon the degree to which female talent is viewed as legitimate, coupled with an awareness among management that the underuse of talent, including the tendency to sponsor men more than women (Morahan, Rosen, Richman, & Gleason, 2011), ultimately reduces organizational competitiveness.

Evidence of the legitimacy of female talent may be found, for example, if the leadership team makes note of the roles junior members play in their communities as well as in the workplace. Hewlett, Luce, and West (2005) present a compelling case for minority professionals in this regard, which can stand alone or be connected in the dialogue on women in senior leadership. Often, according to Hewlett et al.,

> minority professionals hold leadership roles outside of work, serving as pillars of their communities and churches and doing more than their share of mentoring. It is time their employers took notice of these invisible lives and saw them as sources of strength.
>
> (Hewlett et al., 2005: 75)

These skill sets and leadership roles could translate into organizational value, but they must first be viewed as legitimate.

This notion was demonstrated in an empirical study by Ely and Meyerson (2010), who examined a shift away from prototypically male leadership behaviors and the resulting impact on workplace safety on offshore oil platforms. Their analysis revealed that an overreliance on typical masculine behavior was leading to high levels of risk-taking and suboptimal decision-making. In the context of workplace safety, viewing extreme masculine behavior as legitimate not only marginalized the women workers, but also led to a higher incidence of accidents for all employees. As part of an effort to improve workplace safety, training was put into place that redefined competency in a way that acknowledged a more balanced mix of masculine, feminine, and gender-neutral traits. Accident rates fell by 84 percent companywide. Similarly, we would suggest that surfacing and reconsidering models of behavior based on race and gender stereotypes could yield sizable benefits for organizations. Continuing the point raised by Hewlett et al.:

> the disproportionate load of care that minority professionals bear in their extended families is also invisible to employers, and neither acknowledged nor supported by corporate benefits packages. The result: Too many high-potential employees end up feeling ignored and diminished, overextended and burned out. At the same time, organizations are being deprived of the strong and diverse leadership they could so easily draw upon.
>
> (Hewlett et al., 2005: 77)

Routines create more occasions for senior members to build personal connections with junior members, and in doing so, greater knowledge of a whole person is available. Junior members, and their talents used outside of the workplace, may be seen more holistically, and their non-traditional talents may be deemed legitimate in their professional lives. Without this expanded view, women's talent is viewed through a prism of unchallenged biases and assumptions. This limits who is identified as a leader worth the investment of professional and personal development.

The expectations and characteristics of decision makers may also be reconsidered. The role of those decision makers who are engaged in sponsoring candidates is to identify talent and then assign that talent in the most efficient and effective way to areas of need in the organization (Hewlett et al., 2010; Price & Howard, 2012). Borrowing the power of an often white, male sponsor can be critical to advancement; so too is a sponsor being able to confidently risk his/her reputation on behalf of an employee. Additionally, Murrell and Zagenczyk's research is instructive:

> Burt's (1998) work on social networks is also quite relevant to our present discussion. He argued that women are unable to duplicate the networks of men because they lack legitimacy in the organization. In order to be successful, women need to effectively "borrow" the social network of a male sponsor who is influential in the organization. This borrowing of social power helps others to perceive that they are actually dealing indirectly with the male manager (power by proxy). Burt's work confirmed,

women who borrowed social networks were promoted more quickly than women who attempted to develop their own networks.

(Murrell and Zagenczyk, 2006: 565)

Thus, for women and especially minority women, proxy power is the greatest source of legitimacy that makes individual talent and professional ambition credible (Murrell et al., 2008). We would recast this as the role of sponsorship, and further suggest that the leadership team is charged with promoting and protecting talent. A reconsideration of female talent necessarily includes a call to re-examine racial identity and other forms of identity so that a more complete and complex view of women of color is up for review. "The picture becomes more complicated when exploring people of color's ability to develop relationships with those who share the same racial group (or racial identity group) membership" (Murrell et al., 2008: 276). Gaining access to professional mentorship/sponsorship with someone of the same race may be difficult for people of color because of their low numbers at higher levels in the organization (Ghosh, 2014). Gaining access to senior members who provide career-focused mentoring means that people of color are thrust into interracial dynamics embedded within the organization to a greater degree than Whites (Ghosh, 2014; McGuire, 2012). In addition, the relationships that people of color form within organizations may not receive the organizational support needed to yield benefits of mentoring (Murrell et al., 2008). The work of diversity and talent leaders is to create adequate space for sponsorship relationships to evolve; in the process, a deeper understanding of race-ethnicity identity in the workplace will emerge. Women, for example, have a perception that male sponsors have an edge over female sponsors, because of their greater external and internal networks (Hewlett et al., 2010). Admittedly, "the real issue may be that women feel they have no choice. If they seem to prefer male sponsors it's because they simply can't find any females—or rather, any females who measure up to their near-impossible ideal" (Hewlett et al., 2010: 13). Sponsorship routines shift the focus from the role of the person to the process and from an individual to a team. Still, the characteristics of the leadership team, that is, a predominantly White, male leadership team versus a predominantly White, female leadership team, would likely impact sponsorship actions absent a mechanism for interrupting existing sponsorship practices.

Disrupting Sponsorship Routines

Routines contribute to "efficiency, legitimacy, accountability, and reliability in organizations" (Geiger & Schröder, 2014: 173). To the extent that sponsorship routines are highly embedded in the organization, they provide stability and may be highly resistant to change. Howard-Greenville states that: "embeddedness of a routine may not prevent actors from improvising individual performances, it may prevent these improvisations from being taken up and perpetuated as an ongoing part of the routine" (2005: 619). Yet an organization that adopts mechanisms for surfacing assumptions and biases may bring about significant positive change. A specific occurrence often sparks the need to interrupt an organizational routine, and thus allows for the possibility of more inclusive selection and identification of top organizational talent. Gersick and Hackman (1990) and Feldman and Pentland (2003) discuss five drivers for change in habitual routines, each of which has applicability for organizations seeking to sponsor women:

1   the record number of women in organizations and/or managerial positions represents a novel state of affairs;
2   organizations may be experienced as failures if they cannot construct robust talent pipelines to advance women into the C-suite;
3   professional women are reaching a natural breakpoint in their careers, causing them to question and evaluate their desired paths forward into the C-suite;
4   societal and governmental pressures are mounting for organizations to develop and implement effective programs to increase the number of women in the C-suite; and
5   the structure of the workplace is changing rapidly as a result of technology, the political climate, and family dynamics, all of which are impacting how women engage with current organizational structures.

There is likely to be significant variation across cultures regarding which driver is most influential. In some countries, societal and governmental pressures may be the primary drivers (Pryce & Sealy, 2013); in others, a marked increase in the number of working women due to social pressures or demographic change may also bring about change. Moreover, the type and intensity of dialogue among decision makers will also impact sponsorship routines. Societies that emphasize group-level decision-making may adopt and adjust routines more readily than those who focus on individual-level action. For example, in a country like Japan, group decisions are embedded in the culture and, as such, the Japanese tend to address and make decisions collectively, whereas in the United States decisions are more individually based.

Thus far, we have discussed sponsorship actions as they relate to characteristics of the individual HPC. But second-order actions are dynamic sets of acts that relate to both men and women. These second-order sponsorship actions, which we call "sequencing," fuel the patterns evident in organizations whereby the gains of women trail those of men. Women may be sponsored and subsequently promoted, but their advancement does not merely impact women only. Second-order actions suggest that concomitant actions occur such that men are also promoted in a way that keeps the status quo intact. Put another way, the actions taken to promote men ensure that their mobility surpasses that of women. Even an organization that has a robust sponsorship program for women in place may find that the gap between male and female gains remains constant over time.

Sequencing is an important stabilizing organizational dynamic that reinforces existing beliefs about the competency levels and leadership capabilities of men versus women. Such beliefs are rooted in deeply held assumptions that undergird organizational life. There is something that is "not quite right" about a woman who is placed in a position that has more status, opportunity, or prestige than a man. Sequencing actions may be intentional, as happened historically when it was widely accepted that women were unsuited for organizational life, save the supportive, nurturing roles prescribed for them by men (Adame, Caplliure, & Miguel, 2016). However, they may also be unintentional byproducts of a non-reflexive decision-making process that privileges men without considered debate. These "gendered social practices become so normalized that the injustices they perpetuate are utterly transparent" (Nugent, Dinolfo, & Giscombe, 2013: 391). Evidence of sequencing may include the following points:

- Women's promotion rates trail those of men;
- Work assignments given to women are viewed as less rigorous than those given to men;
- Performance ratings given to women are lower than those of men.

Absent human or social capital explanations for such patterns, sequencing may influence decisions across gender in order to maintain the accepted pattern of gender participation and differentiation in the organization.

A great deal of attention has been paid to the persistent gender pay gap, particularly given that decision makers are typically male who are determining the pay of subordinate women (Newton & Simutin, 2014). However, we would suggest that sequencing is an organizational and cultural phenomenon that makes it likely that women would make similar choices, perhaps not at the same rate. Challenges to those beliefs—for example, if a woman progresses at a rate that eclipses men—may be viewed as illegitimate and would engender negative responses ranging from disbelief to dissent to intentional sabotage. This may also contribute to the extreme and often distorted attributions applied to women in leadership positions—the "damned if you do, doomed if you don't" double-bind (Catalyst, 2007). Reversing "problematic" patterns of advancement that threaten core beliefs can be seen as an imperative, as necessary to "make things right." Thus, organizations seeking to effect change in the advancement patterns of women recognize the group-level dynamic that operates in alignment with the existing organizational order. Interrupting first- and second-order sponsorship routines, if the efforts are to be effective and sustainable, will be linked to important organizational outcomes and to the core functions and desired processes of the business. Moreover, the new routines must enrich the organization's sense of vitality and expand possibilities, rather than deflate and contract performance and influence.

Sponsorship of Women: Disruptive Organizational Routine

As Table 6.1 summarizes, key aspects of our framework offer potential for advancing more women into leadership positions. As we have argued, a process-based, routine approach to sponsorship requires that decision makers surface and examine assumptions operating within their specific context.

Not only are decision makers accountable collectively for the sponsorship process, they are also called upon to create a culture that cultivates and supports routines necessary to promote sponsorship. As social leaders, they are charged with getting "members of the team excited about their task, increasing the energy level around accomplishing an assignment, instilling team spirit, and reducing conflict" (Price & Howard, 2012: 34). They also emphasize the importance of "cultivating relationships with mentors, participating in professional and community organizations, taking calculated career risks, surrounding oneself with talented people, and maintaining a positive mental attitude" (Price & Howard, 2012: 34). In addition, social leaders can promote, interrupt, and alter sponsorship routines in a way that furthers talent management objectives and signals cohesion to the rest of the organization.

Though the research shows that routines rely on the individuals within an organization remaining vigilant about learning, a similar dynamic can happen at the group level when senior leaders hold each other accountable for holding transparent conversations. According to Edmondson, Bohmer, and Pisano (2001), leadership teams can use a four-step process to leverage collective learning techniques in order to alter routines: (1) enrollment (careful selection of team members), (2) preparation (off-line practice sessions), (3) trials (trials of new routines), and (4) reflection (debriefing to learn from trials). In addition, members who have successfully changed routines have "used enrolment to

TABLE 6.1 A Framework for Creating Change in Current Approaches to Advancing Women into the C-Suite

Dimension	Role-Based, Non-Routine	Process-Based, Routine
Level of Analysis	Individual	Group
Mechanism	Matching based on characteristics	Questioning assumptions
Time	Episodic	Routine
Scope	Ad hoc and localized/individualized	Systemic and generalized/group-level
Practice	Sponsors as individuals	Sponsorship as a patterned behavior

motivate the team, conducted preparatory practice sessions and early trials to encourage psychological safety and promote new behaviors, and developed shared meaning and process improvement through reflective practices" (Vilkas, 2013: 190). This four-step process, especially the last step, aligns and complements our view that it is important for leaders to continuously check their assumptions and beliefs as they determine who should be recommended for endorsement within an organization.

Engaging leaders in a dialogue about the value of sponsorship and how it currently is conducted in the organization may provide the foundation for introducing sponsorship routines. Decision makers and women candidates may also need ongoing development, support, and guidance in order to avoid the setbacks that can occur with cross-gender mentoring or sponsorship relationships. As Hewlett et al. point out,

> women's reluctance to seek out and actively engage senior colleagues as allies is amply justified. Sponsorship, which often involves an older, married male spending one-on-one time, often off site and after hours, with a younger, unmarried female, can look like an affair; and the greater the power disparity between the male and female, the more intense the speculation becomes that the relationship is more than professional.
>
> (Hewlett et al., 2010: 78)

As we have suggested, sponsorship of women as a routine is coupled with the need to reconsider how legitimacy is ascribed to attributes of talent in the workplace. In many cases, organizations "recognize the cultural and organizational factors working against inclusiveness and women's advancement," and many are optimistic about the number and breadth of initiatives aimed at women's advancement (Morahan et al., 2011: 393). This view can provide a starting point for adopting and sustaining routines, with the potential to increase the number of women moving from middle to upper management.

Implications for Contemporary Organizations

This chapter has focused on the premise that because the concept of organizational routines has been around for some time, they have become the de facto means for organizations to accomplish their work: "Since the concept was introduced ... organizational routines have been regarded as the primary means by which organizations accomplish much of what they do" (Feldman & Pentland, 2003: 94). For organizations focused on accomplishing the task of increasing the number of women and minorities at the highest levels of business leadership, routinizing the sponsorship process may prove useful.

The benefits of sponsorship are practically clear, yet it is the implementation within the workplace that requires a commitment to learning and ensuring the talents of women are valued. With the support of management, social leaders can cultivate a learning culture where it is possible to routinize sponsorship within the workplace. Unsuccessful efforts often begin with a "failure of commitment by staff management [...] and the operating departments" (Fottler, 1977: 75). There are many functional aspects to routines but establishing new norms and revisiting outcomes guards against an unexamined reliance on routines.

However, this type of research notes a number of potential problems, such as routines becoming sources of inertia and inflexibility (Foss, Heimeriks, Winter, & Zollo, 2012). For example, Hewlett et al. (2010) have noted that the threat of gossip and scandal, the intense scrutiny about one's personal and professional choices, the pressure to maintain one's composure, and the need to be judicious about which comments should evoke a response work together in order to decrease the likelihood that a woman will be identified as having leadership potential. Thus, women may need assurances that the sponsorship process will not require them to seek out a sponsor or otherwise put themselves at increased risk. Because recruiting is a core talent management function, HR professionals can continue to ask: "if women and minorities truly have access to positions in which they can exercise visible power or if they continue to function as a marginalized group" (O'Brien & Janssen, 2005: 353). Addressing both recruitment and retention will allow for both functionality and vitality to exist in a routinized nature. Looking forward, Catalyst (2009: 25) provides the following recommendations:

- Examine current forms for gender stereotypes and biases;
- Develop worldwide leadership competency models;
- Review practices from other companies;
- Continue to develop, recruit, and retain all employees;
- Foster and build trusting relationships between managers and employees;
- Ensure that women and people of color thrive within the company;
- Empower managers to run performance management processes; and
- Address individual biases at all levels of the organization.

Research indicates that where women do occupy senior managerial positions, they have been found to focus more than men on the development and mentoring of their subordinates, encouraging them to reach their full potential and rewarding them for good performance (Eagly & Carli, 2003). Thus, a woman has good reason to believe that the presence of diverse top management teams is a critical factor for her likely success at a firm.

Indeed, researchers have argued that the presence of a woman on the corporate board indicates that, whatever barriers to advancement by women may exist in society, the culture of the firm is hospitable for women and committed to the advancement of women at all levels (Bilimoria, 2006). This in turn enhances the motivational and organizational commitment of women who occupy lower-level management positions within the organization (Dezso & Ross, 2012). Still, we would maintain that the existence of a routinized process is a critical additive component that, coupled with diverse organizational leadership, can create meaningful and lasting change. In this chapter, we argue that establishing sponsorship routines is strategic and integrated with existing culture-change processes in the organization. It has been further observed that some organizations produce identifiable patterns of activity related to their decentralized coordination of implicit and explicit knowledge within the employees. These activities appear to follow a script, though no ostensible script exists (Gioia & Poole, 1984). "Individuals' knowledge remains fragmentary but, in a stable environment, the collective performance becomes increasingly patterned and efficient over time" (Miller, Pentland, & Choi, 2012: 1554). A coordinated effort to ensure behavior is standardized is a necessary component in any effort to improve outcomes for women and diverse employees as future leaders of the organization.

We propose a new framework about sponsorship of women as a way to ensure that those who aspire to become corporate officers and CEOs can do so. We suggest that embedded sponsorship routines align with, and offer opportunities to disrupt, existing talent management efforts in ways that expand opportunities for a wider segment of the high potential talent pool. Our framework further illustrates the mechanisms that facilitate leadership development for senior women, with the ultimate goal of eradicating the obstacles that block talented women from advancing to the upper echelons of organizational life.

Future conceptual and empirical research opportunities should examine gender, legitimacy, and sponsorship routines, as well as the notion of leadership development as "gendered routine" that ascribes legitimacy differently for women. Drawing these connections around a specific set of research questions focused on leadership development and succession for senior women and areas for organizational practice could enrich our understanding of talent management processes that drive advancement opportunities.

Note

1 The authors thank Laurin Hodge for assistance with an early version of this chapter.

References

Adame, C., Caplliure, E. M., & Miquel, M. J. (2016). Work-life balance and firms: A matter of women? *Journal of Business Research, 69*(4), 1379–1383.

Barsch, J., & Yee, L. (2011). *Unlocking the full potential of women in the US economy.* Retrieved from www.google.com/?gws_rd=ssl#q=Barsch%2C+J.%2C+and+Yee%2C+L.+(2011).+Unlocking+the+full+potential+of+women+in+the+US+economy.+Retrieved+from+www.mckinsey.com.

Bilimoria, D. (2006). The relationship between women corporate directors and women corporate officers. *Journal of Managerial Issues, 18*(1), 47–62.

Burt, R. (1998). The gender of social capital. *Rationality and Society, 10*, 5–46.

Carter, N., & Silva, C. (2010). Women in management: Delusions of progress. *Harvard Business Review, 88*(3), 19–21.

Catalyst (2007). *The double-bind dilemma for women in leadership: Damned if you do, doomed if you don't.* Retrieved from www.catalyst.org/system/files/The_Double_Bind_Dilemma_ for_Women_in_Leadership_Damned_if_You_Do_Doomed_if_You_Dont.pdf.

Catalyst (2009). Cascading gender biases, compounding effects: An assessment of talent management systems. *Profiles in Diversity Journal, 11*(3), 9.

Cotter, D., Hermsen, J., Ovadia, S., & Vanneman, R. (2001). The glass ceiling effect. *Social Forces, 80*(2), 655–682.

Cuadrado, I., Garcia-Ael, C., & Molero, F. (2015). Gender-typing of leadership: Evaluations of real and ideal managers. *Scandinavian Journal of Psychology, 56*, 236–244.

DelCampo, R., & Blancero, D. (2008). Perceptions of psychological contract fairness of Hispanic professionals. *Cross Cultural Management: An International Journal, 15*(3), 300–315.

Dezso, C., & Ross, D. (2012). Does female representation in top management improve firm performance? A panel data investigation. *Strategic Management Journal, 33*(9), 1072–1089.

Eagly, A., & Carli, L. (2003). The female leadership advantage: An evaluation of the evidence. *The Leadership Quarterly, 14*(1), 807–834.

Eagly, A., & Carli, L. (2007). Women and the labyrinth of leadership. *Harvard Business Review, 85*(9), 63–71.

Edmondson, A. C., Bohmer, R. M., & Pisano, G. P. (2001). Disrupted routines: Team learning and new technology implementation in hospitals. *Administrative Science Quarterly, 46*(4), 685–716.

Ely, R. J., & Meyerson, D. E. (2010). An organizational approach to undoing gender: The unlikely case of offshore oil platforms. *Research in Organizational Behavior, 30*, 3–34.

Federal Glass Ceiling Commission (1995). *A solid investment: Making full use of the nation's capital.* Retrieved from www.dol.gov/dol/aboutdol/history/reich/reports/ceiling2. pdf.

Feldman, M. (2000). Organizational routines as a source of continuous change. *Organization Science, 11*(6), 611–629.

Feldman, M. S., & Pentland, B. T. (2003). Reconceptualizing organizational routines as a source of flexibility and change. *Administrative Science Quarterly, 48*, 94–118.

Feldman, M. S., Pentland, B. T., D'Adderio, L., & Lazaric, N. (2016). Beyond routines as things: Introduction to the special issue on routine dynamics. *Organization Science, 27*(3), 505–513.

Festing, M., Knappert, L., & Kornau, A. (2015). Gender-specific preferences in global performance management: An empirical study of male and female managers in a multinational context. *Human Resource Management, 54*(1), 55–79.

Foss, N. J., Heimeriks, K. H., Winter, S. G., & Zollo, M. (2012). A Hegelian dialogue on the micro-foundations of organizational routines and capabilities. *European Management Review, 9*(4), 173–197.

Fottler, M. D. (1977). Management commitment and manpower program success. *California Management Review, 19*(3), 71–77.

Foust-Cummings, H., Dinolfo, S., & Kohler, J. (2011). Sponsoring women to success. *Catalyst*. Retrieved from www.catalyst.org/system/files/sponsoring_women_to_success.pdf.

Friday, E., Friday, S., & Green, A. (2004). A reconceptualization of mentoring and sponsoring. *Management Decision, 42*(5), 628–644.

Geiger, D., & Schröder, A. (2014). Ever-changing routines? Toward a revised understanding of organizational routines between rule-following and rule-breaking. *Schmalenbach Business Review, 66*(2), 170–190.

Gersick, C. J., & Hackman, J. R. (1990). Habitual routines in task-performing groups. *Organizational Behavior and Human Decision Processes, 47*(1), 65–97.

Ghosh, R. (2014). Antecedents of mentoring support: A meta-analysis of individual, relational, and structural or organizational factors. *Journal of Vocational Behavior, 84*(3), 367–384.

Gioia, D. A., & Poole, P. P. (1984). Scripts in organizational behavior. *Academy of Management Review, 9*(3), 449–459.

Gupta, V. K., & Turban, D. B. (2012). Evaluation of new business ideas: Do gender stereotypes play a role? *Journal of Managerial Issues, 24*(2), 140–156.

Hayes, C. (2006). African American: Still chipping away at the concrete ceiling. *Black Enterprise, 36*(7), 147–150.

Hewlett, S. A., Luce, C. B., & West, C. (2005). Leadership in your midst: Tapping the hidden strengths of minority executives. *Harvard Business Review, 83*(11), 74–82.

Hewlett, S., Peraino, K., Sherbin, L., & Sumberg, K. (2010). The sponsor effect: Breaking through the last glass ceiling. *Harvard Business Review, 12*(1), 1–85.

Higgins, M. C., & Kram, K. E. (2001). Reconceptualizing mentoring at work: A developmental network perspective. *Academy of Management Review, 26*(2), 264–288.

Howard-Grenville, J. A. (2005). The persistence of flexible organizational routines: The role of agency and organizational context. *Organization Science, 16*(6), 618–636.

Hurst, J., Leberman, S., & Edwards, M. (2016). Women managing women: Intersections between hierarchical relationships, career development and gender equity. *Gender in Management: An International Journal, 31*(1), 61–74.

Ibarra, H., Carter, N., & Silva, C. (2010). Why men still get more promotions than women. *Harvard Business Review, 88*(9), 80–126.

Johnson, S., Murphy, S., Zewdie, S., & Reichard, R. (2008). The strong, sensitive type: Effects of gender stereotypes and leadership prototypes on the evaluation of male and female leaders. *Organizational Behavior and Human Decision Processes, 106*, 39–60.

Kaczmarek, S., Kimino, S., & Pye, A. (2012). Antecedents of board composition: The role of nomination committees. *Corporate Governance: An International Review, 20*(5), 474–489.

Kalev, A., Dobbin, F., & Kelly, E. (2006). Best practices or best guesses? Assessing the efficacy of corporate affirmative action and diversity policies. *American Sociological Review, 71*(4), 589–617.

Kesler, G. C. (2002). Why the leadership bench never gets deeper: Ten insights about executive talent development. *Human Resource Planning, 25*(1), 32–44.

McGuire, G. M. (2012). Race, gender, and social support: A study of networks in a financial services organization. *Sociological Focus, 45*(4), 320–337.

Miller, K. D., Pentland, B. T., & Choi, S. (2012). Dynamics of performing and remembering organizational routines. *Journal of Management Studies, 49*(8), 1536–1558.

Morahan, P. S., Rosen, S. E., Richman, R. C., & Gleason, K. A. (2011). The leadership continuum: A framework for organizational and individual assessment relative to the advancement of women physicians and scientists. *Journal of Women's Health, 20*(3), 387–396.

Mundy, L. (2014, November). Cracking the bamboo ceiling: Can Asian American men learn from *Lean In? The Atlantic.* Retrieved from www.theatlantic.com/magazine/archive/2014/11/cracking-the-bamboo-ceiling/380800/.

Murrell, A. J., Blake-Beard, S., Porter, D. M. Jr., & Perkins-Williamson, A. (2008). Interorganizational formal mentoring: Breaking the concrete ceiling sometimes requires support from the outside. *Human Resource Management, 47*(2), 275–294.

Murrell, A. J., & Zagenczyk, T. (2006). The gendered nature of role model status: An empirical study. *Career Development International, 11*(6), 560–578.

Nelson, R. R., & Winter, S. G. (1982). *An evolutionary theory of economic change.* Cambridge, MA: The Belknap Press.

Newton, D., & Simutin, M. (2014). Of age, sex, and money: Insights from corporate officer compensation on the wage inequality between genders. *Management Science, 61*(10), 2355–2375.

Nugent, J. S., Dinolfo, S., & Giscombe, K. (2013). Advancing women: A focus on strategic initiatives. In S. Vinnicombe, R. J. Burke, S. Blake-Beard, & L. L. Moore (Eds.), *Handbook of research on promoting women's careers* (pp. 391–404). Cheltenham: Edward Elgar.

O'Brien, S. P., & Janssen, K. N. (2005). Internships for women in higher education administration: Springboards for success? *Work, 24*(4), 353–361.

Pentland, B. T., Feldman, M. S., Becker, M. C., & Liu, P. (2012). Dynamics of organizational routines: A generative model. *Journal of Management Studies, 49*(8), 1484–1508.

Price, A. R., & Howard, D. M. (2012). Connect for success: Social leadership, mentorship, and the female healthcare executive. *Frontiers of Health Services Management, 28*(4), 33–38.

Pryce, P., & Sealy, R. (2013). Promoting women to MD in investment banking: Multi-level influences. *Gender in Management: An International Journal, 28*(8), 448–467.

Rothwell, W. J. (2011). Replacement planning: A starting point for succession planning and talent management. *International Journal of Training & Development, 15*(1), 87–99.

Sandberg, S., & Scovell, N. (2013). *Lean in: Women, work and the will to lead.* New York: Alfred A. Knopf.

Scott, K., & Brown, D. (2006). Female first, leader second? Gender bias in the encoding of leadership behavior. *Organizational Behavior and Human Decision Processes, 101*(2), 230–242.

Silva, C., & Carter, N. (2011, October 6). New research busts myths about the gender gap. *Harvard Business Review.* Retrieved from https://hbr.org/2011/10/new-research-busts-myths-about.

Silva, C., & Ibarra, H. (2012, November 14). Study: Women get fewer game-changing leadership roles. *Harvard Business Review.* Retrieved from https://hbr.org/2012/11/study-women-get-fewer-game-changing.html.

Turner, R. H. (1960). Sponsored and contest mobility and the school system. *American Sociological Review, 25*(6), 855–862.

Vilkas, M. (2013). The role of emergent networks in a planned change of organizational routines. *Transformations in Business and Economics, 13*(2), 188–206.

Wayne, S. J., Liden, R. C., Kraimer, M. L., & Graf, I. K. (1999). The role of human capital, motivation and supervisor sponsorship in predicting career success. *Journal of Organizational Behavior, 20*(5), 577–595.

7

MENTORING AS A MEANS TO ACHIEVE INCLUSION

A Focus on Practice and Research on Women in India

Nisha Nair and Neharika Vohra

While the concept of mentoring is not new and organizations have long reaped the benefits of informal mentoring (Weinberg & Lankau, 2011), there is growing interest in the mentoring function (Kram, 1985) with formal mentoring programs becoming more popular and abounding in organizations today. Formal mentoring is also viewed as a human resource development strategy (Hegstad, 1999), with organizations realizing the benefits of mentoring and investing in formal programs for employee development. Typically, a mentor is someone who uses his or her experience and influence to help with the advancement of the protégé. The term mentor is thought to describe a "relationship between a younger adult and an older more experienced adult, that helps the younger individual learn to navigate the adult world and the world of work" (Kram, 1985: 2). The key dimensions of mentoring are often discussed in terms of career and psychosocial mentoring functions (Kram, 1985). The former relates to career-related support, which enhances the protégé's advancement in the organization. Associated mentor functions include sponsorship, coaching, exposure, visibility, protection, and challenging assignments. Psychosocial support relates to the interpersonal level of interaction that influences an individual's identity, efficacy, and effectiveness in a professional role. The psychosocial functions include role modeling, acceptance and confirmation, couseling and friendship.

Research shows that protégés receive more career and psychosocial support if mentors and protégés have similar personalities (Menges, 2016), with career support linked to mentor and protégé similarity in the openness to experience trait, and psychosocial support linked to openness to experience and conscientiousness. Other studies also support this similarity-attraction paradigm with regard to gender (Weinberg & Lankau, 2011).

In this chapter, we will review the research on inclusion, draw connections for mentoring, and discuss implications of mentoring and inclusion for work organizations in India. While the topic of inclusion is broad, this chapter focuses on gender and draws a linkage to the need for additional research on the unique experience of women in India as an emerging segment within the global workforce.

Increasingly, the mentoring relationship is being conceptualized as a developmental network with mentoring emerging as a multiple relationship phenomenon rather than a dyadic relationship between mentor and mentee (Higgins & Kram, 2001; Srivastava, 2015). Studies have shown that formal mentoring relationships cutting across organizational boundaries in the form of inter-organizational formal mentoring programs provide important access to mentoring relationships, besides forging psychosocial support and developing social capital (Murrell, Blake-Beard, Porter, & Perkins-Williamson, 2008). From the point of view of the protégé, some (Horvath & Bradley, 2008) suggest that protégés have a preference for mentoring programs where they get to choose a mentor rather than have one assigned to them, and ones that highlight both career related and psychosocial functions. Protégés' internal locus of control has also been positively associated with the extent of career-related and psychosocial support reported by the protégé (Wang, Tomlinson, & Noe, 2010).

Mentoring has been linked to superior career outcomes for protégés such as more positive employee attitudes, as evidenced by meta-analytic research (Allen, Eby, Poteet, Lentz, & Lima, 2004). Access to mentoring has been associated with higher career satisfaction, higher commitment, lower turnover intention, increased personal learning, greater compensation, and more promotions for protégés (Allen, Eby, O'Brien, & Lentz, 2008; Allen et al., 2004; Blake-Beard, 1999; Dreher & Cox, 1996; Lankau & Scandura, 2002; Wanberg, Welsh, & Hezlett, 2003). Protégés' perceived psychological safety is also thought to mediate the relationship between formal mentoring and both affective commitment and turnover intention (Chen, Liao, & Wen, 2014). The act of providing mentoring has been associated with career success and positive work attitudes across occupational, professional, and organizational boundaries (Bozionelos, Bozionelos, Kostopoulos, & Polychroniou, 2011).

Outcomes of the mentoring process have been discussed (Hegstad & Wentling, 2005) in terms of the individual (psychosocial and career support), as well as desirable outcomes for the organization (employee motivation, leadership development, retention, commitment etc.). Supportive organizational cultures where mentoring is championed at the top level and where there is a culture of open communication are seen as more conducive to effective mentoring outcomes (Bally, 2007; Gibson, 2006).

There is some research that examines differential mentoring experiences based on gender and race (Blake-Beard, 1999; Dreher & Ash, 1990; Hu, Thomas, & Lance, 2008; Spalter-Roth, Shin, Mayorova, & White, 2013). Blake-Beard's research suggests that mentoring experiences and outcomes differ for Black and

White women. Access to mentoring, derived benefits, and outcomes of mentoring have been shown to differ for minority members when compared to majority members (Ragins, 1997). Factors such as stereotyping, perceptual differences in competence, and negative work group reactions and visibility, all restrict access to mentoring relationships for minority members. Diversity programs can help correct this imbalance and address issues of access to mentoring by including mentoring programs as part of diversity management and inclusion efforts in organizations (Kossek, Lobel, & Brown, 2006; Madera, 2013).

One of the areas which has received less attention is that of mentoring as a tool for facilitating inclusion (more so in the Indian context) where both formal mentoring and inclusion have yet to be fully integrated in organizational processes (Blake-Beard, 2015; Budhwar, 2001; Budhwar & Baruch, 2003; Mohapatra, 2012). Blake-Beard's (2015) research points to the particular opportunities that mentoring can offer to professional Indian women. The specific cultural context within India should be taken into account when examining diverse mentoring relationships.

Indian organizational culture has been characterized as high in power distance (House, Hanges, Javidan, Dorfman, & Gupta, 2004; Hofstede, 2011; Hofstede, Hofstede, & Minkov, 2010). Research has indicated that power distance orientation is a moderator of the mentoring relationship and perceived psychological safety, in that the relationship is stronger when protégés have low levels of power distance orientation (Chen et al., 2014). How mentoring could be used as an effective tool in Indian work settings which are largely patriarchal (Chakravarti, 1993), and women employees are perceived to have less power and prestige (Chakravarti, 1993; Kandiyoti, 1988) will be explored in this chapter. Specifically, we will review the research on inclusion, draw connections for mentoring, and discuss implications of mentoring and inclusion for work organizations in India.

Inclusion in Organizations

The focus of literature in organization studies has seen a shift from the language of "diversity" management to "inclusion" in more recent years (Hays-Thomas & Bendick, 2013). Diversity and inclusion are closely tied; however, the two concepts are distinct but interrelated. While diversity focuses primarily on the demographic make-up of groups and organizations, inclusion emphasizes encouraging participation and moving beyond merely appreciating diversity toward leveraging and integrating diversity into everyday work life (Roberson, 2006; Stevens, Plaut, & Sanchez-Burks, 2008). Inclusion focuses on employee involvement and ways to increase the participation of all employees and to leverage diversity effects for the benefit of the organization (Roberson, 2006).

It has been argued that if just 10 percent more employees feel included, the company would increase work attendance by almost one day per year per employee (Deloitte, 2012). A Catalyst report found that in India, employee perceptions of inclusion accounted for 43 percent of team citizenship behavior (Prime & Salib, 2014). The same Deloitte report found that when employees think their organization is committed to and supportive of diversity and they feel included, they report better business performance in terms of their ability to innovate, their responsiveness to changing customer needs, and their level of team collaboration (Deloitte, 2012). It has been found that those who feel included are more likely to experience greater self-worth and more likely to extend help to their co-workers and show initiative at work (Cottrill, Lopez, & Hoffman, 2014). Thus, the need for focusing on inclusion in addition to diversity is clearly important.

Roberson argues that inclusion refers to "the removal of obstacles to the full participation and contribution of employees in organizations" (2006: 217). Elsewhere, it is defined as "the extent to which employees believe their organizations engage in efforts to involve all employees in the mission and operation of the organization with respect to their individual talents" (Avery, McKay, Wilson, & Volpone, 2008: 6). A clear implication of all these definitions is that mentoring can serve as an important vehicle for providing access to information, removing obstacles, supporting fairness, and serving as a formal means of integrating minority members into the organization.

Underlying the notion of inclusion is an individual's need to belong to a larger social group, which in turn is related to employees' psychological well-being (Ferdman & Davidson, 2002). Feelings of inclusion or exclusion have been associated with self-esteem, anxiety, satisfaction/dissatisfaction, and motivation (Mor Barak, 2011). Being included signals to employees that they are important, valued, and trusted (Cottrill et al., 2014). Central to the notion of inclusion is the culture or climate of inclusion. A culture of inclusion is defined as existing when "people of all social identity groups have the opportunity to be present, to have their voices heard and appreciated, and to engage in core activities on behalf of the collective" (Wasserman, Gallegos, & Ferdman, 2008: 176). Similarly, a multicultural, inclusive organization is defined as "one in which the diversity of knowledge and perspectives that members of different groups bring to the organization has shaped its strategy, its work, its management and operating systems, and its core values and norms for success" (Holvino, Ferdman, & Merrill-Sands, 2004: 249). However, some argue that mentoring across diverse groups can actually make difference more salient, which suggests that understanding social or identity group dynamics is relevant to our current discussion.

Thus, in conceptualizing inclusiveness, some researchers draw on social identity theory, optimal distinctiveness theory, and the need for belongingness. According to social identity theory (Tajfel, 1982; Tajfel & Turner, 1986) one's self concept is derived from being members of specific social groups, especially those groups which have higher perceived social identities. As per the optimal distinctiveness theory (Brewer, 1991), individuals seek to be accepted by valued groups to optimize their need for belongingness and individuation (Pickett, Bonner, & Coleman, 2002; Shore, Randel, Chung, Dean, Ehrhart, & Singh, 2011). Therefore, inclusion may be facilitated when individuals feel a strong sense of acceptance and belonging through diverse mentoring relationships.

Inclusion has been identified as focusing on the psychological experience of feeling accepted and being treated as an insider in the workplace while maintaining one's uniqueness (Pelled, Ledford, & Mohrman, 1999; Shore et al., 2011). Focused on the need for belongingness, Lirio, Lee, Williams, Haugen, and Kossek define inclusion as "when individuals feel a sense of belonging and inclusive behaviors such as eliciting and valuing contributions from all employees are part of the daily life in the organization" (2008: 443). Focusing on recognizing and valuing the uniqueness of diverse individuals for fostering inclusion, Chavez (2008) calls it celebrating the "me" within the "we." A more widely accepted approach to viewing inclusion is offered by Shore et al., who define inclusion as "the degree to which an employee perceives that he or she is an esteemed member of the work group through experiencing treatment that satisfies his or her needs for belongingness and uniqueness" (Shore et al., 2011: 1265). They argue that individuals can vary in their experience of exclusion or inclusion depending on the degree of uniqueness and belongingness that employees experience. When both uniqueness and belongingness needs are met, the individual experiences inclusion. Therefore, mentoring relationships that are supportive of differences should facilitate individuals' experience of and an overall culture of inclusion.

On the other end of the inclusion spectrum is exclusion where individuals experience both low belongingness and low uniqueness. When there is high belongingness but low value in uniqueness, the state of assimilation exists. This is when the individual is treated as an insider in the work group only when they conform to organizational or dominant culture norms and downplay their uniqueness. On the other hand, where there is high value in uniqueness and low belongingness, the state of differentiation exists. Under this condition, the individual is not treated as an organizational insider but their unique characteristics are seen as valuable and required by the organization or work group, resulting in negative mentoring experiences similar to those described by Eby and her colleagues (Eby, McManus, Simon, & Russell, 2000).

Exclusion in Organizations

Mor Barak notes that:

> employee perception of inclusion–exclusion is conceptualized as a continuum of the degree to which individuals feel a part of critical organizational processes; these processes include access to information and

resources, connectedness to supervisor and co-workers and ability to participate in and influence the decision making process.

(Mor Barak, 2000: 52).

A social psychological perspective for understanding exclusion and inclusion has been offered by some authors (Abrams, Hogg, & Marques, 2005; Mor Barak, 2008). Prejudice, discrimination and exclusion are seen as psychological processes that influence the inclusion of employees (Mor Barak, 2008).

Offering a framework for understanding social inclusion and exclusion, Abrams et al. (2005) discuss the various psychological effects of exclusion, motives invoked by it, and potential responses and interventions to address them. The psychological effects may vary from a contraction of the self, threat to the self-concept, lowered self-esteem, anger, frustration, and emotional denial, to even cognitive impairment. These in turn may invoke motives of need to belong, need for positive self-concept, and the need for meaningfulness, validity, and distinctiveness. Reputation management or even avoidance of threat or discomfort may also occur. Responses to exclusion vary from attempting re-inclusion, finding alternative bases of inclusion or alternative sources for validation, redrawing boundaries or expressing hostility by way of prejudices. Withdrawing in the form of reducing contact with the source of exclusion or engaging in self-defeating behavior are also possible reactions. Either way, exclusion almost always carries negative psychological and behavioral outcomes for individuals, groups, and mentoring relationships. From visible manifest segregation and communicative practices that epitomize it, exclusion can also be in more abstract forms that are ideologically grounded and based on popular societal representations, which are harder to identify and manage (Abrams et al., 2005). At one level, exclusion can be transnational, based on geographical, religion, culture, nationality, or ethnic differences. At the societal level, this can manifest in the stigmatization of certain groups of people who don't subscribe to a particular norm, social class, or physical appearance. Exclusion could also happen at the institutional level, where basis for inclusion and exclusion get defined by different institutions or organizational boundaries (e.g., level, professional, education). The most common are the intergroup and intragroup levels where exclusion is directed at those outside the group prototype or even those within, who don't conform or who are not deemed legitimate members. Interpersonal and even intrapersonal exclusion exist, with interpersonal referring to the exclusionary cognitions and behaviors that exist between people, and intrapersonal referring to the cognitive and emotional frames of an individual that serve as a basis of exclusion. For example, a White person not having the necessary mental frames to think and feel like a person of color. Clearly whether at the transnational, societal, or interpersonal level, lack of inclusion poses significant obstacles and challenges for diverse mentoring relationships.

Mentoring and Inclusion

Mentoring can serve as an important area for developing inclusive workplaces through both formal and informal mechanisms. For example, there is evidence to suggest that mentoring of minority teachers has had an impact on the recruitment and retention of minority teachers (Holloway, 2002; Meyers & Smith, 1999). We argue that effective mentoring relationships can enable inclusiveness via facilitating belongingness, while fostering a sense of uniqueness and belongingness throughout the organization. We base our perspective on Shore et al.'s (2011) model of inclusiveness, conceptualized along the intersection between uniqueness and belongingness. When high belongingness and uniqueness are present, inclusion happens and the minority member feels cherished and accepted, and simultaneously celebrates his/her unique identity. When neither of the needs of uniqueness or belongingness is high, exclusion is the result. When only uniqueness is valued or emphasized, in that minority members are recognized or valued only for their minority status or demographic but do not feel integrated or accepted as an equal organizational member (low belongingness), then there is the risk of marginalization. On the other hand, when minority members are accepted and belongingness is high but comes at the cost of abandoning their uniqueness where minorities feel pressurized to assimilate

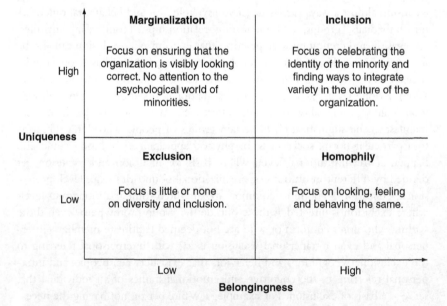

FIGURE 7.1 Inclusion Model*

Note

* Based on Shore et al.'s (2011) conceptualization of inclusion along the dimensions of belongingness and uniqueness.

and discard their unique identities in order to belong, it represents the fourth quadrant of homophily.

In drawing a connection between inclusion and mentoring, we adapt Shore's model to the specific context of diverse mentoring relationships. This revised model can provide critical insight into the research questions and implications for practice as we move across the intersection of belongingness and uniqueness. Relating this inclusion model to mentoring and also drawing on the acculturation work of Berry (2005), we explain the impact of these two dimensions on mentoring, as well as the organizational climate of inclusion. Thus, Figure 7.2 provides our revised model with the mentoring outcomes as a function of the intersection between fostering belongingness or maintaining uniqueness. Similar to the overall model, this intersection produces four different states of experience or outcomes for mentoring relationships. The adaptation of this model to the specific content of mentoring can also identify potential challenges, obstacles, and opportunities that may emerge within diverse mentoring relationships (see Figure 7.2).

When mentors offer psychosocial support by relating to the protégés at an interpersonal level, influencing their efficacy, and offering acceptance and confirmation, they are essentially extending opportunities for belongingness. On one end of the spectrum is protégé integration and inclusion, when the mentor

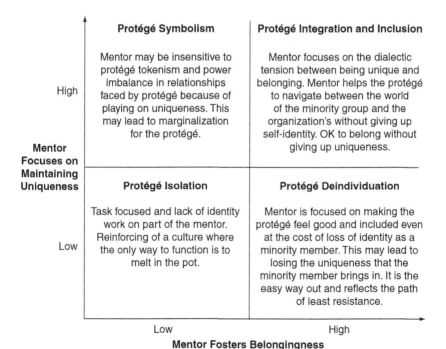

FIGURE 7.2 Inclusion Model Applied to Mentoring Relationships

focuses on both fostering belongingness and maintaining uniqueness for the protégé, representing effective or positive mentoring relationships. Effective psychosocial mentoring can result in feelings of affirmation and belongingness that do not take away from the protégé's unique identity or sense of self. On the other end of the spectrum is protégé isolation or exclusion, where the mentor does not focus on either fostering belongingness or addressing the uniqueness of the protégé. Such mentoring would be ineffective with minimal or no investment/engagement of the mentor with the protégé and lack of identity work on the part of the mentor.

When mentors focus exclusively on the uniqueness of minority protégés and do not invest enough on fostering belongingness, they encourage protégé symbolism. Mentors primarily focusing on the fact that the protégé is unique, helping him/her gain maximum advantage out of their uniqueness may in fact, encourage tokenism. Such a relationship does not draw any substantial benefits from the mentoring and the protégé is likely to feel marginalized. The final quadrant represents protégé deindividuation where the mentor excessively focuses on fostering belongingness for the protégé at the cost of his/her uniqueness. This is also a negative mentoring relationship characterized by in-group biases and closed networks that force the protégé to assimilate and subscribe to the world-view and identities imposed by the mentor to the detriment of the protégé's own self-worth. There is some research that points to dysfunctional mentoring relationships with potential for abuse (O'Neill & Sankowsky, 2001).

Translating the notion of "theoretical abuse" from the field of psychotherapy, O'Neill and Sankowsky (2001) focus on the misuse of influence with regard to interpretation of events and coloring the meaning making of the protégé in ways that are harmful for the protégé's self-worth. When a mentor imposes his/her own meaning-making needs at the expense of the protégé's interpretations or sense making, it results in protégé deindividuation (Figure 7.2). One way to address this problem is to focus beyond assimilation toward the inclusion of protégés. In other words, by encouraging simultaneous attention to the twin needs of belongingness and uniqueness and the development of voice among protégés, effective mentoring relationships can be nurtured to temper the potential for theoretical abuse in a mentoring relationship (Eby et al., 2000).

Mentoring and Inclusion within a Global Context: A Look at Women in India

The Indian context offers a complex and yet largely unexplored area for the examination of diversity and inclusion. India as a country is inherently diverse in terms of languages spoken, the religious affiliation of its people, their customs, traditions, art forms, and even variety of cuisines (Sorman, 2001). Some have argued that India is a country that handles cultural diversity well (Panda &

Gupta, 2004). Given the inherently diverse context of India, organizations in India have a challenge to manage this diversity and gender diversity is increasingly receiving more attention (Ali, Kulik, & Metz, 2011; Blake-Beard, 2015; Cooke & Saini, 2010; de Jonge, 2014; Haynes & Alagaraja, 2016). Even so, representation of women in work organizations in India has been far from promising. While the Indian constitution has provisions for the reservation of various under-represented minority groups in publicly funded organizations (Haynes & Alagaraja, 2016), and the Securities and Exchange Board of India (the regulatory authority for all publicly trading organizations) has called for the mandatory appointment of at least one woman corporate board member by the year 2015, many companies are still struggling to comply with this requirement (Shaw, 2015). With about 5 percent representation at the board level (Shaw, 2015), women in India account for about one-third of the workforce (Prime & Salib, 2014), filling less than 9 percent of leadership roles (Dubey, 2015). Organizations have much to do to further gender diversity in the Indian work context and with the increasing presence of multinational corporations in India and Indian firms going global (Cooke & Saini, 2010; Som, 2010), it is not just diversity in terms of representative numbers that has become an imperative, but also the inclusion of women. Blake-Beard (2015) points to the curious paradox that professional Indian women face, of navigating their professional careers in a changing economy and increasing participation of women in the workforce while still facing traditional conceptions of familial role expectations. In such a context, mentoring can offer huge opportunities to support women through their careers.

Studies on inclusion and mentoring are few in the Indian context. Various researchers (Baruch & Budhwar, 2006; Budhwar, 2001; Bhatnagar, 2007; Ramaswami & Dreher, 2010) have noted the lack of studies on mentoring in India. Mentoring as an interpersonal reciprocal relationship of guidance, counselling, advice, and feedback (Eby, Rhodes, & Allen, 2007) between a senior and more experienced personnel and the less experienced protégé tends to be somewhat less formal in the Indian context. While the lexicon of "inclusion" and "mentoring" are only beginning to enter the popular management discourse in the Indian context, informal practices geared toward them have been part of the pluralistic ethos and fabric of the society, and as Blake-Beard (2015) notes, the family too serves as an important mentor source in the collectivist cultural context of India.

For the most part, formal mentoring has received less attention among Indian organizations and managers, and mentoring with a focus on inclusion remains largely unexplored. There is some research (Ibarra, Carter, & Silva, 2010; Drexler, 2014) that indicates formal mentoring is far more beneficial than informal mentoring and that the benefits of mentoring differ for men and women. Mentoring in the form of executive coaching for grooming leaders is slowly catching up in India (Mohapatra, 2012; Pande, 2013). Vohra, Sharma, and Nair (2015) showed that those organizations who provided for mentoring of the members of minority groups also were better able to achieve inclusion in their oganizations.

Sensing the need for formal mentoring programs for professional women, dedicated organizations like BizDivas (BizDivas India), WIL Forum (Women in Leadership Economic Forum), and Women's Leadership Forum of Asia (WLFA) offer a variety of programs to mentor women. BizDivas (BizDivas India) offers formal mentoring programs for women, with a five-pronged strategy including: (1) dedicated mentors for six months; (2) panel of coaches providing coaching sessions if flagged by mentors; (3) webinars and learning series; (4) networking forums; and (5) building visibility by highlighting the achievements and success stories of mentors and protégés. To increase awareness, advocate mentoring, and help initiate new mentoring relationships and networks, BizDivas also organizes a "mentoring walk," initiated as a concept when Geraldine Laybourne, founder and former CEO of Oxygen media (the mother company of Nickelodeon) yielded to mentoring requests by asking young women to join her in her morning walk every morning. Inspired by the idea, a mentoring walk gathers together experienced women leaders and emerging women leaders to walk together, engage in discussions regarding their professional challenges and successes, and establish a mentoring relationship. It is expected that possibly long-lasting relationships develop with the first purposeful meeting. Protégés are urged to pay it forward and become mentors to young women leaders. Initiatives such as these are an important resource for the mentoring and inclusion of women and some researchers (e.g., Banerjee, 2015) even highlight the importance of mentoring for women in patriarchal societies such as that of India. Similar mentoring initiatives need to be extended to other forms of diversity such as social class or aspects of regional culture within India. Especially with regard to women, there is a call for cross–gender mentoring (Ghosh & Haynes, 2008) for women's career growth in Indian organizations, suggesting that for women in business a better way forward may be to focus on mentoring constellations involving numerous mentors (including men) rather than the traditional dyadic relationship between mentor and protégé.

While mentoring can serve as an important career management tool, it has been observed (Budhwar & Baruch, 2003) that in India, mentoring is not commonplace among tools and strategies for employee development. Some researchers (Blake-Beard, 2015; Ramaswami & Dreher, 2010) have noted that Indian views of mentoring and the experience of it likely differs from Western models and interpretation of mentoring. They suggest that while mentor roles and behaviors in India are conceptualized by research based on Western models, certain elements of the mentoring process and expectations are influenced by Indian cultural norms, specifically those of high power distance, collectivism, and paternalistic behavior expectations. For example, Srivastava and Jomon (2013) focused on formal and supervisory mentoring in an Indian manufacturing organization. They found that protégés expected mentoring relationships to help them cope with life and job challenges, and fulfill performance expectations with little differentiation between mentor and supervisor. Mentoring in India is frequently limited to newcomers and their socialization. In a separate study (Arora & Rangnekar, 2014), career mentoring was not found to be a significant predictor of career resilience among Indian managers, indicating that mentoring support is possibly less received, or alternatively, perceived less favorably among Indian managers once they have passed the initial stages of organizational socialization. Thus, several aspects of Indian culture should be explored in more detail.

It has also been shown (Ramaswami, Huang, & Dreher, 2014) that cultural values of power distance and the demographic of gender moderate the relationship between mentoring and outcomes of career attainment. In their research, Ramaswami et al. (2014) found that in hierarchical cultures, mentored women with high power distance report higher career returns, while women who display lower power distance (the opposite of the Indian culturally expected norms), reported lower career gains. The opposite pattern was also reported in the USA, where mentored women with low power distance reported higher career gains, and those with high power distance (deviating from the prevalent cultural norms), reported lower career returns. Clearly in both cases, deviating from strong cultural norms had a negative impact on the outcomes of mentoring relationships. The influence of the socio-cultural context in the mentoring dynamic is also highlighted by Srivastava and Jomon (2013) and Blake-Beard (2015). Thus, it appears that for reaping the benefits of inclusion, mentoring as a medium is likely to be beneficial, only if it works within the socio-cultural norms related to power dimensions.

Given the collectivistic characteristic of the Indian culture, there appears to be a greater emphasis on belongingness, which can produce both positive and negative outcomes. Patriarchal tendencies may fuel homophily (see Figure 7.1). Collectivism could imply that the belongingness dimension of inclusion is more central than the uniqueness dimension in the given cultural context, or alternatively, that there is greater opportunity for exclusion given that seeking uniqueness can run counter to the dominant cultural norms. For example, a woman who tends to stand out both because of her gender and her behavior (violating traditional Indian cultural norms) would be penalized and have negative mentoring experiences as a result. Effective training and sensitization of mentors and careful selection of mentors would be necessary to ensure that she does not suffer from in-group biases, tokenism, or power imbalances. On the other hand, a woman organizational member who has high belongingness needs and low uniqueness needs may end up behaving in a way that she gives low centrality to her identity as a woman and thus depriving the group or the organization of the benefit of her diverse background. Such a woman may not be excluded given that her behavior fits in with the cultural norms. Effective and culturally competent mentors can help show women the need to be more open about their unique perspectives and move mentoring experiences away from marginalization or isolation, and toward integration and inclusion especially within collectivist cultures.

A way to address the inclusion of diverse perspectives for women protégés within an Indian cultural context is for women to be mentored by diverse mentoring relationships (gender, culture, position, etc.), each serving a different purpose. For example, male mentors could open doors to traditional old boys' networks and help decode the culture for women, thereby allowing them to understand how they are being viewed and what can be done to lose neither their individualities nor their potential opportunities for success in the organization. Women mentors on the other hand, can offer role modeling with reduced power distance and provide for belongingness that fuels inclusion and satisfaction. Similarly, a person with a disability, may be best mentored by diverse mentors, such as a mentor who may also have a disability (helps in identification and developing belongingness) and someone without a disability (helps in developing perspective for both parties and building other shared identities while allowing for the maintenance of protégé's unique identity). The use of diverse mentoring relationships illustrated by these examples can help support Indian women as they navigate between the intersection of inclusion and belongingness.

Future Agenda for Inclusion and Mentoring

Achieving inclusion is beyond achieving the representative numbers. As noted by Macan Kandola, Meriac, and Merritt (2013), it involves interactions, belongingness, acceptance of unique identities, and support across both career and interpersonal dimensions. Diversity management must fundamentally address the way people deal with each other and the way leaders engage with all in the organization, including the role that leaders play in creating and sustaining effective mentoring relationships. At the interpersonal level, inclusion calls for respect and acceptance, empathy from the dominant groups, trust in the capability of the minority group, and providing access to information to persons belonging to minority groups (Daya, 2014; Hays-Thomas, Bowen, & Bourdreaux, 2012). Many of these interpersonal needs may be met by putting in place positive mentoring relationships between the members of the diverse groups that support high belongingness and foster uniqueness.

Inclusive environments are places where individuals of all backgrounds feel fairly treated, valued for who they are, and are also made part of important decision making. Attempts to create inclusive workplaces must consider individual differences, needs, and perceptions as well as focus on creating structures, systems, and processes that make people feel valued and treated equitably (Ferdman & Davidson, 2002). Employee resource groups (Derven, 2014), are essentially established networks (e.g., group mentoring) to promote a welcoming environment for minority or under-represented groups. Such employee resource groups offer a formal means of mentoring diverse employees that may play a unique role and fit especially within cultures that are group-orientated or collectivistic. This would suggest that traditional one-to-one mentoring used significantly within a US cultural environment may be limited in its ability to capture the full range of benefits for women in an Indian cultural context.

We argue that sensitivity to cultural context is critically important in achieving inclusion. Derven's (2014) research on best practices across six global companies indicates diversity and inclusion initiatives must be adapted to each region, requiring a multifaceted approach across the organization's policies and practices. Taking a Western-centric model for driving diversity and inclusion initiatives globally has been cautioned as a sure recipe for failure (Goodman, 2013). This notion is highlighted by emerging research on the unique experience of mentoring within an Indian cultural context.

Thus, there are several routes that future research on inclusion and mentoring could take. First is to move beyond examining the differing meanings of inclusion in cultural contexts besides the current dominant US cultural perspective. It would also mean exploring inclusion across other aspects of diversity and examining the specific strategies and practices that are liable to work in different cultural contexts toward inclusive mentoring. A specific area that warrants exploration is the culture specific and cross-cultural level of analysis for inclusion and mentoring studies. Since diversity management has also been linked to few undesirable outcomes (Chavez, 2008; Holvino, 2008; Nishii, 2013), and there is also potential for abuse of mentoring relationships (O'Neill & Sankowsky, 2001), future research could examine both conceptually and empirically what specific strategies and practices of mentoring and under what conditions the management of visible differences can in fact be counterproductive. Lastly, exploring the nature of re-categorization in multi-identity mentoring relationships may require different strategies for overcoming exclusion and ineffective mentoring relationships.

Another factor that warrants greater attention by future research is the role that leadership plays in creating and supporting inclusive mentoring within the workplace. One of the ways leaders can contribute to creating inclusive climates is through conscious mentoring of under-represented groups. The work of Shore et al. (2011) indicates that inclusive leadership and inclusive practices can be viewed as antecedents of a range of positive outcomes. By formally acknowledging the sources of differing employee identities and by instituting and championing diverse mentoring relationships for differing identity groups, leaders can send a strong signal of acknowledging and supporting differences. Leaders who wish to create inclusive cultures need to value the diversity of talents, experiences, and identities that employees bring while finding common ground (Prime & Salib, 2014), balancing both uniqueness and belongingness, and supporting inclusive mentoring that drives overall organizational effectiveness.

Ayman and Korabik (2010) argue that one of the ways that leaders contribute to being less inclusive is pretending that organizations are gender, racially, or culturally neutral. Some (Chorbot-Mason, Ruderman, & Nishii, 2013) even suggest that the failure of the leader to recognize that the gender, race, or cultural background of an individual is important, can negatively impact employees' feeling of uniqueness. Even if the individual feels a sense of belongingness, if his/her unique identity is not acknowledged or accepted, the employee is forced to assimilate to the dominant social identity rather than truly experience inclusion and integration in the work group. Inclusive leadership requires that leaders understand the social identities that exist throughout the organization and be self-aware of their impact in a relational context. Blindness to other's social identities can be damaging in a diverse work context. It is here that mentoring can play an important role through leader driven mentoring practices and behaviors. For example, mentoring relationships with senior level leaders through formal mentoring programs for leadership development are thought (Olson & Jackson, 2009) to influence the career movement of protégés from diverse backgrounds (in terms of gender, race, culture etc.) into higher level leadership positions.

Conclusion

Diversity is leveraged through inclusion, which requires employees to feel valued and connected within their organization. It calls for simultaneously recognizing differences in, while valuing uniqueness across, people throughout the organization. On their part, individuals have a need to belong, to be appreciated, to be treated fairly, and to be acknowledged from whatever source or basis their identity is derived. Arguably, when organizations invest in policies and practices that support diversity and inclusion, they stand to gain in economic, organizational, and relational terms, that all support overall effectiveness. Mentoring can play an important role in increasing inclusion, preventing exclusion, and reducing negative outcomes for individuals and the overall organization.

Our chapter focuses on the intersection between belongingness and uniqueness using a revised model as it applies to mentoring as a tool for an inclusive workplace. This perspective is applied to the unique cultural experience of women in India as an emerging workforce segment. The need for future research in this area is based on previous research (Prime & Salib, 2014), and is illustrated by data from the recent Catalyst survey in India. These participants did not report the uniqueness and belongingness dimensions as distinct elements of inclusion. It is therefore also worth exploring what meaning and interpretation, diversity and inclusion hold in differing cultural contexts of work such as that of India, where multiple identities jostle with each other for relevance. With the myriad identities that abound in a country that is as diverse such as India, do workers here have a different notion of diversity and inclusion? How do these different notions impact on mentoring relationships and their outcomes? What are appropriate mentoring approaches and strategies that are both effective and culturally sensitive? When can mentoring be counter-productive or dysfunctional in a particular cultural context? What role do individual differences play in perceptions of inclusion and how do leader behaviors influence inclusion and mentoring in a culturally sensitive manner? What specific leader behaviors are required to foster inclusion in other cultural contexts? Lastly, how can mentoring inform and shape the practice of inclusion in the Indian context? These are just some of the questions that bear further exploration by future research in this important area of study.

References

Abrams, D., Hogg, M. A., & Marques, J. M. (2005). A social psychological framework for understanding social inclusion and exclusion. In D. Abrams, M. A. Hogg, & J. M. Marques, *The social psychology of inclusion and exclusion* (pp. 1–24). New York: Psychology Press.

Abrams, D., Hogg, M. A., & Marques, J. M. (Eds.) (2005). *The social psychology of inclusion and exclusion*. New York: Psychology Press.

Ali, M., Kulik, C. T., & Metz, I. (2011). The gender diversity-performance relationship in services and manufacturing organizations. *The International Journal of Human Resource Management, 22*(7), 1464–1485.

Allen, T. D., Eby, L. T., O'Brien, K. E., & Lentz, E. (2008). The state of mentoring research: A qualitative review of current research methods and future research implications. *Journal of Vocational Behavior, 72,* 269–283.

Allen, T. D., Eby, L. T., Poteet, M. L., Lentz, E., & Lima, L. (2004). Career benefits associated with mentoring for proteges: A meta-analysis. *Journal of Applied Psychology, 89*(1), 127–136.

Arora, R., & Rangnekar, S. (2014). Workplace mentoring and career resilience: An empirical test. *The Psychologist-Manager Journal, 17*(3), 205–220.

Avery, D. R., McKay, P. K., Wilson, D. C., & Volpone, S. (2008). Attenuating the effect of seniority on intent to remain: The role of perceived inclusivess. *Academy of Management Conference*, Anaheim.

Ayman, R., & Korabik, K. (2010). Leadership: Why gender and culture matter. *American Psychologist, 65*(3), 157–170.

Bally, M. G. (2007). The role of nursing leadership in creating a mentoring culture in acute care environments. *Nursing Economics, 25*(3), 143–148.

Banerjee, S. (2015, April). *Women and the Business of Leadership.* Retrieved October 16, 2015, from *The Leadership Review*: http://theleadershipreview.org/column/women-and-the-business-of-leadership/.

Baruch, Y., & Budhwar, P. S. (2006). A comparative study of career practices for management staff in Britain and India. *International Business Review, 15*(1), 84–101.

Berry, J. W. (2005). Acculturation: Living successfully in two cultures. *International Journal of Intercultural Relations, 29,* 697–712.

Bhatnagar, J. (2007). Talent management strategy of employee engagement in Indian ITES employees: Key to retention. *Employee Relations, 29*(6), 640–663.

BizDivas India. (n.d.). Retrieved October 16, 2015, from BizDivas: http://mentoring.bizdivas.in/.

Blake-Beard, S. (2015). Confronting Paradox: Exploring mentoring relationships as a catalyst for understanding the strength and resilience of professional Indian women. In P. Kumar (Ed.), *Unveiling women's leadership: Identity and meaning of leadership in India* (pp. 25–43). London: Palgrave Macmillan.

Blake-Beard, S. D. (1999). The costs of living as an outsider within: An analysis of mentoring relationships and career success of Black and White women in the corporate sector. *Journal of Career Development, 26*(1), 21–36.

Bozionelos, N., Bozionelos, G., Kostopoulos, K., & Polychroniou, P. (2011). How providing mentoring relates to career success and organizational commitment: A study in the general managerial population. *Career Development International, 16*(5), 446–468.

Brewer, M. B. (1991). The social self: On being the same and different at the same time. *Personality and Social Psychology Bulletin, 17,* 475–482.

Budhwar, P. (2001). Employment relations in India. *Employee Relations, 25*(2), 132–148.

Budhwar, P., & Baruch, Y. (2003). Career management practices in India: An empirical study. *International Journal of Manpower, 24*(6), 699–719.

Chakravarti, U. (1993). Conceptualising brahmanical patriarchy in early India: Gender, caste, class and state. *Economic and Political Weekly, 28*(14), 579–585.

Chavez, C. I. (2008). Beyond diversity training: A social infusion for cultural inclusion. *Human Resource Management, 47*(2), 331–350.

Chen, C., Liao, J., & Wen, P. (2014). Why does formal mentoring matter? The mediating role of psychological safety and the moderating role of power distance orientation in the Chinese context. *International Journal of Human Resource Management, 25*(8), 1112–1130.

Chorbot-Mason, D., Ruderman, N. M., & Nishii, H. L. (2013). Leadership in a diverse workplace. In M. Q. Roberson (Ed.), *The Oxford Handbook of Diversity and Work* (pp. 315–340). New York: Oxford University Press.

Cooke, F. L., & Saini, D. S. (2010). Diversity management in India: A study of organizations in different ownership forms and industrial sectors. *Human Resource Management, 49*(3), 477–500.

Cottrill, K., Lopez, P. D., & Hoffman, C. C. (2014). How authentic leadership and inclusion benefit organizations. *Equality, Diversity & Inclusion, 33*(3), 275–292.

Daya, P. (2014). Diversity and inclusion in an emerging market context. *Equality, Diversity & Inclusion, 33*(3), 293–308.

de Jonge, A. (2014). The glass ceiling that refuses to break: Women directors on the boards of listed firms in China and India. *Women's Studies International Forum, 47* (Special Issue on Gender, Mobility and Social Change), 326–338.

Deloitte (2012). *Waiter, is that inclusion in my soup? A new recipe to improve business performance.* Australia: Deloitte Research Report.

Derven, M. (2014). Diversity and inclusion by design: best practices from six global companies. *Industrial & Commercial Training, 46*(2), 84–91.

Dreher, G. F., & Ash, R. A. (1990). A comparative study of mentoring among men and women in managerial, professional, and technical positions. *Journal of Applied Psychology, 75*(5), 539–546.

Dreher, G. F., & Cox, T. H. (1996). Race, gender, and opportunity: A study of compensation attainment and the establishment of mentoring relationships. *Journal of Applied Psychology, 81*(3), 297–308.

Drexler, P. (2014, March 4). *Can Women Succeed Without A Mentor? Forbes.* Retrieved October 16, 2015, from www.forbes.com/sites/peggydrexler/2014/03/04/can-women-succeed-without-a-mentor/.

Dubey, J. (2015). India Inc takes baby steps to break the glass ceiling. *Business Today.*

Eby, L. T., McManus, S., Simon, S. A., & Russell, J. E. A. (2000). An examination of negative mentoring experiences from the protégé's perspective. *Journal of Vocational Behavior, 57,* 1–21.

Eby, L. T., Rhodes, J., & Allen, T. D. (2007). Definition and evolution of mentoring. In T. D. Allen, & L. Eby (Eds.), *The Blackwell handbook of mentoring: A multiple perspective approach* (pp. 7–20). Malden, MA: Blackwell.

Ferdman, B. M., & Davidson, M. N. (2002). A matter of difference: inclusion: What can I and my organization do about it? *The Industrial-Organizational Psychologist, 39*(4), 80–85.

Ghosh, R., & Haynes, R. K. (2008). *Cross gender mentoring in the era of globalization: Implications for mentoring the organizational women of India.* Panama: Academy of Human Resource Development International Research Conference in the Americas.

Gibson, K. S. (2006). Mentoring of women faculty: The role of organizational politics and culture. *Innovative Higher Education, 31*(1), 63–79.

Goodman, N. R. (2013). Taking diversity and inclusion initiatives global. *Industrial & Commercial Training, 45*(3), 180–183.

Haynes, R., & Alagaraja, M. (2016). On the discourse of affirmative action and reservation in the United States and India: Clarifying HRDs role in fostering global diversity. *Advances in Developing Human Resources, 18*(1), 69–87.

Hays-Thomas, R., & Bendick, M. (2013). Professionalizing diversity and inclusion practice: Should voluntary standards be the chicken or the egg? *Industrial & Organizational Psychology, 6*(3), 193–205.

Hays-Thomas, R., Bowen, A., & Bourdreaux, M. (2012). Skills for diversity and inclusion in organizations: A review and preliminary investigation. *The Psychologist-Manager Journal, 15*(2), 128–141.

Hegstad, C. D. (1999). Formal mentoring as a strategy for human resource development: A review of research. *Human Resource Development Quarterly, 10*(4), 383–390.

Hegstad, C. D., & Wentling, R. M. (2005). Organizational antecedents and moderators that impact on the effectiveness of exemplary formal mentoring programs in Fortune 500 companies in the United States. *Human Resource Development International, 8*(4), 467–487.

Higgins, M. C., & Kram, K. E. (2001). Reconceptualizing mentoring at work: A developmental network perspective. *Academy of Management Review, 26*(2), 264–288.

Hofstede, G. (2011). Dimensionalizing cultures: The Hofstede model in context. *Online Readings in Psychology and Culture, 2*(1). Retrieved from http://dx.doi.org/10.9707/2307-0919.1014.

Hofstede, G., Hofstede, G. H., & Minkov, M. (2010). *Cultures and organizations: Software of the mind: Intercultural Cooperation and Its Importance for Survival* (3rd ed.). Maidenhead: McGraw-Hill.

Holloway, J. H. (2002). Mentoring for diversity. *Redesigning Professional Development, 59*(6), 88–89.

Holvino, E. (2008). Intersections: The simultaneity of race, gender and class in organization studies. *Gender, Work & Organization, 17*(3), 248–277.

Holvino, E., Ferdman, B. M., & Merrill-Sands, D. (2004). Creating and sustaining diversity and inclusion in organizations: Strategies and approaches. In M. S. Stockdale, & F. J. Crosby (Eds.), *The psychology and management of workplace diversity* (pp. 245–276). Malden, MA: Blackwell.

Horvath, M. W., & Bradley, J. L. (2008). The effect of formal mentoring program characteristics on organizational attraction. *Human Resource Development Quarterly, 19*(4), 323–349.

House, R. J., Hanges, P. J., Javidan, M., Dorfman, P. W., & Gupta, V. (Eds.) (2004). *Culture, Leadership and Organizations: The GLOBE study of 62 societies.* Thousand Oaks, CA: Sage Publications.

Hu, C., Thomas, K. M., & Lance, C. E. (2008). Intentions to initiate mentoring relationships: Understanding the impact of race, proactivity, feelings of deprivation, and relationship roles. *Journal of Social Psychology, 148*(6), 727–744.

Ibarra, H., Carter, N. M., & Silva, C. (2010, September). Why men still get more promotions than women. *Harvard Business Review, 88*(9), 80–85.

Kandiyoti, D. (1988). Bargaining with patriarchy. *Gender & Society, 2*(3), 274–290.

Kanungo, A. (2013). Social exclusion of women in India—A step towards social inclusion of women in mining industry. *International Research Journal for Social Science and Corporate Excellence.*

Kossek, E. E., Lobel, S., & Brown, J. (2006). Human resource strategies to manage workforce diversity. In A. M. Konrad, P. Prasad, & J. K. Pringle (Eds.), *Handbook of workplace diversity* (pp. 53–74). London: Sage.

Kram, K. E. (1985). *Mentoring at work: Developmental relationships in organizational life.* Glenview, IL: Scott, Foresman.

Lankau, M. J., & Scandura, T. A. (2002). An investigation of personal learning in mentoring relationships: Content, antecedents, and consequences. *Academy of Management Journal, 45*(4), 779–790.

Lirio, P., Lee, M. D., Williams, M. L., Haugen, L. K., & Kossek, E. E. (2008). The inclusion challenge with reduced-load professionals: The role of the manager. *Human Resource Management, 47,* 443–461.

Macan, T., Kandola, B., Meriac, J., & Merritt, S. (2013). Learning from others: Expanding diversity and inclusion across our borders. *Industrial & Organizational Psychology, 6*(3), 233–236.

Madera, J. M. (2013). Best practices in diversity management in customer service organizations: An investigation of top companies cited by Diversity Inc. *Cornell Hospitality Quarterly, 54*(2), 124–135.

Menges, C. (2016). Toward improving the effectiveness of formal mentoring programs. *Group & Organization Management, 41*(1), 98–129.

Meyers, H., & Smith, S. (1999). Coming home—Mentoring new teachers: A school-university partnership to support the development of teachers from diverse ethnic backgrounds. *Peabody Journal of Education, 74*(2), 75–89.

Mohapatra, P. K. (2012). Don't forget the corner office! *Human Capital, 16*(1), 66–70.

Mor Barak, M. E. (2000). Beyond affirmative action: Toward a model of diversity and organizational inclusion. *Administration in Social Work, 23*(3/4), 47–68.

Mor Barak, M. E. (2008). Social psychological perspectives of workforce diversity and inclusion in national and global contexts. In R. Patti (Ed.), *Handbook of human services management* (pp. 239–254). Thousand Oaks, CA: Sage Publications.

Mor Barak, M. E. (2011). *Managing diversity: Toward a globally inclusive workplace.* Thousand Oaks, CA: Sage Publications.

Murrell, A. J., Blake-Beard, S., Porter, J. D., & Perkins-Williamson, A. (2008). Interorganizational formal mentoring: Breaking the concrete ceiling sometimes requires support from the outside. *Human Resource Management, 47*(2), 275–294.

Nishii, L. H. (2013). The benefits of climate for inclusion for gender-diverse groups. *Academy of Management Journal, 56*(6), 1754–1774.

Olson, D. A., & Jackson, D. (2009). Expanding leadership diversity through formal mentoring programs. *Journal of Leadership Studies, 3*(1), 47–60.

O'Neill, R. M., & Sankowsky, D. (2001). The Caligula Phenomenon: Mentoring relationships and theoretical abuse. *Journal of Management Inquiry, 10*(3), 206–216.

Panda, A., & Gupta, R. K. (2004). Mapping cultural diversity within India: A meta-analysis of some recent studies. *Global Business Review, 5*(1), 27–49.

Pande, S. (2013, October 13). A girl's best workplace friend. *Business Today India.* Retrieved October 16, 2015, from www.businesstoday.in/magazine/careers/career-news-mentor-for-women-employees-at-workplace/story/198805.html.

Pelled, L. H., Ledford, G. E., & Mohrman, S. A. (1999). Demographic dissimilarity and workplace inclusion. *Journal of Management Studies, 36*(7), 1013–1031.

Pickett, C. L., Bonner, B., & Coleman, J. M. (2002). Motivated self-stereotyping: Heightened assimilation and differentiation needs result in increased levels of positive and negative self-stereotyping. *Journal of Personality and Social Psychology, 82*(4), 543–562.

Prime, J., & Salib, E. R. (2014). *Inclusive leadership: The view from six countries.* New York: Catalyst.

Ragins, B. R. (1997). Diversified mentoring relationships in organizations: A power perspective. *Academy of Management Review, 22*(2), 482–521.

Ramaswami, A., & Dreher, G. F. (2010). Dynamics of mentoring relationships in India: A qualitative exploratory study. *Human Resource Management, 49*(3), 501–530.

Ramaswami, A., Huang, J. C., & Dreher, G. (2014). Interaction of gender, mentoring, and power distance on career attainment: A cross-cultural comparison. *Human Relations, 67*(2), 153–173.

Roberson, Q. M. (2006). Disentangling the meanings of diversity and inclusion in organizations. *Group & Organization Management, 31*, 212–236.

Shaw, K. M. (2015, April 6). Women on boards: Why India Inc. needs the "diversity edge." *DNA.*

Shore, L. M., Randel, A. E., Chung, B. G., Dean, M. A., Ehrhart, K. H., & Singh, G. (2011). Inclusion and diversity in work groups: A review and model for future research. *Journal of Management, 37*(4), 1262–1289.

Som, A. (2010). Emerging human resource practices at Aditya Birla Group. *Human Resource Management, 49*(3), 549–566.

Sorman, G. (2001). *The genius of India.* New Delhi: Macmillan India.

Spalter-Roth, R., Shin, J. H., Mayorova, O. V., & White, P. E. (2013). The impact of cross-race mentoring for "ideal" PhD careers in sociology. *Sociological Spectrum, 33*(6), 484–509.

Sreenath, K. C. (n.d.). *Breaking barriers: Towards inclusion.* Retrieved from www.equip123.net/docs/E1-REACHInclusion.pdf.

Srivastava, S. B. (2015). Network intervention: Assessing the effects of formal mentoring on workplace networks. *Social Forces, 94*(1), 427–452.

Srivastava, S., & Jomon, M. G. (2013). Outcome linkage in formal and supervisory mentoring in a business organization. *Indian Journal of Industrial Relations, 49*(1), 82–96.

Stevens, F. G., Plaut, V. C., & Sanchez-Burks, J. (2008). Unlocking the benefits of diversity: All-inclusive multiculturalism and positive organizational change. *Journal of Applied Behavioral Science, 44*(1), 116–133.

Tajfel, H. (1982). *Social identity and intergroup relations.* Cambridge: Cambridge University Press.

Tajfel, H., & Turner, J. C. (1986). The social identity theory of intergroup behavior. In S. Worchel, & L. W. Austin (Eds.), *Psychology of intergroup relations*. Chicago, IL: Nelson-Hall.

Vohra, N., Sharma, S., & Nair, N. (2015, November). *Diversity and inclusion: Insights from India*. Paper presented at the Sustainable HRM and Employee Well-Being: An International Research Symposium, Sydney, Australia.

Wanberg, C. R., Welsh, E. T., & Hezlett, S. A. (2003). Mentoring research: A review and dynamic process model. In G. R. Ferris, & J. J. Martocchio (Eds.), *Research in personnel and human recourses management*, Vol. 22 (pp. 39–124). Oxford: Elsevier.

Wang, S., Tomlinson, E. C., & Noe, R. A. (2010). The role of mentor trust and protege internal locus of control in formal mentoring relationships. *Journal of Applied Psychology, 95*(2), 358–367.

Wasserman, I. C., Gallegos, P. V., & Ferdman, B. M. (2008). Dancing with resistance: Leadership challenges in fostering a culture of inclusion. In K. M. Thomas (Ed.), *Diversity resistance in organizations* (pp. 175–200). New York: Taylor & Francis Group.

Weinberg, F. J., & Lankau, M. J. (2011). Formal mentoring programs: A mentor-centric and longitudinal analysis. *Journal of Management, 37*(6), 1527–1557.

WLFA. (n.d.). Women Leadership Forum of Asia. Retrieved October 16, 2015, from http://wlfa.in/.

Women in Leadership Economic Forum. (n.d.). Retrieved October 16, 2015, from www.wilforum.com/.

8

CREATING EFFECTIVE FORMAL MENTORING PROGRAMS FOR WOMEN OF COLOR

Katherine Giscombe

> *The assignments and the sponsorship and the buzz around people who are considered brilliant and so forth. All of those sorts of factors don't seem to come together for women of color here the way they do for other groups.*
>
> Bagati (2009)

Women of color in the private sector have experienced greater career progress over the years. For example, more have mentors than in prior years and they see less evidence of overtly biased workplaces (Giscombe, 2012). Yet, women of color (defined here as women in the USA who self-identify as Black, Hispanic, Asian, or Native American; and in Canada as those who self-identify as indigenous, Black, East Asian, Filipino, Latin American, Middle Eastern, South Asian, Southeast Asian, and West Indian) continue to grapple with workplace cultures that are not fully inclusive. While some research has identified attitudinal similarity as more important than demographic similarity in forging positive or strong mentor–protégé bonds (Brown, Zablah, & Bellenger, 2008), most research supports the "like preferring like" dynamic in workplace cultures (McPherson, Smith-Lovin, & Cook, 2001). This dynamic refers to those who look and sound like the dominant culture (in US- and Canadian-based organizations typically represented by White men) having a relatively uncomplicated time establishing informal mentoring or sponsorship relationships (Bagati, 2008). While this body of research analyzed the satisfaction with the mentor–protégé relationship, the work did not look at the initial *formation* of the relationship. How mentor–mentee relationships are formed can shape factors critical for the nature of these interactions such as expectations, perceptions of fit, and overall level of engagement. This issue is (or should be) of concern not just to the women who are overlooked, but also to business organizations that are struggling to effectively manage their talent in an increasingly competitive global economy. Being included in the formation process also has benefits. For example, recent research indicates that when co-workers feel included by their manager—such that they feel a sense of both uniqueness and belongingness in the work team—the result is greater innovation and satisfaction (Prime & Salib, 2014).

In this chapter, I address how formal mentoring programs can be used as an entry point for women of color to establish developmental relationships that will become more beneficial over time both for them and for the organization. I stress the fluidity and dynamism of such relationships and provide strategies for formal mentoring programs to be effective for women of color in the long term. I include examples of mentoring practices that address unique challenges for women of color and other people of color.

The practices included in this chapter come from Catalyst's work with Diversity & Inclusion (D&I) practitioners. Catalyst is the leading non-profit organization with a mission to expand opportunities for women and business. In addition to Research and Consulting, the organization has instituted recognition programs that include the Catalyst Award. The Catalyst Award for a D&I program is given after stringent vetting, including on-site assessment of the program's business alignment, accountability, and impact.

This chapter will also touch on implications for formal mentoring programs for marginalized groups in other countries.

A Look at Mentorship vs. Sponsorship

While some theorists position sponsorship as an activity distinct from mentoring (e.g., Ibarra, Carter, & Silva, 2010; Hewlett, 2013), sponsorship was initially conceived as one facet of mentoring (Kram, 1985). This line of thought is continued into the current day by several mentoring theorists. While specific definitions of mentoring do vary, mentoring support is often classified into two categories: psychosocial functions and career functions (which includes sponsorship) (Haggard, Dougherty, Turban, & Wilbanks, 2011).

By contrast, a sponsor is defined as someone at a high level within an organization who has strong influence over decision-making as it relates to employees. Sponsors, at the outset of sponsoring relationships, assist employees in getting visibility for assignments or assist them in getting specific promotions or positions. Sponsors introduce their protégés to their network, expose them to influential others, and advocate for them (Foust-Cummings, Dinolfo, & Kohler, 2011).

Keeping sponsorship within the mentoring domain is particularly relevant for women of color, as well as for others from "outsider" groups. While informal relationships with mentors and sponsors can be quite powerful and have been found in some research to be more effective than formalized relationships

(Underhill, 2006), as noted above, women of color may not have the same access to such informal relationships. Formalized programs then become a critical avenue for their development. However, formal *sponsorship* programs are relatively rare and in Catalyst's experience, we find that organizations set stringent criteria for protégés to have access to these programs, such as prior identification as employees regarded as "high potentials." Thus, women of color are more likely to be excluded at the outset from such formal programs. By contrast, entry into general mentoring programs is typically more open.

As with any relationship, mentoring is not static but is dynamic and can change over time. Those who start out as mentors providing primarily psychosocial support may be able to transition at a later point to provide career support, perhaps as sponsors. Empirical research has shown that mentors of minority executives often became powerful sponsors later in the minority executives' careers, even recruiting them repeatedly to new positions (Thomas, 2001). One final reason to keep sponsorship within the mentoring framework is that mentoring programs represent a typical "entry" by organizations into the sphere of formal diversity and inclusion programs. We have seen this in Catalyst consulting engagements—particularly for clients who are fairly new to the diversity and inclusion space.

Sponsorship can be a normally occurring outgrowth of mentoring relationships and one that can become more accessible to out-groups, such as women of color, if the capacity for the transition from mentoring to sponsorship is supported by formal mentoring efforts. In addition, if the program can address both challenges for women of color and challenges in developing the mentor–protégé relationship, then this "sponsorship-type" of mentoring relationship should prove to be mutually beneficial. This chapter examines the important role that formal mentoring programs play for women of color, using the original framework of mentoring functions as a way to capture these diverse and dynamic relationships.

Diverse Mentorship Experiences for Women of Color

Prior research and practice consistently reveal that women of color tend to lag behind White women as beneficiaries of diversity and inclusion programs. For example, White women have indicated significantly higher levels of satisfaction with formalized mentoring as part of diversity and inclusion programs as compared with the experiences for women of color. Over one-third of women of color believe that diversity and inclusion programs fall short in addressing subtle gender or racial bias (Giscombe, 2007b; Bagati, 2009).

Over time, the number of women of color with mentors has grown. In the late 1990s, only one-third of women of color reported having a mentor. With growth in the number of formal mentoring programs, more women of color are being mentored—up to one half by 2009. However, women of color are much more likely than White women to have mentors that lack power. In a Catalyst study, 62 percent of women of color with mentors cited "lack of an influential mentor or sponsor" as a barrier to advancement in comparison with 39 percent of White women (Bagati, 2009). This is a crucial gap, given that powerful mentors can act as sponsors by influencing decision-making for key positions and providing coaching for stretch assignments as preparation for moving into senior roles and responsibilities.

Having a powerful mentor who actively shares his/her power with the mentee should help the mentee in turn become more powerful. As Ragins noted in her influential work on mentorship and power:

> Mentoring is intricately tied to the protégé's development of resources for power within and between organizations.... Mentors may help their protégés recognize the importance of developing power resources within and between organizations, and can provide training in political skills and influence strategies. By providing challenging assignments and placing protégés in visible positions, mentors can help protégés develop expert power and obtain visibility within and outside organizational boundaries ... (M)entors provide "reflected power" to their protégés; the mentor's organizational influence augments the protégé's influence, and the mentors' power allows them to provide resources for their protégés and buffer their protégés from adverse organizational forces.
>
> (Ragins 1997: 487–488)

Similarly, Catalyst research found that women of color with influential mentors are more likely than those with non-influential mentors to experience the workplace in advantageous ways (e.g., greater satisfaction with career advancement), and the organization benefits as well (lower intent to leave and higher organizational commitment). However, women of color with influential mentors still lag behind their White women counterparts (those with influential mentors) on a number of dimensions (Giscombe, 2012) including:

- Satisfaction overall with the mentoring relationship
- Trust and mutual understanding within the mentoring relationship
- Help with navigating organizational politics
- Recommendations for assignments that increase contact with higher level managers

Thus, the need to have formal mentoring programs that fill these important gaps for women of color remains as a critical need. Next, I outline several key issues that should be taken into account in addressing this mentoring gap as organizations prepare diverse leaders of the future.

The Need for Assessment

Organizations should consider collecting targeted employee survey data to examine any unique needs of women of color. These needs may be indicated by: low engagement or commitment; low satisfaction with career advancement potential; a perceived lack of access to senior executives, mentors, or sponsors; perceptions of inequity in opportunities or lack of access to key assignments; and, low satisfaction with direct managers. Similarly, examination of employee data could also reveal negative outcomes for women of color, such as disproportionately high turnover or lack of career mobility. Thus, organizations may want to tailor existing programs or create new ones for women of color to address issues that are revealed from these targeted assessments.

When considering formalized mentoring in a global context, diversity and inclusion practitioners should be cognizant that there will be differences based on the cultural settings that may be revealed from assessments that come from sources external to the organization. For example, within Catalyst's Consulting Services engagements, we often find that expatriates from dominant national cultures and/or where multinational organizations are headquartered (e.g., USA or UK) are placed in positions of leadership in regional offices in countries dominated by people of color (e.g., Asia or Africa), rather than encouraging or allowing regional talent to rise to the top of their offices. Given that women in these countries are typically less empowered than their male colleagues, formalized mentoring that seeks to break down national silos along with gender and ethnicity could benefit from diverse expatriate utilization.

If there is an existing mentoring program in place, participant feedback should be gathered indicating how well current mentoring programs meet the needs of women of color. For example, it would be useful to know how satisfied women of color are with the mentoring program based on their rating of aspects of the program or informal comments using both quantitative and qualitative metrics. This may include how well program goals and individual outcomes have been met for women of color in areas such as engagement, commitment to organization, turnover rate, promotion rate, assignment to high visibility projects, and performance reviews. Feedback could be sought from assigned mentors as well, which is rarely done as part of the assessment of formal mentoring programs.

While these broad assessments can be useful, there is also a need to get even more detailed data in assessing how formal mentoring programs work to equalize outcomes for diverse employee groups. Often the traditional assessments for the effectiveness of mentoring programs for women of color participants are incomplete. Those who oversee mentoring programs need to explore the dynamics of how individuals in positions of power are willing or unwilling to engage in the sharing of this power or, as Burt (1998) describes it, sharing of social capital for women employees.

For example, one area for more detailed assessment is how equally mentees are provided with knowledge of organizational politics, informal rules regarding organizational culture, and access to senior individuals with influence as part of their mentoring relationships. These, and other more specific metrics to assess the needs for women of color, are necessary for designing more effective formal mentoring programs within organizations.

Thoughts on Program Design

Once a comprehensive assessment has been done, attention can turn to program design. Undergirding formal mentoring programs involving women of color are the needs to address unconscious and other forms of bias while building trust within the mentor–mentee relationship. Effective program design should also proactively seek to address potential barriers that have been identified by the initial assessment. This aspect would also include data provided by general research showing that women of color still experience lack of high visibility assignments, lack of influential mentors, and lack of access to influential networks. These barriers may be structural or motivated by individual unconscious bias that often underlies discriminatory behavior (Devine, Plant, Amodio, Harmon-Jones, & Vance, 2002). To be able to address, or eventually dismantle, these biases, aspects of awareness and cultural competence should be included as part of program design and mentor training. Unconscious bias over time can become more covert and subtle, and more difficult to recognize; thus, the need for ongoing awareness and training is important (Thomas & Plaut, 2008). For example, women of color are subject to intense scrutiny, have failures attributed to overall incompetence, and may face stereotyped judgments that can damage professional reputation and performance evaluations (Giscombe, 2015). By incorporating training for mentors, awareness of these biases can be raised and the potential negative impact can be reduced.

Thus, developmental programs for women of color—and their mentors— need to drill down and address any biased behavior or attitudes that may affect the relationship. A critical step for program design is to include awareness of any implicit biases that may exist on the part of the mentor or mentee that could reduce effectiveness and trust, especially during the early stages of relationship cultivation.

While unconscious bias training should be part of program design, awareness of other types of biases should also be included. For example, types of covert bias include "social distancing" or avoidance, application of double standards (e.g., giving those from majority groups the benefit of the doubt in performance evaluation), and the withholding of full support (Utsey, Ponterotto, & Porter, 2008; Bobo, Kluegel, & Smith, 1997). Empirical research shows that mentors of women of color in essence withhold support—by being less likely to coach women of color on how to become politically savvy or recommend them for high-visibility assignments, as compared with their White counterparts (Giscombe, 2012). Thus, program design must not only take into account what is revealed by the initial assessment, but also proactively attempt to reduce the negative impact of biases on diverse mentoring relationships.

Matching Diverse Mentees and Mentors

A special aspect of program design that has received considerable attention is the matching or selection of diverse mentors and mentees. Because unconscious biases have an impact on these relationships, organizations should consider opening up mentoring programs beyond high-potential or other elite groups within the organization. Diverse criteria should be used as indicators of strong performance in addition to conventional methods. Manager assessment of subordinates may not be completely unbiased in the case of women of color, and as a result other sources of information should be used, such as heads of employee networks, peer reviews or external evaluators.

In terms of selection, mentors are often recruited based on their interest in developing others, with specific criteria dictated by the goals of the program or as part of an overall leadership development effort within the organization. Developers of programs may want to take account of the challenges faced by women of color and not always use similarity of interest or individual preference to match mentors and mentees. For instance, women of color face more negative stereotyping and double standards than other groups. They also tend to be less satisfied with opportunities for advancement in their organizations. Some potential mentors may be wary and seek to avoid these complex dynamics. Mentor behaviors that indicate awareness and understanding of the unique characteristics and challenges faced by women of color mentees should therefore be a criterion. Past work on formal mentoring for women suggests that mentor behaviors that indicate sensitivity to characteristics of mentees (such as gender) are associated with mentor program effectiveness (Giscombe, 2007a).

Beyond expanding the criteria for recruitment and matching, providing ongoing support and skilled intervention in conflictual situations should be included as part of program design. Training for mentors on topics such as speaking up on behalf of women of color who are being disrespected in meetings, managing bias in the workplace, and awareness of micro-aggressions at work are a few examples of what should be included as part of standard training and preparation for mentors.

Ongoing Support for Mentor–Mentee Relationships

Given the relational dynamics involved in diverse relationships, there is a need to focus on the dyadic nature of mentoring. Developing reciprocal relationships between mentors and mentees is key to overall program effectiveness and requires support, especially within formal programs. More specifically, trust has been shown to be a crucial element of successful sponsor–protégé relationships (Foust-Cummings et al., 2011), but trust-building between diverse women and those from majority groups can be difficult. Ongoing support in these instances is vital given the fact that, compared with White women with influential mentors, women of color counterparts are less likely to have a trusting relationship with their mentors (Giscombe, 2012).

Within the scope of the program, building trust (which is an iterative process) can take many different forms. For example, encouraging mentors to take the lead in sharing information about themselves can be an essential first step in developing trust. More specifically, the senior person should model self-disclosing behavior, particularly in relating anecdotes of how he or she learned from mistakes or missteps, in an effort to build trust and encourage women of color to do the same. The senior person can also model the importance of candor within relationships by honestly disclosing his or her opinions on topics such as organizational culture or current workplace issues. Women of color as mentees can strive for more open communication by asking for feedback as well as balancing self-presentation of a weakness with strengths, thereby reducing feelings of vulnerability (Giscombe, 2012).

One difficult obstacle that many formal mentoring programs face is that they are time restricted to a one-year maximum. Given that it generally takes a longer time for open, trusting relationships to develop among diverse pairs (Turban, Dougherty, & Lee, 1999), a longer period for formal mentorship programs for women of color may be beneficial. This longer format would provide a greater chance of success in cultivating relationships and produce mutual benefits for mentees, mentors, and for the organization.

Regardless of the length of the program, there is little evidence that supports a reliable method or formula for matching mentors and mentees especially within diverse mentoring relationships. Thus, a potential limitation to any formal program would be the ongoing management of relationships between the mentors and mentees, especially if they were not well-matched initially. In such instances, mentors and mentees could be given the opportunity to be paired with a new person as part of this ongoing program support. Another drawback could be protégé desires for greater exposure to a variety of functions in the organization that may not be supported by the assigned mentor. In this case, women of color could benefit by being exposed to a different mentor from another area within the firm. Thus, to provide ongoing support to diverse mentoring relationships, it may be necessary to include additional resources that can be accessed by mentors and mentees.

One technique for facilitating this ongoing support is to supply a coach to the mentoring relationship. Two organizational practices, at PepsiCo, Inc. and Goldman Sachs, are worth noting that have had success with third-party involvement in facilitating close working relationships across differences.

For example, within PepsiCo, in 2007, the Multicultural Women of Color Alliance put into place a program for women of color. This initiative was a strategic support and resource group aligned with the business, targeting women of color in middle and senior management ranks (Bagati, 2008). One of the initiative's first components was a program called Power Pairs®, which was a customized coaching program for women of color, their immediate managers, and their second-level managers. The program used facilitated dialogue to create more authentic and honest relationships by enabling participants' understanding of their work styles, career goals, and interests. The women of color participants were able to discuss their career plans and goals while receiving direct feedback. The program showed strong results, with turnover among women of color participants one-half that of executive women of color employees not participating in the program (Bagati, 2008).

A potential drawback to a program like this is its cost. Hiring outside facilitators can be costly and often outside the realm for many organizations. However, some attention to the development of a strong dyadic relationship is important.

A second example, the Goldman Sachs' Emerging Leaders Program (ELP), launched in 2014. ELP is a career management program designed to enhance the progression and retention of strong-performing black and Latino/Hispanic vice presidents. The program was developed jointly by Goldman Sachs' Office of Global Leadership and Diversity and Goldman Sachs University, the learning and development arm of the firm (Catalyst, 2014a). A core component of ELP is a coaching session led by an external facilitator that focuses on strengthening the relationship between participants and their managers. In advance of this session, participants complete a questionnaire that assesses their workplace experience across several dimensions, including: opportunities for contribution, sense of recognition, teamwork and inclusion, organizational resources, open communication, and organizational climate. The manager completes the same survey, but does so from the employee's perspective, answering the questions as she or he believes the direct report would. The facilitator reviews the survey data, analyzing any gaps between the employee's experience and the experience the manager perceives the direct report to have.

The employee and manager then participate in a coaching dialogue with the facilitator. This discussion is designed to identify and close gaps in perception by improving communication, heightening disclosure, and utilizing trust. The session helps to align the business, professional, and performance expectations of both parties. Anecdotal feedback suggests that revealing and exploring these different perceptions provides managers and employees with tools to build authentic relationships with each other. With the coach's help, participants and managers create an action plan that includes commitments to next steps.

The success of this type of activity depends on the skill of the facilitator. If the expense of an external facilitator is prohibitive, one alternative is to engage peer facilitators from within the organization to provide this ongoing support. One example is Kimberly-Clark Corporation's global, enterprise-wide initiative, "Unleash Your Power: Strengthening the Business with Women Leaders" (Catalyst, 2014b). As part of this initiative, mentoring and sponsoring are driven through the employee resource groups (ERGs). For example, the company's women's ERG, Women's Interactive Network (WIN) pairs pipeline women with a senior-level coach to undergo a year-long professional development training curriculum through its WIN Matters program. In addition, through Mentor Up the WIN leadership team nominates women considered high potential to serve as reverse mentors to senior leaders. Lastly, WIN developed Advancement Through Leadership and Sponsorship (ATLAS), a formal sponsorship program that accelerates the development of women to leadership roles through cross-function, cross-sector partnerships between high-potential women and senior leaders.

When Formal Programs Close

Program administrators should consider what happens after the formal program concludes. At the end of the program, some mentors may be willing to continue to work with their mentees and possibly expand their role as mentors to include sponsorship. While research indicates that women of color are less likely to have informal or influential mentors than their White counterparts, there has been little research that examines the "post-program" phase of formal mentoring relationships. In particular, within firms, there has been little follow-up on whether formal mentoring relationships continue and/or develop into informal sponsorship. Developing assessments to track the incidence of mentors continuing the relationship, and moving toward informal sponsorship, would be an important way for formal mentoring programs to demonstrate impact. This can be accomplished by having former mentors and mentees check in with program administrators on a semi-annual basis on the relationship's progression (or lack thereof). One study of inter-organizational formal mentoring programs, developed as part of a diverse leaders pipeline program, included such a follow-up assessment and found results useful to future program development (Murrell, Blake-Beard, Porter, & Perkins-Williamson, 2008). In a study of effective mentoring programs, one program deemed successful ensured that mentors were able, at least potentially, to act as sponsors for mentees by requiring that mentors be well-networked within the organization (Giscombe, 2007a). Thus, program administrators may wish to consider how to measure and reward ongoing sponsorship for women of color once formal programs have ended.

Conclusions

This chapter explored ways to enhance the effectiveness of formal mentoring programs that provide development and support for women of color as diverse leaders. To better support the nuances of growth in diverse mentoring relationships, attention needs to be paid to the relational aspects of diverse mentor–mentee dyads. According to Allen et al., "Mentoring relationships are … inherently dyadic and the failure to consider both partners' perspective greatly limits our understanding of mentoring" (Allen, Eby, O'Brien, & Lentz, 2008: 344).

There are gaps in both research and organizational practice that need to be filled. While studies have shown that attitudinal similarity predicts satisfaction among mentees with their mentors to a greater extent than does racial or gender similarity, these studies have not looked at the initial formation of the mentor–mentee relationship. This is in contrast to findings within the Catalyst study that reported that women of color had less influential mentors than White women. This suggests that powerful mentors do not often choose racially diverse women as mentees at the same rate that they choose their White counterparts, which has implications for formal programs in which choice is part of the matching process.

To effectively guide the provision of mentoring for women of color, additional research and examples of best practices in organizations are needed to examine these complex dynamics. Such research has been done in the past (e.g., Thomas, 2001), but little has focused on the unique experiences of women of color.

Future directions for research that examine the dynamics of dyadic relationships when other issues of difference are considered, such as class, would also be beneficial. For example, are there instances in which a demographic similarity on class might interact differently with race or gender? How might protégés access various identities they may have in common with their formal mentor, in the most effective way to gain support and advocacy? Finally, while the presence of third-party facilitators to oversee development of relationships is appealing, we need to understand more about the relationship dynamics that develop involving a third party, and build robust theory that can enhance the overall effectiveness of formal mentoring programs for women of color as diverse leaders.

References

Allen, T. D., Eby, L. T., O'Brien, K. E., & Lentz, E. (2008). The state of mentoring research: A qualitative review of current research methods and future research implications. *Journal of Vocational Behavior, 73*, 343–357.

Bagati, D. (2008). *Women of color in U.S. securities firms—Women of color in professional services series*. New York: Catalyst.

Bagati, D. (2009). *Women of color in U.S. law firms—Women of color in professional services series*. New York: Catalyst.

Bobo, L., Kluegel, J. R., & Smith, R. A. (1997). Laissez-faire racism: The crystallization of a kinder, gentler, antiblack ideology. In S. A. Tuch, & J. K. Martin (Eds.), *Racial attitudes in the 1990s: Continuity and change* (pp. 15–42). Westport, CT: Praeger.

Brown, B. P., Zablah, A. R., & Bellenger, D. N. (2008). The role of mentoring in promoting organizational commitment among black managers: An evaluation of the indirect effects of racial similarity and shared racial perspectives. *Journal of Business Research, 61*(7), 732–738.

Burt, R. (1998). The gender of social capital. *Rationality and Society, 10,* 5–46.

Catalyst (2014a). Practices: Goldman Sachs—Fostering Trusting Relationships and Investing in the Pipeline: A Multi-Pronged Approach to Developing Diverse Talent.

Catalyst (2014b). Practices: Catalyst Award Winner Kimberly-Clark Corporation— Unleash Your Power: Strengthening the Business with Women Leaders.

Devine, P. G., Plant, E. A., Amodio, D. M., Harmon-Jones, D. H., & Vance, S. L. (2002). The regulation of explicit and implicit race bias: The role of motivations to respond without prejudice. *Journal of Personality and Social Psychology, 82* (5), 835–848.

Foust-Cummings, H. Dinolfo, S., and Kohler, J. (2011). *Sponsoring women to success*. New York: Catalyst.

Giscombe, K. (2007a). Advancing women through the glass ceiling with formal mentoring. In B. R. Ragins & K. E. Kram (Eds.), *The handbook of mentoring at work: Theory, research, and practice* (pp. 549–571). Thousand Oaks, CA: Sage Publications.

Giscombe, K. (2007b). *Women of color in Accounting—Women of color in professional services series*. New York: Catalyst.

Giscombe, K. (2012). *Optimizing mentoring programs for women of color*. New York: Catalyst.

Giscombe, K. (2015). Emotional resilience and failure. In M. Davidson, L. Wooten, & L. M. Roberts (Eds.), *Positive organizing in a global society: Understanding and engaging differences for capacity-building and inclusion* (pp. 85–95). New York: Taylor & Francis.

Haggard, D. L., Dougherty, T. W., Turban, D. T., & Wilbanks, J. E. (2011). Who is a mentor? A review of evolving definitions and implications for research. *Journal of Management, 37*(1), 280–304.

Hewlett, S. A. (2013). *Forget a mentor, find a sponsor: The new way to fast-track your career.* Boston, MA: Harvard Business School Press.

Ibarra, H., Carter, N. M., & Silva, C. (2010). Why men still get more promotions than women. *Harvard Business Review, 88*(9), 80–85.

Kram, K. E. (1985). *Mentoring at work: Developmental relationships in organizational life.* Glenview, IL: Scott, Foresman.

McPherson, M., Smith-Lovin, L., & Cook, J. M. (2001). Birds of a feather: Homophily in social networks. *Annual Review of Sociology, 27,* 415–444.

Murrell, A. J., Blake-Beard, S., Porter, D. M., and Perkins-Williamson, A. (2008). Inter-organizational formal mentoring: Breaking the concrete ceiling sometimes requires support from the outside. *Human Resource Management, 47*(2), 275–294.

Prime, J., & Salib, E. (2014). *Inclusive leadership: The view from six countries.* New York: Catalyst.

Ragins, B. R. (1997). Diversified mentoring relationships in organizations: A power perspective. *Academy of Management Review, 22*(2), 482–521.

Thomas, D. A. (2001). The truth about mentoring minorities: Race matters. *Harvard Business Review, 79*(4), 99–107.

Thomas, K. M., & Plaut, V. C. (2008). The many faces of diversity resistance in the workplace. In K. Thomas (Ed.), *Diversity resistance in organizations* (pp. 6–8). New York: Taylor & Francis Group.

Turban, D. B., Dougherty, T. W., & Lee, F. K. (1999). The impact of demographic diversity and perceived similarity on mentoring outcomes: The moderating effect of time. *Academy of Management Proceedings*, E1–E6.

Underhill, C. M. (2006). The effectiveness of mentoring programs in corporate settings: A meta-analytical review of the literature. *Journal of Vocational Behavior, 68*(2), 292–307.

Utsey, S. O., Ponterotto, & Porter, J. S. (2008) Prejudice and racism, year 2008—still going strong: Research on reducing prejudice with recommended methodological advances. *Journal of Counseling & Development, 86*, 339–347.

PART III
Creating Change for Paradigms

9

CLIMBING THE LADDER OR KICKING IT OVER?

Bringing Mentoring and Class into Critical Contact

Maureen Scully, Stacy Blake-Beard, Diane Felicio, and Regina M. O'Neill

Socio-economic class is a defining feature of the very structure of the workplace. Class is itself determined in large part by location on the organizational job ladder and the wages associated with that rung of the ladder (Baron, Davis-Blake, & Bielby, 1986). Class is inextricably intertwined with race and gender, so studies of climbing the job ladder have examined specific impediments by race (e.g., Westcott, 1982) and by gender (e.g., DiPrete & Soule, 1988; Warihay, 1980). Mentoring is one of several strategies that can help employees to climb the ladder, and thereby increase socio-economic class for themselves, their families, and even their communities. Mentoring, of course, involves more than upward mobility; it has come to be understood as a more well-rounded approach to developing a whole sense of self, career, and impact. Similarly, socio-economic class—while indeed primarily an economic marker—also has many facets beyond economic capital, including different levels and types of social capital (who do you know?), educational capital (what does your schooling signify?), and cultural capital (what kind of style and savvy do you have?). Our goal in this chapter is to bring mentoring and class into critical contact.

While keeping a broad view of both mentoring and class, we also focus on this simple connection: that mentoring moves people up the ladder of socio-economic class, and as such, mentoring presupposes and implicates class. It is noteworthy that past examinations of mentoring have been surprisingly silent on the effects of class on mentoring relationships, particularly because mentoring is essentially a practice designed to help people traverse the class landscape by moving upward in a career. We argue that this connection between mentoring and class deserves richer attention.

What is at stake? Mentoring is offered as one remedy for inequality, particularly in studies of gender and race in organizations. However, without taking the context of mentoring seriously, mentoring may just redistribute a diverse population across a structure of inequality. In an era when inequality is acute, and the low end of the class spectrum faces serious deprivation, it is vital to examine closely any processes that might accidentally rely upon and reproduce inequality. Our aim in this chapter is to guide researchers, mentors, and mentoring program managers toward fresh ways of thinking about mentoring and about how it can be mobilized to remedy rather than reproduce steep stratification.

We open with a look at the ladder metaphor and then examine mentoring and class in four sections. We examine where the literature has connected mentoring and class, finding the focus to be largely on mentoring in educational systems rather than workplace settings and drawing lessons from across disciplines. We contextualize mentoring in the mythic meritocracy. The idea of meritocracy pushes the belief that class is a personal achievement, and if this belief lurks in a mentoring relationship, it may become awkward, as we will explore. We then examine how the concept of mentoring is itself "classed," with its focus on the highest rungs of the ladder; we open space for inquiry about mentoring at the "bottom of the ladder." Finally, we consider mentoring in the contemporary employment landscape, where there are fewer and shorter organizational ladders and where employees face unstable career scenarios, such as jumping across ladders or staying stuck in low rungs of a ladder. By considering these multiple angles on the question of how mentoring and class intersect, we hope to generate new research agendas and implications for practice.

The Ladder Metaphor

As our title suggests, we start from the simple observation that mentoring has deep origins in the idea of climbing the ladder and pursuing upward mobility. Researchers began in the 1970s to uncover how gender and race impede advancement in large organizations with classic career ladders. Article titles have invoked the image of the ladder and the upward climb, for example, "climbing the corporate ladder: do female and male executives follow the same route?" (Lyness & Thompson, 2000) and "factors affecting the upward mobility of black managers in private sector organizations" (Nkomo & Cox, 1990). One factor affecting advancement is that women and people of color do not have access to the networks and insider knowledge (Warihay, 1980) that can propel advancement. Mentoring was proposed as a solution to blocked advancement, for "moving up through mentoring" (Van Collie, 1998). Senior mentors would serve as guides through the maze of bureaucracy and corporate culture, supporting more junior employees trying to succeed in the upward climb. As one implementation manual averred, capturing the spirit of these programs, "finding a mentor is the most important strategy for climbing the professional ladder" (Rawlins & Rawlins, 1983). "Successful mentoring, including that which successfully crosses class boundaries, has a genuine impact on the life of the mentee" (Muskal, 2007: 280). Having a mentor was indeed found to relate to advancement and career success (Dreher & Ash, 1990).

The language of mentoring studies is replete with references to the upward climb of advancement, and indeed, assistance with advancement becomes a key part of the crystallizing definition of mentoring, as summarized by Crosby (1999). In an early paean to the benefits of mentoring, Collins and Scott (1978) proclaimed, "everyone who makes it has a mentor." A mentor is "committed to providing upward mobility" (Ragins & McFarlin, 1990). Survey items to capture mentoring activity include "groom me for promotions" (Goh, 1991). A model mentor ensures that the "protégé is recommended by a mentor for promotion" (Zey, 1984: 8). These upward moves benefit all protégés, and especially those who leap upward across class lines.

Of course, this very basic approach to mentoring now reads as a bit dated, with the "old career definition of climbing the ladder" being replaced by notions such as the "learning alliance" mentor who helps in navigating fulfilling as well as remunerative careers that may span organizations and occupations (Poulsen, 2006). But we start from the premise that mentoring has deep origins in the ideas of a "climb" toward success—whether taking steps up a classic ladder or scaling a personally defined mountain. Mentoring also aims to expand economic opportunity—especially for women and people of color—as a remedy to inequality. Mentoring more people toward economic stability affects more than individual economic outcomes, because opportunities for good jobs and good wages also redistribute resources toward historically underprivileged communities. Bringing class into the conversation about mentoring at once recognizes that class has always been there—and that class is too infrequently mentioned explicitly.

Though mentoring and class have this natural link, there are also tensions between climbing the ladder versus kicking it over. Kicking over the ladder is a potentially more radical vision of shared power, flatter organizations, less punishing vertical authority relationships, worker empowerment, and gainsharing rather than steep wage inequality. The idea for this paper was sparked at an annual meeting of the Academy of Management many years ago, in a session that surfaced these tensions. During the session, researchers from two distinct traditions had an opportunity to share ideas (we thank Stella Nkomo and Paul Adler for creating the space for this fresh discussion). Researchers studying gender and diversity in organizations were concerned about advancement and blocked opportunities. They were looking at how more women and people of color could make it to the top of organizations, whereupon they might manage differently, or use their "institutional position to perform discrimination-ameliorative tasks for those on the bottom" (Carbado & Gulati, 2004: 1645). Researchers taking a "critical management studies" perspective were concerned about power in organizations and about continually reproducing a top and bottom per se. They were examining how organizations might become flatter, with shorter or even no ladders, lower authority distance from top to bottom, and more opportunities for employee participation and shared governance. Interestingly, these two groups of researchers accepted one another's similar commitments to equal opportunity and economic justice, while seeing how they tackled issues differently. The puzzle began in thinking about specific practices, such as mentoring: *Are climbing the ladder and kicking over the ladder fundamentally at odds?* Or in other words, can mentoring address inequalities without getting entangled in inequalities? In addressing such questions, we can learn more about mentoring and about underlying goals like contesting power dynamics and equitably distributing livelihoods, meaningful work, and personal and social development.

The Literature

We looked to see where the literature has linked mentoring and class. A landmark study that included class background in modeling how several variables affect mentoring outcomes found that mentoring raised the probability of increased wages and promotions for individuals from middle-class and upper-class origins, but the effects did not hold for those coming from working-class origins (Whitely, Dougherty, & Dreher, 1991). This study has been cited nearly 600 times, and some follow-up research picks up the thread on class. Class is often mentioned in a list of "race, gender, and class" as intersectional, which may at once be the only way to think about class authentically (Holvino, 2010) but also, ironically, a way to obscure class, unless the focus is trained on intersectionality at lower levels of the wage structure (Weaver, Crayne, & Jones, 2016). Researchers observe that employees from lower socio-economic class backgrounds face barriers in finding a mentor and reaping benefits from mentoring (Blickle, Schneider, Meurs, & Perrewé, 2010; Johnson-Bailey & Cervero, 2002).

In reviewing the literature, a particularly powerful call to consider the mechanisms by which class can distort the mentoring experience stands out. Hoyt (1999) explores mentoring and class in academia and uncovers how class differences create discomfort in the mentoring relationship. Her article exposes stereotypes of lower- or working-class people, which include traits that are not regarded by middle- and upper-class people as appropriate for high-status positions. In the context of a putative meritocracy, to which we return below, it is often assumed that people "earn" their class status and that class standing is therefore a good indicator of their merit. In fact, upward mobility from generation to generation is quite limited, as shown in calculations of limited "elasticity" of mobility (Corak, 2011). Nonetheless, the idea of meritocracy is tenacious, and it sets up a "logical syllogism" (Huber & Form, 1973), whereby it follows that lower class indicates lower merit. Meritocracy thus makes class not just a material stratum, but also a judgment of worthiness. The fear of such judgments is at the heart of Hoyt's (1999) discussion of the desire to hide class background and the discomfort that can result when working-class markers, like accent, are looked down upon.

> There is a real fear to being discovered as having working- or lower-class origins, a fear that is not paranoia. Any person who is an outsider, the Other, or marginalized knows that there can be serious consequences for those who are different from the norm. Stereotypes and attributions do not stay in the theoretical for people; they are often acted upon to become discrimination and abuse.
>
> (Hoyt, 1999: 204)

Since Hoyt issued her compelling call in 1999, there have been substantial advances in the literature on mentoring across differences (e.g., Blake-Beard, Bayne, Crosby, & Muller, 2011) as well as significantly more organizational research that names class (e.g., Gray & Kish-Gephart, 2013). However, these two streams have flowed separately. There is little research where class and mentoring connect, or even clash, when the message is that working-class identity is something to shed in the climb upward. As of 2016, Hoyt's chapter has received twenty-one citations, spanning the seventeen years since it was published. Most of these citations are in the area of the psychology of class and poverty, the dynamics of exclusion, and mentoring for urban youth. The uptake in the literature on mentoring in the workplace is markedly missing.

Before springing from Hoyt's (1999) insights and taking a deeper dive into the specific challenges of mentoring in the context of meritocracy, we consider other places in the literature where mentoring and class are linked. We found studies that considered class and mentoring in three distinct settings: for youth and college students, for entrepreneurs starting a small business, and across global contexts. We briefly review these studies, appreciating directions for future research, while also noting that they stop short of probing the potential painfulness of troubled cross-class mentoring relationships that Hoyt (1999) revealed.

The interest in mentoring for relatively underprivileged youth sprang from early research, which found that high school students from low income backgrounds had fewer mentors, sometimes had negative influences rather than positive mentoring, relied more upon teachers for mentoring, and often recalled singular incidents of mentorly advice in their youth that stayed with them (Chairez, 1990). Since then, mentoring has been formalized, more widely offered, and has been pursued as a purposive policy for equalizing educational opportunity and workforce preparedness, especially for youth of color (Blake-Beard & McGowan, 2000). Longer duration mentorships benefit low-income urban youth who have experienced hardships, while mentorships that are terminated early actually deter these youth; they may experience defeat and despair, or feel judged. Given the stressors of class, lower-income mentors may ironically be the ones who have to terminate relationships earlier (Grossman & Rhodes, 2002). Mentors from a higher social class could bring their social capital and easier life circumstances to bear to support lower-class youth, but may lack the interpersonal sensitivity and commitment for their mentoring to remain supportive (Gaddis, 2012). Cross-class mentoring necessarily involves power dynamics and can provoke feelings of "relative deprivation" (Hu, Thomas, & Lance, 2008). Smaller-scale and in-depth mentoring partnerships, particularly when they take the intersectionality of race, ethnicity, and class into account, may build trust, help participants shape an approach to future aspirations and communication styles, and offer concrete financial deals that help make dreams more real and immediate (Muskal, 2007). As evident in essays by college-bound students (Lieber, 2015), meaningful dialogues about class-based experiences can enrich a mentoring context, including family history of work and class, a student's own early experiences in the workplace, and the process of coming to experience the "Otherness" of wealth.

Class and mentoring also come together in the domain of mentors for start-up businesses. The spirit of entrepreneurship in the mentoring relationship is a new focus, and indeed, in the revised version of the classic text on mentoring (Kram, 1985), Murphy and Kram (2014) aim to support the "entrepreneurial protégé." Starting a new business can require a kind of cultural capital that is often nurtured in the upper classes, especially to make pitches, court investors and customers, and keep a hopeful stance. Using three case studies on mentoring, Greenbank (2006) was surprised to uncover some class differences. He found cross-class mentoring to be challenging, characterizing working-class business owners as "fatalistic," lacking a "future orientation," and instead "liv[ing] for today." They regarded being ambitious as "pretentious" and "getting above oneself." He examines these findings using Bourdieu's (1977) concepts of cultural capital and habitus, which explain how working-class experiences naturally create an expectation of barriers. Even while acknowledging constraints, it is possible to take a more "asset based" view of resilience and lower socio-economic class. Working-class entrepreneurs may take the discourse of the American Dream as a challenge to get ahead, showing optimism and an "upbeat" attitude (Gill, 2014) about entrepreneurial possibilities. Below we return to the question of whether showing a positive attitude is a way that working-class people comply with middle-class expectations of cheerfulness and hide their legitimate worries about obstacles and business failure.

In another vein, the literature links mentoring and class transnationally. Thus far, our discussion of the literature is anchored in the United States. Class dynamics vary transnationally, and the dynamics of mentoring and class thus vary as well. A study of 512 formally assigned mentors in a Chinese manufacturing firm shows that mentors themselves benefit from the experience of mentoring as does their team's cohesiveness (Liu, Liu, Kwan, & Mao, 2009). This study is distinctive in focusing on mentors and teams, not just on individual mentees' career advancement, showing the benefit of cross-cultural perspectives.

A study of Indian women's mentoring experiences (Blake-Beard, 2015) brought to life the "tug of war between cultural legacies and global mindedness" (Reis, Fleury, Fleury, & Zambaldi, 2015: 55), pitting the global neoliberal value of individual success against local beliefs about whether changing class status is possible or desirable. The "tug of war" appears as Indian women appreciate the opportunities that mentoring relationships offer, but also face internal questioning and external censure when mentoring pushes against traditional cultural boundaries of expected gender roles and appropriate career aspirations. Within the bounded scope of this chapter, we focus mainly on mentoring and class in the USA, while noting that US approaches to individualistic human resource management practices are diffusing transnationally (e.g., Weinstein & Obloj, 2002) as is US educational socialization to have faith in meritocracy (Krishna-murty, Carberry, & Scully, 2015). Thus, the tensions we identify in this chapter may appear transnationally, particularly between individualistic and collective notions of career success, between leaving a class and staying loyal to a class, and between striving for personal gain and sharing the fruits of collective labor.

Overall, the studies we review here show us the value of a transdisciplinary approach to mentoring, across education, entrepreneurship, international management, and sociology. Three future directions for research and practice stand out. First, we can link school-based and workplace-based mentoring, by considering mentoring across the life cycle. Longer-term mentoring relationships have high dividends, particularly when building trust across class differences, but may be especially vulnerable to the strains of class. Second, there is room to look at mentoring outside the top rungs of organizations, as is done in the studies of a manufacturing setting (Liu et al., 2009), workforce entry (Muskal, 2007), and "industrial training" (Greenbank, 2006). Third, transnational views of careers and human resource systems show places where meritocracy is taking hold but also where the individualism that is a hallmark of elite classes can be resisted and reframed. Next, we turn directly to the context of meritocracy.

Mentoring in the Mythic Meritocracy

A meritocracy is a system that offers equal opportunities to develop and display merits and then rewards individuals on the basis of merit (Scully, 1997). The idea of meritocracy pushes individuals to understand their socio-economic class position as their own fault or their own achievement (Sennett & Cobb, 1972), and not to see how the structures of race, gender, and class distribute opportunities unequally. We refer to the "mythic" meritocracy both because it is based on myths about equal opportunity and has mythic stature in making individuals unsure about where they stand in the class system and why. When corporations and societies claim they are offering individuals abundant opportunities for upward mobility, those who do not advance may experience a sense of personal failure. If the promises of meritocracy are strong, there may not be space for an alternative discourse of unequal opportunities that reveals class standing as inherited more than achieved. Class is therefore not a simple identity, but one that invokes everything from shame to bragging, from hiding to display. Essays by college-bound students in the United States explain how work experiences and class assumptions in their family systems affect their sense of themselves, revealing internal struggles by both the poor and the wealthy (Lieber, 2015). The latter sometimes recognize that privilege, not personal merit, drives their success, another factor that can introduce awkwardness when mentors give counsel on "how to get ahead."

Mentoring aims to help people move within the class structure, but building mentoring relationships is complex when class comes freighted with so many societally shaped meanings. Mentoring relationships are strengthened by trust and even by willingness to be reciprocally vulnerable, so that mentoring becomes not just instrumental but also more fully developmental (Kram, 1985; Murphy & Kram, 2014). In this section, we discuss how mentoring across class differences may present both barriers and buffers. There may be barriers to meaningful reciprocity in mentoring relationships, especially if people are hiding their class backgrounds or counseling mentees to lose or "fix" their working-class identity. At the same time, mindful mentoring relationships might provide buffers to the stings of class biases, by decoding upper-class norms or offering ways to balance assimilation and authenticity. Taking this dual perspective—of barriers as well as buffers—we can understand more richly the intersection of mentoring and class.

We return to Hoyt's (1999) notion that class can enter a mentoring relationship in invisible but insidious ways. For illustrations, we draw upon examples from Hoyt (1999), from the literature, as well as from one of the co-author's workshops in workplaces and universities on class as an aspect of diversity. The lived experience of class, for many, is a "complex weaving of shame, fear and cultural expectations" (Brown, 2007: xiv). In college, working-class students start learning how to "draw and transgress class boundaries" (Lehmann, 2009). Armor is needed, because class-based micro-aggressions permeate organizational life, just as they do around race and gender (Smith & Redington, 2010). A young man in a workshop talked fondly about working in his brother's motorcycle shop during high school. He had numerous tattoos and explained that looking at them anchored his working-class identity. However, his boss told him to cover up his tattoos with long sleeves, even in the back office with no clients around and even in the heat of summertime, so he would not "look like some hippie dropout from *Easy Rider*," a reference to the 1969 movie that the junior person did not at first grasp, but felt the sting of later.

Why is class background a source of shame? Hoyt (1999) notices subtle ways in which working-class characteristics are put down, from accent to style of dress to ways of thinking. Local kids at her university lived at home to save money and "weren't looked upon favorably by elite students or professors" (Hoyt, 1999: 193). While mentoring may help a mentee to elevate their current socio-economic status upward from their class of origin, a working-class background is an enduring identity, which at once triggers shame and pride. The shame comes from the "hidden injuries of class" (Sennett & Cobb, 1972), which show up as a lurking sense of failure, both internalized and placed upon individuals by a judgmental meritocracy. That is, while having a lower-class status is surely about the injury of material deprivation and economic precariousness, it can also involve shame and even scorn. A woman from a very poor neighborhood who is now working at a university explained in a workshop, "I get that look, the minute I pronounce a word wrong." Hoyt (1999: 192) shared that she, like many people in the US, just thought she was middle class, until someone pointed out a working-class stereotype, she realized it fit, and then in her mind, "I had just gone down the class ladder one rung."

Shame about class background can surround and impede the mentoring relationship. Recent work on shame in organizational contexts proposes that: "felt shame signals to a person that a social bond is at risk, and it catalyzes a fundamental motivation to preserve valued bonds," which may be why there is such persistence of organizational pressures to conform to shared norms that are comfortable and familiar (Creed, Hudson, Okhuysen, & Smith-Crowe, 2014: 275). This sense that a valued bond is at stake might trigger mentees to hide their class backgrounds. To preserve a treasured mentoring relationship and steer away from shame, mentors and protégés alike might avoid discussion of class and seek social ease. Mentoring is a dyadic process that affects who "fits" in an organization; those who do not "fit" the dominant ideal of the straight, White, middle- to upper-class male may engage in some adjusting and improvising to preserve the social bond. As an example, a mentor warms up a meeting with some small talk about summer vacationing and favorite places to travel. The protégé from a lower-class background may not have had these experiences, but plays along to continue the banter with the mentor and keep open the lines of valued mentoring.

To understand the challenges of coping with shame, we first explore the pressures for assimilation and then consider processes for preserving cherished aspects of lower-class identities. The acculturation or assimilation function of mentoring is well documented in the literature (Blake-Beard et al., 2011; Kram, 1983; Scandura & Williams, 2001). Indeed, acculturation is how mentors unlock some of the secrets of organizational life for those who were not born into privilege. Mentoring can be a "supplement" for individuals who do not have the right "pedigree" (Rivera, 2015), but that very formulation opens up questions about the need for and costs of "fitting in," particularly by attempting to make class background invisible. Mentoring research has deep foundations in classic studies that link it to gender (e.g., Burke & McKeen, 1990; Giscombe, 2007; Morrison, White, & Van Velsor, 1987; Ragins, Townsend, & Mattis, 1998) and to race (e.g., Bell, Denton, & Nkomo, 1993; Blake-Beard, 1999; Blancero & Del-Campo, 2005; Cox & Nkomo, 1990; Nkomo & Cox, 1989; Thomas, 1993).

These studies examine how mentoring with respect to gender, race, and their intersections often involves implicit or explicit strategies for assimilation, and researchers have evaluated, exposed, and critiqued these strategies.

Hoyt asks, "Can the working- or lower-class person ever become middle class? Isn't the attempt to appear middle class always just 'passing?' If it goes beyond 'passing' has the person sold out?" (1999: 203). Class is distinct in that it can be an "invisible" dimension of identity and hence raises questions of "coming out" versus "passing," terms drawn from the long history of taking on a privileged identity to avoid serious risks, such as lighter-skinned black people passing as White or LGBTQ people passing as straight. The place of the "coming out" process in mentoring has been discussed with respect to sexual orientation (Hebl, Tonidandel, & Ruggs, 2012; Ragins, 2008). The "coming out" formulation is not so neat, because there are cues that enable co-workers to "guess" at invisible identities, and moreover, passing or coming out does not happen in a singular moment but in multiple encounters throughout a workday and a career (Creed & Scully, 2000; DeJordy, 2008).

Whether they passed or did not, there are often feelings of guilt, anxiety, and betrayal that overwhelm those who are moving up. Hoyt (1999) described her own feelings of hostility that she felt toward members of the middle and upper class for some of the values embedded in their cultures that she did not want to embody. She spoke of the ambivalence that people may have about deserting their class background, and she also recalled working-class folks who did not pass (either because they did not know how or chose not to). For those who chose to retain their working-class styles of being, she saw that it made them stand out in a negative way, triggering her own discomfort, and re-opening the question of how visible to be.

Organizational scholarship has considered how employees manage "invisible social identities" in the workplace, but remains interestingly silent on the dimension of socio-economic class: "Visible characteristics usually include sex, race, age, ethnicity, physical appearance, language, speech patterns, and dialect. Nonvisible characteristics usually include differences like religion, occupation, national origin, club or social group memberships, illness, and sexual orientation" (Clair, Beatty, & MacLean, 2005: 78). While class is not named, it is often the case that "physical appearance, language, speech patterns, and dialect" can carry and reveal class background (Fussell, 1992), making class at once curiously visible and invisible. A study that asked Americans to guess the socio-economic class of people whom they watched in video clips found that Americans were remarkably good at pinpointing an individual's class from these body language and linguistic cues, even as many Americans insist that the USA is a "classless" society (Coleman & Rainwater, 1979). Although the effect of class on our everyday lives in organizations is both pervasive and impactful, "it is rarely discussed directly or with legitimacy" (Holvino, 2002: 28). Class is at once always there and hard to broach.

When mentoring is done more mindfully, and with a critically aware class-consciousness, it can become precisely the space where issues surrounding class can be raised in a safe and empowering way. The mentoring process can provide buffers from the loss of identity that accompanies assimilation. Being oneself—when one is different from the dominant organizational identity—might be an act of "tempered radicalism" (Meyerson & Scully, 1995). It opens spaces for others who are different to come forward, making mentoring not just an individualistic but also a more collective process. Tempered radicals balance the challenges of fitting in and selling out, and moreover, they can mobilize class-consciousness to bring alternative ways to divide labor and share rewards. In a sense, they can climb the ladder *in order to* kick it over. A more collective orientation to rising up or falling down the economic ladder is a hallmark of working-class communities, and this collective orientation buffers judgments about economic status (Newman, 1988). Mentors can raise candid consideration of how choosing *not* to assimilate has potential tactical costs but also the emotional benefits of bolstering a feeling of authenticity, preserving all that they value in their working-class identity, and standing up as an agent for change.

The very emotionally fraught choices about hiding or disclosing a class identity are interjected into a mentoring relationship, perhaps with high stakes for the relationship. The mentoring relationship can involve both practical career advice and psychosocial support (Kram, 1985). The term "developmental" is used to describe support that goes beyond skill mastery to embrace the holistic growth of an individual into a career identity. Mentoring is often conceptualized as a relationship between a more senior and a more junior person (typically in terms of age and work experience), over a series of phases that require both individuals to invest considerable time, effort, trust, and emotional work (Kram, 1983). Where class identity is involved, the relationship is more than a senior/junior dyad. We have considered how a junior person might want to avoid stigma and please a mentor by hiding class background.

However, class could play out in multiple ways and directions in a mentoring relationship. It could be that the senior person feels awkward about their own lower-class background, and thus unsure of how to serve as a guide to a junior person, even more so a junior person who already has a ready stash of upper-class cultural capital. Mentoring dynamics where the senior person is from the less dominant social identity group can be awkward, as with a female mentor and male protégé (O'Neill & Blake-Beard, 2002). With invisible social identities, two people of working-class origins may each be hiding their class background when they could instead form a bond. One man in a workshop described how he and his mentor both spoke very obliquely about their family backgrounds, only to discover that their parents had grown up in the same working-class ethnic enclave.

Once arriving at the CEO position, a story of humble origins almost confers bragging rights. CEOs are celebrated for coming from humble beginnings.

"Perhaps it is our cultural infatuation with rags-to-riches stories and anything-is-possible examples in business that aids in the elevation of CEOs to celebrity status" (Ketchen, Adams, & Shook, 2008: 530). While managers ascending toward the CEO suite might still downplay their class origins, once at the top, coming from a working-class background becomes a badge of honor in the mythic meritocracy. Because of this constant impulse to retell "rags to riches" stories in the USA (Naveh, 1991), senior mentors who did not rise from the mailroom to the boardroom may feel awkward that they do not have such a story to tell. They may be reluctant to reveal class privilege or that an uncle got them their first job in the company. Indeed, they may be admiring of the resilience and drive of their mentee who has come from a lower-class background, not casting scorn or judgment toward them.

Mentoring with class awareness might permit affirmations of class differences. Recent theorizing on doing "class work" in organizations points out that cross-class relationships can involve both anxiety and rituals that reduce anxiety. "Cross-class encounters generate existential anxiety among one or both participants in the interaction (Crocker, Major, & Steele, 1998). Class work serves as an antidote to quell this anxiety" (Gray & Kish-Gephardt, 2013: 671). While class work often keeps all the players in their class roles, there can be emancipatory class work that opens new possibilities. Consider an example told by a workshop participant from a working-class background. She described going to a fancy restaurant for a work dinner and, when her bowl of soup was served, she started eating, recalling her grandmother handing around the bowls and telling each person to get started and "enjoy it while it's hot." The senior partner from the other company asked, rather pointedly and snidely, "Are we hungry?" She had, she suddenly realized, broken the unspoken rule about waiting until everyone was served. Her mentor, she could see, was visibly embarrassed on her behalf. Later in the office, she found it difficult to broach the incident, get his feedback, and move on. Here is where training for mentors and mentees in doing mindful class work would provide them both with a way to discuss, learn from, and move beyond such incidents.

As a buffering space, a positive mentoring relationship might permit people from lower-class backgrounds not only to learn upper-class norms but also to preserve and share those working-class qualities they value. As Hoyt concludes, "After all, there are many things that the middle-class could learn from the working-class culture as well" (1999: 209). Working-class culture holds its own cherished values about work. Willis (1977) found that the working-class "lads" valued hard work and getting the job done. They had little tolerance for the superficialities of politeness and posturing that marked the upper classes and that seemed to them to have nothing to do with work. The work ethic, determination, and connection to "real life experiences" of working-class students have been shown to be assets for first-generation students in universities (e.g., Lehman 2009), in the way that "street smarts" are regarded as an asset in the workplace, particularly in sales. Research on gender differences has moved from repair of deficits, to valuing differences, to learning across differences about making change and working more effectively (Ely & Meyerson, 2000). Taking such an appreciative and learning-oriented approach to class is rare but certainly possible and warranted (Scully & Blake-Beard, 2005).

Mentoring is "Classed"

We opened by discussing how the image of "climbing the ladder" imbues the concept of mentoring. The ladder extends from the lowest rungs to the very top, but most of the mentoring literature in organizations and management focuses on advancement from the middle- or upper-middle rungs to the top. This focus is not surprising, as corporate mentoring programs were created to help groom people for the demands of top roles, and in the realm of diversity management, to help women and minorities move toward the top from being plateaued at midway rungs. At the same time, inasmuch as mentoring focuses on the top levels, we argue that it could be said that mentoring is itself a "classed" concept.

What does it mean when a concept is "classed?" The concept introduces a difference where there may not be a real difference in order to impart a "classiness" to elite experience and preserve class distinctions. This imagined distinctiveness remains unchecked and separates the classes. Instead of a ladder with linked rungs, there is an impasse from lower to upper rungs. Most important in an era of widening inequality, preserving distinctions about what is appropriate for the upper versus lower classes helps to legitimate the widening of inequality, as if it has a basis in wide differences in merit. In the USA, the pay ratio of CEOs to workers who are called "unskilled" is 354:1, while most Americans think it is 30:1 and believe 7:1 would be desirable (Kiatpongsan & Norton, 2014); these ratios support our investigation into assumptions that those on the bottom are entirely "Other" from those on the top.

Class in the USA is often enacted by calling essentially the same things something different. A simple example of this subtlety is offered by Fussell (1992: 162) in his decoding of US class customs. "Proles [proletarians] say *tux*, middles *tuxedo*, but both are considered low by uppers who say *dinner jacket* or (higher) *black tie*," for basically the same "costume." Are we as researchers doing the same thing in naming "mentoring" for elites and "on-the-job training" for the proletarians? These linguistic distinctions make it harder to see and expose class, and we argue that researchers have a special obligation to be mindful about where their own terminology might be classed.

The way to check on whether mentoring versus on-the-job training (Barron, Black, & Loewenstein, 1989) is a "difference that makes a difference" is to examine what each involves. Both involve more than skills training and focus instead on the "tacit knowledge" required to do a job, and moreover, do it with excellence and perhaps get recognized and promoted (Doeringer & Piore, 1985). Tacit knowledge is distinct from explicit knowledge, which can be more readily codified. It is acquired through experience and exception management, and can include savvy about politics and how to play the game as well as insights about how to troubleshoot technical problems (Gilsdorf, 1998). Sharing tacit knowledge is a "social process" (Smith, 2011: 313). Both mentoring and on-the-job training have psychosocial and not just instrumental functions. Psychosocial functions are related to "those aspects of the relationship that enhance an individual's sense of competence, identity, and effectiveness in a professional role" (Kram, 1985: 32). While the qualifier "professional" points to upper levels, the sense of competence, identity, and effectiveness are also imparted in on-the-job training. Psychosocial functions include role modeling, acceptance and confirmation, counseling and friendship, and learning the ropes, and decoding the organization's cultural codes. In short, both the mentoring that happens at the top and the on-the-job training that happens at the bottom of the ladder fit the definition from Levinson and colleagues' (1978) classic work on mentoring, *Seasons of a Man's Life*, where the more senior person "may be a host and guide, welcoming the initiate into a new occupational world and acquainting him with its values, customs, resources, and cast of characters" (quoted in Crosby, 1999). Is all this just job socialization, with mentoring being something more?

Something about mentoring seems naggingly different than on-the-job training. Mentoring might warrant its distinct name and distinct domain nearer the top of the ladder. Mentoring sounds more personal, more about artisan and protégé, less instrumental. It is easy to associate on-the-job training with just the handing down of the brass tacks of an accounting system or the technical details of how to run a particular machine. While these are surely elements of on-the-job training, important insights about this process have emphasized how political hints, local norms, and unwritten codes are also passed along during on-the-job training. Indeed, it is the failure to pass along these subtle customs that has often resulted in the exclusion of women and minorities from the best unionized working-class jobs in internal job ladders (Reskin & Padavic, 1988). That is the same "presenting problem" that begat mentoring programs aimed at opening up the secret box for women and people of color. Perhaps it is that the skills at the higher levels are more abstract. But is that just an upper management mythology about its own special value, to create a cult of charisma that justifies high wages (Khurana, 2004)? Considering mentoring to be about broad, intangible skills and on-the-job training to be about narrow, technical skills might just be a class-anchored bias about the division of labor and the legitimacy of wide wage differences.

A critical re-reading of these processes, by bringing mentoring and class into critical contact, asks us to consider that the reproduction of class differences may be at the heart of the distinction between mentoring and on-the-job training, not some more formally justifiable distinction. This reproduction of class differences benefits elites, legitimates inequality by making these distinctions appear taken-for-granted and natural, and seeks to preserve a false harmony at work by neutralizing the inequality and even pain behind class differences. This examination of mentoring and on-the-job training does not have a definitive resolution. It is a thought experiment that raises questions about how forms of socialization at the top and at the bottom may not be as far apart as they initially might appear.

Mentoring in a World without Ladders

We open with the idea of job ladders and close with a coda on a world without job ladders. Kicking over the job ladder used to seem like a bid for alternative types of employment, with more team-based and empowered workers (Deming, 1986), and "pay for performance" schemes that recognized contributors at any level for generating results (Schuler & Jackson, 1987). However, instead of being the change agents who kicked over the ladder in a quest for empowerment, employees found the ladder kicked over by employers, in ways that created precariousness of employment. The world without ladders has its own challenges, as discussed in the now substantial literature on the "boundaryless career" (Arthur & Rousseau, 1996), and its benefits and limitations. How do mentors play a role in a world where the economic structure itself has changed, and the task of climbing upward is no longer the prominent—or even available—career goal? How are class differences exacerbated when there is differential access to the "host and guide" who can help a person navigate when economic standing is precarious?

Now that advancement is less and less likely to take place in one organization, the notion of a single mentor who can guide and decode an organization is fading somewhat. Instead, we hear more today about "coaching," with its mix of political savvy and search for personal expression through work. Coaching is both alike and distinct from mentoring. It is sometimes arranged and paid for by organizations for high-level employees, but often is engaged privately by individuals seeking a foothold in the shifting employment relations of the contemporary economy. Sponsorship is another emerging practice that appears elite, instrumentally careerist, and difficult to access. People from working-class backgrounds are even less likely to have access to the resources and connections that compose the worlds of coaching and sponsorship. While it is structural changes in the nature of employment that are making work more precarious, people in the USA still take an individualistic view and blame themselves. "Unemployed Americans overwhelmingly describe their predicament as an individual and private challenge, and not as a public issue with structural causes and political solutions" (Sharone, 2007: 403). The robust reproduction of class—the inability of people to move upward and the accompanying ideology that everyone lands in the place they deserve—is only strengthened.

Bringing class and mentoring together serves as a reminder to look at the very structures of employment, rather than just the processes for navigating them. Inequality lives in the structures. For example, just as women began to claim equal pay for equal work, often verified as gender equity for those with the same job title, new idiosyncratic job titles began to appear (Miner, 1987). A mentor could help a woman get to the next job title, but the real action was in these idiosyncratic jobs, which were more likely to be held by White men with the same credentials and more likely to be highly paid (Baron & Newman, 1990). For example, all senior software engineers, male and female, might be paid the same, and a mentor might help a woman access the engineering stronghold. But the one person bearing the title of "senior software engineer for special projects" might be the most highly paid, and it might be beyond the ken of mentors or aspiring women to access those elusive and customized titles. This example shows how the dynamics of advancement are located, at least in part, in the structural features of an organization that are determined by a mix of old routines and continuously evolving politics. For those from working-class backgrounds, accessing these hidden pockets in the ladder may be especially difficult. With people jumping among ladders and doing "gigs" (Bowe & Bowe, 2009) that are brokered by connections, access to the best opportunities will only become more elusive.

Once the ladder is reconsidered, the essential function of mentoring—to help individuals climb upward—needs to be reconsidered as well. Research on mentoring has always had a parallel emphasis on helping individuals find good and rewarding careers, which might be through meaningful work, lateral moves, career changes, or a variety of activities that are not strictly about upward climbing. When mentoring and class come into critical contact, this notion of crafting a good career must be considered for those at lower levels of the organization as well, which is a new direction for mentoring research and practice. When ladders are kicked over, individuals are encouraged to "manage your own employability" (Scully, 2000), perhaps through searching for savvy mentors and coaches, but structural factors continue to create differential opportunities across class. It is important not to obscure inequalities with a patina of meritocracy that legitimates them.

By including class in our study of mentoring at work, we not only see mentoring differently, such as the experiences of mentoring across class, but we also see the features of organizational life and its assumptions differently. For example, we can look at who gets to have mentoring or other forms of socialization that are differently named and coded, who gets to find the pockets of privilege when job titles in the ladder are juggled, and who may or may not find economic opportunity when the ladders are kicked over in the so-called "post-bureaucratic organization" (Heckscher & Donnellon, 1994). We close with some implications for research and for practice of bringing mentoring and class into critical contact.

Implications for Future Research

The mentoring literature can be expanded by considering class across three levels: individuals, processes, and structures. In surveys of individuals, the literature should return to early inclusion of socio-economic class (Whitely et al., 1991), both to explore how class infuses mentoring relationships and how mentoring does or does not open up the opportunity structure of organizations. Class is more than a control variable; it deserves its own substantive focus.

Research can examine how the processes of mentoring are altered or expanded by connections and dialogues across class in mentoring relationships. Recognizing that tentativeness about class may come from awkward notions about merit and worth, researchers can help to decode where mentoring of youth makes promises such as "you can be anything you want" or where mentoring of adults inserts class-based cultural capital unthinkingly. Examining the content and modes of mentoring will surface how "class work" creates barriers or buffers for people of working-class origins. The structures surrounding mentoring also deserve deeper attention. Mentors help mentees navigate a landscape of employment, and that landscape is changing. As the nature and shape of job ladders change, mentoring and its efficacy will adapt as well, and research can trace that change process.

Our scan of the literature found that much of the existing work on mentoring and class is focused on youth and college students (e.g., Gaddis, 2012; Hu et al., 2008), while research on mentoring and class later in life is more scarce. This imbalance may arise because of faith in meritocracy, which makes the promise that youth can become "anything they want to be" more interesting than the career plateaus and disappointments later in a career. Taking a critical look at how class limits advancement opportunities requires questioning the structure of opportunity and the promises of meritocracy, which remains a politically volatile topic.

The idea of kicking over the ladder is one that should be further investigated, in two ways. The active verb "kicking" over the ladder serves as a reminder that employees themselves may have agency in reshaping the opportunity structure. The shifting employment relationship is a macro-economic phenomenon that is often beyond workers' control. Nonetheless, employees have had an active role in advocating for greater participation, more transparent promotion policies, and higher pay. For example, temporary workers at Microsoft were not on the formal job ladder, but filed and won a lawsuit that recognized that they were working like regular employees and deserved benefits accordingly (Greenhouse, 2000). As we consider issues of class and employee inequality, there is opportunity to expand the existing body of research by considering the ways that employees can envision their careers and the settings in which they might mobilize for career opportunities.

Researchers also need to supplement survey research as a methodological framework. Qualitative and action-oriented research methods will help reveal the sometimes subtle ways in which class dynamics play out in dyads, groups, and organizations. Stories, often of those on the margins of organizations, go beyond the main effects of research studies and surface hidden obstacles—as well as the best ideas for how to remedy these inequities.

Researchers also need to be mindful of the language we use and how it might carry class connotations. The divide between elite and working-class experience in organizations is perpetuated when researchers deploy and diffuse different names for a similar phenomenon at different organizational levels. It is the language of research that has distinguished "mentoring" from "on-the-job training" and distinguished "coaching" from "apprenticeship." While the differences among these experiences may be informative, insisting on different names for them is one way in which researchers participate in drawing class lines in organizations.

Bringing mentoring and class together serves as a reminder to researchers that we sometimes take organizational advancement processes and structures of rewards and status for granted. We divert our attention to how people move within these structures, rather than problematizing the structures themselves. A class re-reading of the mentoring literature asks not just about how people climb the ladder, but also what purpose the ladder serves, whose interests it advances over the interests of others, and how careers—and economic livelihoods—will develop if ladders are kicked over.

Implications for Practice

Mentors can expand their awareness of how socio-economic class may enter the mentoring relationships. Hoyt (1999) presented tips for mentors of all class backgrounds that hold relevance for the workplace. She suggested becoming class conscious, not dismissing or trivializing class, sharing information that helps to uncover middle-class assumptions, and paying attention to how organizational policies may disadvantage or penalize one class over another. Surprisingly, although there have been active efforts in the workplace to raise consciousness across issues of race, gender, and identity issues, the "how-tos" of talking about (and mentoring through) class distinctions are much less evident. New research is shining light on cross-class relationships at work (Gray & Kish-Gephardt, 2013) and may offer suggestions for how to support mentors, particularly to make them more aware of the dynamics of hiding, assimilation, shame, and pride that we have discussed.

Mentoring has been conceptualized as a dyadic relationship between a more senior and a more junior person. Re-reading mentoring through the lens of class, we can see that mentoring has had an individualistic approach to the success of the mentee. Working-class orientations toward collectivity open the door for mentoring programs that are more collaborative learning spaces. Multiple mentors and mentees might work together to decode advancement and the root structures of opportunities that are available. Instead of moving one person up toward the narrowest point of a pyramid, the total flows of employees into decent jobs and livelihoods can be considered. By taking a learning stance toward mentoring programs and processes, more careers and voices might be included.

This alternative approach has training implications as people set up formal mentoring relationships. It may also provide a fresh perspective on the employment relationship—learning from the different aspirations of people at all levels about what it means to belong to an organization and have meaningful work. It is too often assumed that working-class people are content where they are, breeding complacency in the policy arena and diminished political will to address low wages and demeaning working conditions. Class differences need not be an excuse for differential treatment—they can be a window for learning about multiple ways to construct meaningful work, not just at the sought-after pinnacle of pyramidal organizations, but also across varied organizational levels, employment relationships, and types of work. Indeed, Wellington (1999: xii) observes that mentoring someone who is different from oneself requires "new feats of empathy and imagination," and these insights are what will open doors to new concepts of the meaningful and remunerative career.

References

Arthur, M. B., & Rousseau, D. M. (Eds.). (1996). *The boundaryless career: A new employment principle for a new organizational era*. New York: Oxford University Press.

Baron, J. N., Davis-Blake, A., & Bielby, W. T. (1986). The structure of opportunity: How promotion ladders vary within and among organizations. *Administrative Science Quarterly, 31*(2), 248–273.

Baron, J. N., & Newman, A. E. (1990). For what it's worth: Organizations, occupations, and the value of work done by women and nonwhites. *American Sociological Review, 55*(2), 155–175.

Barron, J. M., Black, D. A., & Loewenstein, M. A. (1989). Job matching and on-the-job training. *Journal of Labor Economics*, 7(1), 1–19.

Bell, E. L., Denton, T. C. & Nkomo, S. (1993). Women of color in management: Toward an inclusive analysis. In E. A. Fagenson (Ed.), *Women in management: Trends, issues, and challenges in managerial diversity* (pp. 105–130). Newberry Park, CA: Sage Publications.

Blake-Beard, S. D. (1999). The costs of living as an outsider within: An analysis of the mentoring relationships and career success of Black and White women in the corporate sector. *Journal of Career Development, 26*(1), 21–36.

Blake-Beard, S. (2015). Confronting paradox: Mentoring relationships as revolutionary in the careers and lives of professional Indian women. In P. Kumar (Ed.), *Unveiling women's leadership: Identity and the meaning of leadership in India*. London: Palgrave Macmillan.

Blake-Beard, S., Bayne, M. L., Crosby, F. J., & Muller, C. B. (2011). Matching by race and gender in mentoring relationships: Keeping our eyes on the prize. *Journal of Social Issues, 67*(3), 622–643.

Blake-Beard, S. D., & McGowan, E. (2000). *Insights from multiple perspectives: Mentor and protégé reflections on a formal high school mentoring program.* Paper presented at the American Educational Research Association national conference, April, New Orleans, LA.

Blancero, D. M. & DelCampo, R. G. (2005). *Employment Relations Today (Wiley), 32*(2), 31–38.

Blickle, G., Schneider, P. B., Meurs, J. A., & Perrewé, P. L. (2010). Antecedents and consequences of perceived barriers to obtaining mentoring: A longitudinal investigation. *Journal of Applied Social Psychology, 40*(8), 1897–1920.

Bourdieu, P. 1977. Cultural reproduction and social reproduction. In J. Karabel, & A. H. Halsey (Eds.), *Power and ideology in education.* New York: Oxford University Press.

Bowe, J., & Bowe, M. (Eds.) (2009). *Gig: Americans talk about their jobs.* New York: Broadway Books.

Brown, B. (2007). Introduction. I thought it was just me (but it isn't): Making the journey from "what will people think?" to "I am enough." New York: Gotham Books.

Burke, R. J., & McKeen, C. A. (1990). Mentoring in organizations: Implications for women. *Journal of Business Ethics, 9*(4–5), 317–332.

Carbado, D. W., & Gulati, M. (2004). Race to the top of the corporate ladder: What minorities do when they get there. *Washington & Lee Law Review, 61,* 1645.

Chairez, M. (1990). *The mobility strategies of successful Hispanic high school students.* Doctoral dissertation, University of the Pacific.

Clair, J. A., Beatty, J. E., & MacLean, T. L. (2005). Out of sight but not out of mind: Managing invisible social identities in the workplace. *Academy of Management Review, 30*(1), 78–95.

Coleman, R., & Rainwater, L. (1979). *Social standing in America: New dimensions of class.* New York: Routledge and Kegan Paul.

Collins, E. G., & Scott, P. (1978). Everyone who makes it has a mentor. *Harvard Business Review, 56,* 89–101.

Corak, M. (2011). *Generational income mobility in North America and Europe.* Cambridge: Cambridge University Press.

Cox, T., & Nkomo, S. M. (1990). Invisible men and women: A status report on race as a variable in organization behavior research. *Journal of Organizational Behavior, 11*(6), 419–431.

Creed, W. E. D., & Scully, M. A. (2000). Songs of ourselves: Employees' deployment of social identity in everyday workplace encounters. *Journal of Management Inquiry, 9*(4), 391–412.

Creed, W. D., Hudson, B. A., Okhuysen, G. A., & Smith-Crowe, K. (2014). Swimming in a sea of shame: Incorporating emotion into explanations of institutional reproduction and change. *Academy of Management Review, 39*(3), 275–301.

Crocker, J., Major, B., & Steele, C. (1998). Social stigma. In D. T. Gilbert, S. T. Fiske, & G. Lindzey (Eds.), *The handbook of social psychology* (pp. 504–553). New York: McGraw-Hill.

Crosby, F. J. (1999). The developing literature on developmental relationships. In A. J. Murrell, F. J. Crosby, & R. J. Ely (Eds.), *Mentoring dilemmas: Developmental relationships within multicultural organizations* (pp. 3–20). Mahwah, NJ: Lawrence Erlbaum Associates.

DeJordy, R. (2008). Just passing through stigma, passing, and identity decoupling in the work place. *Group & Organization Management, 33*(5), 504–531.

Deming, W. E. (1986). *Out of the crisis.* Cambridge, MA: Center for Advanced Engineering Study, Massachusetts Institute of Technology.

DiPrete, T. A., & Soule, W. T. (1988). Gender and promotion in segmented job ladder systems. *American Sociological Review, 53*(1), 26–40.

Doeringer, P. B., & Piore, M. J. (1985). *Internal labor markets and manpower analysis.* London: Routledge.

Dreher, G. F., & Ash, R. A. (1990). A comparative study of mentoring among men and women in managerial, professional, and technical positions. *Journal of Applied Psychology, 75*(5), 539–546.

Ely, R. J., & Meyerson, D. E. (2000). Theories of gender in organizations: A new approach to organizational analysis and change. *Research in Organizational Behavior, 22,* 103–151.

Fussell, P. (1992). *Class: A guide through the American system.* New York: Touchstone.

Gaddis, S. M. (2012). What's in a relationship? An examination of social capital, race and class in mentoring relationships. *Social Forces, 90*(4), 1237–1269.

Gill, R. (2014). "If you're struggling to survive day-to-day": Class optimism and contradiction in entrepreneurial discourse. *Organization, 21*(1), 50–67.

Gilsdorf, J. W. (1998). Organizational rules on communicating: How employees are-and are not-learning the ropes. *Journal of Business Communication, 35*(2), 173–201.

Giscombe, K. (2007). Advancing women through the glass ceiling with formal mentoring. In B. R. Ragins, & K. E. Kram (Eds.), *The handbook of mentoring at work: Theory, research, and practice* (pp. 549–571). Thousand Oaks, CA: Sage Publications.

Goh, S. C. (1991). Sex differences in perceptions of interpersonal work style, career emphasis, supervisory mentoring behavior, and job satisfaction. *Sex Roles, 24,* 701–710.

Gray, B., & Kish-Gephart, J. J. (2013). Encountering social class differences at work: How "class work" perpetuates inequality. *Academy of Management Review, 38*(4), 670–699.

Greenbank, P. (2006). Does class matter? Mentoring small businesses' owner-managers. *Journal of European Industrial Training, 30*(8), 639–652.

Greenhouse, S. (2000, December 13). Temp workers at Microsoft win suit. *New York Times.* Retrieved from www.nytimes.com/2000/12/13/business/technology-temp-workers-at-microsoft-win-lawsuit.html.

Grossman, J. B., & Rhodes, J. E. (2002). The test of time: Predictors and effects of duration in youth mentoring relationships. *American Journal Of Community Psychology, 30*(2), 199–219.

Hebl, M. R., Tonidandel, S., & Ruggs, E. N. (2012). The impact of like-mentors for gay/lesbian employees. *Human Performance, 25,* 52–71.

Heckscher, C., & Donnellon, A. (Eds.) (1994). *The post-bureaucratic organization: New perspectives on organizational change.* Thousand Oaks, CA: SAGE Publications.

Holvino, E. (2002). Class: "A difference that makes a difference" in organizations. *Diversity Factor, 10*(2), 28–34.

Holvino, E. (2010). Intersections: The simultaneity of race, gender, and class in organization studies. *Gender, Work and Organization, 17*(3), 248–277.

Hoyt, S. K. (1999). Mentoring with class: Connections between social class and developmental relationships in the academy. In A. J. Murrell, F. J. Crosby, & R. J. Ely (Eds.), *Mentoring dilemmas: Developmental relationships within multicultural organizations* (pp. 189–210). Mahwah, NJ: Lawrence Erlbaum Associates.

Hu, C., Thomas, K. M., & Lance, C. E. (2008). Intentions to initiate mentoring relationships: Understanding the impact of race, proactivity, feelings of deprivation, and relationship roles. *The Journal of Social Psychology, 148*(6), 727–744.

Huber, J., & Form, W. H. (1973). *Income and ideology: An analysis of the American political formula.* New York: Free Press.

Johnson-Bailey, J., & Cervero, R. M. (2002). Cross-cultural mentoring as a context for learning. *New Directions for Adult and Continuing Education, 2002*(96), 15–26.

Ketchen Jr, D. J., Adams, G. L., & Shook, C. L. (2008). Understanding and managing CEO celebrity. *Business Horizons, 51*(6), 529–534.

Khann, N., & Johnson, C. (2010). Passing as black: Racial identity work among biracial Americans. *Social Psychology Quarterly, 73*(4), 380–397.

Khurana, R. (2004). *Searching for a corporate savior: The irrational quest for charismatic CEOs.* Princeton, NJ: Princeton University Press.

Kiatpongsan, S., & Norton, M. I. (2014). How much (more) should CEOs make? A universal desire for more equal pay. *Perspectives on Psychological Science, 9*(6), 587–593.

Kram, K. E. (1983). Phases of the mentor relationship. *Academy of Management Journal, 26*(4), 608–625.

Kram, K. E. (1985). *Mentoring at work: Developmental relationships in organizational life.* Glenview, IL: Scott, Foresman.

Krishnamurty, K., Carberry, E., and Scully, M. (2015). The tenacity *and* tenuousness of meritocracy: The legitimation of status and inequality in Indian management education. Paper presented at the annual meeting of the European Group on Organization Studies (EGOS), Athens, Greece, July.

Lehmann, W. (2009). Becoming middle class: How working-class university students draw and transgress moral class boundaries. *Sociology, 43*(4), 631–647.

Lieber, R. (2015, May 21). Essays about work and class that caught a college's eye. *New York Times.* Retrieved from www.nytimes.com/2015/05/23/your-money/essays-about-work-and-class-that-caught-a-colleges-eye.html.

Levinson, D. J., Darrow, C., Klein, E., Levinson, M., & McKee, B. (1978). *The seasons of a man's life.* New York: Ballantine Books.

Liu, D., Liu, J., Kwan, H. K., & Mao, Y. (2009). What can I gain as a mentor? The effect of mentoring on the job performance and social status of mentors in China. *Journal of Occupational and Organizational Psychology, 82*(4), 871–895.

Lyness, K. S., & Thompson, D. E. (2000). Climbing the corporate ladder: Do female and male executives follow the same route? *Journal of Applied Psychology, 85*(1), 86–92.

Meyerson, D. E., & Scully, M. A. (1995). Tempered radicalism and the politics of ambivalence and change. *Organization Science, 6*(5), 585–600.

Miner, A. S. (1987). Idiosyncratic jobs in formalized organizations. *Administrative Science Quarterly, 32*(3), 327–351.

Morrison, A. M., White, R. P., & Van Velsor, E. (1987). *Breaking the glass ceiling: Can women reach the top of America's largest corporations?* New York: Basic Books.

Murphy, W., & Kram, K. E. (2014). *Strategic relationships at work: Creating your circle of mentors, sponsors, and peers for success in business and life.* New York: McGraw Hill Professional.

Muskal, F. (2007). Mentoring across social class boundaries: Empirical lessons. In M. C. Brown (Ed.), *Still not equal: Expanding educational opportunity in society* (pp. 279–296). New York: Peter Lang.

Naveh, E. (1991). The transformation of the "rags to riches" stories: Business biographies of success in the Progressive Era and the 1920s. *American Studies International, 29*(1), 60–80.

Newman, K. S. (1988). *Falling from grace: The experience of downward mobility in the American middle class.* New York: Free Press.

Nkomo, S. M., & Cox, T. (1989). Gender differences in the upward mobility of Black managers: Double whammy or double advantage? *Sex Roles, 21*(11–12), 825–839.

Nkomo, S. M., & Cox, T. (1990). Factors affecting the upward mobility of black managers in private sector organizations. *The Review of Black Political Economy, 18*(3), 39–57.

O'Neill, R. M., & Blake-Beard, S. D. (2002). Gender barriers to the female mentor–male protégé relationship. *Journal of Business Ethics, 37*(1), 51–63.

Poulsen, K. M. (2006). Implementing successful mentoring programs: Career definition vs mentoring approach. *Industrial and Commercial Training, 38*(5), 251–258.

Ragins, B. R. (2008). Disclosure disconnects: Antecedents and consequences of disclosing invisible stigmas across life domains. *Academy of Management Review, 33*(1), 194–215.

Ragins, B. R., & McFarlin, D. B. (1990). Perceptions of mentor roles in cross-gender mentoring relationships. *Journal of Vocational Behavior, 37*(3), 321–339.

Ragins, B. R., Townsend, B., & Mattis, M. (1998). Gender gap in the executive suite: CEOs and female executives report on breaking the glass ceiling. *The Academy of Management Executive, 12*(1), 28–42.

Rawlins, M. E., & Rawlins, L. (1983). Mentoring and networking for helping professionals. *Personnel & Guidance Journal, 62*(2), 116–118.

Reis, G. G., Fleury, M. T. L., Fleury, A. C. C., & Zambaldi, F. (2015). Brazilian multinational competences: Impacts of "tug of war" between cultural legacies and global mindedness. *Brazilian Business Review, 12*(1), 55–79.

Reskin, B. F., & Padavic, I. (1988). Supervisors as gatekeepers: Male supervisors' response to women's integration in plant jobs. *Social Problems, 35*(5), 536–550.

Rivera, L. (2015). *Pedigree: How elite students get elite jobs.* Princeton, NJ: Princeton University Press.

Scandura, T. A., & Williams, E. A. (2001). An investigation of the moderating effects of gender on the relationships between mentorship initiation and protege perceptions of mentoring functions. *Journal of Vocational Behavior, 59*(3), 342–363.

Schuler, R. S., & Jackson, S. E. (1987). Linking competitive strategies with human resource management practices. *The Academy of Management Executive (1987–1989), 1*(3), 207–219.

Scully, M. (1997). Meritocracy. In R. E. Freeman, & P. H. Werhane (Eds.), *Dictionary of business ethics* (1st ed.). London: Blackwell Publishers.

Scully, M. (2000). "Manage your own employability": Meritocracy and the legitimation of inequality in internal labor markets and beyond. In C. Leana, & D. Rousseau (Eds.), *Relational wealth: The advantages of stability in a changing economy* (pp. 199–216). New York: Oxford University Press.

Scully, M., & Blake-Beard, S. (2005). Locating class in organizational diversity work: Class as structure, style, and process. In A. Konrad, P. Prasad, & J. Pringle (Eds.), *The handbook of workplace diversity* (pp. 431–454). London: Sage Publications.

Sennett, R., & Cobb, J. (1972). *The hidden injuries of class.* New York: W. W. Norton.

Sharone, O. (2007). Constructing unemployed job seekers as professional workers: The depoliticizing work–game of job searching. *Qualitative Sociology, 30*(4), 403–416.

Smith, E. A. (2011). The role of tacit and explicit knowledge in the workplace. *Journal of Knowledge Management, 5*(4), 311–321.

Smith, L., & Redington, R. M. (2010). Class Dismissed: Making the case for the study of classist microaggressions. In D. W. Sue (Ed.), *Microaggressions and marginality: Manifestation, dynamics, and impact* (pp. 269–286). Hoboken, NJ: Wiley and Sons.

Thomas, D. A. (1993). Racial dynamics in cross-race developmental relationships. *Administrative Science Quarterly, 38*(2), 169–194.

Van Collie, S. C. (1998). Moving up through mentoring. *Workforce, 77*(3), 36–39.

Warihay, P. D. (1980). The climb to the top: Is the network the route for women? *Personnel Administrator, 25*(4), 55–60.

Weaver, K., Crayne, M. P., & Jones, K. S. (2016). IO at a Crossroad: The value of an intersectional research approach. *Industrial and Organizational Psychology, 9*(1), 197–206.

Weinstein, M., & Obloj, K. (2002). Strategic and environmental determinants of HRM innovations in post-socialist Poland. *International Journal of Human Resource Management, 13*(4), 642–659.

Wellington, S. W. (1999). *Creating women's networks: A how-to guide for women and companies.* San Francisco, CA: Jossey-Bass.

Westcott, D. N. (1982). Blacks in the 1970's: Did they scale the job ladder? *Monthly Labor Review, 105*(6), 29.

Whitely, W., Dougherty, T. W., & Dreher, G. F. (1991). Relationship of career mentoring and socioeconomic origin to managers' and professionals' early career progress. *Academy of Management Journal, 34*(2), 331–350.

Willis, P. E. (1977). *Learning to labor: How working class kids get working class jobs.* New York: Columbia University Press.

Zey, M. (1984). *The mentor connection.* Homewood, IL: Irwin Professional Publishing.

10

USING CRITICAL MANAGEMENT STUDIES TO ADVANCE MENTORING THEORY AND PRACTICE

Michelle Ann Kweder

Mentoring is most often seen as an organizational good—a "win–win" for both mentors and mentees where mentors provide "young adults with career-enhancing functions" while mentors gain "satisfaction in enabling a younger colleague to learn how to navigate in the organizational world" (Kram & Isabella, 1985: 111). Although the exact parameters of the relationship can vary, mentoring is commonly understood as the "developmental relationship that is embedded within the career context" (Ragins & Kram, 2007: 5).

The literature on mentoring has evolved substantially over the past several decades (see Allen, Eby, Poteet, Lentz, & Lima, 2004). Some researchers have examined new models such as peer mentoring (e.g., McManus & Russell, 2007), reverse mentoring (Murphy, 2012), and e-mentoring (Hamilton & Scandura, 2002). Other have named less than ideal situations including "serious relational problems" such as "sabotage, exploitation, harassment, deception, and manipulation" (Eby, 2007: 326). However, few have critically and theoretically examined the possible role of mentoring in assimilation at the individual level and in the reproduction of various forms of inequality (social, economic, racial, gender, etc.) at the organizational and societal level. This critical examination is important given that mentoring is described by researchers as having "the capacity to transform individuals, groups, organizations, and communities" (Ragins & Kram, 2007: 5). Unfortunately, mentoring theory and practice have not evolved in a way that moves us from a traditional developmental model toward transformation or emancipation. Utilizing a critical management studies (CMS) lens on mainstream mentoring research allows for creative possibilities and engaging in a dialog which questions fundamental assumptions within the existing literature such as the "subordinate status of participants as its central warrant" (Brewis & Wray-Bliss, 2008: 1543).[1]

While CMS has been described as a "big tent," contemporary scholars mostly agree on three areas of critique: questioning the performativity of intent, denaturalizing taken-for-granted organizational knowledge or practice, and expecting a high level of reflexivity from researchers and other actors (Fournier & Grey, 2000). These three elements will be used to theorize critically about current as well as future mentoring theory and practice. This work is my attempt to move the theorizing of mentoring relationships from the traditional approach to a critical analysis in order to both inform and shape our dialog moving forward.

From Critical Management Studies to Critical Mentoring Studies

Although criticism of organizations and management is not a new phenomenon, its recognition as a serious scholarly study is more recent. In 1992, Alvesson and Willmott edited *Critical Management Studies*, a book that brought together a group of scholars predominately from the UK under one theoretical umbrella. In the following years, CMS has broadened its scope to become increasingly global and include those teaching, learning, and researching in places considered more and less developed. This foundation work has shaped the formation of CMS thought and inquiry moving forward.

More recently, CMS scholars have come from a diversity of theoretical positions including neo-Marxism, post-structuralism, deconstructionism, literary criticism, feminism, psychoanalysis, cultural studies, and environmentalism. Many share all or some of three key elements: non-performative intent, denaturalization of taken-for-granted organizational knowledge, and emphasis on reflexivity (Fournier & Grey, 2000). CMS has been used to theorize and analyze various subfields of organizational studies such as accounting (e.g., Collier, 2001; Neu, Cooper, & Everett, 2001; Moore, 1991); information technology (e.g., Kvasny & Richardson, 2006); CSR (e.g., Costas & Kärreman, 2013); diversity and inclusion (e.g., Banerjee & Linstead, 2001; Kalonaityte, 2010; Zanoni, Janssens, Benschop, & Nkomo, 2010); and leadership (Collinson, 2012; Sinclair, 2004). However, little has been done in linking "critical mentoring studies" with the extant literature on mentoring, with a few exceptions.

Darwin (2000) critiques the traditional functionalist mentoring practices of helping younger protégés advance their careers. This process typically involves the mentor showcasing their work and modeling competencies in order to develop a mentee's self-confidence that defines their fit for future leadership positions. This traditional approach also draws attention to recycled power relationships, thus reinforcing models of hierarchal leadership. Darwin's critique is located in the field of adult education, informed by Freirian pedagogy, and anchored by radical humanist theory. She questions both the notion of the learning organization and the processes of mentoring: "Is this an organization that has embraced the social democratic ethos of lifelong education or a fancy name applied to well-oiled corporatism of the new right?" (Darwin, 2000: n.p.)

Thus, Darwin begins the process of foregrounding issues of power, social justice, and reflexivity while both calling for and doubting assumptions embedded in traditional mentoring approaches that "the possibility of a co-learning, interdependent activity—which encourages authentic dialogue and power sharing across cultures, genders, and hierarchical levels." (Darwin, 2000: n.p.).

While the initial critique by Darwin first problematized mainstream mentoring, it also served as a catalyst for theorizing the mentoring relationship as a site of social change, privilege traitorship, and resistance. This chapter seeks to destabilize and problematize mentoring at this moment because *it is necessary*. By disrupting the pattern of recycled power relationships embedded within traditional views, a CMS perspective argues that mentoring has the possibility of having emancipatory qualities in a societal context where abuses of power continue. In the USA, those abuses are most obviously exemplified by the prison industrial complex and its mass incarceration (especially of Black men), state-sanctioned violence including torture, and growing income inequality and poverty, including 1.6m households with 3.5m children living in extreme poverty[2] (Shaefer & Edin, 2014). These abuses of power are neither limited to these issues or contained within US borders as the USA continues an aggressive project of global capitalization. As Mohanty writes, "people of and from the Third World live not only under Western eyes but also within them" (2002: 516). Thus, the three key tenants of CMS provide an illuminating framework by which contemporary mentoring studies can move forward toward critical mentoring studies.

Questioning the Performativity of Intent

When thinking and theorizing through a CMS lens, mentoring can be seen as a mechanism of the historically contextualized contemporary capitalist organization. Thus, traditional mentoring approaches prioritize performativity over the authenticity of the individual, part of or similar to what Fleming and Spicer (2003) term "corporate culture engineering." CMS sees the questioning of performativity as not taking "management as a desirable given, seeking to pinpoint the inequalities and problematics that management-as-discourse (re)produces" (Brewis & Wray-Bliss, 2008: 1521). To gain insight into their perspective, I describe and compare to mentoring the workings of three similar and related mechanisms of this engineering: CSR, multiculturalism (also referred to as diversity and inclusion), and "performative reflexivity" (Hancock & Tyler, 2004).

Costas and Kärreman (2013) write of the "aspirational control" and "identity regulation" of CSR as part of an HRM function:

> CSR initiatives mostly derive their persuasive power from the assumption that they provide a path for organizational members to engage in "good" causes and morally worthy activities, thereby fulfilling the ideal of a

"good" person. They offer clear definition of instruction on how to be good. On one level these instructions can be interpreted as a rather blunt way of exercising technocratic control: specific guidelines on what to do and procedures and policies for how to act. [...] However, the technocratic edge is softened by the fact that a lot of CSR activities are supposed to be voluntary or operate on a symbolic level and are not really enforced in a strong sense by management. Here CSR initiatives mostly exercise control in the socio-ideological mode.

(Costas & Kärreman, 2013: 406)

The mentoring relationship may be seen in a similar fashion. A mentor, in fact, may use the relationship to shape goals and outcomes (aspirational control) or define culture and organizational realities (identity regulation) through the use of formal, reference, or other persuasive forms of power. If a mentor's role is to help a protégé learn the ropes (Ragins & Kram, 2007: 5), that assistance may be done through a lens similar to what is used for CSR initiatives where being a "good" person and "good" employee are intertwined into what Kärreman and Alvesson (2010, in Costas & Kärreman, 2013) term ethical sealing.

The second illustration is taken from Banerjee and Linstead, who write critically of multiculturalism as it is applied in both national and organizational settings. As these authors state:

This notion of multiculturalism is problematic and, as we shall see, perpetuates hegemonic modes of relations in a global context. It does not acknowledge, let alone challenge, existing material inequalities of opportunity and access.

(Banerjee and Linstead, 2001: 703)

and

Cultural diversity therefore is seen as a market opportunity whether it is in the form of niche marketing efforts directed at "ethnic" communities [...] or using "authentic" cultural knowledge to exploit foreign markets.

(Banerjee and Linstead, 2001: 707)

Like CSR, diversity and inclusion initiatives enforce both aspirational control and "identity regulation." The standards of what determines multiculturalism are defined, enacted, and validated by those in domination or powerful positions. As long as the terms of inclusion are dictated by those in positional power and norms of neoliberal capitalism are not disrupted, then diversity is tolerated and valued. For example, diversity and inclusion are celebrated when they are framed as a way to reduce costs (e.g., CSR initiatives that reduce packaging of goods), or open markets (e.g., diversity and inclusion initiatives that reach "the bottom of the pyramid"), or help the organization remain in compliance with regulations (e.g., avoiding law suits for discrimination). However, when critically examined, this business case for diversity has been shown to "de-emphasizes [*sic*] management's complicity in the history of exclusion and focuses on the economic and functionalist side of workplace diversity [...] [h]omogeneity is created, but not change" (Kalonaityte, 2010: 33).

The learning the ropes view of mentoring is validated by similar mechanisms as those that are driving CSR or multiculturalism efforts. Doing good or valuing difference are often defined in exclusively instrumental terms that are rarely disruptive to the dominant culture or structures that both create and perpetuate social imbalance and injustice. Mentoring has its own mechanistic role where the elder person trains the junior person to not only learn the ropes but also to "toe the line" concerning taken-for-granted organizational knowledge, processes, and cultural rituals that are deeply infused with normative ideals of individual, group, organizational, and national definitions of success.

"Performative reflexivity" differs from the reflexivity called for by CMS in that it is neither critical in form nor purpose (Hancock & Tyler, 2004). A clear example is provided by Hancock and Tyler, who have researched the "ongoing managerialist colonization of the everyday life world" (2004: 619). They both describe and problematize the performativity of intent embedded with the oxymoronic practice of the managerial class:

> a posited colonization of everyday life by managerial discourse, and the proliferation of a performance imperative by which it is underpinned means, therefore, that the freedom to pursue our sense of self through genuinely inter-subjective social relations devoid of mass-mediated performance pressures and linear purposiveness, of "the creation—and a maintenance—of a BRAND CALLED YOU" (Peters, 1997: 6),[3] is largely denied as authentic experiences of being are increasingly excluded from the ensuing pseudo-individualizing hegemony. The aggregate effect of which, we would argue, is entirely commensurate with both atomization of the individual and the individualization of system contradiction, leaving many people feeling literally "beside themselves" (see Benhabib, 1992).
>
> (Hancock & Tyler, 2004: 640)

Traditional mentoring, as largely described in mainstream literature is one of the core inter-subjective workplace relationships infused with both performance pressures and linear purposiveness as defined by its often touted metrics of success such as promotions, status, and higher incomes (Dougherty & Dreher, 2007). Questioning the intent of mentoring involves questioning the likely coexistence of performative reflexivity and its colonizing consequence on individuals, which ultimately has repercussions for organizations, communities, and society.

Much of CMS scholarship can be used to re-conceptualize how organizational tools are used to colonize (Casey, in Fleming & Spicer, 2003: 2) workers' identities so that they are more productive and less recalcitrant (Fleming & Spicer, 2003: 2). For example, formal mentoring programs can be seen as tools of assimilation and control where mentees and mentoring relationships are disempowered and bound by the assumption that mentoring is done to mold individuals and cultures rather than transform or disrupt them. Thus, mentoring can be critiqued as a process that will supplant or compromise workers' unique identities along one or more axes (gender, gender identity, religion, language fluency, citizenship status, religion, and other factors) in the name of organizational effectiveness.

The Denaturalization of Taken-for-Granted Organizational Knowledge

Part of the global nature of organizations including diverse mentoring relationships, is that they are necessarily racialized (Nkomo, 1992), gendered (Acker, 1990), and embedded in other invisible social identities at work (Clair, Beatty, & MacLean, 2005). The shaping of these identities should be viewed in tandem with a critical "analysis of the political economy of contemporary capitalism" (Azmanova, 2012: 148). Denaturalizing taken-for-granted mentoring knowledge begins with problematizing *both* the largely individualistic dual aims of developing both career and psychosocial skills for career advancement and longevity. This critique involves moving from a model of equality to equity.

The practice of mentoring high potentials or rising stars, or the practice of mentors selecting protégés on the basis of their competency and potential (Singh, Ragins, & Tharenou, 2009), can mean that the mechanism of mentoring reproduces inequality by continually promoting those who have had early advantages such as education, training, and the acquisition of social capital through privileged intersectional social identity factors (race, class, gender, etc.). Additionally, Turban and Dougherty found that workers with "an internal locus of control, high self-monitoring, and high emotional stability" were more likely to initiate and therefore be engaged in mentoring relationships (1994: 688). Both would privilege mentees with established social capital resources and disadvantage those without access to these connections, including those who think differently or elect to respond differently to organizational demands. In fact, mentors may see protégés who experience isolation, anger, or stress-related illness as a liability (Turban & Lee, 2007: 41). This disadvantaging builds a type of ableism into the mentoring relationship. Those who need mentoring the most may be the least likely to receive it in the context of unspoken judgments of deservingness embedded within global political economies of capitalism.

A better understanding of the mechanism for assimilation and the pitfalls of the traditional merit-based approach to mentoring practices can lead to uncovering embedded ableism within the dual aims of improving career skills and providing personal development as the definition of effective mentoring. These aims often result in promotions and higher incomes (Dougherty & Dreher, 2007). The challenge arises when we ask *for whom* and *at the expense of whom* are these existing practices and outcomes exercised? When contextualizing these outcomes in today's political economy, the answer is likely for *the already economically privileged* and at the expense of the *economically disadvantaged*. The valued outcome results in amplified material consequences and increased economic inequality both within and between people and organizations.

From the Margins: Reflexivity for Social Justice

Critical reflexivity "aims, even if only ideally, at a full understanding of the researcher, the researched and the research context" (Rose, 1997: 305). As a theorist, I will apply the same aims, paying most careful attention to "the differences that matter" within the context of mentoring (Ahmed, 1998).

Understanding the Theorist

Understanding "what matters" is not understanding the typical intersection identity categories. As a CMS research and theorist, I usually easily disclose (race, citizenship, socio-economic status, gender, and sexuality which happen to be White, US, mixed having moved from a low-income SES to an upper-middle-class SES, female, and lesbian). Rather, I can identify three "differences that matter" which shape as well as inform the current analysis: my primary and secondary areas of scholarship, my relationship to one of the Editors, and my personal experience with mentoring.

First, while I critically study "Mainstream Graduate Management Education" (MGME), I do not primarily study mentoring practice or theory. Specially, I used critical discourse analysis (CDA) as a methodology to examine existing work (e.g., subsets of the cases and interdisciplinary intertextual readings) and an epistemology of intersectionality distinguishes my methodology. I have no doubt that my larger body of work of MGME and much of the intertextual reading I have done (feminist and anti-colonial theory) inform my critique of mentoring. Moreover, my emerging secondary area of research focuses, in part, on "organizations of confinement" (e.g., prisons, detention centers, military prisons, and involuntary mental health facilities). While many readers might immediately place mentoring as a helpful process in global corporations, I immediately think of the psychologists who "mentored" the torturers at Guantanamo. Thus, my research is situated on the margins of traditional management and organizational studies. It is from these realities that I research and write.

Second, you are reading this work because of a mentoring relationship. My former MBA professor, friend, mentor, and dissertation committee member is co-editor Stacy Blake-Beard. Critical work—especially CMS in the USA—is mainly siloed in specific journals and collections often still controlled by White British men. This critical work can stand next to more normative work because of the sisterly "sponsorship" embedded in my mentoring relationship with Stacy Blake-Beard.

Third, with one exception (my only formal mentoring experience), I have had wonderful experiences as both a mentor and a protégée. In my fifteen-plus years before entering the academy, I had multiple informal mentoring relationships. There was one stand-out relationship that both helped me negotiate normative success (promotion and increased income) while helping maintain my ethical center. As a consultant, I continue to pride myself on spotting "talent"—often somehow marginalized by identity (lesbian, bisexual, and/or of color)—and helping them make the transition from administrative staff to program or management staff while always acknowledging the issues of oppression at work in their organizations. My experience as a protégée in the academic experience is mixed. This is in part because of my vocal criticism of my graduate training that seemed overly functionalistic, intent on naturalizing the acceptance of rapid research production (at the expense of teaching and everyday life), and representative of a reflexivity that, again, seemed performative. My mentors have largely remained my MBA professors, with the exception of my dissertation chair and multiple critical women from across the globe who share an interest in intersectional, anti/post-colonial feminisms, and making change within the academy and in broader society. Yet, when I am in the space of the academy, I find myself "beside myself." The experience of expressing truth comes (mostly) from a practice that is not of my body. My cis-gendered female body is left behind to present through strictly policed formats that can only occasionally be left under the guise of being a "public intellectual."

Understanding the Theorizing and the Context

> One of the many challenges of globalization is preventing perpetuation, or increase, of the inequitable distribution of wealth and resources.
>
> (Banerjee & Linstead, 2001: 711)

Questioning the concept of a sovereign nation state[4] allows for a redefining of the concept of global. A taken-for-granted concept of "global" can become a trope where the West is seen as an advantaged group of organizations and knowledge traveling to the "other," a less advantaged place lacking organizations and knowledge where resources are extracted, imported, and monetized by the West. When indigenous practices from other areas, especially less developed nations, are imported, they are generally tolerated if they are cost-neutral, benign, or appropriate—if they are able to meet the goal of "maximum output for minimum input" (Fournier & Grey, 2000: 180). In a redefined "global," where not all people, organizations, knowledge, and resources are the property of a single nation state, can exist in multiple spaces, and are not static, we can begin to understand the complexity of relationships, including mentoring relationships. In this *global* context, relationships are infused with power and politics. Additionally, US management practice and theory is leaky. Taken-for-granted profit-centered motives are purposefully diffused within and across borders entering the spaces of NGOs, governments, families, and everyday life.

The idea of place stability is increasingly interrupted by migration (forced and chosen), travel, virtual communication, and other global factors. Although CMS views on mentoring may not at times seem explicitly global, they are heavily reliant on Mohanty's (2002) ideas of *One-Third/Two-Thirds Worlds* that exist both *within* and between nations and indigenous communities. Sassen (in Banerjee & Linstead, 2001) argues similarly that the national/global binary does not fully capture the complexities of globalization processes. Global is neither a "brand" nor a "strategy" but a reality with a historical context and current economic implications for individuals, families, and communities. Thus, mentoring must be situated within the global, historical, and cultural context that exists both inside and outside of traditional organizational boundaries.

The "global organization" is not just relevant to for-profit organizations but also the family-owned Guatemalan coffee shop in Valencia, Spain (where I have been writing this chapter), the agency that my neighbors use to procure a new nanny each year, and the many nameless workers who make my clothes, process my online purchases, and exist somewhere along a global supply chain that is marred by some of the worst practices in global business. Global is not only the stereotypical scenario of a White Western male manager remotely supervising "ethnic" male employees in a call center in the global South (and similar examples) but is also embedded in everyday practices including the purchases we make, the global footprint we leave behind, the policies we vote for (directly or by representation), and the world we construct through our own discourses.

Thus, my intent with these illustrations is not to geographically situate the mentor-protégée relationship but to remind us that each mentor–mentee relationship exists in a larger historical, cultural, and contemporary context. For example, the increase in income that the protégée gets at any global firm may allow her to more regularly purchase coffee at her local coffee shop; however, she may also make improvements to her flat in East London accelerating gentrification of her neighborhood causing the coffee shop to not be able to afford the rent. When followed down the supply chain, this spiraling process may have negative impacts for the source of coffee, a Guatemalan women's coffee coop.

Critical Mentoring Studies and the Future

Brewis and Wray-Bliss posit that the "researcher's central task as seeking not just to articulate but also practically change the marginalized status of certain research participants" (2008: 1531). I would argue that this should be the same intent of the theorist. So how can we rethink mentoring to include a different set of people and practices not currently included in mainstream theory, research, and practice?

Azmanova, when writing of social justice, calls for an "emancipation from structural injustice—the injustice of submitting to the operative logic (rules of the game) of the social order under considerations" (2012: 148). On a very basic level, that could mean individual workers resisting organizational mechanisms such as CSR, diversity and inclusion initiatives, and mentoring programs. That is certainly one possibility.

Mentoring relationships can also be theorized as a space for resistance. Resistance is not a new or undocumented theme in organizational studies (e.g., Roy, 1959; Prasad & Prasad, 2000). Resistance is generally thought of as a collective movement of dissent or actions taken by a leader and followers. The possibility of resistance in or supported by mentoring relationships and what it means for transformative disruptions are provocative.

Mentoring relationships could become (and likely already are for some) a "critical space" (Kalonaityte, 2010: 32) of reflexivity where participants continually ask the questions *for whom* and *at the expense of whom* is our relationship occurring? (See also, Banerjee & Linstead 2001). This questioning can lead to action and a change in how we design, develop, and define effective diverse mentoring relationships.

Drawing from Delgado's theory of the "race traitor,"[5] I suggest that the role of the "privilege traitor" within the mentoring relationship (Delgado, 1997) should be examined in future work. Tangibly, "traitorship" can lead to a number of justice-supporting and producing actions such as a rising-star mentee who opts out of a mentoring relationship to allow a less privileged colleague the advantage, mentors and mentees refusing pay increases while advocating for intra-organizational pay equality (Kweder, 2014), or a protégée taking a promotion with the *sole* intent on centering social justice practices in the workplace. These actions are likely to fall along a continuum of "organizational shocks" (Weick in Mills, Thurlow, & Mills, 2010: 183) helpful in beginning or supporting larger movements external to the organization of origin.

Drawing on social movement theory, mentor pairs or groups show promise in supporting efforts of workplaces' justice. McAdam and Paulsen conclude that individuals are likely to join a movement based on:

> four limiting conditions: (1) the occurrence of a specific recruiting attempt, (2) the successful linkage of movement and identity, (3) support for that linkage from persons who normally serve to sustain the identity in question, and (4) the absence of strong opposition from others on whom other salient identities depend.
>
> (McAdam and Paulsen, 1993: 662)

Conditions three and four are key to participation. Informal mentoring relationships have the possibility of supporting the link between movement and identity. It is likely that these relationships played roles in some recent high-profile acts of resistance in the USA, including the Market Basket strike[6] or the increasingly successful efforts of Adjunct Action.[7]

Further Considerations and Conclusion

> If your success is defined as being well adjusted to injustice and well adapted to indifference, we don't want successful leaders.
>
> (Cornell West in Serwer, 2011)

> place consciousness [...] encourages us to come together around common, local experiences and organize around our hopes for the future of our communities and cities. While global capitalism doesn't give a damn about the people or the natural environment of any particular place because it can always move on to other people and other places, place-based civic activism is concerned about the health and safety of people and places.
>
> (Boggs 2000: 19, in Mohanty, 2002: 515)

Additional work—I would argue interdisciplinary work—needs to be done within and beyond critical management studies and mentoring studies to begin to imagine the majority of our organizations as emancipatory and equity producing. Having taken this initial theoretical attempt at a "critical mentoring studies," it is easy to begin to identity the unfinished business of this work.

First, much has been done in the area of Critical Leadership Studies. Much of mentorship operates on the assumption of leadership as a universally desired attribute. Particularly intriguing is the possible intersection of Sinclair's concept of leadership as "seduction" (2009) and the mentoring relationship. Can mentoring interrupt a cycle of leadership that appears, as West articulates, as "well adjusted to injustice"? How are organizational mechanisms such as CSR, diversity and inclusion, performative reflexivity, mentoring and, I would add onboarding, used independently and in combination to "socialize" workers to the brand culture and naturalize managerial practices as a universal, agreed-upon common good? And is it possible that these mechanisms "back-fire" and play a role in workplace resistance? Are there "positive deviants" (Pascale, Sternin, & Sternin, 2010) who remain critically reflexive throughout the processes? Third, is a new attention to global *place*. We know how a T-shirt operates in a global economy (Rivoli, 2005), but how does mentoring impact the global economy? Can we follow, in empirical detail, the global impacts of a protégée's career success to better understand if the mentoring relationship is inequality enabling, status quo upholding, social change producing, or some combination? Finally, by entertaining the thought of mentoring as a critical practice with the aim of emancipation at the individual level and social justice at the organizational and, aspirationally, at the societal levels, we can further broaden the definition of "diverse leaders" to those who resist the mostly hegemonic careerist aims of (increasingly global) society often at the expense of larger societal goods such as economic, environmental, racial, and gender justice.

Notes

1 Brewis and Wray-Bliss are arguing this possibility for research participants. Here I use this concept more broadly to talk about participants in informal and formal mentoring relationships and the larger organizations, communities, and society in which they reside.
2 In the USA, extreme poverty is defined as living on $2 or less per person per day.
3 There continues to be much unproblemitized discussion of "the personal brand" in workplaces, management schools, and the mainstream media. Ulrich and Smallwood write to an executive audience:

> Ultimately, for culture to permeate a company, it must shift what leaders know and do. Leaders send signals to employees about what matters and how to approach work. Leadership brand implies that leaders' knowledge, skills, and values are shaped by customer expectations. A leadership brand exists in a company when customers' expectations translate to employee actions because of leadership practices.
>
> (Ulrich & Smallwood (2008: 27)

Here the conflating of customer expectation and leadership values do not consider the authentic experiences of the individual and the cultural and historical contexts in which leadership is occurring.
4 Problematizing the nation state is beyond the scope of this paper and has been well written by theorists such as Mbembe and Nuttall (2004) and Comaroff and Comaroff (2009). However, for the sake of this work, I accept the premise that scholars such as the aforementioned put forward.
5 Delgado best explains the concept of the race traitor with an example:

> If you refuse to be white you begin the process of destabilizing this construction that society relies on to preserve the current system of racial subordination. So, suppose a neatly dressed white person, who happens to be a race traitor, is pulled over by a police officer and then let go with a warning. The person ought to question the officer, "Would you have done this if I had been black?"
>
> (Delgado 1997: 615)

6 Market Basket workers (managers, warehouse workers, truck drivers, cashiers, and others) when on strike to bring back their boss after he was "sacked in a long-running family feud" (Gittleson, 2014). Market Basket is known regionally as an organization with a "family" feel where employees earn living wages, have sick time, and receive bonuses. Many are also immigrants who may share other important organizational ties (religious affiliation, neighborhood identity, communities formed through local schools, etc.).
7 From the Adjunct Action website:

> Adjunct Action is a campaign that unites adjunct professors at campuses across the country to address the crisis in higher education and the troubling trend toward a marginalized teaching faculty that endangers our profession. At most colleges and universities, adjuncts are a majority of all teaching faculty yet we still face low levels of compensation, no benefits, lack of institutional support for research and scholarship, and exclusion from the governance of our institutions.

References

Acker, J. (1990). Hierarchies, jobs, and bodies: A theory of gendered organizations. *Gender and Society, 4*(2), 81–95.

Adjunct Action: A project of SEIU. About Us. Retrieved from http://adjunctaction. org/about-us/.

Ahmed, S. (1998). *Differences that matter: Feminist theory and postmodernism.* Cambridge: Cambridge University Press.

Allen, T. D., Eby, L. T., Poteet, M. L., Lentz, E., & Lima, I. (2004). Career benefits associated with mentoring for protégés: A meta analytic review. *Journal of Applied Psychology, 89,* 127–136.

Alvesson, M., & Willmott, H. (Eds.) (1992). *Critical management studies.* London: Sage.

Azmanova, A. (2012). De-gendering social justice in the 21st century: An immanent critique of neoliberal capitalism. *European Journal of Social Theory, 15*(2), 143–156.

Banerjee, S. B., & Linstead, S. (2001). Globalization, Multiculturalism and Other Fictions: Colonialism for the New Millennium? *Organization, 8*(4), 683–722.

Brewis, J., & Wray-Bliss, E. (2008). Re-searching ethics: Towards a more reflexive critical management studies. *Organization Studies, 29*(12), 1521–1540.

Clair, J. A., Beatty, J. E., & MacLean, T. L. (2005). Out of sight but not out of mind: Managing invisible social identities in the workplace. *Academy of Management Review, 30*(1), 78–95.

Collier, Paul M. (2001). The power of accounting: A field study of local financial management in a police force. *Management Accounting Research, 12*(4), 465–486.

Collinson, D. (2012). Prozac leadership and the limits of positive thinking. *Leadership, 8*(2), 87–107.

Comaroff, J. L., & Comaroff, J. (2009). *Ethnicity, Inc.* Chicago, IL: University of Chicago Press.

Costas, J., & Kärreman, D. (2013). Conscience as control—managing employees through CSR. *Organization, 20*(3), 394–415.

Darwin, A. (2000). Critical reflections on mentoring in work settings. *Adult Education Quarterly, (50)*3, 197–211.

Delgado, R. (1997). Rodrigo's eleventh chronicle: Empathy and false empathy. In R. Delgado, & J. Stefancic (Eds.), *Critical white studies: Looking behind the mirror.* Philadelphia, PA: Temple University Press.

Dougherty, W., & Dreher, F. (2007). Mentoring and career outcomes: Conceptual and methodological issues in an emerging market. In B. R. Ragins, & K. E. Kram (Eds.), *The handbook of mentoring at work: Theory, research, and practice* (pp. 51–94). Los Angeles, CA: SAGE Publications.

Eby, L. (2007). Understanding relational problems in mentoring: A review and proposed investment model. In B. R. Ragins, & K. E. Kram (Eds.), *The handbook of mentoring at work: Theory, research, and practice* (pp. 323–334). Los Angeles, CA: SAGE Publications.

Fleming, P., & Spicer, A. (2003). Working at a cynical distance: Implications for power, subjectivity and resistance. *Organization, 10*(1), 157–179.

Fournier, V., & Grey, C. (2000). At the critical moment: Conditions and prospects for critical management studies. *Human Relations, 53*(1), 7–32.

Fortune. Global 500 (2014). Retrieved from http://fortune.com/global500/royal-dutch-shell-2/.

Gittleson, K. BBC News Business. (2014, August 1) Market Basket: Workers risk it all for their boss. *BBC News Business.* Retrieved from www.bbc.com/news/business-28580359.

Hamilton, B. A., & Scandura, T. A. (2002). E-mentoring: Implications for organizational learning and development in a wired world. *Organizational Dynamics, 31*(4), 388–402.

Hancock, P., & Tyler, M. (2004). "MOT your life": Critical management studies and the management of everyday life. *Human Relations, 57*(5), 619–645.

Kalonaityte, V. (2010). The case of vanishing borders: Theorizing diversity management as internal border control. *Organization, 17*(1), 31–52.

Kram, K., & Isabella, L. (1985). Mentoring Alternative: The Role of Peer Relationships in Career Development. *Academy of Management Journal, 25*(1), 110–132.

Kvasny, L., & Richardson, H. (2006). Critical research in information systems: Looking forward, looking back. *Information Technology & People, 19*(3), 196–202.

Kweder, M. A. (2014) Principled Leadership: A case for paid nonprofit internships. *Management Magazine.* Boston: Simmons College. Retrieved from www.simmons.edu/som/docs/Management_Magazine_-_Spring_2014(1).pdf.

McAdam, D., & Paulsen, R. (1993). Specifying the relationship between social ties and activism. *American Journal of Sociology, 99*(3), 640–667.

McManus, S. E., & Russell, J. E. A. (2007). Peer Mentoring Relationships. In B. R. Ragins, & K. E. Kram (Eds.), *The handbook of mentoring at work: Theory, research, and practice* (pp. 273–298). Los Angeles, CA: Sage Publications.

Mbembe, A. and Nuttall, S. (2004). Writing the World from an African Metropolis. *Public Culture, 16*(3), 347–372.

Mills, J. H., Thurlow, A., & Mills, A. J. (2010). Making sense of sensemaking: The critical sensemaking approach. *Qualitative Research in Organizations and Management: An International Journal, 5*(2), 182–195.

Mohanty, C. (2002). "Under Western Eyes" Revisited: Feminist Solidarity through Anticapitalist Struggles. *Signs, 28*(2), 499–535.

Moore, D. C. (1991). Accounting on trial: the critical legal studies movement and its lessons for radical accounting. *Accounting, Organizations and Society, 16*(8), 763–791.

Murphy, W. M. (2012). Reverse mentoring at work: Fostering cross-generational learning and developing millennial leaders. *Human Resource Management, 51*(4), 549–573.

Neu, D., Cooper, D. J., & Everett, J. (2001). Critical accounting interventions. *Critical Perspectives on Accounting, 12*(6), 735–762.

Nkomo, S. (1992). The Emperor Has No Clothes: Rewriting "Race in Organizations." *Academy of Management Review, 17*(3), 487–523.

Pascale, R. T., Sternin, J., & Sternin, M. (2010). *The power of positive deviance: How unlikely innovators solve the world's toughest problems,* Vol. 1. Boston, MA: Harvard Business Press.

Prasad, P., & Prasad, A. (2000). Stretching the iron cage: The constitution and implications of routine workplace resistance. *Organization Science, 11*(4), 387–403.

Ragins, B. R., & Kram, K. E. (2007). The roots and meaning of mentoring. In B R. Ragins, & K. E. Kram (Eds.), *The handbook of mentoring at work: Theory, research, and practice* (pp. 3–15). Los Angeles, CA: Sage Publications.

Rivoli, P. (2005). *The travels of a T-shirt in the global economy: An economist examines the markets, power, and politics of world trade.* Hoboken, NJ: John Wiley & Sons.

Rose, G. (1997). Situating knowledges: Positionality, reflexivities, and other tactics. *Progress in Human Geography, 21*(3), 305–320.

Roy, D. F. (1959). "Banana Time": Job satisfaction and informal interaction. *Human Organization, 18*(4), 158–168.

Serwer, Adam (2011, September 21). All the president's frenemies. *The American Prospect.* Retrieved from http://prospect.org/article/all-presidents-frenemies.

Shaefer, H. L, & Edin, K. (2014). The rise of extreme poverty in the United States. Retrieved from http://web.stanford.edu/group/scspi/_media/pdf/pathways/summer_2014/Pathways_Summer_2014_ShaeferEdin.pdf.

Sinclair, A. (2004). Journey Around Leadership. *Discourse: Studies in the Cultural Politics of Education, 25*(1), 7–19.

Sinclair, A. (2009). Seducing leadership: Stories of leadership development. *Gender, Work & Organization, 16*(2), 266–284.

Singh, R., Ragins, B. R., & Tharenou, P. (2009). Who gets a mentor? A longitudinal assessment of the rising star hypothesis. *Journal of Vocational Behavior, 74*(1), 11–17.

Turban, D. B., & Dougherty, T. W. (1994). Role of protégé personality in receipt of mentoring and career success. *Academy of Management Journal, 37*(3), 688–702.

Turban, D. B., & Lee, F. K. (2007). The role of personality in mentoring relationships: Formation, dynamics, and outcomes. In B. R. Ragins, & K. E. Kram (Eds.), *The handbook of mentoring at work: Theory, research, and practice* (pp. 21–50). Los Angeles, CA: Sage Publications.

Ulrich, D., & Smallwood, N. (2008). Aligning firm, leadership, and personal brand. *Leader to Leader, 47*(Winter), 24–32.

Zanoni, P., Janssens, M., Benschop, Y., & Nkomo, S. M. (2010). Unpacking diversity, grasping inequality: Rethinking difference through critical perspectives. *Organization, 17*(1), 9–29.

11

NEW PATHWAYS AND ALTERNATIVE SETTINGS

Applying Social Justice Principles to Mentoring in the Academy

Meg A. Bond, Maureen O'Connor, and Amanda Clinton

The original "Mentor" was a man entrusted by Odysseus to care for his family and serve as a tutor to his son, Telemachus, when the King left to fight in the Trojan War. Ultimately, however, it was Athena, the Goddess of Wisdom and War, who took the form of Mentor to provide Telemachus the guidance he needed to find Odysseus (Koocher, 2002). The term "mentor" has come to mean trusted advisor, teacher, sage, and friend. Yet at its root, there is the feminist notion that the process of mentoring is not necessarily a singular one-on-one relationship and, thus, approaches need to adapt to current realities (Allen, 1996; Buzzanell, Long, Anderson, Kokini, & Batra, 2015; Colley, 2001).

Even though the word "mentor" continues to refer to an individual who provides assistance and personal knowledge in support of the growth and ability of another, there is increasing recognition that we need to pay attention to needs that vary "across the boundaries of gender, ethnicity, and social class" (Crosby, 1999: 5). Mentorship can take on particular importance when it is employed to lessen disparities and increase life-changing opportunities most notably when enhancing access for members of historically marginalized groups (Rayburn, Denmark, Reuder, & Austra, 2010; Neville, 2015). This chapter will highlight mentoring approaches that push the margins of more traditional programs—both in terms of the specific strategies adopted and in terms of outcomes targeted.[1] Our examples explicitly incorporate social justice principles that emphasize attention to the collective and the importance of provoking change within the individual, social, and organizational contexts. Such efforts can simultaneously improve career success for women and under-represented minorities *and* lead to more fundamental change in the systems in which mentees and mentors work. We hope to encourage a re-imagining of individualized mentoring models and argue that both the process and the product of mentoring can be guided by social justice principles.

Our particular focus is on promoting success in higher education, though we believe that the overall framework could translate to other contexts as well. Our examples include programs designed to support the research and scholarship of diverse faculty and to promote innovations in academic administration, both of which are intended to support a broader vision for advancement of under-represented groups in academic positions. The examples include attention to individual growth alongside efforts that can shift the culture of the academy to be more in sync with varied professional development needs. These efforts also create new settings, promote collective arrangements for support, and challenge prevailing definitions of "success"—all of which ultimately help to pave a path toward sustained success for diverse members of the academy.

We suggest here that attending to the *process* of mentoring (i.e., how it is done) and expanding the targeted *outcomes* of mentoring (i.e., beyond individual mentee outcomes) can lead to systems-change that promotes under-represented groups and diverse leaders in addition to enhancing individual skill sets and advancement.

The Context of Inequality in Academia

Education systems around the world are plagued by well-documented inequal-ities (Cubillo & Brown, 2003; Knights & Richards, 2003). Many of these inequalities start in early childhood and persist throughout a person's life. For example, in the United States, youth of color enter college at lower rates (Horn & Nevill, 2006), and among those minority students who gain admission to post-secondary programs, fewer graduate, and degree completion takes longer than majority peers (Boykin & Noguera, 2011; Darling-Hammond, 2010). These inequalities carry over to faculty and administrators within academic institutions as well. At every juncture in the progression toward higher-level positions and leadership in academia, fewer and fewer women and members of under-represented racial and ethnic groups move to the next level. This leaky-pipeline pattern has been observed in institutions of higher learning around the world (e.g., Cubillo & Brown, 2003; Knights & Richards, 2003; Van den Brink & Stobbe, 2009).

Within this context, it is understandable that much of the literature on men-toring in academe focuses on increasing individuals' skills to facilitate individual educational or career success. Some work has grounded this individualized approach in awareness of gender, privilege dynamics, and multicultural perspec-tives (Bowman, Kite, Branscombe, & Williams, 1999; Denmark & Klara, 2010; Shields, 2012) and recognized the value of advancing psychosocial outcomes such as a sense of competence, identity, and confidence (Thomas, 1990). Nevertheless, it is our contention that simply coaching targeted individuals from diverse groups to advance in their profession will not change systems and thus accomplish the broader goals of equity and justice. Instead, we need to both create new pathways for under-represented groups to succeed and, even more importantly, challenge the structures and social norms that impede their progress. Specifically, we propose an expanded model of mentoring that supports a commitment to social change as part of the explicit purpose (see, e.g., Bridges, 2010; Moore, 1984). Many people use the metaphor of a leaky pipeline, with its implied linear progression toward "success," that assumes both a singular pathway and a rigid endpoint. Rather than a pipeline, we envision a sprinkler that, with effective and broad leadership vision, can nourish and help grow expanded images of success and endpoints for each individual.

Principles of Social Justice Mentoring

By adapting and applying principles of feminist, multicultural, community, and social psychology to the manner in which we mentor, we suggest making social justice principles explicit within mentoring scholarship and practice (see, e.g., Bridges, 2010; Goodman, Liang, Helms, Latta, Sparks, & Weintraub, 2004). Specifically, proponents of a social justice mentoring model resist encouraging mentees to succeed by simply mastering the current rules.[2] Instead, those who subscribe to a social justice model: (1) *question criteria for success by* introducing new pathways and challenge some previously unquestioned assumptions about what constitutes success; (2) *adopt mentee-centered approaches by* working diligently to identify mentees' interests, goals, and life challenges and to work collaboratively on how to creatively achieve those goals (i.e., mentee-centered mentoring that can include support for non-traditional pathways); (3) *create new settings for mentoring by* adopting a variety of approaches and establishing new settings where, for example, there is value for horizontal—in addition to hierarchical—relationships, encouraging learning in all directions and incorporating collaborative and collective mentoring (e.g., Clifford, 2003, cited in Paludi, Martin, Stern, & DeFour, 2010); and (4) *promote institutional change by* explicitly adopting approaches that provoke positive change in the immediate institution and in the larger social context to support more diverse participants in the academy.

Shifting the Context for Mentoring among University Faculty

Faculty in most colleges and universities are expected to shine in the three areas of research and scholarship, teaching, and service. Excelling in all three and learning how to balance these priorities is extraordinarily difficult, and faculty are often provided little support and guidance (Taylor & Martin, 1987). Finding appropriate mentorship as faculty navigate these sometimes-conflicting demands is particularly challenging for people who are outside the majority (i.e., often people of color and/or women) and for people who are interested in studying issues that are value-based (e.g., topics considered non-mainstream such as applied, action-oriented work explicitly connected to social justice). Moreover, traditional (formal) models of mentoring are suggested to be less helpful for those in under-represented statuses or with alternative career aspirations (Smith, 2000). A mentoring relationship imposed through formal programs can lead to discomfort and resentment, and can be influenced by underlying stereotypes and biases (Smith, 2000). Even informal mentoring, particularly in cross-race relationships, may be less likely to overcome historical differences and lead to psychosocial support (Blake, 1999).

In this section of the chapter, we highlight an approach to mentoring university faculty doing research relevant to social justice. Since its inception in 1998, the Center for Women and Work (CWW) at the University of Massachusetts Lowell has demonstrated its commitment to addressing equity at work in several key ways: by designing and implementing programs and projects that foster new ways of thinking about the gendered conditions of work; by encouraging and supporting interdisciplinary linkages among scholars with relevant expertise; and by bringing to the forefront the reciprocal relationship between women's work and the well-being of families and communities. At the heart of CWW is an Associates Program that serves as a hub for innovative scholarly projects related to the center's mission. CWW fosters a dynamic and growing, multi-disciplinary community of scholars who are actively involved in pursuing their individual projects related to women and work. Associates have come from the fields of anthropology, English, economics, education, history, management, nursing, political science, public health, engineering, labor relations, psychology, and sociology. What is most distinctive about CWW, however, is not the simple affiliation of such a diverse group of faculty with diverse areas of scholarship. Rather, it is a deliberate effort to foster a community of scholars who are invested in supporting one another in their professional development and success. At one level, the structure of the Associates Program is very simple in that faculty meet about once a month to talk about their work with one another. However, the foundation for such meetings is built upon numerous deliberate strategies to create a setting that allows for multi-directional support and guidance and that counters some of the isolating aspects of traditional academic cultures and traditional mentoring relationships (University of Massachusetts Lowell CWW).

The Culture of the Academy: Questioning Existing Criteria for Success

One of the values promoted within the academy that can present particular challenges for mentoring of any kind revolves around how success is defined (Bond & Sladkova, 2014; Braxton, Luckey, & Helland, 2006; Eddy & Mitchell,

2012). The strength of one's contributions within the academy is typically based upon one's *individual* research program. In many disciplines, particularly social sciences and humanities, solo authorship is the most highly valued sign of productivity. One's contributions to shared authorships are often deemed "less than" sole authorship or, even worse, considered illegitimate. In other fields, like many sciences, there are different norms about number and order of authors with tenure and promotion decisions based upon having one's *own* distinctive research agenda (Bozeman & Boardman, 2004; Frost, Jean, Teodorescu, & Brown, 2004). This aspect of academic culture can contribute to faculty member isolation. Further, in this context, while collaborating with a senior mentor may be enriching, having one's areas of research overlap too much can lead to questions about the junior member's specific contributions (the risk being that the productivity will be credited to the mentor while the mentee's contributions may be questioned). The silos within many academic institutions do not facilitate exchange across or even within disciplines but encourage faculty to work in isolation (Bozeman & Boardman, 2004; Bok, 1986). The risks associated with these norms are particularly high for faculty who already experience themselves as marginalized or without access to the role models and/or informal mentoring that are available to faculty who see their gender, race, and/or ethnicity as similar to their more seasoned colleagues.

Even though there is a preference for solo ownership of a body of work in academia, there can be tremendous value in thinking aloud with others and sharing ideas while they are still in the formative stage. Establishing a distinctive research contribution does not need to be done in isolation. Thus an issue that guided the creation of CWW's Associates Program was: how can we create an alternative setting that fosters opportunities for lively, interdisciplinary exchange and mentoring while also being syntonic with the academic reward system (Kezar & Eckel, 2002). In other words, CWW's program was designed to:

> simultaneously embrace *and* challenge academic norms about definitions of success, faculty exchange, and mentoring—more specifically, to create a new setting where *individual* scholarship was supported (i.e., culturally syntonic with broader academic culture) in the context of *community* (somewhat countercultural).
>
> (Bond & Sladkova, 2014)

Balancing Mentee-Centered and Community-Driven Norms

In order to carve out mentoring space within the potentially isolating and individually oriented culture of the academy, the structure and processes of the Associates program were carefully and intentionally designed. CWW is explicit about requirements for membership and about expectations around participation. To apply for membership, faculty need to articulate an *individually driven* research or action project connected to the theme of women and work. At the same time, they also need to make a commitment to forwarding one another's work. These expectations are, at one level, quite straightforward. However, within the context of the academy, these expectations can mark a radical departure from traditional approaches. Each Associate's individual research agenda needs to be articulated in her/his letter of application, and Associates are held accountable for their progress vis-à-vis submitting an annual report in which they report on their progress related to their articulated project.

Expectations about commitments to contribute to the CWW community are also explicit. Associates make a pledge both to regularly attend meetings and to come prepared to discuss the work of whichever Associate has asked for time in that meeting. Each Associate is also asked to take on what we call an "infrastructure role," with the idea being that everyone makes a commitment to sustaining the community. The aim is to build upon the natural interests and talents of each associate in a way that will benefit the entire CWW community (e.g., by helping to organize an event, engaging social media, editing a newsletter, or advocating for a parent-friendly campus). Associates also report on their contribution to the CWW community in their annual report.

Regular meetings are designed to simultaneously foster a community of support and provide faculty members with substantive feedback on their individual work. Most monthly meetings start with a check-in for all members, where members share professional success as well as personal updates. This process provides opportunities to celebrate and strengthen personal bonds, which challenges the notion that faculty should establish rigid boundaries between personal and professional lives. The majority of meeting time is, however, devoted to discussion of specific Associate projects or questions. The only hard and fast rule is that the presenting Associate should not present finalized work, but rather bring a dilemma, a question, and/or an impasse for discussion. Taking the risk to share work at preliminary stages requires trust that colleagues will not prematurely judge the quality of the work, react by pushing their own agenda for the scholarship, or "steal" their colleagues' ideas. Yet, it is at such formative stages that people can most easily incorporate new perspectives into ongoing projects, which significantly adds to the usefulness of the group discussions for all presenters. Further, the stipulation to take risks by sharing ideas in progress is a deliberate effort to counter academic pressures to "perform" or demonstrate individual achievement as an outcome that requires little support from others. Thus, we start with the belief that everyone is qualified, smart, and capable; we also assume that everyone, no matter how accomplished, will hit sticking points in their work and benefit from others' perspectives and expertise. We have sought to hold meetings frequently enough to foster connection without contributing too much to faculty overload. Thus, meetings tend to last one and a half hours and are held monthly.

Meetings also include time for helping group members to address professional development issues; we have sought to foster norms that encourage participants to bring their whole selves to the table. We do this not only through our regular check-ins described above, but also through allowing Associates to ask for meeting times to strategize professionally. For example, Associates have asked for feedback on their tenure and promotion materials, input for dealing with departmental politics, and strategic advice around managing various work and life commitments. It can be invaluable to use the group for "reality checks" around micro-aggressions and the subtle dynamics that can make one feel devalued. These norms are particularly critical to the goals of mentoring women and faculty of color who may be more likely to have marginalizing experiences but can benefit from a safe and supportive community of scholars.

A New Setting to Foster a Collaborative Model of Mentoring

Faculty mentoring programs often focus on matching a junior with a senior professor. Such arrangements can work well, but have limitations. They tend to be less successful when the substance of the research of the two is not synergistic, when the senior member experiences the mentoring job as a distraction from her/his own research, or within university cultures that do not provide tangible rewards for mentoring junior colleagues (Ragins, 1996; Rayburn et al., 2010). Further, even under the best circumstances, the mentoring needs of faculty can rarely be addressed by a single relationship given the range of issues on which faculty need support and guidance (Kezar, 2001).

The mentoring that occurs within the context of the CWW Associates Program is grounded in a philosophy of mentoring as collaborative and multidirectional as well as focused on the whole person (including managing work-family-life demands as discussed above). Given the ways in which the CWW program is organized, senior faculty can provide support and guidance for junior faculty, while at the same time, junior faculty provide support and unique perspectives back to senior faculty and to each other as peers. In fact, rarely are people labeled as either senior or junior; there is simply an expectation that all participants can benefit from this cross-status exchange.

Institutional Change

While institutional change has not been an explicit component of the CWW Associates Program, our collective approach to mentoring has been so successful that we are now considered a model for other research centers on campus. We have developed and "exported" our model through what we refer to as IDEA (InterDisciplinary Exchange and Advancement) Communities (Bond & Sladkova, 2014) which promote similar mentoring around topics other than women and work. To truly push the boundaries around institutional values and forward the broader social justice goals espoused in this chapter, however, it is helpful when enduring infrastructures can be put into place to support those goals. For example, the CWW Associates program benefits from being housed within a university-recognized research center with the formally accepted goal of "promoting scholarship for social change."

Across institutions, having people in administrative positions who can initiate and support (or at least not block) mentoring that adheres to social justice principles needs to be a high priority. Therefore, mentoring to expand and reshape academic leadership is an essential partner to models like CWW. We look at this issue in the following section.

Leadership to Support Social Justice Mentoring

Leaders have a critical role to play in creating innovative pathways and settings both to support individual success for diverse students, faculty, and staff, *and* to establish an institutional culture that can be the foundation for such efforts. At a Nag's Heart meeting attended by a co-author (O'Connor) described by Stockdale, Chrobot-Mason, Chance, and Crosby (2017: Chapter 12), senior women in higher education administration of both large and small institutions discussed challenges they face in their leadership positions. Attendees included under-represented minority women and White women in or planning to move into department chair, dean, provost, and university president positions. While they encounter personal challenges and barriers in order to reach their current positions, they also face ongoing challenges in efforts to reshape their institutions. In particular, women in these powerful positions often felt compelled to mask or downplay their explicit efforts to develop feminist and inclusive leading and mentoring strategies by developing and implementing policies, procedures, relationships, and structures that would allow a diverse set of people to succeed. These leaders recognize the structural barriers that impede success for women and other under-represented minorities in academe and are working to transform their institutions.

When addressing these issues, however, they reported either doing so surreptitiously or by embedding their efforts into a larger strategic agenda of overall benefit to the campus, students, and/or faculty. In other words, even for women in positions of formal authority, it was challenging to promote institutional shifts that could serve to support more diverse participants in the academy. We will discuss the importance of academic leadership by reviewing ways in which the principles for social justice mentoring summarized in our introduction can infuse the work of leaders.

The Culture of the Academy: Transforming Criteria for Success

Academic leaders are in an optimal position to pave the way for not just questioning but also transforming the criteria by which faculty (and student) success can be envisioned and achieved. Especially in the current outcomes assessment-driven context of higher education, academic leaders must recognize that terms such as "merit" and "success" are not neutral terms, but are value-laden, often in ways that reproduce the existing systems and structures. Without innovative articulation of goals and proactive management strategies to achieve those goals, equity and pathways to success for diverse members of the institution cannot be achieved.

In terms of challenging definitions of success at the institutional level, leadership across all levels can work with their institution's personnel or faculty review committees to ensure that multi-authored work is highly valued for recognition of the time and effort required to collaborate with peers, mentors, and/or guide students as co-authors. Similarly, a colleague with non-traditional or boundary-pushing approaches (e.g., commitment to applied work) can be assisted by a leader who truly understands and values the transformative impact of that work and who will advocate where necessary to show how it is consonant with the overall goals of the institution.

Relevant to the current chapter, academic administrators can also leverage strategic goals and outcome measures to advance a social justice mentoring framework. Utilizing current tools and systems for social change requires creative leadership. For example, department leaders can influence a search committee by specifying "qualifications" or "preferences" for an open faculty line to prioritize candidates with demonstrated multicultural and diversity commitments. In mentoring and guiding search committees in this way, tremendous gains can be achieved by authentically drafting position descriptions to support multicultural and intersectional curriculum commitments rather than including vague language that does not signal an authentic value for diversity and social justice.

Similar change can be realized through inspired leadership in professional organizations or associations. In academic settings, for example, much can be accomplished through the articulation of learning goals for the training provided by departments, colleges, and large institutions. Leaders who do a close reading of the American Psychological Association's (APA) *Learning Goals for the Undergraduate Psychology Major 2.0* (2013), for example, will find strong support for and articulation of social justice commitments. One goal specifically targets "Ethical and Social Responsibility in a Diverse World," and is explained as "relevant to the full range of human diversity, including race, ethnicity, gender, sexual orientation, age, religious affiliation, disability status, social class, culture, and other identities associated with sociocultural diversity" (see APA, Goal #3: 12). Moreover, this strong statement from the profession of psychology urges infusion of these concerns throughout undergraduate and graduate training by leveraging accreditation requirements such as:

> Each set of guidelines raises awareness about social oppressions associated with specific minority statuses, identifies methods for increasing awareness

and knowledge of diverse social identities and associated sociocultural issues, and articulates methods for *working toward social justice*. We believe that individuals, departments, and programs who follow and use Guidelines 2.0 to improve teaching and learning will best serve their students by ensuring that diversity is not just a stand-alone experience but a central feature of all student learning goals.

(APA, Goal #3: 13, *emphasis added*)

Explicit commitment to social justice learning goals underscores the necessity of offering courses and conducting meaningful research on intersecting diversity issues and of valuing the faculty who can do such work well as part of the execution and implementation process.

The APA approach serves as one model that provides administrators with a strong platform to advance important social-justice-related goals, which can in turn create an environment that supports the success of diverse students and faculty. Parallels can be found in other disciplines, for example, the American Sociological Association's report on the undergraduate major, which includes specific recommendations on diversity to guide departmental decisions (McKinney, Howery, Strand, Kain, & Berheide, 2004). Similarly, the field of teacher education has been discussing whether and how to include social justice considerations in teacher education, thereby potentially shaping coursework, practical experiences teacher-trainees receive, and outcome measures for determining success (see, e.g., Cochran-Smith, 2004).

Mentee-Centered Leadership for Individual and Institutional Advancement

In her Society for the Psychological Study of Social Issues (SPSSI) presidential address, O'Connor complained that higher education had:

allowed a culture and environment that is NOT grounded in basic social justice and small "d" democratic processes, but instead is top-down, needlessly bureaucratic, needlessly impatient, needlessly individualistic, and which fails to give voice to the diverse and challenging perspectives that should allow great universities to thrive.

(O'Connor, 2015: 206)

Rather than simply preparing faculty to succeed in such an environment, academic leaders need to simultaneously support multiple paths to success *and* alter the environment so that more pathways are possible.

One way to approach this challenge is to make mentoring more protégé-centric, that is, draw on the person who is developing her career to articulate the outcomes that would lead to her own definition of success. So, rather than mentoring that is guided by institutionally defined templates of success, such as those espoused in traditional handbooks or mentoring guides or those driven by external rating agencies, a social justice approach would allow for alternative definitions of and pathways toward success. This position draws on a key principle underlying a number of critical approaches, including the constructivist mentoring approach developed in counseling psychology (Bridges 2010; Goodman et al., 2004; Neville, 2015), and participatory action research approaches to research (see, e.g., Fine, 2013; Lykes, forthcoming; Massey & Barreras, 2013; Torre, Fine, Stoudt, & Fox, 2012). In these approaches, traditional paradigms are challenged and—rather than acting *upon* the "subject" (either the client or the research participant)—the participating person(s)/communities develop a stake by contributing to the questions asked, the methods used, and the articulation of desired outcomes.

Translating this approach into the role of academic department chair or dean, for example, means that one must take the time to find out what the mentee's (whether student, faculty, or administrator) goals are for her/his own life and career, then strategizing ways in which those goals could be achieved within the current institutional context and within the pragmatics of the position. If, however, existing policies and structures could impede a preferred approach (especially where a student or colleague is bringing new and different perspectives to the institution), then someone with administrative authority can open up possibilities in ways that those without legitimate power cannot. One Chair, for example, in a department in which this social justice approach is modeled, worked with a junior faculty member over several years to craft both a teaching workload and professional development opportunities (e.g., online course development skills) that ultimately supported that faculty member's goal to have a family *and* stay in academe.

New Settings to Foster Innovative Models of Mentoring

Administrators are exceptionally busy people. Some may argue there is simply no time for them to mentor others for success, or spend time supporting the success of a diverse faculty or student body, or take on these additional goals. Taking guidance off the shelf or simply checking off the box indicating that tasks are done (e.g., Task—Increase diversity; Action—Diversity Officer hired—CHECK; Task—Stay within Budget; Action—Hire contingent faculty to solve budget crisis—CHECK) has not produced the working environment that many of us seek as equitable and inclusive institutions. As long as 4 percent of faculty are Latina, only 20 percent of faculty at research/graduate institutions are women, and only one in four university presidents are women (June, 2015), the work is not done. Relying on mentoring strategies that truly expose the barriers and then using the authority and responsibility allotted to those in administrative positions to reduce those barriers will move us forward.

Institutional Change

Creative and collaborative mentoring programs, such as CWW and Nag's Heart, can be critical to creating atmospheres of support and community. Yet, without academic leadership to enact the change envisioned by such programs, ultimately the status quo remains. As Meyers so clearly articulates:

> For the past 40 years, women faculty have been working to eliminate the many inequities they face in getting their work published; getting hired, tenured, and promoted and getting the same salaries, research leaves, and other resources as their male colleagues so that they can compete on a relatively level playing field. All of this has taken time, energy, and a toll—physically, emotionally, and financially. The end result of 50 years of struggle is that women faculty are still far from the Promised Land.
>
> (Meyers, 2012: 3)

Moreover, she laments that those in power will not "be able or willing to view institutional structures as inherently discriminatory—or [...] will want to change those policies from which they have benefitted" (Meyers, 2012: 12). We argue that for any mentoring strategy to be successful, academic leaders MUST be willing to "promote institutional change" that doesn't simply recreate what worked historically, but honors and enacts what will allow for authentic success, including both personal and career satisfaction. Without this leadership commitment, particularly in the face of the corporatization of higher education (Meyers, 2012), mentoring alone will not create the change needed to increase gender and racial equity in the academy.

Supporting Entrance into the Academy

As a final point, it is imperative that the social justice principles discussed above also be embedded at points much earlier in the pipeline. Establishing innovative pathways and establishing new settings for promoting success for women and under-represented racial and ethnic minority groups cannot just focus on those who have already been privileged enough to gain entry into the faculty and/or leadership of the academy.

Models that support under-represented minority students to enter university well prepared for the academic rigors include, for example, bridge programs that build individual skills (both academic and work–study skills) for easing the transition to college and/graduate school. Bridge programs often address insufficient preparation by offering short courses in fundamental skills prior to the start of the semester (Douglas & Attewell, 2014). Such programs can also help students establish academic momentum through orientations to campus life so that students are ready to focus on academics as soon as their semester begins (Attewell,

Lavin, Domina, & Levey, 2006). The aims of such programs are, fundamentally, to address factors critical to retention and graduation rates of under-represented minority students by counteracting barriers to their individual success (Murphy, Gaughan, Hume, & Moore, 2010). We are suggesting that these programs can be positively supplemented by building upon social justice principles in the same way we have discussed for faculty and academic leaders.

For example, the Puerto Rican Education Preparation (PREP) is a pilot program sponsored by the University of Puerto Rico Mayagüez aimed at improving graduate school admissions and success for under-represented minorities (Clinton, 2014). It was designed as a short-term, intensive graduate school application mentoring program that provides detailed instruction and individualized support regarding career/program decisions, application components (essays, interviewing, etc.), and other related aspects of the graduate school application process. It offers a model that combines some features of many other existing bridge programs, but it also emphasizes the creation of new sustainable networks of support. To anchor the program in the particular cultural and lived experiences of Puerto Rican students, involvement was sought from a network of recent graduates from the University of Puerto Rico Mayagüez who had successfully entered graduate programs in the USA. These role models shared strategies with program participants to address critical pitfalls and challenges, such as how to address second-language issues as they affect standardized admissions tests and what to expect in personal interviews. Furthermore, interaction between recent graduates and current students involved in PREP was established electronically to broaden the web of mentors from an island-based professor to peers throughout the USA, who directly understood the challenges of being a bilingual, bicultural graduate student of color. These networks were essentially new settings for support—ones that were sustained over time after the conclusion of the formal training aspects of the mentoring program.

Conclusions

Progress for female and minority faculty at research universities, which has been supported by multiple past efforts, has been too slow (Valian, 1998). If significant progress is to be made in the near future, new and innovative approaches to addressing the barriers facing women and minority faculty are needed (Nelson & Rogers, 2005). Without question, effective mentoring is essential to reaching our goal of greater inclusiveness in higher education, particularly at leadership levels. In determining whether a particular higher education mentoring program has succeeded, however, the traditional outcome discussed is whether the mentees were able to move into or up in a particular organizational setting (see, e.g., Speizer, 1984). While these inclusion outcomes are critically important to ensuring diverse leaders and potentially reducing structural inequalities, they are not enough. Career mobility alone cannot satisfactorily account for the barriers faced once under-represented groups gain access (see, e.g., Glenn, 2012; Yoshino, 2007), nor can they explain or repair the leaky pipeline that allows too many women and people of color at all levels to drain out before achieving their dreams.

Helping members of under-represented groups to succeed also requires paying attention to intersectionalities (Crenshaw, 1991). Current approaches do not, for example, necessarily address the significant and distinctive barriers faced by women of color. Such barriers are painstakingly portrayed in the book titled, *Presumed Incompetent: The Intersections of Race and Class for Women in Academia* (Gutiérrez y Muhs, Niemann, González, & Harris, 2012), and include the adobe ceiling (which unlike a glass ceiling, is dense and impenetrable, cf., Alicea, 2003) so well described by Latina education leader, Cecilia Burciaga, as well as other powerful critics. We still need to heed the experience of those who described the feeling as "not fitting in," as if entering a "fraternal and paternalistic institution" (Gutiérrez y Muhs, 2012: 502; see also Yoshino, 2007).

The examples summarized in this chapter point to very practical mentoring innovations that have the potential to provoke cultural shifts that can make a critical difference. Returning to the principles for social justice mentoring outlined in the introduction, we argue that in any effort, it is critical to: (1) challenge the established criteria for success and traditional "wisdom" about preferred pathways; (2) adopt mentee-centered mentoring, that is, define mentoring goals in line with the expressed needs of the focal individuals rather than trying to shoehorn participants into models developed in other contexts; and, (3) expand to new settings to free ourselves up to think beyond the dyadic matching of senior mentors and junior mentees. These three principles contribute to the fourth overarching principle: (4) to enhance efforts to mentor strategically for individual *and* institutional change.

The efforts summarized here are just a few among many models that promote social justice mentoring by incorporating these principles. The CWW Associates Program incorporates collaborative, multi-directional mentoring, while also establishing a community of support that counters the solo, silo, and heroic definitions of success that currently exist within the academy. The approaches to academic leadership we describe include going beyond offering individual coaching to thinking strategically about how to shift the norms of the academy. Across our examples, even something as seemingly mundane as "setting aside time" can signal an important change in business as usual. The CWW Associates meetings provide the opportunity for faculty to prioritize time away from other academic demands to talk about research and scholarship— something that many faculty want to do but find difficult in the tumult of daily teaching, service, and administrative pressures. Creative academic leadership requires the time to listen to the goals (both work and life/family) of junior faculty to best strategize paths toward achieving *those* goals and not merely advancing the standing of the department or institution. Our examples all emphasize the importance of creating alternative settings alongside our existing academic structures, that is, creating new settings that expand communities of support and that chart new pathways to success. In sum, establishing new norms and structures can not only provide invaluable guidance for members of under-represented groups, but these innovative approaches can also change the culture of the overall institution such that it truly fosters the professional success of faculty and leaders from diverse backgrounds.

Notes

1 This chapter grew out of an Interactive Discussion titled, "Mentoring initiatives to mobilize social action and change," held at the Society for the Psychological Study of Social Issues Biennial Conference, Portland, OR, June 2014. Participants included Maureen O'Connor (chair), Meg A. Bond, Amanda Clinton, and Margaret Stockdale.
2 See, in contrast, *The Compleat Academic: A Career Guide* (2003) edited by Darley, Zanna & Roediger, which addresses how to succeed under existing parameters, assuming everyone can become an insider, if they simply follow the rules.

References

Alicea, I. P. (2003, February). The dense, impenetrable adobe ceiling; Sage advice from seasoned Latina Cecilia Preciado Burciaga. *The Hispanic Outlook in Higher Education, 13*, 16–17.

Allen, B. (1996). Feminist standpoint theory: A black woman's (re)view of organizational socialization. *Communication Studies, 47*(4), 257–271.

Attewell, P., Lavin, D., Domina, T., & Levey, T. (2006). New evidence on college remediation. *Journal of Higher Education, 77*(5), 886–924.

American Psychological Association. (2013). *APA guidelines for the undergraduate psychology major: Version 2.0.* Retrieved from www.apa.org/ed/precollege/undergrad/index.aspx.

Blake, S. (1999). At the crossroads of race and gender: Lessons from the mentoring experiences of professional black women. In A. J. Murrell, F. J. Crosby, & R. J. Ely, *Mentoring dilemmas: Developmental relationships within multicultural organizations* (pp. 83–104). Mahwah, NJ: Lawrence Erlbaum Associates.

Bok, D. (1986). *Higher learning.* Cambridge, MA: Harvard University Press.

Bond, M. A., & Sladkova, J. (2014). *The IDEA Community Initiative: Mentoring and capacity building for scholarship through fostering unique interdisciplinary communities.* Working paper of the University of Massachusetts Lowell Center for Women & Work.

Bowman, S. R., Kite, M. E., Branscombe, N. R., & Williams, S. (1999). Developmental relationships of black Americans in the academy. In A. J. Murrell, F. J. Crosby, & R. J. Ely (Eds.), *Mentoring dilemmas: Developmental relationships within multicultural organizations* (pp. 21–46). Mahwah, NJ: Lawrence Erlbaum Associates.

Boykin, A. W., & Noguera, P. (2011). *Creating the opportunity to learn.* Alexandria, VA: Association for Supervision & Curriculum Development.

Bozeman, B., & Boardman, C. (2004). The NSF Engineering Research Centers and the university-industry research revolution: A brief history featuring an interview with Erich Bloch. *The Journal of Technology Transfer, 29*, 365–375. DOI: 10.1023/B:JOTT. 0000034128.39526.6b.

Braxton, J. M., Luckey, W. T., & Helland, P. A. (2006). Ideal and actual value patterns toward domains of scholarship in three types of colleges and universities. *New Directions for Institutional Research, 129*, 67–76. DOI: 10.1002/ir.172.

Bridges, S. (2010). Constructivist mentoring as social justice. In J. D. Raskin, S. K. Bridges, & R. A. Neimeyer (Eds.), *Studies in Meaning 4: Constructivist Perspectives on theory, practice, and social justice* (pp. 185–204). New York: Pace University Press.

Buzzanell, P. M., Long, Z., Anderson, L. B., Kokini, K., & Batra, J. C. (2015). Mentoring in academe: A feminist poststructural lens on stories of women engineering faculty of color. *Management Communication Quarterly, 29*(3), 440–457. DOI: 10.1177/089331 8915574311.

Clifford, V. (2003, May). Group mentoring: An alternative way of working. Paper presented at the Second National Conference on Women in Science, Technology, and Engineering, Sydney, Australia. In C. A. Rayburn, F. L. Denmark, M. E. Reuder, & A. Meteria Austria (Eds.), *A Handbook for Women Mentors: Transcending barriers of stereotype, race, and ethnicity*. Santa Barbara, CA: Praeger.

Clinton, A. (2014, June). *Puerto Rican education preparation (PREP): Initial program evaluation results*. Paper presented at the national conference of Society for the Psychological Study of Social Issues Biennial Conference, Portland, OR.

Cochran-Smith, M. (2004). Defining the outcomes of teacher education: What's social justice got to do with it? *Asia-Pacific Journal of Teacher Education, 32*, 193–22.

Colley, H. (2001). Righting rewritings of the myth of Mentor: A critical perspective on career guidance mentoring. *British Journal of Guidance & Counselling, 29*, 177–197.

Crenshaw, K. (1991). Mapping the margins: Intersectionality, identity politics, and violence against women of color. *Stanford Law Review, 43*(6), 1241–1299.

Crosby, F. J. (1999). The developing literature on developmental relationships. In A. J. Murrell, F. J. Crosby, & R. J. Ely (Eds.), *Mentoring dilemmas: Developmental relationships within multicultural organizations* (pp. 1–20). Mahwah, NJ: Lawrence Erlbaum Associates.

Cubillo, L., & Brown, M. (2003). Women into educational leadership and management: International differences? *Journal of Educational Administration, 41*, 278–291.

Darley, J. M., Zanna, M. P., & Roediger, H. L. (Eds.) (2003). *The Compleat Academic: A Career Guide* (2nd ed.). Washington, DC: American Psychological Association.

Darling-Hammond, L. (2010). Restoring our schools. *The Nation*, pp. 14–20.

Denmark, F. L., & Klara, M. D. (2010). Women mentors and their effect on educational and professional career development. In C. A. Rayburn, F. L. Denmark, M. E. Reuder, & A. Meteria Austria (Eds.), *A Handbook for Women Mentors: Transcending barriers of stereotype, race, and ethnicity* (pp. 3–20). Santa Barbara, CA: Praeger.

Douglas, D., & Attewell, P. (2014). The bridge and the troll underneath: Summer bridge programs and degree completion. *American Journal of Education, 121*(1), 87–109.

Eddy, P., & Mitchell, R. (2012). Faculty as learners: Developing thinking communities. *Innovative Higher Education, 37*, 283–296.

Fine, M. (2013). Echoes of Bedford: A 20-year social psychology memoir on participatory action research hatched behind bars. *American Psychologist, 68*, 687–698.

Frost, S., Jean, P., Teodorescu, D., & Brown, A. (2004). Research at the crossroads: How intellectual initiatives across disciplines evolve. *Review of Higher Education, 27*(4), 471–479.

Glenn, C. L. (2012). Stepping in and stepping out: Examining the way anticipatory careers socialization impacts identity negotiation of African American women in academia. In G. Gutiérrez y Muhs, Y. F. Niemann, C. G. González, & A. P. Harris

(Eds.), *Presumed incompetent: The intersections of race and class for women in academia* (pp. 133–141). Boulder, CO: University Press of Colorado.

Goodman, L. A., Liang, B., Helms, J. E., Latta, R. E., Sparks, E., & Weintraub, S. R. (2004). Training counseling psychologists as social justice agents: Feminist and multicultural principles in action. *The Counseling Psychologist, 32*, 793–837.

Gutiérrez y Muhs, G. (2012). Afterword. In *Presumed incompetent: The intersections of race and class for women in academia* (pp. 501–504). Boulder, CO: University Press of Colorado.

Horn, L., & Nevill, S. (2006). Profile of undergraduates in U.S. postsecondary education institutions, 2003–2004: With a special analysis of community college students (NCES 2006–184). U.S. Department of Education. Washington, DC: National Center for Education Statistics.

Gutiérrez y Muhs, G., Niemann, Y. F., González, C. G., & Harris, A. P. (2012). *Presumed incompetent: The intersections of race and class for women in academia.* Boulder, CO: University Press of Colorado.

June, A. W. (2015, March 16). Despite progress, only 1 in 4 college presidents are women. Chronicle of Higher Education. Retrieved from http://chronicle.com/article/Despite-Progress-Only-1-in-4/228473.

Kezar, A. (2001). *Understanding and facilitating organizational change in higher education in the 21st century.* San Francisco, CA: Jossey-Bass.

Kezar, A., & Eckel, P. (2002). The effect of institutional culture on change strategies in higher education: Universal principles or culturally responsive concepts? *The Journal of Higher Education, 73*(4), 435–460.

Knights, D., & Richards, W. (2003). Sex discrimination in UK academia. *Gender, Work, and Organization, 10*, 213–238.

Koocher, G. (2002). Mentor revealed: Masculinization of an early feminist construct. *Professional Psychology: Research and Practice, 33*, 509–510.

Lykes, M. B. (forthcoming). Community-based and participatory action research: Community psychology collaborations within and across borders. In M. Bond, I. Serrano-García, C. Keys, & M. B. Shinn (Eds.), *Handbook of Community Psychology Volume 2: Methods of Community Psychology in Research and Applications* (pp. 43–58). Washington DC: American Psychological Association Press.

Massey, S. G., & Barreras, R. E. (2013). Introducing "Impact Validity." *Journal of Social Issues, 69*, 615–632.

McKinney, K., Howery, C. B., Strand, K. J., Kain, E. L., & Berheide, C. W. (2004). *Liberal learning and the sociology major updated: Meeting the challenge of teaching sociology in the twenty-first century.* Washington, DC: American Sociological Association.

Meyers, M. (2012). Women in higher education: The long, hard road to equality. In M. Meyers with D. Rios (Eds.), *Women in Higher Education: The fight for equity* (pp. 3–18). New York: Hampton Press.

Moore, K. (1984). Careers in college and university administration: How are women affected?. In A. Tinsley, C. Secor, & S. Kaplan (Eds.), *Women in higher education administration* (pp. 5–15). San Francisco, CA: Jossey-Bass.

Murphy, T. E., Gaughan, M., Hume, R., & Moore, S. G. (2010). College graduation rates for minority students in a selective technical university: Will participation in a summer bridge program contribute to success? *Annals of Education, Policy, and Evaluation, 32*(1), 70–83.

Nelson, D. J., & Rogers, D. C. (2005). *Nelson diversity surveys: A national analysis of diversity in science and engineering faculties at research universities.* Norman, OK: Diversity in

Science Association. Retrieved from http://users.nber.org/~sewp/events/2005.01.14/Bios+Links/Krieger-rec4-Nelson+Rogers_Report.pdf.

Neville, H. (2015). Social justice mentoring: Supporting the development of future leaders for struggle, resistance, and transformation. *The Counseling Psychologist, 43*, 157–169.

O'Connor, M. (2015). SPSSI Presidential Address: Embodied social justice: Warm tea, flexed muscles, and enacting SPSSI's mission. *Journal of Social Issues, 71*, 203–217.

Paludi, M., Martin, J., Stern, T., & DeFour, D. C. (2010). Promises and pitfalls of mentoring women in business and academia. In C. A. Rayburn, F. L. Denmark, M. E. Reuder, & A. Meteria Austria (Eds.), *A Handbook for Women Mentors: Transcending barriers of stereotype, race, and ethnicity* (pp. 79–108). Santa Barbara, CA: Praeger.

Ragins, B. R. (1996). Jumping the hurdles: Barriers to mentoring for women in organizations. *Leadership & Organization Development Journal, 17*, 37–41. http://dx.doi.org/10.1108/01437739610116984.

Rayburn, C. A., Denmark, F. L., Reuder, M. E., & Austria, A. M. (Eds.) (2010). *A Handbook for women mentors: Transcending barriers of stereotype, race, and ethnicity*. Santa Barbara, CA: Praeger.

Shields, S. A. (2012). Waking up to privilege: Intersectionality and opportunity. In G. Gutiérrez y Muhs, Y. F. Niemann, C. G. González, & A. P. Harris (Eds.), *Presumed incompetent: The intersections of race and class for women in academia* (pp. 29–39). Boulder, CO: University Press of Colorado.

Smith, P. (2000). Failing to mentor Sapphire: The actionability of blocking Black women from initiating mentoring relationships. *UCLA Women's Law Journal, 10*(2), 373–467.

Speizer, J. J. (1984). The administrative skills program: What have we learned?. In A. Tinsley, C. Secor, & S. Kaplan (Eds.), *Women in higher education administration* (pp. 35–45). San Francisco, CA: Jossey-Bass.

Stockdale, M. S., Chrobot-Mason, D. M., Chance, R. C., & Crosby, F. J. (2017). Peer mentoring retreats for addressing dilemmas of senior women in STEM careers: The Nag's Heart Model. In A. J. Murrell, & S. D. Blake-Beard (Eds.), *Mentoring diverse leaders: Creating change for people, processes, and paradigms*. New York: Routledge.

Taylor, S. E., & Martin, J. (1987). The present-minded professor: Controlling one's career. In M. P. Zanna, & J. M. Darley (Eds.), *The compleat academic: A practice guide for the beginning social scientist* (pp. 23–60). New York: McGraw-Hill.

Thomas, D. A. (1990). The impact of race on managers' experiences of developmental relationships (mentoring and sponsorship): An intra-organizational study. *Journal of Organizational Behavior, 11*(6), 479–491.

Torre, M. E., Fine, M., Stoudt, B. G., & Fox, M. (2012). Critical participatory action research as public science. In H. Cooper, P. M. Camic, D. L., Long, A. T. Panter, D. Rindskopf, & K. J. Sher (Eds.), *American Psychological Association Handbook of Research Methods in Psychology, Vol. 2: Research designs: Quantitative, qualitative, neuropsychological, and biological* (pp. 171–184). Washington, DC: American Psychological Association.

Valian, V. (1998). *Why So Slow? The Advancement of Women*. Cambridge, MA: The MIT Press.

Van den Brink, M., & Stobbe, L. (2009). Doing gender in academic education: The paradox of visibility. *Gender, Work, and Organization, 16*, 451–470. DOI: 10.1111/j.1468-0432.2008.00428.x.

Yoshino, K. (2007). *Covering: The hidden assault on civil rights*. New York: Random House.

12

PEER MENTORING RETREATS FOR ADDRESSING DILEMMAS OF SENIOR WOMEN IN STEM CAREERS

The Nag's Heart Model[1]

Margaret S. Stockdale, Donna M. Chrobot-Mason, Randie C. Chance, and Faye J. Crosby

Researchers and practitioners know that mentoring relationships can help both individuals and organizations change and prosper (Allen, Eby, Poteet, Lentz, & Lima, 2004; Eby et al., 2013; Eby, Durley, Evans, & Ragins, 2006). As some chapters in this volume emphasize, those who become leaders have often benefited from having been mentored; and from the research presented in other chapters, we conclude that good mentoring programs can serve leaders who wish for their organizations to make the most of all the talent available (see also, Gentry, Weber, & Sadri, 2008).

The current chapter examines one small but highly effective mentoring program that has focused on fortifying feminists and has thus helped create and sustain change among people, processes, and paradigms. The chapter starts with a brief critique of traditional mentoring forms and discusses newer formats including "mentoring circles." It then moves to a detailed description of the particular mentoring program known by the curious of *Nag's Heart* in which mentoring circles are formed and run according to a strict protocol. The third section of the chapter presents evidence on the effectiveness of Nag's Heart using data from a recent study of women in the academic fields of Science, Technology, Engineering, and Math (STEM). In the final section, we point to implications of the Nag's Heart model for how one might think about the role of mentoring circles like the Nag's Heart model, in multicultural, multi-gender contexts.

Traditional Mentoring Structures: Impact and Pitfalls

There is no doubt that mentoring is effective for career development and success, but a one-size-fits-all mentoring model may not be ideal. The traditional model of mentoring is characterized by a dyadic relationship differentiated by status in which the benefits of mentoring flow from an experienced, senior individual who shares his or her wisdom, advice, and sponsorship with a younger, inexperienced but high-potential protégé (Holbeche, 1996; Kram, 1985). Mentors also experience enhanced career success, organizational commitment, and job performance from their mentoring activities (Ghosh & Reio, 2013). Mentoring relationships develop over time and tend to follow predictable developmental stages (Kram, 1985). Career and psychosocial benefits for the protégé tend to be strongest when such relationships develop naturally or informally, but high-quality formal mentoring programs in which mentors and protégés are matched also lead to positive outcomes compared to non-mentored individuals (Murrell, Blake-Beard, Porter, & Perkins-Williamson, 2008; Ragins & Cotton, 1999).

Good as they are, traditional forms of mentoring have been criticized for a variety of reasons (Kram & Higgins, 2008). Relying on a single mentor may prove ineffective in complex environments, where the answers to important organizational and career dilemmas cannot be answered by one person (Kram & Higgins, 2008). Finding suitable mentors may turn out to be difficult for individuals from demographic groups who are highly under-represented in their occupations (particularly women and minorities; Cox, Blaha, Fritz, & Whitten, 2014), especially given the tendency for homosocial reproduction (Darwin, 2000; Darwin & Palmer, 2009; Hansman, 2002). Conflicts may arise from the disparate goals and expectations of mentors and protégés, especially perhaps when one member of the power-asymmetric pair comes from an under-represented group or a group that is new to the organization.

Given the importance of similarity in attraction, spontaneously formed mentoring dyads often involve individuals who resemble each other on demographic characteristics and thus end up privileging those who are already privileged by virtue of their gender or ethnicity (Darwin, 2000; Hansman, 2002). Women and ethnic minorities can experience difficulty in finding suitable mentors whom they trust (Cox et al., 2014). Mentors and protégés may have different, if not conflicting goals for self-advancement. Sometimes protégés feel disrespected, abused, or otherwise diminished by their associations with a senior person who was meant to be their mentor (Eby, McManus, Simon, & Russell, 2000). Finally, the traditional mentoring model reinforces the structure of paternalistic power hierarchies that ultimately sustain the subordination of women and minorities (Darwin & Palmer, 2009).

Alternative Mentoring Models

Alternative mentoring models have flourished, including inter-organizational mentoring, peer mentoring, mentoring networks, and group mentoring. Inter-organizational mentoring programs (see Murrell et al., 2008) match mentors and protégés at professional conferences, training programs, or workshops and provide guidance to dyads on ways to facilitate their mentoring relationship over time and space. Such programs have been found to be particularly beneficial for persons of color who typically cannot access powerful same-race/same-gender mentors within their own institution (Murrell et al., 2008).

Peer mentoring models address the concerns of power differentials in traditional mentoring relationships, and are considered especially useful to help women combat under-representation, isolation, and lack of support in STEM fields and careers (Amelink, 2009; Cox et al., 2014; Langdon, 2001). Whether dyadic or group-based, peer mentoring functions flow two ways and are mutually beneficial when they involve enhanced career and psychosocial support including coaching, career strategizing, information sharing, counseling, and professional-development role modeling (Amelink, 2009; Holbeche, 1996; Kram & Isabella, 1985). This type of mutual relationship is thought to be especially impactful in developing competence, responsibility, and career identity for all members of the peer mentoring relationship (Kram & Isabella, 1985).

One form of peer mentoring is the mentoring circle (Dansky, 1996) in which a group of colleagues, guided by a facilitator, provide feedback, advice, and support to each other (Palermo, Hughes, & McCall, 2010). Most mentoring circles include one or two members who are senior in their organizations or professions and eight to twelve junior members. Sometimes a separate facilitator helps run the mentoring sessions. Sometimes members take turns running the group or facilitating discussions. Mentoring circles are especially useful when people's "lived experiences" (as opposed to their conceptual understandings) are important and when demographic characteristics are likely to influence the lived experiences of people in an organization. If, for example, women experience subtle shunning in an organization, a circle composed exclusively of women will discuss the issue of subtle shunning in a different (and deeper) way than a circle in which women are in the minority.

Perhaps the first published report of a mentoring circle came from Ellen McCambley (1999). McCambley reported on her experiences in setting up and helping to run a program for women who worked in a telecommunications company in New England. Because there were only a tiny number of women in senior management at that time, the decision was made to set up ten mentoring circles that met regularly over a one-year period. The pilot project was not without some mishaps, but overall the project proved to be a huge success. At the close of the year, eight of the ten groups elected to continue to meet on their own time. Very high levels of mutual trust were established. "For the first time," reported McCambley, "we had an old boys' network among the girls" (McCambley, 1999: 179). Even more importantly, organizational changes were implemented. Some were small and easy to effect—like cordoning off a section of the women's room as a nursing station. Others, like a program to identify young talent among diverse populations and help that talent accelerate through the ranks, were harder to implement and more far-reaching. A reported downside to mentoring circles has been difficultly in sustaining the momentum and commitment to membership in the group (Darwin & Palmer, 2009).

The benefits of implementing mentoring circles in a business setting (McCambley, 1999) have also been reported more recently in academic settings. Darwin and Palmer (2009) and Palermo et al. (2010) reported on mentoring circle programs instituted at Australian universities. In both studies, groups were composed of junior faculty or practitioners led by a senior professional or facilitator. Groups determined what topics they would pursue such as learning competencies, research support, building collaborations, managing work/life balance, and other career development issues. At the end of the program, participants regarded their opportunities to interact with others, to engage in peer mentoring, and to share experiences to be the most valuable benefits of the program.

The Nag's Heart Model

An organization that has made intensive use of mentoring circles is Nag's Heart. Nag's Heart retreats have been held since the early 1990s, with about ninety retreats held to date. Currently, the term "Nag's Heart" refers both to an organization and to the retreats sponsored by the organization. As we describe below, Nag's Heart retreats embody the essential elements of status attenuation, mutual support and trust, and network enhancement found in peer mentoring models and mentoring circles. Moreover, Nag's Heart retreats are commonly interorganizational in structure, providing access to powerful colleagues and their networks, which is particularly important for traditionally marginalized professionals, such as women in science, engineering, and math, as well as for underrepresented minorities in almost all disciplines (Murrell, et al., 2008).

As an organization, Nag's Heart has evolved rather organically and at times a bit haphazardly. Take the strange name. The name came about after the organization had been functioning for a couple of years and members felt the need for a moniker other than "meeting at Faye's place." One member of the group, a professor named Louise Kidder, offered "Nag's Heart" as the name because the very first meeting occurred when some members appeared to have been excluded from a small scholarly retreat program situated in Nag's Head, North Carolina. It seemed at the time that the Nag's Head retreats embraced strict hierarchy and shunned the core concepts of feminism, and thus group members cheered Louise Kidder's idea of replacing the word "head" with the warmer word of "heart." Now, more than twenty years since the first retreat was held, virtually all those who have participated in a retreat seem to resist the suggestion—regularly put forward by others who have not yet been to a retreat—to change the name to something less easy to confuse with either old female horses or the practice of harping on something.

In 1997, Nag's Heart found a home at the University of California, Santa Cruz when one of the founders of Nag's Heart (FC) joined the faculty there. Soon an endowment was established, and by the mid-2000s a "leadership collaborative" (LC) was formed. By-laws came into being as did a sometimes outdated website. At around the same time, the processes of facilitating a Nag's Heart retreat were more or less solidified.

Nag's Heart currently hosts two to six workshops or retreats in a given year. In each retreat a group of six to fourteen individuals meet over a period of one to four days to tackle together their dilemmas concerning a specified topic. The length of any specific workshop is determined by the needs of the participants. All participants need to be present for the entire time. Given the press of work and other demands on many women, meetings are frequently shorter (one to two days) than one might wish in an ideal world.

Topics that have been addressed in meetings include: ethical issues in research; balancing home and work; spirituality in academia; ethnic diversity among feminist academics; feminist agendas in the law; and detecting and resisting sexism. Every topic is one that touches feminists, defined as those who care about equality for women and men. Every topic can be approached from both a personal and a professional vantage point.

Once a retreat is approved by the LC and a convener is identified, announcements are sent out via professional networks. Retreat organizers take care to make sure that everyone invited knows the "rules of engagement." Unlike the standard professional retreat, a Nag's Heart retreat involves a great deal of interdependence, and organizers make sure that all potential participants are prepared to be wholly present for the duration of the retreat.

Those invited to attend a retreat are informed that the retreat will revolve around each participant coming with a dilemma and will follow a structured format. Cell phones and laptops are to be left at the front door. No PowerPoint presentations are allowed. In addition, each participant is told that the group eats together and, if time permits, engages jointly in free-time activities. For overnight retreats, sleeping arrangements often entail "bunking" with one or more participants. Funding for each Nag's Heart conference is typically a combination of participant fees, which may be supported by her home institution, and a Nag's Heart Foundation fund built up by donations from past participants.

For each retreat a list of participants and alternates is made. Names and institutional affiliations are exchanged in advanced of the meeting. Travel arrangements are coordinated. Every attempt is made to help the participants feel "pampered but not spoiled." Individuals are treated as individuals, but everyone is reminded gently of the interdependence of all members of the group. If one participant's plane is late to arrive, for example, the others in her van need to wait.

Once the group assembles, we strictly follow procedure so as to allow the magic of a group to emerge. After an initial introduction of each individual's problem or situation she would like to discuss, the facilitators of a Nag's Heart retreat create sessions on the basis of issue similarity (loosely defined). All participants of the Nag's Heart are present for every session, and they agree to be fully engaged.

At the start of the first session (and the start of subsequent sessions as needed), the group facilitator states the rules. First, everything is confidential. Second, everyone is present for all parts unless prior arrangements are made. Third, everyone needs to promise to speak only the truth. No lies, white or otherwise. Fourth, no one should feel compelled to say anything that she or he does not want to say. Thus, even though everyone speaks only the truth, no one is obligated to speak "the whole truth." That is, while a participant may not want to reveal the whole story or situation, what she says must be truthful. Following these rules is essential because trust is at the core of all exchanges. Even with all the chauffeuring and tailor-made cuisine, the greatest luxury of any Nag's Heart retreat is the ability to speak the truth and to know that everyone else is speaking the truth. Trust—that basic element of any healthy life (Stroh, 2010)—is a cherished asset of every Nag's Heart retreat.

A typical session during a workshop focuses on three participants. Each individual participant has thirty minutes in which to present her dilemma and receive feedback on it. She may use a small portion of the time to present her dilemma and use the remaining time to get feedback and dialogue from the group; or she may spend most of her time describing her dilemma with little time for group input. The choice is hers. When the timer goes off after thirty minutes, the conversation on her dilemma ends.

In any session, after all participants have spoken, there is a thirty-minute "bucket" session. In the bucket session, the entire group can return to any of the participants' issues and provide further input or discussion, and/or identify common themes among dilemmas and strategies for addressing them. Knowing that the bucket session will allow for a return to interrupted thoughts, the retreat facilitators can be strict in cutting off conversations when the timer goes off and participants can feel relaxed that they will be able to complete their incomplete thoughts.

The next session begins after a break, which can be brief or extended. During extended breaks, meals may be served and/or free-time activities may be offered. Free-time activities typically include hikes, visits to local attractions, yoga, massage, or time alone.

In a one-day Nag's Heart retreat, we typically seek to keep attendance to nine or fewer participants. In a multi-day Nag's Heart retreat, we can go as high as twelve or even fourteen participants and try to keep the sessions to only two per day. Multi-day retreats seem to have more impact than one-day retreats; but even a one-day retreat can have a special effect.

When all of the sessions have been completed, the group reconvenes for a final ceremony. During this ceremony, the timer is turned off, but a strict protocol is still followed. The ceremony is based on a Native American practice introduced some years ago by a participant named Candace Fleming, a Native American psychologist who worked with Native American populations. First, the facilitator reminds the group of the rules of confidentiality, honesty, and trust. Then the facilitator explains the process. During the closing ceremony, participants sit in a circle and pass around a token (e.g., a rock, a feather, a glass heart) selected by the facilitator. Only the person holding the token may speak.

The token-holding speaker may reflect on what the Nag's Heart retreat has meant to her and what insights she has learned or she may reach out to a particular participant to say something personal to her. The token holder may also choose not to speak and to simply pass the token to the next person in the group. The token proceeds around the group with each person given as much time to talk as she likes. The number of circulations is not usually limited, and often the token goes through the entire circle ten or more times. The session ends when the token has made two complete passes around the circle with no one speaking. This signifies that all has been said and that closure has been met. A silent period of person-to-person expression of thanks ends the retreat.

It is clear that Nag's Heart retreats are similar to mentoring circles in many ways and also unlike most mentoring circles in other ways. The most notable difference between Nag's Heart and other mentoring circles concerns duration. While many organizations might have a mentoring circle in place for three to twelve months, the Nag's Heart circles last one to four days. Nag's Heart might be conceived as a "mentoring intervention" meant to jump-start some processes.

In other ways, Nag's Heart retreats resemble what one might find in a corporation or university. Each retreat has a facilitator and either a co-facilitator, or a "helper" or both. The facilitator (typically the host) develops the sessions, helps to facilitate the dialogues within the session, and monitors the time. The co-facilitator also helps with the dialogues and handles other logistics. The helper typically manages the meals and snacks. Similar to a mentoring circle, the role of the facilitator and possibly co-facilitator is to explain the structure of the sessions, help maintain the flow of the dialogue, and keep the timer. On rare occasions, the facilitator has to help resolve interpersonal conflicts that might otherwise compromise the success of the Nag's Heart process.

For Nag's Heart retreats, like most mentoring circles, the structure of the formal group sessions is intended to normalize the existence of problems or dilemmas and to reinforce that most problem-solving occurs in groups. Every attention is given to the building of trust, because without trust, mentoring efforts are doomed to failure (Thomas, 1990). Nag's Heart retreats go further than most mentoring circles in the effort to attenuate status differences. The rigid structure of the sessions is important: All participants get the same amount of time in which attention is focused on their problem. All participants focus fully on each participant's issue during the allotted time. Participants who may hold more junior positions in their occupations are relieved of the burden of deference, and participants holding more senior positions are relieved of the burden of being wise elders to care for younger colleagues. Indeed, usually within the space of the first hour, the junior-senior distinctions tend to fall away without losing the wisdom of the senior members.

The Effectiveness of Nag's Heart Retreats for Women in Academic STEM Fields

Since its inception, Nag's Heart has attracted psychologists and related social scientists—reflecting the discipline of its founding mothers, but recently the focus has expanded. In the first decade of the twenty-first century, the Leadership Collaborative (LC) recognized the opportunity to expand Nag's Heart retreats to women in STEM due to national attention being focused on the career dilemmas of this uniquely situated population. The LC also recognized an opportunity to advance the research agenda on women and mentoring.

The Situation of Women in Academic STEM Fields: Facts and Figures

It is well recognized that White women and racial minorities are underrepresented in STEM academic disciplines. Even though the numbers of STEM degrees earned by White women and racial minorities have slowly increased (Burke, 2007; McNeely & Vlaicu, 2010), disparities persist at all levels of academia. The problem is particularly prominent at the faculty level, with female and minority individuals consistently comprising only a small proportion of university STEM professors. Statistics from the National Science Foundation (2012) indicate that in recent years, women have held 32.3 percent of the associate and assistant professorships and 22 percent of the full professorships in the life sciences, and only 17.5 percent of assistant/associate professorships and 5 percent of full professorships in engineering. The percentage of full-time STEM faculty who are female lags behind both the educational pipeline and the percentage of women in STEM-related professions in industry (Hill, Corbett, & Rose, 2010). Whereas in 2000 over 44 percent of biological professionals were women, only 34 percent of faculty in life sciences were women (Di Fabio, Brandi, & Frehill, 2008; Hill et al., 2010). The comparable figures for women in math professions generally versus math university faculty are 30 percent and 19 percent, respectively. In engineering, the dearth of women has been consistent in both industry and academic professions: roughly 11 percent (Di Fabio et al., 2008; Hill et al., 2010). Hill et al. (2010) also showed that in 1996, women earned 12 percent of doctoral degrees in engineering, but in 2006 (allowing ten years to begin an academic job and earn tenure) only 7 percent of tenured engineering faculty were women. The comparable figures for biology—now a female-dominated college major—were 42 percent of earned doctorates in 1996 but less than 25 percent of tenured faculty in 2006. Similar disparities and career barriers are found for women in STEM academic careers around the globe (see Barone, 2011; Mody & Brainard, 2005).

Women are also more likely than men to exit STEM careers (Hewlett et al., 2008; Xu, 2008). Over half of women in STEM-related professions leave their jobs by mid-career, compared to less than 20 percent of men. Xu (2008) analyzed data from a national probability study of faculty, focusing specifically on STEM disciplines and found that female STEM faculty expressed a stronger intention to seek another full-time position in academia than male STEM faculty.

Those who are from an under-represented racial or ethnic group (URM) are at an even greater disadvantage as STEM faculty members. Of non-social science STEM PhD recipients in 1996–1995, between 5.5 percent (Earth Sciences) and 8.2 percent (Computer Science) were URM (Nelson & Brammer, 2010). Yet representation of URMs among full professors at top 100 research universities across a host of non-social science STEM disciplines by 2007 ranged from 2.5 percent (physics) to 5.6 percent (chemical engineering) (Nelson & Brammer, 2010). Nelson and Brammer (2010) further reported that out of 14,400 tenured or tenure-track faculty employed in the nation's top fifty STEM departments, 1,678 of these were women and only eighty-eight—about 0.5 percent—were women of color. Women of color in STEM face dual prejudices due to their race/ethnicity and gender (Ong, Wright, Espinosa, & Orfield, 2011). As a result, the number of female URM STEM faculty members is remarkably low.

Women in STEM: Explaining the Facts and Figures

Researchers have sought to understand why White and URM women are so much less likely to be employed as faculty members in STEM departments, especially research-focused departments. Valian (2005) has delineated the range of processes that serve to marginalize women in STEM, from the almost imperceptible but accumulative social-cognitive effects of categorization and stereotyping to the disparaging, hostile acts of sexual harassment and bullying. Implicit biases still wreak havoc on the career trajectories of women in STEM. As recently as 2012, researchers found that STEM faculty in top research-intensive universities demonstrated a preference for hiring a man over a woman for a laboratory assistant position (Moss-Racusin, Dovidio, Brescoll, Graham, & Handelsman, 2012).

Women keenly feel the negativity. In Rosser's (2004) survey of nearly 400 STEM faculty members, social isolation was mentioned as one of the most significant barriers to career advancement. McNeely and Vlaicu (2010) also found that exclusion from social networks was a problem, indicating that social isolation and lack of connectivity has persisted for female STEM faculty. Women not only feel the negativity; they also sometimes internalize it: Holleran, Whitehead, Schmader, and Mehl (2011) found that female STEM faculty experienced stereotype threat (confirming that a group stereotype is true of oneself) when discussing research with men, which was linked to career disengagement.

Surveys of women who have departed or who intend to depart from academic STEM fields show the same patterns as the studies of women who, against the odds, remain. Xu's (2008) study linked women's departure from STEM fields to their dissatisfaction with advancement opportunities, with research support, and with the ability to freely express ideas. Other researchers (e.g., Trower, 2008, as cited in Hill et al., 2010) cited unsupportive workplaces, ambiguous rules for career advancement, lack of mentoring by senior colleagues, extreme work schedules, and the inability to balance work and family demands as major factors in women's disproportionate exit from STEM fields.

Assessing the Effectiveness of Nag's Heart Retreats

During the first decade of the existence of the Nag's Heart retreats, periodic assessments occurred. Participants were asked about their experiences. The vast majority of participants found the experience to be wholly positive. Most sought to attend another retreat when possible. But during the first decade most of the participants were social scientists, or lawyers, or managers in large organizations. Only a few, including some physicians, were employed in the "hard" sciences.

The question arose: Would the sort of experience provided to participants by a Nag's Heart retreat prove beneficial to women scientists who, by virtue of their training and their inclinations, might tend to feel suspicious of something so "touchy-feely" or who, by virtue of their work, might find it hard to spend too much time on group process? Without denying the obvious benefits of Nag's Heart retreats for one type of woman, we had reason to doubt the efficacy of the method for women with different habits of thought. And yet, knowing that social and professional isolation figured so largely in the experiences of women in STEM fields, we thought that a Nag's Heart retreat might prove especially important for women in STEM fields.

Aided by a seed grant from her then-institution, Southern Illinois University (SIU), one of the authors (MS) organized a study of the effectiveness of our mentoring intervention for women in STEM. The grant permitted some members of the LC to get together with administrators from SIU and permitted the running of two sessions for early-career women (mostly post-doctoral scholars) in STEM. The grant also allowed the running of three Nag's Heart retreats for middle to senior women in academic STEM fields for which attendance fees were waived. Finally, assistants were paid to help with data collection and data analysis.

The three focal retreats took place in different locations at different times for varying durations and with different facilitators. In June 2012, nine women came together for two days in Cincinnati, Ohio. Four were Asian-American/ Asian, and five were European-American/White. Ages ranged from thirty-five to fifty-eight years of age for the participants. The group included four assistant professors, three associate professors, and two full professors. A few weeks later, six African-American/Black, two European-American/White, and two Asian-American/Asian professors gathered in Boston for an evening followed by a full day. Their ages ranged from thirty-eight to sixty-three years of age, and the group included one assistant professor, one associate professor, and seven full professors. Finally, in June 2013, seven full professors, two associate professors, and one research administrator came to a three-day retreat in Santa Cruz, CA. Eight of the women self-identified as White and two as mixed-ethnicity. Their ages ranged from forty-two to sixty-five years of age.

Each participant in each workshop was sent a questionnaire one week after the retreat and a second one after three months. The surveys contained both close-ended and open-ended questions. Closed-ended items assessed participants' sense of empowerment, perceptions of social support, and intentions for career persistence. Open-ended questions asked participants about the impact of the experience, about anticipated positive outcomes, and about anticipated negative outcomes. Participants were also asked if there was any critically important event that occurred for them during the retreat.

Response rates were very high to the questionnaire sent one week after the retreat. One hundred percent of the women in Cincinnati and Santa Cruz responded, as did seven of the nine women in Boston. Response rates dropped for the three-month follow-up: six of the nine women from Cincinnati, five of the nine women from Boston, and nine of the ten women from the Santa Cruz retreats replied.

What We Found from the Surveys

To understand the data from the post-retreat questionnaires, we relied on methods of qualitative data analysis prescribed by Maxwell (2013) and Merriam (2009). Two researchers independently reviewed the data to identify potential themes for coding. The two researchers shared their independently generated themes and discussed each to develop a preliminary codebook. The researchers next independently coded the data and then met to discuss discrepancies and potential revisions to the codebook. Coding definitions were refined and two additional codes were added to the codebook. In the final step of data analysis, the researchers coded the data once again using the revised codebook and met to discuss any discrepancies in coding. Once consensus was achieved, frequencies for each code were calculated.

Retreat Impact

Analyses of answers to an open-ended question about how and why the retreat impacted them suggested that attendees were largely affected by the advice they received from other retreat attendees. Respondents mentioned advice was provided in a variety of ways including how to handle various dilemmas, strategies to succeed in academia, new ideas or creative coping strategies, and available resources. Related to this was the other most frequently coded response to this question which dealt with increased feelings of confidence. This suggests that participants were impacted by the advice they received such that they felt greater empowerment, enhanced inner strength, and stronger confidence in their ability to deal with the professional and personal dilemmas they faced. Two other frequently coded categories include validation and clarity. Thus participants were strongly impacted by learning that other women struggle with similar dilemmas. Women reported feeling validated that they were not alone in facing certain types of struggles, nor were their perceptions of situations deemed inappropriate by others. This validation in turn facilitated greater clarity in how to articulate the dilemmas they were facing and in some cases, greater clarity in how to handle specific issues. One respondent shared how she felt validated as a result of attending the retreat.

> Hearing about others' problems that are similar to mine was reassuring (if depressing) that my problems are not unique and therefore are unlikely to be due to my specific shortcomings. Meeting strong successful women and having the chance to build the start of friendships was extremely valuable. [The retreat] increased my confidence—if these women think I can go far, then maybe [...I can].

Positive and Negative Outcomes

The most frequent response to the question of positive outcomes from the retreat was confidence, followed by both mentorship and a positive outlook. Thus respondents indicated they left the retreat with greater confidence to tackle their dilemmas and a more positive perspective or attitude when approaching their challenges. A large number of women also reported that they anticipated the mentoring they received at the retreat to be a lasting positive outcome of the retreat experience. Other positive outcomes coded were a sense of renewal, greater awareness of the struggles facing women in academia, a sense of community and friendship with other participants, strategies, and clarity as to how to approach their personal dilemma. As for negative outcomes, responses were sparse. Some felt it was difficult to return to their home institutions without powerful allies to support the concerns raised in the retreat.

Critical Events

Our analysis showed that participants were particularly impacted by the stories that were shared during the retreat and the candidness and genuineness of those sharing their stories. Respondents mentioned how strongly they were impacted by other women's stories of pain, isolation, and alienation. They also were struck by the fact that the women attending the retreat and sharing such stories were so honest, open, and trusting of one another. For example, one respondent stated that a critical event was:

> feeling comfortable sharing the challenges you are experiencing in your career and getting tangible feedback of how to move forward [...] As a trained scientist I was skeptical as to how effective this retreat would be. I was pleasantly surprised by both the openness and trust I experienced.

Three Months Later

Three months after the retreat, participants were asked to respond to the fourth question: To what extent did the retreat impact your life and career? Many respondents shared how when they think back to the retreat, they experience a sense of fondness for the retreat, its organizers, and attendees. Several respondents also reported wanting to reconnect with retreat participants and to have follow-up meetings. Finally, a large number reported lessons learned, meaning that they learned something meaningful as a result of their participation in the retreat.

One respondent seemed to summarize the feelings of many of the women who attended the Nag's Heart retreat:

> I was challenged with a very significant career decision at the time of the retreat, and the interactions there provided me with strong support and thoughtful advice that made my decisions easier and implications of the decisions more clear to me. Hearing about the problems and challenges of the other participants made me realize the universality of some of the issues I deal with in my career. Therefore, enhanced awareness and direct input into my challenges were immediate impacts that the retreat had for me. In addition, knowing that this community of women exists and that I can call on them for help, feedback, and support in the future is a huge advantage.

Implications and New Questions

Our findings suggest that mentoring experiences such as the Nag's Heart retreat for women are meaningful and impactful because they provide participants with the opportunity to gain perspective and feel validated. Such experiences allow participants to remove the proverbial mask that seems to be all too common for women working in highly professional and competitive work environments. Providing women with the opportunity to hear one another's heartfelt stories of pain and triumph makes it possible for them to mentor one another with special effectiveness. We were glad to find that the Nag's Heart retreats prove effective for women in the hard sciences just as they have proven effective for women in other fields.

The Nag's Heart model has varied in many ways and stayed constant in others. Retreats have been held for as little as one day and as long as two weeks (a hike through the Himalayas constituted one Nag's Heart). Retreats have been held in homes, bed and breakfasts, hotel conference rooms and suites, and retreat centers. They have piggy-backed onto other conferences and have been stand-alone events. Retreats have also varied on the extent to which participants have previously known each other. The core principles of structured sessions, truthfulness, and trust, however, have been consistent with each retreat.

A model that has not yet been tested is to start a longer lasting mentoring circle with a Nag's Heart retreat; but the idea of continuing the discussion over email or by recurring annual retreats is promising. A Nag's Heart retreat would be a powerful way to establish trust and commitment among mentoring circle participants. Norms of listening, truthfulness, and status attenuation develop within the Nag's Heart process that may be sustained throughout the life of the mentoring circle. The anticipation that Nag's Heart participants will work with each other over time may alleviate some of the concerns we heard from past participants that they may not see each other again.

Some other big questions remain. Three seem especially important for the researchers and practitioners reading the present volume.

a How might language facility influence group dynamics and mutual under-standing? For example, it is likely that not all participants are adept in being able to accurately articulate their feelings and ideas. Does the Nag's Heart structure create a barrier for them, or can this be overcome?

b How well might the Nag's Heart model work for those from completely different cultural backgrounds? Nag's Heart retreats have had participants residing in the USA from many different cultural and international back-grounds, but to date, no Nag's Heart retreat has been held exclusively with non-US participants. The internationalization of the Nag's Heart model is a promising horizon, but intentional focus on how the model may or may not generalize in other cultures is needed.

c   What would happen to the dynamics if men were included? A few men have participated in Nag's Heart retreats in the past because they too need to replenish the feminist spirit. But a more intentional focus for men in Nag's Heart retreats, or Nag's Heart retreats for men is warranted in this era when a focus on building "allies" is promising (e.g., Fabiano, Perkins, Berkowitz, Linkenbach, & Stark, 2003).

It is our sincere hope that we might find answers to these questions. By continuing to take great care in whom we invite to join our circles and in how we prepare newcomers for the intensity of the experience, we expect to minimize the risks that might otherwise arise when one seeks to bring together people with different backgrounds. Surely, we will always acknowledge and salute those aspects of individual identity that emanate from demographic characteristics. And just as surely we will always probe for the ways that each individual carries in herself the basic human impulses to strive for fulfillment and to link with love and trust to other humans in whom she can recognize similar strivings.

Note

1 Funding for the research reported in this chapter was provided by an Interdisciplinary Collaboration grant from Southern Illinois University to the first author. The authors thank Stacy Blake-Beard, Yvonne Rodriguez, Crystal Steltenpohl, Courtney Laughman, Audrey Murrell, Maureen O'Connor, Olaf Einarsdottir, Karen Renzaglia, and Lizette Chevalier for their roles in facilitating Nag's Heart retreats, research assistance, grant co-PIs, and leadership in the Nag's Heart collaborative. Address correspondence to the first author.

References

Allen, T. D., Eby, L. T., Poteet, M. L., Lentz, E., & Lima, L. (2004). Career benefits associated with mentoring for proteges: A meta-analysis. *Journal of Applied Psychology, 89*, 127–136.

Amelink, C. (2009). Overview: "Mentoring and Women in Engineering." *SWE-AWE Applying Research to Practice Series, CASEE Overviews.*

Barone, C. (2011). Some things never change: Gender segregation in higher education across eight nations and three decades. *Sociology of Education, 84*(2), 157–176. DOI: 10.1177/0038040711402099.

Burke, R. J. (2007). Women and minorities in STEM: A primer. *Women and minorities in science, technology, engineering, and mathematics: Upping the numbers* (pp. 3–27). Northampton: Edward Elgar Publishing.

Cox, A. J., Blaha, C., Fritz, L., & Whitten, B. (2014, October 18). For Female Physicists, Peer Mentoring Can Combat Isolation. *Voices, Scientific American Blog Network.* Retrieved from http://blogs.scientificamerican.com/voices/2014/10/18/for-female-physicists-peer-mentoring-can-combat-isolation.

Dansky, K. H. (1996). The effect of group mentoring on career outcomes. *Group and Organization Management, 21*(1), 5–17.

Darwin, A. (2000). Critical reflections on mentoring in work settings. *Adult Education Quarterly, 50*(3), 197–211.

Darwin, A., & Palmer, E. (2009). Mentoring circles in higher education. *Higher Education Research & Development, 28*(2), 125–136.

Di Fabio, N. M., Brandi, C., & Frehill, L. M. (2008). *Professional women and minorities: A total human resources data compendium.* Washington, DC: Commission on Professionals in Science and Technology.

Eby, L. T., Allen, D. T., Hoffman, T. D., Baranik, B. J., Sauer, L. E., Baldwin, J. B., S., Morrison, M. A., Kinkdale, K. M., Maher, C. P., Curtis, S., & Evans, S. C. (2013). An interdisciplinary meta-analysis of the potential antecedents, correlates, and consequences of protégé perceptions of mentoring. *Psychological Bulletin, 139*(2), 441–476. DOI: 10.1037/a0029279.

Eby, L. T., Durley, J. R., Evans, S. C., & Ragins, B. R. (2006). The relationship between short-term mentoring benefits and long-term mentor outcomes. *Journal of Vocational Behavior, 69*(3), 424–444. DOI: 10.1016/j.jvb.2006.05.003.

Eby, L. T., McManus, S. E., Simon, S. A., & Russell, J. E. A. (2000). The protégé's perspective regarding negative mentoring experiences: The development of a taxonomy. *Journal of Vocational Behavior, 57*(1), 1–21.

Fabiano, P. M., Perkins, H. W., Berkowitz, A., Linkenbach, J., & Stark, C. (2003). Engaging men as social justice allies in ending violence against women: Evidence for a social norms approach. *Journal of American College Health, 52*(3), 105–112.

Gentry, W. A., Weber, T. J., & Sadri, G. (2008). Examining career-related mentoring and managerial performance across cultures: A multilevel analysis. *Journal of Vocational Behavior, 72*(2), 241–253. DOI: 10.1016/j.jvb.2007.10.014.

Ghosh, R., & Reio, T. G., Jr. (2013). Career benefits associated with mentoring for mentors: A meta-analysis. *Journal of Vocational Behavior, 83*(1), 106–116. DOI: 10.1016/j.jvb.2013.03.011.

Hansman, C. A. (2002). Diversity and power in mentoring relationships. In C. A. Hansman (Ed.), *Critical perspectives on mentoring: Trends and issues* (pp. 39–48). Columbus, OH: ERIC Clearinghouse on Adult, Career, and Vocational Education.

Hewlett, S. A., Luce, C. B., Servon, L. J., Sherbin, L., Shiller, P., Sosnovich, E., & Sumberg, K. (2008). *The Athena Factor: Reversing the brain drain in science, engineering and technology* (Harvard Business Review Research Report). Boston, MA: Harvard Business Publishing.

Hill, C., Corbett, C., & St Rose, A. (2010). *Why So Few? Women in Science, Technology, Engineering, and Mathematics.* American Association of University Women. 1111 Sixteenth Street NW, Washington, DC 20036.

Holbeche, L. (1996). Peer mentoring: The challenges and opportunities. *Career Development International, 1*(7), 24–27.

Holleran, S. E., Whitehead, J., Schmader, T., & Mehl, M. R. (2011). Talking shop and shooting the breeze: A study of workplace conversation and job disengagement among STEM faculty. *Social Psychological and Personality Science, 2*(1), 65–71.

Kram, K. E. (1985). *Mentoring at work: Developmental relationships in organizational life.* Glenview. IL: Scott, Foresman.

Kram, K. E., & Higgins, M. C. (2008, September 22). A new approach to mentoring. *Wall Street Journal*, R10.

Kram, K. E., & Isabella, L. A. (1985). Mentoring alternatives: The role of peer relationships in career development. *Academy of Management Journal, 28*(1), 110–132.

Langdon, E. A. (2001). Women's colleges then and now: Access then, equity now. *Peabody Journal of Education, 76*(1), 5–30.

McCambley, E. (1999). Testing theory by practice. In A. J. Murrell, F. J. Crosby, & R. J. Ely (Eds.), *Mentoring dilemmas: Developmental relationships within multicultural organizations* (pp. 173–188). Mahwah, NJ: Lawrence Erlbaum Associates.

McNeely, C. L., & Vlaicu, S. (2010). Exploring institutional hiring trends of women in the U.S. STEM professoriate. *Review of Policy Research, 27*(6), 781–793.

Merriam, S. B. (2009). *Qualitative research: A guide to design and implementation.* San Francisco, CA: Jossey-Bass.

Mody, P. N., & Brainard, S. G. (2005, June 12–14). Successful international initiatives promoting gender equity in engineering. In *Proceedings of the international symposium on Women and ICT: Creating global transformation* (p. 5). Baltimore, MD, ACM. Retrieved from http://dl.acm.org/citation.cfm?id=1117422.

Moss-Racusin, C. A., Dovidio, J. F., Brescoll, V. L., Graham, M. J., & Handelsman, J. (2012). Science faculty's subtle gender biases favor male students. In S. Tilghman (Ed.), *Proceedings of the National Academy of Sciences, 109*(43), 16474–16479. DOI: 10.1073/pnas.1211286109.

Murrell, A. J., Blake-Beard, S., Porter, D. M. Jr., & Perkins-Williamson, A. (2008). Interorganizational formal mentoring: Breaking the concrete ceiling sometimes requires support from the outside. *Human Resource Management, 47*(2), 275–294. DOI: 10.1002/hrm.20212.

National Science Foundation (NSF) (2012). *ADVANCE: Increasing the Participation and Advancement of Women in Academic Science and Engineering Careers (ADVANCE).* Program Solicitation. Retrieved August 30, 2012 from www.nsf.gov/funding/pgm_summ.jsp?pims_id=5383?

Nelson, D., & Brammer, C. (2010). *A national analysis of minorities and women in science and engineering faculties at research universities.* Norman, OK: Diversity in Science Association and University of Oklahoma. Retrieved October 5, 2012 from http://cheminfo.ou.edu/~djn/diversity/Faculty_Tables_FY07/FinalReport07.html.

Ong, M., Wright, C., Espinosa, L. L., & Orfield, G. (2011). Inside the double bind: A synthesis of empirical research on undergraduate and graduate women of color in science, technology, engineering, and mathematics. *Harvard Educational Review, 81*(2), 172–208.

Palermo, C., Hughes, R., & McCall, L. (2010). A qualitative evaluation of an Australian public health nutrition workforce development intervention involving mentoring circles. *Public Health Nutrition, 13*, 1458–1465. DOI: 10.1017/S1368980010002491.

Ragins, B. R., & Cotton, J. L. (1999). Mentor functions and outcomes: a comparison of men and women in formal and informal mentoring relationships. *Journal of applied psychology, 84*(4), 529–550.

Rosser, S. V. (2004). Using POWRE to ADVANCE: Institutional barriers identified by women scientists and engineers. *NWSA Journal, 16*(1), 50–78.

Stroh, L. (2010). *Trust rules: How to tell the good guys from the bad guys in work and life.* Westport, CT: Praeger.

Thomas, D. A. (1990). The impact of race on managers' experiences of developmental relationships (mentoring and sponsorship): An intra-organizational study. *Journal of Organizational Behavior, 11*(6), 479–492.

Trower, C. A. (2008, October). Competing on culture: Academia's new strategic imperative. Unpublished presentation. Retrieved from www.advance.iastate.edu/conference/conferencepdf/2008_10-11trower_hoc.pdf.

Valian, V. (2005). Beyond gender schemas: Improving the advancement of women in academia. *Hypatia, 20*(3), 198–213.

Xu, Y. J. (2008). Gender disparity in STEM disciplines: A study of faculty attrition and turnover intentions. *Research in Higher Education, 49*(7), 607–624.

13

POSTFACE

Reflections on the Multiple Faces of Mentoring in the Twenty-First Century

Ella L. J. Edmondson Bell-Smith and Stella M. Nkomo

In its original definition, a mentor was a wise teacher or advisor, usually an elder who provides counsel to a younger and less experienced junior. With its classic origins in how it was practiced in Greece by great philosophers like Socrates who mentored Plato, the advisor was usually male as well as the protégé (Sullivan, 2004).[1] As the concept emerged in the organization behavior and management fields in the twentieth century, mentors in organizations were predominantly males who primarily mentored other males. This configuration was a reflection of the times. Leadership and management positions in organizations globally were filled by men. In fact, the available pool of mentors to provide wise guidance to those new to managerial and leadership roles in the United States workplace were largely White males. This was the reality at the time of Kathy Kram's pioneering work on mentoring published in the 1980s. Kram (1985) positioned mentoring as a developmental relationship between two people. Inherent in her model was the implicit assumption that the mentor was the wise senior who not only possessed the knowledge, power, and skills that juniors needed for success but also had the requisite ability to engage their socio-emotional needs.

Much has changed in the last thirty years since Kram (1985) presented her model of mentoring. The new scholarship introduced by Blake-Beard (1999, 2001) and Murrell, Crosby, and Ely (1999) questioned whether a one-size-fits-all model of mentoring could address the developmental challenges of women of color and others who did not fit the dominate leader prototype. A growing body of research shows diverse leaders and managers faced additional developmental challenges embedded in issues of race, gender, ethnicity, and class (e.g. Blake-Beard, Murrell, & Thomas, 2007; Murrell, Blake-Beard, Porter, & Perkins-Williamson, 2008; Scully & Blake-Beard, 2006; and Thomas, 1990).

Publication of *The Handbook of Mentoring at Work: Theory, Research, and Practice* in 2007 and the recent *Blackwell Handbook of Mentoring: A Multiple Perspectives Approach* (Allen & Eby, 2007) reflect the growing importance of mentoring (Ragins & Kram, 2007).

Forces Driving Changes in Mentoring

The concept of mentoring, as well as who and where mentoring is done, has continued to expand in multiple directions. As the chapters in this volume illustrate, mentoring is no longer limited to the younger protégé seeking counsel from the wise senior (White male) elder, but has increasingly become more diverse and inclusive, crossing global and cultural boundaries, generations, careers, genders, and employee groups. Clearly, the face of mentoring has transformed in response to the changing demographics in the workplace but also through globalization and technological innovations. Before elaborating on how the concept and practice of mentoring has evolved, we discuss the forces contributing to new forms of mentoring relationships.

The predictions of an increasingly diverse labor force in the United States made in the widely influential Workforce 2000 Report (Johnston & Packer, 1987) have materialized. New predictions signal growing diversity. For example, recent reports estimate that by 2030, the USA will be a majority minority nation (i.e., ethnic minorities including African-Americans, Hispanic-Americans, Asian-Americans, Native Americans will become the majority of the population, see US Bureau of Census, 2015). As a result, many US organizations will employ a large number of ethnic minority group members, and will face the challenge of attracting, motivating, and retaining employees who are ethnically and culturally diverse. This is also true in other parts of the world. European countries are becoming increasingly more diverse with the growing inflow of migrants. Countries once thought to be fairly homogenous now find themselves with more heterogeneous populations and workforces (Vertovec, 2007). Forecasters predict that if current migration and birth trends prevail, between 26.5 percent and 34.6 percent of the European population will be of foreign origin. The figure is even higher (50%) for Belgium, Germany, Spain, and Austria (Coleman, 2013). These global changes have given birth to the concept of "superdiversity" to describe the new multicultural condition of the twenty-first century (Meissner & Vertovec, 2015).

Perhaps the most significant global change in the workplace, particularly in the management and leadership workforce, has been the increasing presence of women. According to the most recent Grant Thornton International Business Report (Lagerberg, 2016), women hold 24 percent of senior management positions globally. But the report also shows the global average varies by designated economic regions and countries. With 35 percent of senior management positions held by women, Eastern European countries top the rankings. Russia, with 45 percent of senior positions held by women, pushes the East European average upwards (Lagerberg, 2016). In the ASEAN countries (e.g., Philippines, Indonesia, Cambodia, Vietnam, and Thailand), women hold 34 percent of senior roles.

Ironically, despite their status as economic powerhouses, in G7 countries (Italy, France, Canada, Germany, United States, United Kingdom, and Japan) just 22 percent of senior positions are held by women (Lagerberg, 2016). The figure for the United States is 23 percent (Lagerberg, 2016). However, women of color continue to lag behind White women in the senior ranks (Catalyst, 2016). At the lower end are countries in the Middle East and Africa, although South Africa stands at 23 percent of senior management positions held by women. The percentage of women in senior roles in India has grown to 16 percent (Lagerberg, 2016). Research also shows an increase in the number of women in senior leadership in the Gulf Cooperative Council (GCC) states— Bahrain, Kuwait, Oman, Qatar, Saudi Arabia, and United Arab Emirates (Sperling, Marcati, & Rennie, 2014).

Globalization, and its companion transnationalism, is also a major societal shift with implications for mentoring. Globalization has been identified as one of the most significant trends in the world today. This force has shrunk boundaries between nations and regions of the world (Friedman, 2000). Although early globalization consisted mainly of multinational firms from the United States and Europe entering markets in the rest of the world, today it embraces the rest of the world. For example, Developing Economy Multinationals are doing more business with each other than in the past (Flemes, 2009). For example, firms located in countries in the global South (e.g., India, South Africa, Australia) are increasingly doing business with each other as well as with countries in the global North (e.g., United States, European Union). Not only are businesses moving across borders but people are also increasingly mobile because of migration and immigration. Consequently, people are having more sustained cross-cultural interactions than ever before in this century (Meissner & Vertovec, 2015).

The growing level of cross-country and cross-region business and services dispersion has given rise to increasing attention to transnationalism. Scholars refer to transnationalism as regular, high intensive cross-border social, economic, political, and cultural exchanges that involve new modes of transacting and contact between countries and people (Portes, Guarnizo, & Landolt, 1999; Vertovec, 1999). While there has always been movement of products and people across borders, globalization combined with technological advances has intensified and sustained transnational exchanges in the twenty-first century. In a transnational world, employees are no longer confined to a permanent location but may take business trips or be assigned to work in a different part of the world— or migrate to work in different country while maintaining connections to home. Organization behavior and management scholars have recently turned their attention to the implications of transnationalism for the workplace, particularly the experiences of migrants (e.g., Ariss, Koall, Özbilgin, & Suutari, 2012) as well as its effects on identity (e.g., Calás, Ou, & Smircich, 2014; Pio & Essers, 2014).

Globalization and technology have been identified as mutually reinforcing trends (Aggarwal, 1999). Technology helps globalization leapfrog traditional national boundaries; it is also an enabler for people, organizations, ideas, culture, products, and services to move rapidly across regions of the world (Aggarwal, 1999: 83). Technological advances in air transport, communication systems, communication devices, and software have made the geographical location of a company less of a hindrance to doing business. Organizations can use smart phone technology and other social media to build virtual teams and networks. Facebook, for example, has allowed individuals to build relationships across time and space.

Several observers have noted that the growing ethnic, racial, and gender diversity of the workplace is even more significant in what is referred to as a VUCA world—volatile, uncertain, complex, and ambiguous (Lagerberg, 2016). Diversity combined with increasing globalization along with technological advances suggest that creative approaches to mentoring that foster development and retention of talent are imperative, not optional.

Mentoring in the Twenty-First Century

What will mentoring look like as we progress in the twenty-first century? First, both mentors and mentees will no longer be homogenous. Organizations and individuals have many opportunities to engage in diverse mentoring relationships across categories of difference. Of course, the issue remains of encouraging such engagements and providing people with the skills to be effective in developmental relationships. Second, mentoring has moved beyond the business world. Mentoring can be found in any organizational context, including among family members, in religious groups, Girl and Boy Scout Clubs, and even among friends. Tucked into the concept of mentoring are the constructs of role models, allies, emotional intelligence, career development, power and influence, trust, and leadership. Third, the forms and usage of mentoring will be as diverse as the individuals in mentoring relationships. For instance, mentoring is being used in patient treatment for chronic illness, for therapeutic purposes in mental health, and student retention in schools and universities. Fourth, communication technology will continue to impact the power of mentoring and also facilitate global mentoring. Cross-border mentoring relationships will be the norm, not an exception for employees working in multinational organizations. Distance is no longer a barrier to mentoring. Fifth, individuals and organizations will pay greater attention to mentoring as a constellation of helping relationships, connecting a diverse cross-section of people across time, space, and disciplines. While Kram's (1985) advice that mentees should have multiple individuals or networks for developmental support was largely overlooked in the twentieth century, it is now being embraced (Higgins & Kram, 2001; Murphy & Kram, 2014). Mentoring pods, where small cohorts serve as a support group beyond a company's doors are also growing. This adaptation is particularly important for groups who are not able to find the developmental support needed within their organizations. Lastly, there will be increasing use of peer mentoring and mentee upward mentoring—where the mentee is the wise sage. These and similar forms of mentoring change the hierarchical and power relationships found in traditional mentoring. One of the benefits of this change will be greater attention to what mentors learn from developmental relationships in addition to focusing on outcomes for mentees.

Impact of Peer Mentoring and Mentor Pods

We want to share our personal experience with two forms of mentoring mentioned above: peer mentoring and mentoring pods. These two forms were successfully combined in a leadership development program offered by ASCENT~Leading Multicultural Women to the Top. ASCENT was founded in 2004 with a mission to "help multicultural women prepare for and build careers in corporations and help corporate partners to attract, advance, and retain women." Its dual mission is accomplished through integrated, progressive programs for *finding*, *building*, and *advancing* talent, and through actionable research that *creates new knowledge* on workplace and career issues. One of its major initiatives is the Mastering Management Program targeted at women who have been identified by their organizations as high potential with at least eight to ten years of managerial or leadership experience. Since its launch in 2008, 160 women have completed the program. Over the years, the program has attracted a diverse group of women in terms of race, ethnicity, function, industry, and societal sector (i.e., business and not-for-profit).

The design of the Mastering Management Program consists of four contact sessions in a five-month period. Participants in the program receive over 100 instructional hours from faculty from top tier business schools across the country. Through simulations, case studies, discussions, and emersion exercises, participants strengthen their repertoire of core technical skills and business knowledge. Communication, influence, gaining a strategic perspective, coalition building, championing, teamwork, and networking are also a large part of the program's content. Throughout the program, the women are encouraged to practice new leadership behaviors and to apply what they learn professionally and personally. The contact sessions are heavily experiential to provide participants with an opportunity to engage the content, reflect, and to set professional and personal goals. Ample supportive space is created for the women to network and to learn from one another. Participants also have the opportunity to engage in dialogue and conversation with "wise women and men"—accomplished leaders who share valuable lessons about career and life fulfillment.

In addition to the classroom modules, participants also benefit from peer coaching and mentoring pods. In each cohort, the women are placed into pods consisting of six to seven women. Professional coaches act as a resource to the pods. The pod discussions focus on the achievement of personal and career growth, with the objective of fostering holistic integration resulting from guidance and instruction received during the program modules. The pods provide a powerful mechanism for deep conversation, reflection, and sharing. It did not take long before the pods transformed into a forum where the women learned how to be peer mentors and coaches to their fellow pod members. Women used the pods for support when dealing with personal challenges as well as work related dilemmas and career decisions. The interactions in the pod have allowed the women to develop mentoring and coaching skills, as noted by one of the women, "I also appreciate and value the pods. Being a coach is important, but learning how to coach is critical. It helps on both ends." A quote from another participant revealed how the mentoring and coaching skills they honed in the pods were transferred to their organization, "I've used the coaching principles to help those on my team and other women in the organization from a mentoring perspective." The mentoring skills developed in the pods became part of the women's approach to leading others.

The networks established in the pods did not dissipate at the end of the program. Instead, the pod groups were sustained by the women themselves and have led to long-term relationships. The words of this participant were heard from several women,

> I met an amazing network of women who have welcomed me into their personal and professional lives as though we met a lifetime ago. Many of us have continued through monthly get togethers to remain connected and to support each other in our personal and career evolution. It is rewarding to know that I have found some phenomenal mentors and life coaches through Ascent.

The pods provided groups of women, who shared a common interest in learning and developing individually and collectively in their leadership roles, a place to do transformative work on themselves. In the end, it was about collaboration, affirmation, learning from each other, communication and sharing, challenging one another, practicing getting and giving real-time feedback to others as captured in the words of another participant, "Before, ASCENT, I struggled with asking for help, advice or guidance, often because I was afraid to appear incompetent. The PODs have broken me of that!"

The ASCENT pod experience provides insights into the benefits of mentoring in peer groups. We believe they were so successful because there were no hierarchical barriers between the women. Additionally, the group composition increased the odds that there would always be someone in the pod who could assist another member. This diversity ensured a wide range of knowledge and skills within the pod. Finally, being amongst peers created a safe environment for the women to reveal vulnerabilities rather than cloaking them. At the beginning of the program, many of the women shared experiences of being isolated and having limited networks. Some were also reluctant to seek support within their organizations out of fear of being judged as incompetent. The peer mentoring pods resulted in developmental networks that continue to provide the women with personal and career support. Women were able to speak about their racial, ethnic, sexual orientation, and class differences not as barriers but as a means to understand what was also common among them. Although the pods were part of a contact program, we believe peer pods could work across borders through effective use of communication technology.

Conclusion

There is no doubt that mentoring has changed from its early conceptualization and practice in the twentieth-century workplace. Several forces have contributed to changing its theoretical base and practice as the chapters in this volume insightfully demonstrate. We expect that before the end of the twenty-first century, mentoring will take on additional forms not imaginable today. However, we do need to offer some cautionary words. One of the poignant insights from the research we conducted for our book, *Our Separate Ways: The Struggle for Professional Identity of Black and White Women in Corporate America* (Bell & Nkomo, 2001) is that mentoring should not be seen as the silver bullet for the advancement of women, and we would add for others who continue to experience inequality in the workplace because of being different to those in the majority. Inequality in the workplace has not been eradicated and ending it will require structural changes and advocates for change. One of the interventions stressed by the women leaders in our book is the importance of sponsorship—being identified and supported for higher-level positions by those in power. We continue to hear this today in our work through ASCENT with talented multicultural women and in South Africa where women, particularly black women struggle to advance.

Our description of the peer pods that were a formal part of the ASCENT Mastering Management Program has implications for formal mentoring programs in organizations. Organizations should consider mentoring groups across divisions and locations, which will increase inclusion and help employees to learn to work across differences. In the ASCENT program, the women continued their relations after the conclusion of the program. Perhaps more research is needed on comparing the effects of informal mentoring and formal mentoring on mentors and mentees. A recent article by Dobbins and Kalev (2016) showing that informal diversity interventions were more effective than formal ones suggests the need for more research that compares formal and informal mentoring outcomes for mentees and mentors.

With the growing number of women and people of color across the world getting a seat at the top of their organizations, we are hopeful they too will actively sponsor and mentor other women. "Lifting as we climb," the words of Mary Church Terrell, founding member in the nineteenth century of the African-American Women's Club Movement, remain relevant for all of us, regardless of our professions, locations, identities, and the spheres in which we mentor others. Finally, mentoring cannot be seen as a single solution to the developmental needs of diverse individuals. It should be part of a holistic approach to helping individuals realize and develop their talents.

Note

1 The actual word mentor is derived from the character "Mentor" in Homer's *Odyssey* (Sullivan, 2004).

References

Aggarwal, R. (1999). Technology and globalization as mutual reinforcers in business: Reorienting strategic thinking for the new millennium. *MIR: Management International Review*, 83–104.

Allen, T. D., & Eby, L. T. (Eds.) (2007). *The Blackwell handbook of mentoring: A multiple perspectives approach*. Malden, MA: Blackwell Publishing.

Ariss, A., Koall, I., Özbilgin, M., & Suutari, V. (2012). Careers of skilled migrants: towards a theoretical and methodological expansion. *Journal of Management Development, 31*(2), 92–101.

Bell, E. L. E., & Nkomo, S. M. (2001). *Our separate ways: Black and White women and the struggle for professional identity*. Boston, MA: Harvard Business Press.

Blake-Beard, S. D. (1999). The costs of living as an outsider within: An analysis of the mentoring relationships and career success of Black and White women in the corporate sector. *Journal of Career Development, 26*(1), 21–23.

Blake-Beard, S. D., Murrell, A. J., and Thomas, D. A. (2007). Unfinished business: The impact of race on understanding mentoring relationships. In B. R. Ragins, & K. E. Kram (Eds.), *The handbook on mentoring at work: Theory, research, and practice*. Thousand Oaks, CA: Sage Publications.

Blake-Beard, S. D. (2001). Taking a hard look at formal mentoring programs: A consideration of potential challenges facing women. *Journal of Management Development, 20*(4), 331–345.

Blake-Beard, S. D., Murrell, A. J., & Thomas, D. A. (2006). *Unfinished business: The impact of race on understanding mentoring relationships*. Division of Research, Harvard Business School.

Calás, M. B., Ou, H., & Smircich, L. (2013). "Woman" on the move: mobile subjectivities after intersectionality. *Equality, Diversity and Inclusion: An International Journal, 32*(8), 708–731.

Catalyst (2016, February 4). Women Of Color In The United States. Retrieved July 20, 2016, from www.catalyst.org/knowledge/women-color-united-states-0.

Coleman, D. (2013, April 17). Immigration, population, and ethnicity: The UK in international perspective. *The Migration Observatory*. Retrieved July 20, 2016, from www.migrationobservatory.ox.ac.uk/briefings/immigration-population-and-ethnicity-uk-international-perspective.

Dobbins, F., & Kalev, A. (2016, July–August). Why diversity programs fail. *Harvard Business Review*.

Flemes, D. (2009). India-Brazil-South Africa (IBSA) in the new global order interests, strategies and values of the emerging coalition. *International Studies, 46*(4), 401–421.

Friedman, T. L. (2000). *The Lexus and the olive tree: Understanding globalization*. London: Macmillan.

Higgins, M. C., & Kram, K. E. (2001). Reconceptualizing mentoring at work: A developmental network perspective. *Academy of Management Review, 26* (2), 264–288.

Johnston, W. B., & Packer, A. E. (1987). *Workforce 2000: Work and workers for the twenty-first century*. Indianapolis, IN: Hudson Institute.

Kram, K. E. (1985). *Mentoring at work: Developmental relationships in organizational life*. Glenview, IL: Scott, Foresman & Co.

Lagerberg, F. (2016, March 8). Women in business: Turning promise into practice. Grant Thornton International.

Meissner, F., & Vertovec, S. (2015). Comparing super-diversity. *Ethnic and Racial Studies, 38*(4), 541–555.

Murphy, W., & Kram, K. E. (2014). *Strategic relationships at work: Creating your circle of mentors, sponsors, and peers for success in business and life*. New York: McGraw Hill Professional.

Murrell, A. J., Blake-Beard, S., Porter, D. M., & Perkins-Williamson, A. (2008). Interorganizational formal mentoring: Breaking the concrete ceiling sometimes requires support from the outside. *Human Resource Management, 47*(2), 275–294.

Murrell, A. J., Crosby, F. J., & Ely, R. J. (1999). *Mentoring dilemmas: Developmental relationships within multicultural organizations*. Mahwah, NJ: Lawrence Erlbaum Associates.

Pio, E., & Essers, C. (2014). Professional migrant women decentring otherness: A transnational perspective. *British Journal of Management, 25*(2), 252–265.

Portes, A., Guarnizo, L. E., & Landolt, P. (1999). The study of transnationalism: pitfalls and promise of an emergent research field. *Ethnic and Racial Studies, 22*(2), 217–237.

Ragins, B. R., & Kram, K. E. (2007). *The handbook of mentoring at work: Theory, research, and practice*. Thousand Oaks, CA: Sage Publications.

Scully, M. A., & Blake-Beard, S. (2006). Locating class in organizational diversity work. In A. M. Konrad, P. Prasad, & J. K. Pringle (Eds.), *A handbook of workplace diversity* (pp. 431–454). London: Sage.

Sperling, J., Marcati, C., & Rennie, M. (2014). *GCC women in leadership—from first to norm*. McKinsey & Co.

Sullivan, C. G. (2004). *How to mentor in the midst of change*. Alexandria, VA: ASCD.

Thomas, D. A. (1990). The impact of race on managers' experiences of developmental relationships (mentoring and sponsorship): An intra-organizational study. *Journal of Organizational Behavior, 11*(6), 479–492.

US Bureau of Census, Population Division (2015) Annual Estimates of the Resident Population by Sex, Age, Race, and Hispanic Origin for the United States and States: April 1,

2010 to July 1, 2014. Retrieved from http://factfinder.census.gov/faces/tableservices/jsf/pages/productview.xhtml?pid=PEP_2014_PEPALL6N&prodType=table.

Vertovec, S. (1999). Conceiving and researching transnationalism. *Ethnic and Racial Studies, 22*(2), 447–462.

Vertovec, S. (2007). Super-diversity and its implications. *Ethnic and racial studies, 30*(6), 1024–1054.

INDEX

Page numbers in **bold** denote figures.